AFRICAN IMPRESSIONS

*Winner of the Walker Cowen Memorial Prize
for an outstanding work of scholarship
in eighteenth-century studies*

AFRICAN IMPRESSIONS

How African Worldviews Shaped
the British Geographical Imagination
across the Early Enlightenment

REBEKAH MITSEIN

UNIVERSITY OF VIRGINIA PRESS
Charlottesville and London

University of Virginia Press
© 2022 by the Rector and Visitors of the University of Virginia
All rights reserved
Printed in the United States of America on acid-free paper

First published 2022

9 8 7 6 5 4 3 2 1

Library of Congress Cataloging-in-Publication Data

Names: Mitsein, Rebekah, author.
Title: African impressions : how African worldviews shaped the British geographical imagination across the early Enlightenment / Rebekah Mitsein.
Other titles: Walker Cowen Memorial Prize.
Description: Charlottesville : University of Virginia Press, 2022. | Series: Winner of the Walker Cowen memorial prize | Includes bibliographical references and index.
Identifiers: LCCN 2022038384 (print) | LCCN 2022038385 (ebook) | ISBN 9780813947891 (hardcover) | ISBN 9780813947907 (paperback) | ISBN 9780813947914 (ebook)
Subjects: LCSH: English literature—18th century—History and criticism. | English literature—Early modern, 1500–1700—History and criticism. | English literature—African influences. | Geography and literature. | Discoveries in geography. | Africa—In literature.
Classification: LCC PR448.A38 M58 2022 (print) | LCC PR448.A38 (ebook) | DDC 820.9326—dc23/eng/20220816
LC record available at https://lccn.loc.gov/2022038384
LC ebook record available at https://lccn.loc.gov/2022038385

Cover art: Detail of *A New Map of Libya or old Africk* by Edward Wells. (Dr. Oscar I. Norwich Collection of Maps of Africa and Its Islands, 1486–ca. 1865, David Rumsey Map Center, Stanford University Libraries)

For Sean

CONTENTS

Acknowledgments   ix

Introduction   1

1. "Wherein the Blacke-Prince Keepes His Residence, Attended by His Jetty Coloured Traine": Impressions of the Western Sudan, 1324–1620   41

2. "A Country of Blacks So Called": The Romance of African Impressions in Aphra Behn's *Oroonoko*   77

3. "A Medium of an Endless Correspondence": Rivers for Want of Empires in the African Impressions of Daniel Defoe's *Captain Singleton* and *Atlas Maritimus and Commercialis*   98

4. "Where the Nile Riseth . . . Where the Queen of Saba Lived": Impressions of Abyssinia, 1327–1759   124

5. "Between the Inland Countries of Africk and the Ports of the Red Sea": African Impressions amid Fact and Fancy in Samuel Johnson's *Rasselas*   150

6. "Descended from the Queen of Saba": African Women as Geographical Authorities in James Bruce's *Travels to Discover the Source of the Nile*   177

Coda   201

Notes   207
Bibliography   239
Index   261

ACKNOWLEDGMENTS

This book is about how books are made before they are written and about how no one knows alone. In that way, it tells its own story and mine. Thanks are due to my early mentors Susan Kubica Howard and Laura Engel for fostering my interest in the eighteenth century. Kristina Bross and Wendy Laura Belcher cracked open what I had assumed one was allowed to say about literature, introducing me to and modeling the methods that made this book thinkable. Christopher Lukasik and Geraldine Friedman offered invaluable feedback on the dissertation from which it grew. The reasons I have to be grateful to Nush Powell, who directed that dissertation, are never ending because she continues to be a wellspring of aid and expertise. To choose only one from the list, she encouraged me to take risks where lesser advisors might have balked.

The sincere support of all my colleagues in the Boston College English Department gave me the courage to write this book by trial and error. What seemed like false starts and entropic wandering turned out to be the road, and I was never wholly lost on it because they were looking out for me. I turned to Elizabeth Kowaleski Wallace for guidance on matters great and small. Alan Richardson, Maia McAleavey, Amy Boesky, and Eric Weiskott offered conscientious comments on one or more chapters. Mary Crane gamely read the first manuscript, and Aeron Hunt was the Harriet Vane to my Miss Lydgate when the final one needed to get out the door. For general advice, cheerleading, solidarity, and troubleshooting, my thanks to Andy Crow, Christy Pottroff, James Smith, Min Hyoung Song, Christina Klein, Carlo Rotella, Stephen Sturgeon, Linda Michel, and Tracy Downing.

Other interlocutors, readers, or people who said the right thing at the right time include Derek Pacheco, Greg Barnhisel, John Duvall, Leah Pennywark, Donald Crummey, Jennifer Reed, Daniel Froid, Joy Howard, Kathleen Lubey, Rivka Swenson, Christopher Loar, and all the members of the Purdue Early Atlantic Reading Group. Without the camaraderie and friendship of Helen Hunt, Slaney Chadwick Ross, Marie Balsley Taylor, Heather Stanger Wicks, Jade Higa, and Emily Rutter this labor would have been lonely indeed. It would have been unimaginable without Mary Beth Harris, who rode out my ideas in conference hotel rooms across the country, cheering when the wheel chain of the clock ran smooth and helping me unstick it when it didn't.

My thinking profited from the exchange of ideas at conferences hosted by the American Society for Eighteenth-Century Studies and its regional affiliates, the Aphra Behn Society, and the Defoe Society. I was pleased to be invited to share pieces of this project as part of a panel hosted by the Eighteenth-Century Studies Seminar at the Mahindra Humanities Center, at a symposium put on by the travel writing reading group at Boston University, as a guest of Tennessee Tech University's Center Stage Speaker Series, at the Boston College English Department Graduate Student Colloquium, and with the Long Eighteenth Century and Romanticism Reading Group at Harvard. The librarians at the National Archives and Library of Ethiopia, the British Library, the David Rumsey Map Center at Stanford, and the Bibliothèque nationale de France answered queries about manuscripts and provided images. The Joseph J. Williams SJ Ethnological Collection in the John J. Burns Library at Boston College has been a trove of unexpected treasures. In Ethiopia, Chris Kurtz and Caroline Kurtz were invaluable translators, and Habtu Tekeba got me where I needed to go.

Angie Hogan at the University of Virginia Press has been the best of guides on this book's path to publication. Out of the academic bedlam of 2020, the two readers who reviewed the manuscript offered feedback that was incisive and deeply engaged. I appreciate all who helped bring the final product into the material real, including the production team at UVA Press, the copy editor, the indexer, and the Dean's Office of the Morrisey College of Arts and Sciences at Boston College. Parts of chapter 2 appeared in "Trans-Saharan Worlds and Worldviews in Aphra Behn's *Oroonoko*," *Eighteenth-Century Fiction* 30, no. 3 (2018): 340–68. My thanks to Eugenia Zuroski, Jacqueline Langille, and the two reviewers for their faith in what that article was and would be. Thanks are likewise due to Adam Sills and the reviewers of "Upon a Voyage and No Voyage: Mapping Africa's Waterways in Defoe's *Captain Singleton*," *Digital Defoe* 10, no. 1 (2018), parts of which appear in chapter 3.

My maternal grandparents, Harold and Polly Kurtz, sought to understand Ethiopia through the stories of those who knew it best, as did my mother, Jane Kurtz, whose love, wisdom, and readerly and writerly eye so thoroughly permeate this book that I couldn't decide where in these acknowledgements to put her. My father, Leonard Goering, taught me how to contemplate liquid ideas. David, Jonathan, Hiwot, Ellemae, and Noh did what families are good at. If anyone has ever earned their dedication, it's Sean Mitsein, who gets the last line because he was there for the first and for each one in between.

AFRICAN IMPRESSIONS

INTRODUCTION

This book is about how African worldviews shaped the British geographical imagination after explorers aspired to describe Africa as it was but before they were able to see it for themselves. It untangles the evidence and methods that travelers and geographers relied on to produce knowledge about the continent in the absence of empirical data or firsthand observation and tells the story of how African expressions—what Africans had to say and show about themselves and their worlds—became encoded in European literature. Covering a range of genres, including travel narratives, geography books, maps, verse, and fiction, it makes the case that African strategies of self-representation and European strategies for representing Africa grew increasingly inextricable across the early Enlightenment, amalgamating into coherent and widely circulated geographical ideas that I call "African impressions."

African impressions are not mimetic reflections of any given African place or people. As ample scholarship has by this point shown, early Enlightenment representations of Africa staged racist thinking and expansionist fantasies of various kinds. But African impressions are also not superficial treatments of or wholly invented projections onto a dark continent. They are the result of a dynamic cycle of discursive reiteration that unfolded across hundreds of years. They not only originated through the incorporation of African expressions into European thought; travelers returned to African contact zones and geographers returned to written accounts of past encounters to evaluate whether their outstanding impressions of the continent were viable. Based on what they were either told by new African informants or saw again in the old record, travel writers and geographers maintained or reshaped their own accounts accordingly, though not necessarily accurately and frequently in service to their own agendas. The creation and perpetuation of African impressions was ongoing, in other words, and certain key notions remained at their core because Africans kept implicitly or explicitly affirming them. Authors of literary representations of Africa put these impressions to aesthetic use, but they often did so in ways that preserved rather than obscured their most striking and enduring elements, which infiltrated the settings, characters, plots, intellectual investigations, social commentary, and form of early Enlightenment poetry, prose, and plays from the obscure to the canonical. These works played an important role in keeping certain aspects of African impressions front and center in the cultural imagination, which meant that travelers continued to verify them and geographical texts continued to reiterate them. African impressions acquired their contours and intellectual weight through these many migrations from interactions in the contact zone to abstract representations and back again.

African impressions are therefore both intertextual and extratextual. They are intertextual in the sense that they arose from hundreds of years of communicative events between Africans and Europeans; from erudite geographical traditions that worked across many languages to blend old knowledge about the continent with new knowledge; and from imaginative representations of Africa that drew from and spoke back to geographical discourse. They are extratextual in the sense that no single representation of any particular region encompasses the body of details that European thinkers and writers came to associate with that region; yet when a critical mass of texts are examined for their patterns and consistencies, a collective entity emerges that can be described and analyzed as coherent literary object that tells a recognizable story. Reconstructing those stories enables scholars to reconsider how literature that may initially appear to be only cursorily engaging with African worlds or projecting European fantasies onto the continent in fact necessarily depend on and regularly allude to a complex transcultural representational tradition.

The following chapters establish how two regions of Africa took the form that they did in the European geographical imagination and show how those impressions impacted the way Britons thought about and wrote about the continent as a whole. The first of these regions is the "Land of the Blacks." Borrowed from Arabic geographical discourse (*Bilad al-Sudan*), this designation first mapped fairly neatly over what were thought to be the territorial boundaries of the medieval and early modern Mali and Songhai Empires. It was subsequently expanded by European geographers to include Nubia and the coastal states of West Africa, ending at the Kingdom of Kongo, only to shrink again as "Guinea" took on its own set of distinct and coherent associations. The other region is Abyssinia, presumed by early modern and eighteenth-century Europeans to be the Christian Kingdom of Prester John and the home of the source of the Nile. Abyssinia exerted a stunning level of influence over the way Europeans thought about Africa's geography more broadly. Even though its territorial boundaries were fairly limited by the early Enlightenment, it was thought to encompass—or at least to have encompassed at one time—as much as a fifth of the continent.

This book focuses on these regions not because they were the only ones that were of interest to European geographers or the only ones that shaped European thinking about the continent but because, of all sub-Saharan regions, they have the longest history of being simultaneously known of and inaccessible to European travelers. They were known of because African elites successfully broadcast expressions of their sovereignty, wealth, right to power, geopolitical clout, and religious exceptionalism that entered Europe long before Europeans entered sub-Saharan Africa. In fact, the impressions Europeans formed from these expressions motivated the first earnest attempts by European nations to gain access to the continent and fueled Europe's desire to find the sources of West Africa's gold and the location of the city-states along the Niger, to establish a relationship with the Christian Kingdom of Prester John, and to discover the source of Africa's most legendary river. Their continuing struggles to accomplish any of these aims only prompted more reliance on what Africans—including inhabitants of the Western Sudan, Abyssinia, the Senegambia, the Gold Coast, and the Swahili Coast—had to say and show about the continent as Europeans sought insight into the interior from wherever they could find it.

African Impressions prioritizes the intellectual and imaginative debts that early Enlightenment literature owes African worlds and worldviews, which are so often deemed irrelevant to the evolution of European culture and thought. African expressions not only filled gaps in geographical knowledge: they infused literary texts on an aesthetic level, informed characterization and narrative action, and dictated the parameters of the settings within which that narrative action occurs. How self-reflexive any text is about this dependence varies, but both scholarly and literary writers frequently recognized and gnawed on the fact that much of what Europeans knew about the continent's interior had come from Africans themselves, mediated by chains of written and spoken discourse through layers of space and time. The African impression was acknowledged as an epistemological form. It became an emblem of the point at which empirical knowledge dissolves into other modes and a figure of thought through which to interrogate the value of "native" testimony and the erudite canon during a time when calls for eyewitness accounts were growing more insistent. In fact, this book offers an in-depth look at how African impressions offered four widely read writers—Aphra Behn, Daniel Defoe, Samuel Johnson, and James Bruce—a figural register through which to conduct investigations into what constitutes true and valuable knowledge about the world and how that knowledge is best represented. Not simply a metaphor or a generic scheme, the African impression as a structural idea could not be deployed without also harnessing the content and the historical scenarios (the descriptive details and narrative action) that made it recognizable as what it was. Thus, I argue that African impressions and the expressions that steered their courses are not adjunct details in these authors' texts but are at the very center of their literary projects.

The rest of this introduction addresses the critical idea that "Africa" was merely an invention of Enlightenment discourse and offers reasons why it is useful and warranted to move beyond this notion. It establishes this book's historical, geographic, and methodological scope. It offers an example of a specific African impression as it was shaped and reiterated through geographical writing—the widespread theory that the Biblical city of Ophir from which King Solomon acquired the resources to build his temple was located in East Africa. It shows how travel and travel writing and how geographical practices and geographical genres operated as the scaffold for African impressions. Lastly, it examines three poems that invoke the idea that Ophir was an African city as an illustration of how texts that initially appear to be cursory engagements with or imaginative projections onto the continent often depend on and allude to African impressions, their most distinct details traceable to the African expressions that kept striking the European geographical imagination.

Beyond Blank Space and Absolute Others

This book's central claim that African worlds and worldviews shaped the European geographical imagination runs counter to some long-held critical ideas about how early Enlightenment Europeans produced knowledge in general and knowledge about Africa in particular. In the aftermath of World War II, critical theorists began to put forth the idea that the Enlightenment impulse to categorize went hand in glove with an Enlightenment impulse to dominate, arguing that the epistemological and discursive structures of the seventeenth and eighteenth centuries cleaved the self from the world and turned the latter into an object to be apprehended as it was comprehended.[1] Initiated by texts like Edward Said's *Orientalism*, scholars of literature and other forms of culture drew on these presumed relationships between knowledge and power, and between discourse and political realities, in order to show that global representations produced through allegedly objective methods were, in actuality, highly if not entirely imaginary, inscribing not the world but the European desire for the world.[2] These theoretical approaches have emphasized that Western knowledge is inevitably and inescapably imperial by the very nature of its means of production.[3] In fact, this way of acquiring the world was much more insidious than was outright, violent conquest because its methods masqueraded as academic disinterestedness and because its biased conclusions were made to seem like self-evident truths.[4] In encountering such representations—circulated on a mass scale through travel writing, geographical texts, histories, imaginative literature, and art—Europeans were trained to think about themselves and the rest of the world through an imperial idiom.[5]

Those who have applied these theories of knowledge, imagination, and power to European discourse about Africa have argued that the continent was invented through an "Africanism" that relied on even more explicit statements of alterity and inversion than Said's Orientalism.[6] "It is in relation to Africa," Achille Mbembe writes, "that the notion of 'absolute otherness' has been taken farthest. It is now widely acknowledged that Africa as an idea, a concept, has historically served, and continues to serve, as a polemical argument for the West's desperate desire to assert its difference from the rest of the world."[7] Two European representations of Africa are frequently pointed to as both iconic manifestations of and perpetuators of this absolute otherness—a colonial call and response and an echo chamber of European ideas about the continent. One is G. W. F. Hegel's *The Philosophy of History* (1837), in which he deemed Africa "the Unhistorical, Undeveloped Spirit, still involved in the conditions of mere nature," existing "only as on the threshold of the World's History."[8] The other is Joseph Conrad's *Heart of Darkness* (1899), in which Marlow tells his fellow sailors about his childhood spent poring over maps of the world, superimposing his daydreams of exploration and adventure over their blank spaces and hungering for "the biggest, the most blank, so to speak," the interior of Africa.[9] But Hegel and Conrad are only particularly illustrative and recognizable stopping points on what is often described as a transhistorical and transdisciplinary tradition of Europeans deploying images of the continent to secure their own sense of racial or cultural superiority and to justify first the enslavement of Africa's peoples and then the colonization of its land.[10] Since its inception as a geographical idea, Christopher Miller writes, Africa "brings Europe face to face with nothing but itself."[11]

Returning for a moment to the European worldview at large, given the crucial role that assumptions about Enlightenment and modernity played in early theories of how the protocols of Western knowledge enabled empire, it was fitting that critics brought them to bear on early modern and eighteenth-century literature and culture.[12] The results confirmed that the global knowledge produced by and circulated through early Enlightenment texts was not politically neutral and that art and literature do not exist outside of cultural and epistemological structures that empower some and oppress others. Yet critics also found that much of what such theories took for granted about early modern and eighteenth-century attitudes and worldviews didn't satisfactorily square with how Europeans at the time actually wrote about nation, culture, empire, the self, or human difference.[13] Scholars have since argued, for instance, that a coherent sense of national or racial identity didn't precede global contact but was constantly being renegotiated in relation to it.[14] Some have seen these renegotiations as acts of desperation by European subjects faced with their own existential fragility or with the fragility of Europe's early imperial or expansionist projects.[15] Others have suggested that European writers and readers turned to representations of faraway people and places as a vehicle for interrogating the self and that these investigations could be facilitated by xenophilia rather than prompted by xenophobia.[16] More attention has been given to the fact that not all non-European geographies or people were depicted as potential objects of conquest, and new analytical models have been developed for studying European encounters with and representations of non-European empires that were at least as powerful if not more powerful than their own and with whom their relationships were primarily diplomatic and economic rather than colonial.[17]

Those who study early Enlightenment literature and culture have also made a concerted effort to develop interpretive frames that take into account the capacity of the global majority to both resist and operate outside of European systems of oppression and thought. Initial attempts to unmask European strategies of domination often foreclosed such analyses because they endowed the European subject with an improbable amount of discursive control guided by a level of foresight described by Olúfẹ́mi Táíwò as an "epistemic competence bordering on clairvoyance on the part of the ruling classes to know what would work and when not to try something."[18] As such, these critical paradigms operated within a worldview as Eurocentric as the one they sought to dismantle, one in which the colonizer's exaggerated sense of their own authority was accepted as much as it was critiqued.¹⁹ Scholars have responded by becoming more attentive to the specific ways that texts produced in contact zones were inevitably shaped by the material realities of those contexts.²⁰ There is increasing recognition, for instance, that European dependence on indigenous knowledges and technologies had a marked influence over how Europeans thought and wrote, not to mention their unavoidable reliance on mediators, translators, and guides.²¹ These acting subjects can be recouped even from a literary record that seeks to repress or erase them, though it sometimes requires reading against the grain, searching for traces, or reading gaps and silences to do so.²² They often become most visible in moments when colonial archives or texts reveal their own representational failures or the failures of colonial efforts on the ground.²³ One way that scholars have sought to recover them more directly is by radically rethinking what constitutes an archive to include material culture, cultural memory, gestures, expressions, bodies, techne, and landscapes.²⁴ Methods have been devised for calculating the agency and capacity for resistance of the global majority into analyses of even imaginative literature by authors who never set foot outside of Europe.²⁵ These approaches are usually cousins of or descendants of what Said calls in *Culture and Imperialism* "contrapuntal reading," in which a reader analyzes a work with a simultaneous awareness of the dominant view that the text narrates and the other experiences and histories at play that made the dominant discourse possible, taking into account how what was excluded, suppressed, or left implied might be as much a part of the text as what was included.²⁶ The interpretive field is established through control points set both inside and outside the literary work, and the interplay among them reveals new things about how texts and contexts speak to one another across space and time.

By changing how literary critics think about modernity and the European self, the material realities of the contact zone, the heterogeneity of imperial and expansionist projects and attitudes toward them, the colonized or oppressed subject's capacity to be an agent of resistance, how political and economic power was distributed on the global stage, and how both archives and imaginative literature might offer insight into these complexities, at least thirty years of scholarship has made it not only possible but imperative to talk about Asia beyond Orientalism and Islamophobia and the Americas beyond manifest destiny, abject slaves, and vanishing Indians. This scholarship ought to change the way we talk about Africa, too, but far less has been done to dismantle the notion that Africa could operate in the early Enlightenment imagination as anything but an absolute other, a sandbox where Europeans worked out ideas about themselves, or a blank space over which they prewrote the nineteenth century. In this sense at least, literary studies today is more the inheritor of Hegel's declaration that Africa existed outside of history than the early Enlightenment texts that this book analyzes were the progenitors of it.

Indeed, Anthony Barker, P. E. H. Hair, Roxann Wheeler, George Boulukos, Adam Beach, and Emily Bartels are among those who have demonstrated that travel writing and other geographical genres from the early Enlightenment represented Africa as one of the most diverse parts of the world and that the racial and cultural categories and language they used to describe its inhabitants were neither simplistic within texts nor uniform across texts.[27] Boulukos and Bartels have specifically cautioned against the tendency to read *Heart of Darkness* backward into early Enlightenment literature, arguing that in flattening out the complex history of contact between Africa and Europe, such analyses themselves perform what they critique in their objects of study.[28] These scholars recognize that Africans exerted agency in the contact zone that affected both encounters on the ground and the representations of those encounters in European texts, if only obliquely. Because this research largely focuses on European attitudes toward human difference and slavery, it doesn't delve substantively into what the African worlds that Europeans sought to represent actually looked like beyond occasional illustrative anecdotes, but this work has made it possible to see that many narratives about Africa coexisted in the early Enlightenment and that, although Europeans did write about Africans as primitive savages, they could accept within the very same texts and without incredulity the notion of sophisticated African kingdoms ruled by legitimate sovereigns that existed at crossroads of global trade. Thus, important groundwork has been laid in literary studies for moving away from a discourse of absolute otherness and blank space and toward scholarship that engages African history and thought in substantive ways.

Historians who have shown Africa's centrality to the early Enlightenment world have likewise laid a crucial foundation for dismantling persistent assumptions about the continent's place (or lack thereof) in early modern and eighteenth-century literature, though the fact that they, too, continue to stress how much work needs to be done in this area indicates the extent to which Hegel's ghost remains a transdisciplinary specter.[29] Most pertinently, increasing attention is being given to how Africans' representations of themselves and their worlds—not simply how Africans inhabited their worlds—dictated the terms of precolonial cultural encounters with outsiders. Cécile Fromont, Herman Bennett, Matteo Salvadore, and Michael Gomez, for instance, have all offered detailed analyses of how elite Africans in the medieval and early modern periods successfully manipulated a range of media—including written texts, artwork, diplomatic performances, coronations, processions, pilgrimages, and acts of religious devotion—to communicate ideas about themselves and their worlds that persuaded outsiders at least on some levels even if they also found them strange, unsettling, or uncouth on others.[30] Each of these scholars has widened the scope of what can be interpreted as a meaningful African expression and challenged the notion that expressions were fundamentally misunderstood by or merely appropriated by outsiders seeking to advance their own agendas in international diplomacy, religious conversion, or trade, and I draw on their conclusions, their methods, or both in my own consideration of the contact zone.

What this book offers in turn is an account of how such African expressions moved from relatively insular European discourse communities into the geographical imaginations of a general reading public, and to that end, Wendy Laura Belcher's *Abyssinia's Samuel Johnson: Ethiopian Thought in the Making of an English Author* has opened several doors. Offering a theory of transcultural intertextuality that centralizes how African discourse made meaning in cultural encounters and that deemphasizes how Europeans made meaning out of cultural encounters, Belcher argues that Europeans enshrined African expressions in their texts even when they didn't intend to or know they were doing so. Because those expressions were enthralling, and because discourse can move contagiously from text to mind to text and remain recognizable, they could enter into the imaginative works of authors who never set foot in Africa. As her case study, Belcher turns to the success of the Habesha—the Highland peoples of what is now Ethiopia—in broadcasting narratives of their exceptionalism into the early modern and eighteenth-century world. She reads several of Samuel Johnson's writings as "discursively possessed" by these narratives not because Johnson consciously chose to adopt and adapt them but because they took over his imagination as he read and translated travel narratives and scholarship on Abyssinia. Because Johnson was invested in ecclesiastical debates about Ethiopian Christianity's theological similarities and differences from Protestantism and Catholicism and because he was struck by grief and other kinds of psychological rupture at key moments in his intellectual and creative life, he was a particularly susceptible host for this discursive possession. As a result, African discourses surface even in Johnson's fictional works that initially appear to have nothing to do with Abyssinia.

One of the most radical implications of Belcher's theory of how African discourse could move from genres that strove to represent the world as it was to genres that had no obligation to do so is that the imaginative work of a literary text doesn't negate or obliterate that discourse. Many critical approaches to European representations of the global—even ones like contrapuntal reading and its cousins and descendants that strive to calculate the worlds, experiences, and thought of the global majority into the interpretive field—take as read that the more imaginative a text is, the farther it moves from the moment of encounter and thus the less probable it is that it retained any element of that encounter. The fact that early Enlightenment representations of Africa are often speculative, romantic, allegorical, rhetorical, or figurative has long been considered a reliable indicator that Europeans were indulging in invention, the continent and its inhabitants transfigured by the author into a set of symbols to serve a larger aesthetic, narrative, or political purpose. But recognizing that African discourse could be speculative, romantic, allegorical, rhetorical, or figurative—considering how Africans transformed themselves and their worlds into symbolic forms to serve their own purposes first—gives scholars an avenue to consider its relationship to European texts beyond positivist tests of historical, anthropological, or geographical accuracy.

Like Belcher's book, *African Impressions* takes as a fundamental premise that Europeans encountered not just Africans and their worlds but African representations or projections of themselves and their worlds; that those expressions shaped the way Europeans thought and wrote; that their mobility across texts is not bound by literary genre or style; and that scholars can only see them if we learn more ourselves about African oral and written traditions. It likewise treats the connections between European writers and African discourse as porous interstices rather than as dividing lines that Europeans were constantly finding savvy ways to negotiate and reinscribe. However, in identifying and analyzing a cultural narrative that any relatively well-read European would have encountered, installed at the cultural level through the generic and disciplinary mechanics of the production of geographical knowledge rather than at the personal level through the functions of human consciousness, it offers a framework for locating African expressions in European literary traditions that accommodates a wider range of texts and authors. Belcher's account of how African discourse was able to possess Johnson's imagination is in part an investigation into his unique set of circumstances. If, as Belcher states (and I agree), "the Western literary canon is a vast graveyard haunted by self-representing others, whose voices become the uncanny language of the very text that participates in constituting the other as an object of knowledge," then Johnson's case must fit into a larger constellation of means through which this came to be.³¹ Given the central role that assumptions about Enlightenment methods of knowledge-making and global representation have historically played in theories of cultural encounter, opening the doors between European texts and the worlds and worldviews of the global majority requires not simply a revision of how we think about the relationship between African expressions and the early Enlightenment subject but a revision of how we think about the means through which geographical ideas were made and circulated on a wide scale from contact narratives to more abstract forms of representation and back again.

Scope and Terminology

Before moving into a concrete example of an African impression, a few practical comments about scope and terminology are warranted. Because this is a book about how writers and thinkers struggled to reconcile the local with the global and about how they drew from a representational tradition that spanned hundreds of years to do so, my broad temporal term (early Enlightenment) and geographical terms (Europe and Africa) are necessarily sweeping, and all three are politically and theoretically problematic. I use the term "early Enlightenment" as a shorthand for the timespan between when Europeans began to aspire to describe the world with empirical accuracy and when they actually had the geopolitical scaffolding in place to explore Africa firsthand. It is intended to be a practical denotation of a set of seventeenth- and eighteenth-century epistemological practices, circumstances, and attitudes as they played out across an era of European-African relations that doesn't fall tidily into traditional academic periodization. In terms of British contact with the continent, this corresponds with the time between their first earnest attempts to send explorers up the west coast rivers (c. 1620) and the founding of the Association for Promoting the Discovery of the Interior Parts of Africa (the African Association) in 1788. However, this book also makes the case that by the time this contact happened, Europeans already had fairly well-entrenched impressions of Africa's interior in their geographical imaginations. And because the production of new knowledge about Africa was slow, and old knowledge about Africa kept getting resuscitated in various forms, including by Africans themselves, several of the historical events and representations of Africa considered here predate the seventeenth century but became and remained major drivers of early Enlightenment impressions of Africa. Therefore, African self-representations and representations of Africa dating from the thirteenth century through the first decades of the seventeenth are included in this book, considered as part of the cycle of discursive reiteration that gave African impressions their staying power.

"Europe" is no less imperfect a term, particularly because the impressions this book ultimately works toward were specifically British, following the path of Britain's expansionist interests and culminating in analyses of texts written in English. I frequently use "European" because the production of early Enlightenment geographical knowledge was an enormous transnational effort. It is true that competition and conflict among European powers played a role in who had access to which global region, what was permitted to be printed, and how certain travel narratives were translated. Geographical compilers framed their work in service to specific national agendas. But much of the substance of any individual geographical text, no matter which country or language it was published in, came from a shared corpus of knowledge. If the idea of a "European" geographical tradition is too broad, it is also too narrow—it doesn't do justice to Europe's debt to Arabic geographical sources, though the centrality of Arabic writing to Europe's impressions of Africa is accounted for in the following chapters. And again, each geographical text, whether written in Dutch, French, German, Portuguese, Spanish, English, Arabic, or some other language, also incorporates African self-representation into its pages.

Pragmatically speaking, Africa has real geological boundaries, but the term also lumps together thousands of ethnic groups and nine terrestrial biomes. I use the term because this book is in part about how this lumping occurred. European thinking about global geography grew increasingly continental in the seventeenth and eighteenth centuries, with geographical texts presenting Africa as a unit and striving to make claims about "Africa in General" before describing the continent's different regions, which were also categories imposed on the continent from the outside. When I describe African peoples, I have endeavored to do so in as specific terms as possible. Some of these peoples are Christian or Muslim or have been culturally and linguistically influenced by heavy traffic with Europe or the wider Islamic world. There is still an ingrained tendency in Western scholarship to imagine these groups as culturally diluted—an assumption that is ironically shared by both the Western intellectual inheritors of Hegel's worldview and political and academic movements that long for an origin story for the diasporic subject that precedes any influence from enslavers or colonizers. But African cultures were wrought through centuries of traffic with each other and with the rest of the world. Ethiopian Highlanders have practiced Christianity since the fourth century. Islam began to spread through sub-Saharan Africa at roughly the same time that Christianity began to spread through Britain, and by the late Middle Ages it was a dominant religion as far down the east coast as Zimbabwe, throughout the entirety of the Western Sudan, and as deep into Guinea as Nigeria. Trade routes, political alliances, colonial systems, and shared language families and literatures connected great swaths of the continent. Much of Africa was cosmopolitan, and cosmopolitan places are culturally hybrid places. In the following pages, an expression is considered "African" when it was deployed by local inhabitants of a particular region often enough that it became a part of how they understood themselves and wanted others to understand them as well.

How African thought spread through the Atlantic world and literary traditions via the African diaspora is outside the purview of this project, though work on this topic has influenced my own understanding of what methods are available for locating African expressions in the Western archive or literary canon and for theorizing their relationships to European discourse.[32] Diasporic Africans certainly shaped how Africa was imagined and vice versa, particularly as authors who were brought or claimed to have been brought from Africa to the Americas began writing and publishing their own texts in European languages. Ideas of Africa were also influenced by debates about race and slavery and shaped those debates in turn.[33] The impressions this book outlines were not the only ways that outsiders thought and wrote about the continent, and they don't negate the strands of geographical discourse that justified the enslavement of its inhabitants and that would ultimately make Hegel's notion that Africa had no history both thinkable and believed. But they were mainstream and widely recognizable and serve as a useful reminder in a field that tends to associate Africa first and foremost with the Middle Passage that the continent is not reducible in reality or in European discourse to a point of departure for the slave trade or to the eastern margin of the Atlantic world.[34] In fact, for early Enlightenment Europeans, part of the appeal of Africa's geographical situation was that it sat in the middle of Asia, Europe, and the Americas, accessible not only by Atlantic routes but also by the Indian Ocean and Mediterranean Sea.

All research projects that seek to demonstrate how the ideas and expressions of one culture influenced another face two methodological tasks. One is identifying and describing what those ideas and expressions were, and this can be particularly tricky if the people under consideration don't have written archives of their histories. The other is explaining how those ideas and expressions crossed what at times might seem like insurmountable cultural barriers, remaining intact enough to be recognizable on the other side. Both these tasks are made easier in this book by the fact that the African expressions considered in the following chapters were produced and circulated by Africa's geopolitical and economic elite. Enslaved voices and perspectives are difficult to locate in the historical record, and when they do appear, they are, in Saidiya Hartman's words, "entangled with and impossible to differentiate from the terrible utterances that condemned them to death."[35] For Gayatri Chakravorty Spivak, the condition of not being able to speak was precisely what made the subaltern subaltern.[36] Elite African discourses, by contrast, had organized networks of textual, oral, and visual engines driving and disseminating them that were not dependent on European mediators.

So, as far as describing African expressions in and of themselves goes, reasonable claims can be made about them and about the worlds and worldviews they reflected and constituted, especially given the academic work that has been put into reconstructing them. Some of this work has been done with the grain of a written archive. Africans were literate and wrote in endemic languages like Ge'ez or Swahili or in European languages or Arabic. Others were what Bruce Hall calls "literacy aware," participating in intellectual conversations in ways that shaped the written archive even if they couldn't read or write themselves.[37] Reconstructing African worlds and thought that don't have a written archive requires a different approach, but the more details on any given region that have been compiled and collated, the clearer precolonial African worlds have become. Such sources include the reportage of European and Arabic travelers, African oral literature whose formal constraints have given it stability over time, local oral histories, historical linguistics, African art and architecture, the evaluation of archaeological evidence, and scientific dating.[38] Articulating African ideas through Western frames always runs the risk of misrepresentation, as scholars who have made visible the limitations and biases of Western epistemological methods argue.[39] However, as Mbembe points out, "In principle, nothing Africa says is untranslatable into a human language," nor, as Táíwò expresses, do we need to talk about Africa in a language different than the ones "with which we routinely talk about the rest of the world."[40] The state of African historiography is such that it is possible to look back at precolonial European and Arabic contact narratives and other kinds of geographical writing and identify where their reports resonate with African ideas of themselves.

Exactly how it is that these expressions cross cultural barriers into European thinking and writing is the substance of the following chapters and is theorized more particularly in my account of travel writing and other forms of geographical representation below, but it is a foundational condition of the transcultural influence that I'm describing that the expressions considered in this book were public discourses intended to say something about local worlds and worldviews to outsiders. They are not Michel de Certeau's everyday practices—talking, reading, moving about, shopping, cooking, and so on—though those acts have their own signifying power in the contact zone, nor are they reducible to Pierre Bourdieu's internalized *habitus*, though they shaped community identities.[41] They are performative—what Diana Taylor defines as expressions that are by their nature distinct from "other forms of cultural expression"—and, as such, are self-consciously discursive.[42] But they are not the kinds of rites or rituals that were notoriously misunderstood by Europeans and cited as evidence of Africans' savage backwardness. They were rather the languages of imperialism and religious superiority and also the languages of diplomacy and trade—narratives that were designed to communicate ideas about the self to others. They successfully did so, some of them reaching Europe before Europeans reached Africa, beginning their global journeys through the trans-Sahara trade and Christian and Muslim pilgrimages to the Holy Lands.

Thus, the African expressions considered in this book are also as politically and culturally complex as any imperial or exceptionalist discourse. I have opted to use the term "local" over "native" or "indigenous" when referring to African groups not only because the relationship between the local and the global is a central theme of the book but also to avoid implicit suggestions about who has proprietary rights to inhabit any given region. My accounts of African political and discursive power are intended to be neither triumphalist nor censuring. Finally, since this book is primarily aimed at scholars of Anglophone literature who may be encountering these peoples, places, and events for the first time, I have opted for search-engine friendly spellings of African words and names throughout.

The Sofala-Ophir Impression and African Expressions of Solomonic Exceptionalism

Two aims of this book are to offer an account of the strategies and practices that early Enlightenment travelers and geographers used to create impressions of a continent to which they had no firsthand access and to show how that knowledge-making process led to and perpetuated a dependency on African expressions about themselves and their worlds. This section offers a compressed but comprehensive example of that. It sketches out the role that African expressions played in shaping the theory that the Biblical city of Ophir was in Sofala (a region on the southeast coast that is now part of Mozambique), it demonstrates how European geographical writers synthesized those expressions into a general impression, and it describes the role that returns to contact zones and to African discourse played in maintaining the impression's core details.

In the wake of the so-called age of discovery, Europeans strove to reconcile their ever-widening understanding of the world with a lingering belief in the historicity of the Bible. One of the holy grails of sacred geography was the location of Ophir—the city from which Solomon acquired the wealth and materials to build his temple. Other than references to some exports like gold, silver, ivory, precious stones, peacocks (or possibly parrots, ostriches, or apes), the only specifics the Bible gives about Ophir are that it was a port city and that it took three years to reach it from Judea and return again.[43] European travelers and armchair geographers alike relied on these details and whatever other evidence they could scrape together in their attempts to pin down its location. Christopher Columbus believed the island he would call Hispaniola was Ophir because of the gold he found there, and Benito Arias Montano made a philological argument that it was Peru based on a passage from Kings that said Solomon's Temple was built with "the gold of Parvaim."[44] John Dee located it in Sumatra because of its ivory and gemstones.[45] Abraham Ortelius included a cartouche and a smaller, inset map in the lower left-hand corner of his *Geographia Sacra* listing possible locations of Ophir, throwing his own lot in with those who said it was in southeast Africa—all the commodities listed in the Bible were to be found there as long as one read "parrots" or "ostriches" for "peacocks," and it was reasonable that one could sail to southeast Africa from Israel and back again in three years in a ninth-century BCE ship.[46] Voyages to the New World would take too long. Voyages to other parts of the Holy Lands and the East Indies would be too short of a trip, and large swaths of that trade were conducted via overland caravans, not by sea at all.

But another category of evidence was routinely cited for why East Africa was Ophir's most plausible location—Africa was the only possibility that met the above criteria where the inhabitants themselves affirmed a Solomonic connection. In fact, there are at least three different African narrative traditions that do so, and all three circulated in widely read early modern and eighteenth-century geographical texts. One comes from the Habesha.[47] They have long contended that the Biblical Queen of Sheba is African, and her story is the centerpiece of the *Kebra Nagast*, the mythopoetic national narrative of the Solomonic Dynasty, manuscripts of which date back at least to the fourteenth century. Recounting the queen's visit to Solomon and prophesizing that Ethiopia will someday rise up as the world's most powerful Christian empire, the narrative does not simply identify the Queen of Sheba as African; it puts her at the center of the story, giving her the name Makeda and endowing her with great wisdom as well as great political and economic clout. Tamrin, Makeda's royal merchant, is commissioned by Solomon to bring the materials for building his temple into Jerusalem, all of which come from Makeda's domains. When Tamrin brings Solomon to Makeda's attention, she resolves to visit Solomon herself and judge whether he is as clever as she has heard.

Versions of Makeda's story circulated in European languages from at least the sixteenth century. To offer only a few examples, Francisco Álvares published an account of seeing the *Kebra Nagast* in a church in Aksum, the presumed seat of Makeda's kingdom (1540), and recorded a synopsis of it given to him by his hosts. A fuller account was written down by a Habesha ambassador to Portugal, Saga za Ab, around the same time and published by Damião de Góis (1561). Translations into English of both these accounts were published by Samuel Purchas (1613, 1625). The Ethiopianist Hiob Ludolf included a summary of the story in his *Historia Aethiopica* (1681), the accuracy of which he confirmed with a Habesha monk named Gorgoryos who came to visit him in Germany. James Bruce, who spent six years traveling in Africa in the 1770s and many more thinking and writing about it after he had returned to Britain, brought the first copies of the *Kebra Nagast* itself into Europe in 1774.

Another East African narrative tradition that connects Africa with King Solomon comes from the Swahili traders who migrated to Sofala from Kilwa (in present-day Tanzania) in the twelfth century.[48] Up the Buzi River where the gold and silver were mined, these traders encountered the structures of Great Zimbabwe, a 2.8-square-mile complex of freestone walls built by the Shona in the eleventh century, including a conical tower that is thirty feet high. The impressiveness of the edifices, the fact that they were constructed entirely without mortar, and their proximity to the mines reminded the Swahili traders of stories in their books of how King Solomon wielded great power over the djinn, compelling them to build his palaces and fortresses stone by stone and to mine precious metals and gems on his behalf. They determined that Great Zimbabwe was built by Solomon, giving rise to a common idea in Islamic texts that East Africa was the source of King Solomon's wealth. Europeans knew about this narrative tradition from what these Swahili traders told Portuguese travelers in the sixteenth and seventeenth centuries. In 1502 the Portuguese traveler Thomas Lopez arrived in Sofala. He reported that "the Moorish merchants were telling us that in Sofala there is a wonderfully rich mine to which, as they find in their books, King Solomon used to send every three years to draw an infinite quantity of gold."[49] When João dos Santos sought to confirm Lopez's account (1586), he was told by local inhabitants of Sofala that the freestone walls upriver, a location they call "Fura," were built by devils.[50] Mysterious writing marked the entryways to the mines, the Swahilis told him, indicating they once belonged to an ancient civilization. This testimony, which offered evidence that included ineluctably local rather than generic details that could describe many places, was part of what swayed Ortelius away from arguments that Ophir was to be found in Peru or Indonesia.[51]

A third East African narrative tradition that locates Ophir near Sofala comes from the Lemba, a Bantu ethnic group local to southeast Africa who claim a Semitic origin.[52] According to their oral traditions, they originate from the land of Sheba, though unlike the Habesha, they locate Sheba's capital on the Arabian Peninsula. They traveled to Africa to set up trading posts along the coast thousands of years ago. When war broke out in their country of origin and they could not return, they took African wives and settled permanently. Just as the Swahili traders told Portuguese travelers that the mines belonged to King Solomon, Santos cites "a Tradition of the Natives" that the mines and the freestone structures upriver from Sofala belonged to either Solomon or the Queen of Sheba.[53] Josiah Burchett (1720) similarly points to accounts of "inhabitants" of the region as evidence for locating Ophir near Sofala. Their oral histories prove them to be of "the Race of *Abraham*," and thus Burchett deems them "doubtless the Descendants of some of the *Hebrews* who either settled there, or suffered Shipwrecks in the time of this intercourse between *Judea* and those Countries."[54] Both Santos and Burchett identify these locals as distinct from the Muslim Swahili.

Habesha, Swahili, and Lemba claims to a Solomonic past are all examples of discourses intentionally projected by Africans about themselves and their worlds to outsiders. And Europeans interpreted all three of them to form comprehensive impressions about the continent's history and geography in ways that stretched and morphed them but also perpetuated them and depended on the truth of their essentials. For instance, João de Barros, the Portuguese historian who compiled and synthesized many early modern Portuguese travel accounts into his *Décadas da Ásia* (1552–63), advocated for locating Ophir in East Africa based on the local testimony he found there, on Saga za Ab's writings and perhaps even on interviews with the ambassador himself, and on other another type of African expression nested within this discursive evidence. Noting the similarities between the ruins of Great Zimbabwe and the ruins of Aksum—the city in the Ethiopian Highlands that early Enlightenment Europeans believed was the seat of Makeda's empire—he put forth the notion that not only were Solomon's mines to be found in southeastern Africa, as the inhabitants of that region said, but that Makeda's domains must have stretched nearly the length of the east coast of Africa.[55] Bruce was similarly persuaded that Makeda's empire had encompassed Sofala, pointing to what he saw as consensus among various African sources as evidence for these historical and geographical claims. "The inhabitants of the Continent, and of the peninsula of Arabia opposite to it, of all denominations agree," he insists, that Africa "was the royal seat of the Queen of Saba, famous in ecclesiastical history for her journey to Jerusalem."[56] They also agree that the mines of Abyssinia "belonged to her, and were erected at the place of her residence," and "that all the gold, silver, and perfumes came from her kingdom of Sofala, which was Ophir, and which reached from thence to Azab, upon the borders of the Red Sea, along the coast of the Indian Ocean."

Neither Barros nor Bruce produced what we would now consider an accurate account of the history of southeastern Africa. They interpreted the expressions of exceptionalism and imperial power projected by the Shona ruins of Great Zimbabwe—which in fact have no Solomonic connections—through the lens of what the Habesha said about Makeda's Solomonic connections and geopolitical reach. Then, using Swahili and Lemba accounts as further justification, they fit a great swath of East Africa into preexisting European ideas of sacred geography. Both writers also interpreted the available evidence to suit Portugal's and Britain's respective geopolitical interests. Europeans were not seeking the location of Ophir for purely intellectual reasons, nor were they seeking an El Dorado. (They were using riches that had already been found to make cases for its location, not searching for its location to find riches.) Rather, claiming to have pinpointed its location glorified and legitimized European expansionist agendas. As the theory went, Solomon was the first great navigator and the first lawful global power because he relied on trade rather than conquest to enrich his kingdom and build his temple.[57] Whichever monarch succeeded in locating and establishing his or her own trade with Solomon's ancient partners would shine as his spiritual successor on the world stage.[58] Thus, Barros and Bruce participated in a tradition of both idealizing imperial expansion and making it appear not only inevitable but divinely ordained. And the notion that Sofala was once Ophir would continue to be put to expansionist and then ultimately colonial ends. Almost a hundred years after Bruce wrote his lengthy defense claiming Ophir for Africa, H. Rider Haggard secured the title, at least literarily speaking, when he wrote *King Solomon's Mines* (1885)—a text to which I will return in the coda of this book—representing this segment of Africa as Sheba's body, which European explorers literally penetrate to find a hidden city full of diamonds.

But such appropriations don't erase the African expressions that comprised these impressions from history, nor do Barros and Bruce obscure them from their texts. They not only considered what Africans had to say and show about themselves and their worlds to be legitimate geographical evidence, they also stressed that such narratives are credible because they come from privileged insiders with knowledge that Europeans could never acquire firsthand, and they preserved as much of the local particulars of these narratives as possible because their utility lay in their specificity. Such narratives were also considered to be credible not because Europeans heard them one time but because their essential elements were repeated, reiterated, and rechecked across a cycle of contact that unfolded over hundreds of years—for instance, Barros confirmed Abyssinia's Solomonic claims with Saga za Ab, Ludolf did the same with the monk Gorgoryos, and Bruce did the same with his Abyssinian hosts and by eventually reading the source text itself and bringing it back to Europe. Each walked away from these encounters with a consistent idea of Makeda's story and Abyssinia's geopolitical reach not because it was noted once and then simply reprinted but because, in addition to being reprinted, it was also confirmed in contact zones between Africans and Europeans. And it was confirmed because it was a living discourse, reiterated within Habesha, Swahili, and Lemba narrative traditions independent of European interest in the story. All three types of repetition—internally within African cultures, in contact zones between Africans and Europeans, and across European texts—make up the engine that gave African impressions not only their substance but also their animation, energy, and literary appeal. Due to this cyclical reengagement, African expressions are not simply fleeting ghosts in the background of history or an absent presence in texts that only become visible by reading gaps and silences. They are discourses that exerted persistent influence over the early Enlightenment geographical imagination.

African Expressions in European Travel Writing

The above analysis made some implicit assumptions about how travel writing (considered here) and other forms of geographical representation (addressed in the next section) work that merit some explanation, not in the least because these genres have been suspected of rendering mute the local inhabitants of the places they sought to represent. In travel writing the empirical turn is held responsible for this. There was a push beginning in the early seventeenth century to turn travelers into what David Livingstone calls "properly trained eyewitnesses," fueled by the hope that if they learned to write, draw, or otherwise record what they saw, exactly as they saw it, they would be able to reproduce the world as it was.[59] By the 1660s scientific organizations like the Royal Society were publishing instruction guides for travelers, like Robert Boyle's *General Heads for the Natural History of a Country Great or Small Drawn out for the Use of Travellers and Navigators* (1666), on what to include in their accounts and how to organize them.[60] This initiative ostensibly transformed travel writing from a wonder-inducing genre in which the lines between the marvelous and the empirical were virtually nonexistent to the handmaiden of navigation and natural history.[61] Mary Louise Pratt termed the authorial figure who emerged from these efforts the "seeing man": "The white male subject of European landscape discourse—he whose imperial eyes passively look out and possess."[62] His pen created the world as colonizable space and the other as a colonizable subject, serving simultaneously as a visionary catalyst for conquest and the justification for it all under the cover of scientific inquiry. Travel writers, of course, always depended on cultural brokers, translators, and guides.[63] But since the account the seeing man produced was supposed to be both objective and monological, he ostensibly took pains to disguise this fact, ensuring that the point of view he offered seemed to be a view from nowhere.[64] When locals do appear, they are either extracted from the landscape and enshrined in ethnographic description where they are rendered objects or they animate the narrative as literary characters, their words and behaviors massaged or outright invented to a narrative end, like making the seeing man appear more credible or more powerful or making the locals seem enthusiastic about expansionist agendas.[65]

Empiricism was undoubtedly gaining ground in the seventeenth and eighteenth centuries and did aspire to discipline language and representation into instruments that could communicate the naked and unvarnished truth of the world. But in part because of these lofty ambitions, both the method and the eyewitness as a figure were also under constant interrogation. One's ability to merely see and write didn't guarantee the viability of one's observations. Packaging oneself as an effective and trustworthy eyewitness was a complicated textual endeavor, and naive empiricists were subjects of satire and objects of scathing critique.⁶⁶ Not all self-proclaimed empiricists understood the self as the penetrator and the world as the penetrated; they often considered themselves to be open to what the world had to show them.⁶⁷ Furthermore, what naturalists wanted from travel writers and what general readers wanted from travel writers were often at cross purposes, as Jonathan Lamb describes, the readerly desire for excitement, novelty, and interesting details often coming in conflict with the expected uniformity of empirical documentation. Anne Thell has shown that under the weight of these pressures and conflicting expectations, travel narratives became sites experimentation in and of themselves and not simply the handmaidens of the Royal Society's taxonomic projects.⁶⁸

When it came to offering insights into Africa's interior or history, "eyewitnesses" were subject to constraints that required them both to rely on external sources, lest they have nothing new or interesting to say on the topic, and to cite them, lest they be accused, as travelers often still were, of telling tales. Bound by the fact that no one but the inhabitants of the continent could claim to know for sure what lay past the point of European or Arabic navigation, travel writers positioned their narratives as joint efforts between themselves as eyewitnesses and the Africans they depended on as sources of local knowledge. To offer a few representative examples from three hundred years of this nearly ubiquitous trope, Álvares assures his reader that he "sought to know a great part of the Countries, Kingdomes, and Signiories of [Abyssinia], and their customs and usages, some by sight, and some others by the report of credible persons."⁶⁹ He swears that his account is reliable because he immediately wrote things down, "delivering such things as I saw, as having seene them; and things reported, as received by hearing." Leo Africanus, whose late sixteenth-century account of the Western Sudan dominated representations of Africa for hundreds of years, did not actually see much of sub-Saharan Africa with his "owne eies"; he relied on the reports of locals to whom the various kingdoms he includes were "sufficiently known and frequented."⁷⁰ When Jean Barbot articulated his approach to gathering knowledge about the Gold Coast in the late seventeenth century, he wrote, "I us'd to pry into every object that occurr'd to the eye," but what he could not see for himself, he learned through conversation "with the discreetest of the natives."⁷¹ In the early eighteenth century, a literal seeing man, the surveyor William Smith, supplemented his surveys with information from local informants who he deemed "generally faithful as to what Account they gave of Things."⁷² In the late eighteenth century, the slave trader turned abolitionist John Newton was not overly bothered by the fact that he could no longer distinguish what he had "seen" from what he had "only heard related"; he was nevertheless willing to "confirm upon oath" the truth of his relation.[73] If travelers' eyewitness claims both reiterate travel writing's burgeoning and then blossoming relationship with empiricism and interrogate it, as Thell suggests, their earwitness claims reiterate geography's much longer relationship with hearsay and offer similar opportunities for reflecting on precisely what counted as convincing geographical evidence, in what contexts, and why.

The local informants cited in these travel narratives are by necessity not mute, but they are curated in the sense that the eyewitness narrator extends his own credibility to them, performing what Parrish calls in a New World context "the obligatory white framing or confirming of native testimony."[74] At one time this kind of curation led critics to interpret them as invented figures rather than referential ones, included in order to validate the European perspective but then contained to avoid any risk of empowering them beyond that. Such is Spivak's "native informant," who is invoked, enlisted in service to colonial master narratives, and then erased again and Stephen Greenblatt's "alien voices," which allow only the illusion of multiplicity in the text so the "monological power" of the European narrator can deny it.[75] As outlined above, more recent critical trends read around this monological power or undercut the idea that it was all that powerful to begin with. The notion has generally taken hold that such analyses problematically assume the truth of the supremacy of the Cartesian authorial subject even as they seek to expose it as a fiction, and non-Europeans in travel narratives are now largely understood to at least be avatars for located, embodied subjects and cues to think through how those subjects might be present in the text in other ways.[76]

In other words, analyses of contact narratives now tend to treat European authors' representations of their informants; who their informants might have been as historical individuals; and the discursive impact of their informants' words and actions on the text as interrelated but distinct inquiries. The questions have thus become what one can justifiably say about any of the three and how they then might shed light on one another, and the answers largely depend on who is being represented, under what circumstances, and through which kind of "eyewitness account" (which turns out not to be a monolithic genre). In Cassander Smith's analysis of how travelers in the Atlantic world attempted to put Black Africans to symbolic use in their anti-Spanish rhetoric, for instance, she locates the presence of Black Africans not through those descriptions but in their ruptures and breaks, which suggest that something happened on the ground that was powerful and startling enough that it interrupted the author's narration or exceeded their ability to smoothly incorporate it into the work's larger agendas. She offers judicious speculations on what that something might have been—not as historical conjectures (she contends that the thoughts and intentions of the individual represented subjects remain unrecoverable in that sense) but as testaments to the fact that early modern Black subjects were multifaceted, complete, and capable of meaningful action. By comparison, in Nicole Aljoe's study of embedded Caribbean slave narratives—the narratives of enslaved peoples recorded and edited by white authors—she notes that the "testimony of the slave narrators" exists on a more fluid continuum with the voice and intentions of the editor since without it "the editor would have no text."[77] They surface in the moments when the editor steps aside for them, and they seize narrative control in ways that the narrator did not anticipate. Aljoe describes what she does as a version of what Hartman termed "critical fabulation," but the genre she is working in justifies taking on faith that the text retained the voice of the enslaved subject at least in some measure.[78]

Travelers also had good reasons for recording in specific and thorough detail the words, gestures, and political rituals of their local interlocutors. Jeffrey Glover argues that this is the case, for example, in early descriptions of European treaties with Native Americans. Travelers sought to capture the diplomatic intentions of Native American leaders so they could prove the terms of those agreements to other European powers.[79] Attending to the specifics of the context and the genre enables Glover to assert with some confidence that intentions are recoverable—in fact, "Europeans only cared about treaties because they captured Native intentions"—though this doesn't mean that they were wholly understood by Europeans themselves. Ultimately, there is always some degree of speculation regarding what a figure mediated by a European text was thinking and feeling, but as Aljoe stresses, the autobiographical accounts of thinking, feeling individuals are not the only kind of accounts capable of being transgressive, and to assume that they are is to fall into the same fetishization of the Cartesian authorial subject that has long been recognized as a key ingredient of imperial worldviews.[80]

I focus on moments when travelers cite what their African informants told them about the continent past the point of navigation not to make the case that Europeans have accurately represented the African subject—though they might have—but because they offer a cue to consider how African expressions are at work in their texts. The traveler is, by the very nature of the trope, flagging that they are offering information they couldn't have possibly known firsthand and—unlike Parrish's European observers in the Americas—could not corroborate themselves, deploying what we might call an obligatory African framing or confirming of white testimony. This information can be identified and assessed not against conjectures of what did or did not happen in the interaction but against what Lisa Brooks calls the broader "narrative field," Taylor calls the "scenario," and Bennett calls the "grammar of politics" of the contact zone—the diorama that emerges when readers pay attention to patterns across many kinds of representations from a range of sources.[81] It can also be assessed against African expressions themselves, which, like African impressions, are not the thoughts or subjective experiences of any one person—they are widespread cultural discourses that have a life and a genealogy of their own outside of the European text. The locus of their transgressive power is their collective nature rather than the agency of an individual.

Concentrating on the way travel narratives participate in a broader, more abstract intercultural conversation enables us to shift attention away from the question of whether European frames can accurately capture what happened in any given contact zone, but it also enables us to rethink the nature of the frame. Travelers did use familiar categories and narratives to make sense themselves of the unfamiliar and to make the unfamiliar familiar to their readers back home.[82] One of this book's aims, though, is to show that an interpretive frame didn't have to be European in origin to be familiar. By the time Europeans arrived on sub-Saharan Africa's shores, they already had fully grown ideas in their heads about what they would find there that had been shaped by African expressions that had entered Europe via the trans-Sahara trade and Christian and Muslim pilgrimages to the Holy Lands. By the early Enlightenment, as demonstrated in the Sofala-Ophir example above, African impressions inflected everything from how Europeans interpreted the landscape to the kinds of questions they asked their local informants. Travelers were never, in other words, wholly strangers but were always thinking and writing through hybrid frames that were already as familiar by the early seventeenth century as any other cultural idea that had hundreds of years to develop.

Geographical Genres and the Consolidation of African Impressions

If travel writing is one genre that has been implicated in packaging subjective and ideological representations of the world as objective truth, geographical genres like grammars, gazetteers, and maps have been even more so. They were, to borrow Robert Mayhew's useful distinction, products of the "study" rather than the "field."[83] This distance is the very thing that has made geographical genres so complicit in the production of imperial ideologies. It was from the study, Said argued, that Western scholars were able to invent an imaginary Orient that floated free from material realities as certain associations and images accumulated critical mass. As scholars have described how locally produced knowledge moved from the field into the study, the process of purification it needed to go through in order to become universal truth ostensibly sought to strip it of all vestiges of its local production.[84] Using the age of discovery as his keystone example, Bruno Latour describes the "cycle of accumulation" through which global knowledge grew increasingly distant from the place it was made and how European outsiders thus gained supremacy over places that they had once been at the mercy of: early Portuguese explorers gathered geographical information from locals (for instance, the best course to sail), preserved it in a stable form (measurements produced through navigational equipment), brought it back to the center of calculation (in this case Europe), and transformed it through a "cascade of inscriptions" into an epistemological artifact (the map) that was then used to send explorers away to bring back more information.[85] Through this process, the knowledge that Europeans produced about a place started to appear universal, outweighing and eventually erasing the existence or even the possibility of local epistemologies from the genealogy of Western thought.[86] Simplification was a necessary part of this transfiguration. Pointing to Boyle's methods as a test case, Lorraine Daston argues that the construction of the "fact" and the universalization of knowledge at the dawn of Enlightenment involved a practice of "description by omission": "Long accounts bristling with particulars" were turned into "concise reports made deliberately bland by summary, repetition, and omission of details."[87] It may seem at first, then, that geographical texts like grammars, gazetteers, and maps would absorb rather than preserve as distinct details any African expressions that contact narratives might manage to capture as each textual transposition moved knowledge farther from the contact zone described above.

Yet even as calls for empirical facts about the world grew louder and even as the "known" world grew larger, throughout the eighteenth century "geography" remained a banner under which many kinds of global representation were collected, and those who study the history of geography are undecided over the extent to which it should rightly be called an empirical discipline during this time.[88] The push toward gathering firsthand observations of the world for the sake of producing the useful knowledges of navigation and trade unfolded alongside and often intersected with a still robust humanist tradition of compiling, excerpting, collating, and synthesizing a wide range of erudite sources into coherent narratives that served a wide range of purposes. Authors of geographical texts drew from eyewitness accounts, but they also drew from Classical geographers, Arabic geographical traditions, Classical and modern histories, the Bible, and any other previously published work that had retained credibility. (By the early Enlightenment, for instance, Mandeville's *Travels* [c. 1357–71] had not, but Muhammad al-Idrisi's work [c. 1154] still had.) Many saw their task as synthesizing these forms of knowledge rather than replacing the old with the new, working to make the pieces fit together as agreeably as possible.[89] This is how Barros—drawing from scripture, Classical geographers, what Lopez, Santos, and Álvares were told by their African informants, and what he himself likely learned from Saga za Ab—arrived at his theory that Sofala was once Ophir, that the Queen of Sheba's domains must have extended far enough south to include Sofala, and that Aksum and Great Zimbabwe were built by the same people. The cycle of discursive reiteration through which Barros's theory accrued is a counterepistemology to Latour's contemporaneous example of the cycle of accumulation—each return to Africa to gather more information resulted not in European global knowledge moving further away from local knowledge but in local knowledge repeatedly infusing European worldviews.

Further into the eighteenth century there was a more concerted push from some quarters for geographers to start replacing erudite geographical representations with what could be empirically verified. In 1717 John Green expressed irritation over "how industrious the Learned have been to adjust the Modern to the Antient Geography, and fond of making Discoveries that way."[90] Yet he contended that no cartographer could draw a map of Africa "without consulting the Ancients, for he will often find they help where the Moderns fail."[91] He also lamented the fact that many travelers were not diligent enough in collecting their observations to be trusted and castigated mapmakers and geographers for being too quick to adopt new ideas before they had been sufficiently confirmed.[92] He offers a list of what he considers to be the most reliable sources on Africa from which geographers should pull instead, which includes a mix of travel accounts, collected geographies, and histories written in both European languages and Arabic.[93] In other words, even empirical geographical practices remained self-consciously enmeshed in citational networks that kept longstanding impressions of Africa alive and took seriously a variety of different categories of knowledge. And though it may seem that travelers were wholly the people of the field, there was an expectation that they, too, would evaluate the existent literature written about the regions to which they traveled and either confirm their contents or make the case for why their own reports were credible enough to overturn precedent.[94] Rather than imagining the movement of knowledge from the field to the study as an uncoupling of text from context, then (a process in which the representation grows increasingly detached from its referent over time), the dynamic among these arenas in the early Enlightenment might be pictured like a figure eight with travelers on one side, geographers on the other, and African expressions in the middle. Geographers and travelers continually relied on one another, and their respective quests for knowledge kept passing through African expressions as key pieces of evidence and affirmation, whether they were expressions that entered the European geographical imagination long ago or whether they were expressions produced through new encounters on the ground.

Geographers did abstract and synthesize, but they did not simply compile navigational data and landscape descriptions—they incorporated historical, anthropological, and theological information into their texts. Many understood themselves to be in the business of representing human life, not of representing empty containers for human life. Herman Moll, for instance, wrote in his *System of Geography* (1704) that "Topography" was "the most necessary Part of Geography": topography meaning not a place's physical features as it does now but the "great Actions" that have happened in a region, like wars, reigns of kings, and "noted Customs," and the "Condition of the Cities," including their "Wealth, Industry, and Populousness."[95] Moll, like Green, is associated with geography's empirical turn, and he was friendly with Royal Society figures like Boyle. Like d'Anville's map considered below, his own map of Africa, addressed in chapter 3 (fig. 4), is less heavily illustrated than ones that came before. But he contended that the writing of place required narrative, not simply fixed descriptions, and he understood geography as a genre shaped as much by time as by space. He was also sensible of the fact that one goal of geographical writing was public instruction. For Moll, without "great Actions," "Geography alone is Dry and Jejune, and makes but small Impression on the Memory." Moll's interest in ensuring that geographical writing was a genre that would delight as well as instruct is a useful reminder that travel writing, maps and atlases, geographical dictionaries, and general descriptions were made not only, or in some cases not even primarily, for travelers and naturalists but also for consumption by a general reading public.[96]

Editors of abstracted collections of travel accounts were also mindful of the evidentiary weight and literary appeal that local detail and narrative action gave geographical writing. The editor and compiler of Thomas Astley's *New General Collection of Voyages and Travels* (1743–47), who may have in fact been Green, considered his task to be to "preserve the useful, and expunge the superfluous."[97] But narrative descriptions of a country's "Genius, Manners and Customs of People" were not considered superfluous; they were considered "some of the most beautiful Articles in Authors" and also crucial to the integrity of the representation.[98] In fact, he accuses geographical accounts that read too much like "bare relations," stripped of their local detail, as sounding like "Hearsay" rather than fact, and he chides them for failing to "strike the Imagination." Even when geographical texts did distill descriptions of places down to bare relations, what was deemed their essential details were not necessarily devoid of the action and beautiful articles that Moll and this compiler call for. Descriptions of the Western Sudan usually tell some version, however truncated, of the wealth of the Mali Empire and the rise of the Songhai Empire, as discussed in chapter 1; accounts of Abyssinia always mention that it is the source of the Nile, that it was once thought to be the Christian kingdom of Prester John, and that it lays claim to the Queen of Sheba, as shown in chapter 4; accounts of the Swahili coast frequently mention that Sofala is thought by some to have been Ophir. Popular geographical texts, in other words, preserved recognizable elements of African expressions that shaped them because their compilers strove to retain distinct and interesting details and because even descriptive geographical writing preserved great actions (like Makeda's journey to Jerusalem, Mansa Musa I's Hajj, and Askia Muhammad I's conquest of the Western Sudan). Popular geographical texts also maintained these recognizable elements across time and spread them far and wide because, as has been frequently noted, they printed and reprinted the same material over and over again in new packaging, though, as some of the following chapters will show, not necessarily mechanically or arbitrarily.[99]

Texts that we think of as belonging more to the mathematical than the descriptive side of geography were also deeply enmeshed in the cycle of discursive reiteration, including maps. One of the first scholars to put pressure on the notion that maps were mirrors of reality or politically neutral products of Euclidean geometry, J. B. Harley stressed that maps are both records and tools of European imperial worldviews: the way they partition off, empty out, and fill up space reveals a great deal about early Enlightenment global thinking and expansionist desire.¹⁰⁰ Just as Africa itself is singled out as the most other of the other in European discourse, maps of Africa are invoked as the ultimate imaginative projections, evidenced by both literary examples (Conrad's blank map) and historical ones (the Berlin Conference [1884–85] during which representatives of Europe's colonial powers literally partitioned off a map of Africa and then used it to alter the political contours of the continent). On the other hand, even Harley himself cautioned against the impulse to read maps as tidy examples of power-knowledge or apparatuses of state control given the enormously complicated historical conditions of their production.¹⁰¹ Maps don't reflect a single gaze any more neatly than they reflect spatial reality. Rather, "Every map codifies more than one perspective on the world"; it comprises a "web of interrelationships, stretching both inside and beyond the map document."¹⁰² This is true about early Enlightenment maps of Africa—even ones that look like protoversions of Marlow's map.

The French mapmaker Jean Baptiste Bourguignon d'Anville, for example, is credited in the history of cartography for being one of the first mapmakers who resisted the impulse to fill in continents with decorative details or with geographical features at a vague guess. Instead, he was committed to including only information that had been verified.¹⁰³ As a result, the middle of his Africa is less heavily illustrated than on maps that came before (fig. 1).¹⁰⁴ However, empirical witness was not the standard by which a detail was considered verified for d'Anville; rather, he judged whether it had stood the test of time and was borne out by a range of credible sources. Despite their sometimes minimalist appearance, he understood his maps to be supported by an exhaustive body of scholastic knowledge.¹⁰⁵ And much of what he did include on the document itself came from the discursive tradition of geographers like Muhammad al-Idrisi and Leo Africanus rather than recent European eyewitness accounts or mathematically derived data.¹⁰⁶ He did not, for instance, believe that Portuguese eyewitnesses who claimed to have reached the source of the Nile in Abyssinia offered enough evidence to overturn the agreement between the ancient geographers and medieval Arab geographers that the source was further inland. He labels the Blue Nile with the Habesha name for the river instead: "*Abawi, ou Pere des Eaux* [Abay, or Father of Waters]." He was also an advocate of the Sofala-Ophir theory. He includes "Fura" on his 1749 map of the whole continent, writing that it is rich in gold, and on his 1727 map of southeastern Africa, which includes more discursive exposition since it covers less ground, he labels "Fura" as "Ophir."¹⁰⁷ Beginning as early as 1755, English versions included this on his map of the whole continent as well, adding a note

FIGURE 1. *Afrique publiée sous les auspices de Monseigneur le Duc d'Orléans Prémier Prince du Sang*, Jean Baptiste Bourguignon d'Anville, cartographer, 1749. (Dr. Norwich Collection of Maps of Africa and Its Islands, 1486–ca. 1865, David Rumsey Map Center, Stanford Libraries)

in the Mozambique channel that "this part of the Continent about Sofala is with great reason supposed to be the antient Land of Ophir."[108] A 1772 version of d'Anville's map offers an illuminating metacommentary on how such erudite traditions could coexist harmoniously with the impulse toward empiricism even by the later eighteenth century. The map includes an "Advertisement" admonishing other mapmakers for filling the "Inland Parts of *Africa*" with absurd "Conjecture" and concluding that "it may be judged how Absurd are the Divisions Traced in some Maps and why they were not followed in this."[109] Yet the map maintains the note that Sofala "is with great probability supposed to be the Ancient Land of Ophir," clearly considering this an amply defended statement even though it was not an empirically verified nor even an empirically verifiable claim.

D'Anville's map and its reprintings and revisions show that African impressions cross many genres and that the African expressions that permeated them are visible and traceable in the web of relationships that are both encoded in and exceed the map itself, as Harley describes. A stylistic or aesthetic minimalism does not de facto denote an absence of or even reduction in a cartographer's dependency on discursive evidence or outstanding impressions. Likewise, heavy illustration on a map does not de facto denote an imaginative projection. Scholars who study the aesthetics of early modern maps have emphasized how mapmakers strove to induce wonder and give their maps exotic appeal, but these aesthetics could be permeated with African expressions just as written texts were.[110] D'Anville's case highlights that though the history of geography in general and of cartographic representations of Africa in particular is often told as if maps leapt from the exotic and wonder-inducing to the empirical and mathematical—from Blemmyes and Monoculi and "elephants for want of towns" to scientifically produced coordinates—there is another category of geographical knowledge that was still highly respected through the early Enlightenment that was considered legitimate even though, or in some cases because, it was built on discourse and description rather than empirically gathered data.[111] Because so much attention has been given to the alleged transition from "wonder" to "science" across the early Enlightenment, and because it is presumed that geographers aspired to leave behind erudition for empiricism as part of this transition, this category is not always considered on its own terms. But it was governed by its own set of disciplinary practices, it could be prioritized over eyewitness accounts or even cited to negate them, and, for obvious reasons, it was the dominant body of knowledge that geographers and cartographers engaged when producing representations of Africa's interior.

Geography's reliance on African expressions and the readiness of certain travelers and geographers to recognize and validate them as viable knowledge didn't mean that geographers were not suspicious, skeptical, or scornful of what Africans had to say and show about themselves and their worlds. Barros and Bruce deferred to Habesha informants in a way that made clear their subject position as geographical insiders was a strength and not a weakness. By contrast, one of Bruce's reviewers read what Bruce had to say about Ophir with interest—perhaps the only part of the *Travels* of which he is somewhat complimentary—but he expressed dissatisfaction with Bruce's use of the local story of the Queen of Sheba as an evidentiary foundation. The reviewer considers this move suspect "in point of veracity and information" since it is grounded only in Abyssinian "reports of themselves (the only foundation of Mr. B.'s annals)."[112] Nevertheless, the reviewer's criticism of Bruce's reliance on African expressions doesn't negate their impact or erase them from the literary record. The reviewer, in fact, excerpts the whole of Bruce's Sofala-Ophir case, which is several pages long, literally reproducing the African foundations of the theory for his own readers even if he is skeptical of it. And if anything, the reviewer's frustration testifies to the continual control African expressions exerted over knowledge about the interior and reiterates that, even if some considered African testimony less than reliable, it was still often the only evidence geographers had to work from.

The Sofala-Ophir Impression in the Literary Imagination

Throughout the early Enlightenment, authors of fiction, drama, poetry, and other literary genres increasingly found geography a compelling subject for literary consideration. They didn't simply raid travel writing, geographical texts, or other forms of representation for descriptions of exotic places or details to add a touch of realism to their work; they entered into a dialog with these genres, conducting their own investigations into how language could be used to recreate the world.[113] In the process, they both remediated the content of geographical texts and forged formal relationships between imaginative and academic techniques of placemaking. Thus, when authors of imaginative literature wrote about Africa, they, too, participated in the cycle of discursive reiteration. Their texts were shaped by African impressions and the expressions that comprised them, and they reinforced or reshaped those impressions in turn. Like travel writers and geographers, they often harnessed impressions to symbolic and even imperial or expansionist ends; however, such appropriations don't negate the influence of African expressions on the texts themselves nor do they necessarily fundamentally alter their effects or meaning.

A brief consideration of how the Sofala-Ophir impression surfaces in John Milton's *Paradise Lost* (1667), Thomas Heyrick's "The Submarine Voyage" (1691), and John Dyer's *The Fleece* (1757) illustrates what I mean by this. As was the case with the geographical writing described above, these works are not perfect mirrors of African discourse, but each nevertheless depends on and affirms Habesha, Swahili, and Lemba ideas about the continent's history and geography. They are part of a larger cycle of epistemological and literary investment in African expressions, staggered, for instance, with Barros's conjectures about Great Zimbabwe's relationship to Aksum, Ludolf's conversations about the Abyssinian Queen of Sheba with Gorgoryos, and Bruce's analyses of Abyssinian literature—all texts that relied on the "Africanness" or local credibility of African informants as a mark of the authenticity of their information and that had a vested interest in preserving as much of the local particulars of their expressions as possible. Significantly, each poem emphasizes different local particulars of the Sofala-Ophir impression with little to no explanation of what those details refer back to, indicating that not only were their authors drawing from a larger, extratextual impression of eastern Africa themselves, they anticipated their readers would make the same connections—necessary connections for experiencing the poems' broader spatial and temporal effects and comprehending their global commentary.

In *Paradise Lost*, when Archangel Michael takes Adam onto the highest hill in Paradise to show him the future of mankind and "all earth's kingdoms and their glory," they look down onto an Africa segmented into four broad quadrants—East Africa, Southwest Africa, North Africa, and the region of West and Central Africa known as the Land of the Blacks—and each quadrant is emblemized through its most recognizable associations. Adam's eye is immediately drawn to East Africa first, specifically to Abyssinia:

> . . . nor could his eye not ken
> The empire of Negus to his utmost port
> Ercoco and the less maritime kings
> Mombasa, and Quiloa, and Melind,
> And Sofala, thought Ophir . . .[114]

Bruce McCleod reads such moments in *Paradise Lost* as Milton "reorganizing (and reconnaissancing) the globe for and from an English perspective," claiming that Milton "names the world into manageable places through the acquisitive and categorizing drive of colonialism and its discursive practices."[115] But considered within the Sofala-Ophir impression described above, it becomes apparent that these lines were shaped by African ways of imagining and talking about Africa. The quadrant's anchor point—in fact, the anchor point for the entire continent since it is mentioned first—is identified not through its name but through a person, the *negus*, emperor of Abyssinia and direct descendant (or so the *Kebra Nagast* says and so descriptions of Abyssinia reiterated) from Sheba and Solomon. And indeed, Abyssinia enjoys the kind of exceptionalism described here in its own founding myth. Adam's eye can't resist being drawn straight to it ("nor could his eye not ken"), and it is characterized through the language of expanse, stretching to the "utmost port," which unequivocally belongs to the *negusa nagast*: it is "his," not simply a place that happens to fall within Abyssinia's boundaries. He is an individual and an actant unlike the "less maritime kings" who are denoted only by the name of the place they occupy. The sense of spatial expansion in these lines is reiterated in the enjambment between "port" and "Ercoco" and by the fact that the reader is being asked to think up geographically (Arkiko is to the north) while simultaneously reading down the poem toward the south. These states below Abyssinia, ruled by "lesser maritime kings," are mentioned in passing as if they are merely stopover points for the ships sailing past them before arriving in another Solomonic space affirmed through Swahili and Lemba expressions—"Sofala, thought Ophir." These Solomonic bookends create a geographical unit, a stand-in for East Africa in general, comprised through narrative layers that both dovetail with African impressions and valorize the expressions that upheld them. This doesn't mean that Milton was not advancing a vision consistent with what he understood to be England's global duties.[116] But like the geographical writing that he avidly read (considering "the study of Geography" to be "both profitable and delightfull"), both the content and the form of his poetic efforts are indebted to African expressions.[117] These were expressions that he apparently expected his reader to be familiar with as well, since he deploys an African word, *negus*, as a metonym for Abyssinia rather than ever naming the country, assuming his reader will immediately orient themselves by it as Adam does.

In their poetic mappings of Africa, Heyrick and Dyer imitate Milton, playing off the line "Sofala, thought Ophir," but they each foreground aspects of the Sofala-Ophir impression that Milton did not include, indicating that they, too, held a comprehensive impression of the region in their geographical imaginations, which they, too, anticipated their readers would share. "The Submarine Voyage" (1691) gives an overview of Africa from a different angle than *Paradise Lost*—its narrator has been transformed by Neptune into a dolphin who meditates, as he swims through the seas, on England's imperial potential. Off the coast of East Africa, "in the Tract, that *Solomon's* Ships did pass,"

> [His] Course to *Sophola* did hold,
> By Wise-Men thought th' *OPHIR* of old,
> And yet Renown'd for Gold.

> Whose Mines even Admiration do surpass:
> Whose Buildings yet do Ancient Greatness bear,
> Engrav'd with many an Antique Character.[118]

Heyrick's variation on Milton—his stretching out of "Sofala, thought Ophir" to fit his meter—likewise connects southeastern Africa to Solomon. But he centers the Swahili and Lemba contributions to the impression that Sofala was Ophir rather than the Abyssinian contributions, focusing on the ruins of Great Zimbabwe and specifically the mysterious writing engraved on the works that Swahili traders offered as proof that they once belonged to an ancient civilization (a detail reported but which Europeans never saw for themselves). As was the case with Milton's reference to the *negus*, there is no explanation of these "Antique Character[s]," only an implicit expectation that the reader will understand it. If Milton's citation of the Sofala-Ophir impression enables spatial expansion as a poetic effect, Heyrick's generates a sense of temporal expansion through what Joseph Hall calls "scenes of ruin-gazing" to establish an ancient foundation from which to imagine Britain's own potential imperial future.[119] The region's "Ancient Greatness" lingers in the location as potential waiting to be reactivated, sealed by the enduring promise of the alleged Semetic characters that mark it as a privileged place in sacred history.

The Fleece—which sketches out Dyer's vision of England's wool trade knitting the rest of the world together in commerce—offers one more variation on this poetic engagement with East African geography. The speaker describes "Sofala thought Ophir" from the deck of a ship, speculating that in Sofala's hills,

> Ev'n yet some portion of it's [*sic*] antient wealth
> Remains, and sparkles in the yellow sand
> Of its clear streams, though unregarded now;
> Ophirs more rich are found.[120]

He then frames the whole region as if it were itself the richly built temple that its raw resources once allegedly comprised:

> ... The flat sea shines like yellow gold,
> Fus'd in the fire; or like the marble floor
> Of some old temple wide. But where so wide,
> In old or later time, its marble floor
> Did ever temple boast as this, which here
> Spreads its bright level many a league around?

> At solemn distances its pillars rise,
> Sofal's blue rocks, Mozambic's palmy steeps,
> And lofty Madagascar's glittering shores...[121]

Though Dyer also borrows Milton's "Sofala, thought Ophir," like Heyrick, he is more focused on the southern half of the impression, and he is the only one of the three to connect the region not only to Solomon himself but to the construction of his temple explicitly, which is a microcosm of the resources the region has to offer, the implication presumably being that "Ophirs more rich" will be found if Britain invests in the global trade. If Heyrick's poem uses the ruins of Great Zimbabwe as a foundation for what Britain's empire could become, Dyer imagines a future equivalent of Solomon's temple to reach the same end. Tita Chico describes Dyer's global vision as transcending "temporal or spatial constraints, seeing the future in the present and the global in the local."[122] By figuring Solomon's temple as only a model or replica of east Africa's shores rather than the ideal instantiation of a temple in and of itself, Dyer suggests it was a prototype that could be not only recreated but improved upon.

Surely not every reader made the connections that Milton, Heyrick, and Dyer's poems invite, but considering them together does suggest a certain widespread cultural familiarity with the specifics of the Sofala-Ophir impression. The references are brief, but as Belcher argues, brevity is not an argument against influence, and as Said, Cynthia Wall, and Laura Brown have argued, passing references can be windows into shared cultural storehouses of knowledge and ideas.[123] In Robert Tally Jr.'s words, "to merely think of a place is to already be mapping," regardless of whether the thinker has ever been to that location or, indeed, regardless of whether the location is even a real place.[124] Furthermore, while the global visions that Milton, Heydrick, and Dyer's poems advance certainly don't hinge solely on the Sofala-Ophir impression, its invocation serves a powerful purpose. As three poems that point to past empires to imagine Britain's future, their deployment of this Solomonic imagery is in line with the arguments seen in Purchas and Dee that Solomon was the ur-example of a lawful navigator, relying on trade rather than conquest to acquire his wealth, and that to be his successor in spirit was to be his successor in fact. The poems are thus appropriating African discourses in service to British global visions, but the impact of these discourses on the poems is also a testament to their signifying power and persistent credibility. The most salient details of the above lines—the ones that make East Africa a specific, identifiable place and not simply a vague elsewhere—are the details traceable to Africa's own Solomonic mythology. Their citation allows Milton, Heydrick, and Dyer to do something poetically, something beyond merely listing locations, that they otherwise wouldn't be able to do. Thus, these examples also show that African expressions connect European texts with African worlds not simply by a string of associations but aesthetically and formally.

Taking into account how Africans transformed themselves and their worlds into symbolic forms through abstraction and fictionalization is one way for literary scholars to analyze continuities between Africa and European literary traditions that goes beyond the struggle between text and context that many readings that seek to recoup the lives and worlds of the global majority have necessarily and justifiably concentrated on. As the Sofala-Ophir example shows, African impressions could certainly be governed by and reiterate imperial idioms. But scholars have also long recognized that part of dismantling the narrative of epistemological dominance and geographical and historical centrality Europe tells about itself involves showing how these global ideas have always been local—situated epistemological constructs in and of themselves that have been formed through the compilation of other locally articulated worldviews.[125] A crucial part of this work is showing how the epistemologies of the global majority did not simply exist alongside of, or as appropriated ingredients of, European worldviews but made meaning in their own right and on their own terms through their explanatory potential, intellectual traction, and imaginative power.

Chapter Overview

The following chapters offer an extended analysis of how impressions of two different regions of Africa evolved across European geographical and literary texts—the Western Sudan or Land of the Blacks and Abyssinia. Chapters 1 and 4 are keystone chapters that offer a genealogical overview of these respective impressions, detailing—as my example of the Sofala-Ophir impression did—how African expressions, contact narratives, geographical genres, and literature came together across space and time to form and reiterate their core features. Chapters 2, 3, 5, and 6 offer in-depth looks at how four writers of the early Enlightenment—Aphra Behn, Daniel Defoe, Samuel Johnson, and James Bruce—engaged these impressions in both content and form. I consider how their texts were shaped by African impressions and the expressions that comprise them, but I also demonstrate how each takes up the African impression as a figure of thought to stage an inquiry into what constitutes truthful, useful, and valuable geography.

More specifically, chapter 1 demonstrates that the "Land of the Blacks" was not a generic term for sub-Saharan Africa but acquired both its geographical contours and cultural associations from a combination of how leaders of the medieval and early modern empires of Mali and Songhai projected expressions about their sovereign right to power and how trans-Saharan and Senegambian merchants and traders talked about the interior states of the Niger valley in their dealings with Europeans. Chapter 2 examines how Aphra Behn's *Oroonoko* (1688) adopts and extends this impression of the Western Sudan to Coramantien on the Gold Coast, following the trend of seventeenth-century geographers who put Guinea under the heading of the Land of the Blacks not based on similarities of complexion among inhabitants but as part of an attempt to reconcile travel accounts about the Gold Coast with what they knew about the interior. In *Oroonoko* this erudite geographical practice is set up in contrast to the Royal Society–style eyewitness account the narrator deploys in the parts of the text set in Surinam, enabling Behn to stage a critique of the limitations of the naked discourse of fact for recreating worlds through text. Chapter 3 argues that Daniel Defoe's frustratingly paradoxical representation of Africa in *Captain Singleton* (1720) and the *Atlas Maritimus and Commercialis* (1728) is the result of a narrative strategy that endeavored to maintain what outstanding impressions of the Land of the Blacks promised about Africa's physical topography—rivers that would enable easy access to copious amounts of ivory and gold—while simultaneously divesting the continent of the political and cultural infrastructure that had warranted those topographical visions in the first place. Engaging African impressions in this way enabled Defoe not only to sketch out a colonial vision but also to make a distinction between geographical knowledge as a practical tool of trade, exploration, and empire and geographical narrative as an imaginative mode.

Chapter 4 shows how Abyssinians' expressions about their unique Christianity, their Makeda-like women, their Solomonic ties, and their claims to possess and even control the source of the Nile shaped European impressions of Abyssinia. The way these Habesha talked about themselves led Europeans to identify the country as having geographical contours that far exceeded its actual boundaries and to deem it the mythical Christian Kingdom of Prester John—impressions that lingered in the literary and cultural imagination long after travel writing and geographical texts began to temper them.

Chapter 5 considers how the Abyssinian setting of Samuel Johnson's *Rasselas* (1759) was shaped by the fact that the historical scope of Abyssinia and the nature of its Biblical connections were still considered pressing geographical questions well into the eighteenth century, necessary for any comprehensive representation of the country to take into account. By writing a narrative that requires readers themselves to think through multiple perhaps counterintuitive points of view, Johnson counters what he considered to be problematic trends in geographical writing by offering a theory of writing and reading representations of the world that prompts minds toward interactive reflection. Chapter 6 delves more deeply into how James Bruce cited Habesha women as authorities on their own history and culture in his *Travels to Discover the Source of the Nile* (1790). By emphasizing his close relationships with the women of the court at Gondar during his years spent in Abyssinia in the 1770s, he sought to harness their authority to bolster his own. He does so by positioning them within a longer lineage of archetypal African women that Europeans had grown familiar with, beginning with the Queen of Sheba. The coda returns briefly to the Sofala-Ophir impression as it appears in the nineteenth century, demonstrating how African impressions changed once Europeans gained the access to the interior yet never truly disappeared.

1

"WHEREIN THE BLACKE-PRINCE KEEPES HIS RESIDENCE, ATTENDED BY HIS JETTY COLOURED TRAINE"

Impressions of the Western Sudan, 1324–1620

Prior to Atlantic contact, the Western Sudan was one of the primary gateways to Africa's gold and slave trades. Its urban centers were cosmopolitan interfaces between the merchants who crossed the Sahara bringing silks, spices, horses, books, and other goods and the local potentates who controlled trade with the continent's interior. Medieval and early modern travelers and geographers writing in Arabic called this region *Bilad al-Sudan* or the "Land of the Blacks." Europeans adopted this designation as "Nigritarum Regio," "Terra Nigritarum," "Negroland," or the "Country of the Blacks." The boundaries of the Land of the Blacks were somewhat malleable as kingdoms and empires coalesced and splintered. In this chapter the designation refers to the Niger, Senegal, and Gambia river valleys, which extend from Lake Chad to the Atlantic coast. It is the region encompassed by the medieval and early modern empires of Mali and Songhai. The Western Sudan was and still is populated by many ethnic groups with distinct languages, cultures, and worldviews, but it has been interconnected via various formalized though not fixed political, economic, and cultural networks from at least the thirteenth century.

In European texts "Land of the Blacks" was not a generic term for sub-Saharan Africa. A set of specific tropes associated with it made it distinct from other parts of the continent. Broadly speaking, by the mid-seventeenth century, Europeans had developed the impression that West Africa's interior was populated with sophisticated kingdoms or empires; that these kingdoms or empires were created through a combination of conquest and state-building orchestrated by rulers who embodied an immense amount of sovereign power; that the enslaved Africans sold to Arab traders were losers in these military conquests; and that the culture of the Western Sudan was a hybridized and often vexed mix of Islamic and traditional religious and cultural practices. These ideas both facilitated and were facilitated by impressions about the continent's physical topography: that the Gambia and Senegal Rivers were branches of the Niger; that this water system was navigable all the way to a large lake in the middle of the continent and was a means by which Europeans could tap directly into the gold trade, subverting the Arab traders who reached it by crossing the Atlas Mountains and the Sahara Desert; that the goldmines themselves were south of the Niger, guarded by a double wall of silence upheld by coastal brokers who would not disclose their locations to outsiders and monstrous inland miners who could not disclose their locations because, according to legend, they literally did not speak.

Some of the constituent elements of this impression are what we would consider historically accurate and some are not. Most occupy a fuzzy space between the two—they were embellished or magnified or were true at one point in history but not at others. This chapter is not about how correct this impression is; rather, it details how a series of African expressions established its essentials and then how those essentials were reiterated over a span of three hundred years, shaping European engagement with and representations of the continent during a time when access to the interior was not yet a reality. These reiterations happened on several levels: internally, as African leaders repeated the political strategies of their predecessors in order to solidify their power base and project narratives about their sovereignty and right to rule to both their subjects and to the wider world; in the contact zone, as European travelers sought and received confirmation of these details from local hosts and guides; and in European texts both scholarly and literary as this geographical information was recycled and built upon.

African Gold and the Shape of Empire: Mansa Musa I's Pilgrimage to Mecca

In 1324 Musa I, tenth *mansa* of the Mali Empire, took the Hajj to Mecca. All who witnessed his journey and all who spoke and wrote about it afterwards agreed that it was a spectacular event.[1] Reports have him accompanied by an entourage ranging from eight thousand to sixty thousand, including, according to some sources, twelve thousand enslaved women clothed entirely in brocade and Yemeni silk.² Eyewitnesses wrote that his entourage included a parade of five hundred enslaved men who each carried a golden staff weighing at least four pounds, and his caravan was laden with up to eighteen additional tons of gold, much of which he gave away in charitable acts. He told the residents of Cairo that this gold came from an inexhaustible supply that grew like plants and could be harvested any time of the year, and he allegedly funneled so much of it into the local economy on his way through the city that the rate of the dinar dropped precipitously.³ Rumor had it that every Friday, he built a mosque in whichever village he was passing through.⁴ On Musa's return from Mecca, he detoured through two important central West African states that had slipped out of Mali's grasp in the past—Gao and Timbuktu—and repossessed them, both states submitting to his authority without bloodshed.

This journey was more than an act of devotion or diplomacy. It was a multivalent pageant designed to speak to audiences both inside and outside the borders of Musa's empire. As Herman Bennett writes, the ceremony and pomp involved in such displays of monarchical power were a kind of political theater through which African leaders "dramatized sovereignty while displaying authority over sacred knowledge, territory, and people."⁵ Scholarly treatments of African sovereignty, Bennett points out, tend to minimize or overlook entirely the political agency deployed through these "symbolic enactments," reducing them to "cultural affects rather than instruments of power."⁶ But in fact they were a means through which African leaders established the terms under which they and their dominions were understood by both their own subjects and outsiders.

Musa had a range of audiences in mind as he planned his pilgrimage, which took at least ten years to orchestrate.⁷ Most obvious is the wider Islamic world that he traveled through. One of Musa's aspirations was to draw merchants and dignitaries from North Africa and the Near East into Mali's cities, transforming them into cosmopolitan centers of trade and learning and anchoring them firmly into transregional economic and religious networks. Signifying his own devotion to Islam was crucial to facilitating this, but so was making a convincing case that his empire was a destination worth the grueling trek across the Atlas Mountains and Sahara Desert. To this end, the spectacle of his retinue and casual distribution of wealth into local economies served as a mobile advertisement for what Mali wanted (cloth, horses, books, gemstones) and what Mali had to offer in exchange (gold and slaves). Musa's display and distribution of the gold sent a fairly one-dimensional if dazzling message—that he controlled an infinite supply of it. But the way he spoke about the gold trade contextualized it in a more complex geographical narrative and offers additional insight into how he manipulated his own image and the image of his domain to offer a plausible geopolitical justification for this message. He admitted to dignitaries in Cairo that the gold mines did not in fact lie under Mali's direct control. When asked why he did not simply seize the gold mines from the "uncouth infidels" if he was as powerful as he claimed to be, Musa explained that he had done so at one time but that the mines' production slowed to a trickle while the amount of gold in the "heathen countries" south of the mines (the region Europe would come to know as Guinea) increased.[8] Realizing that he received more gold through trade and tribute than through coercion, he made the strategic decision to relinquish total authority over the region in the interest of maximizing gains. If Musa's aim was to communicate his sophistication as a trade partner and a statesman, the anecdote might have spoken to his keen understanding and good judgment. Furthermore, in portraying the trade as a delicate operation that must be handled in just the right way lest it dry up, and in portraying himself as the person who understood how to consistently coax the most gold out of the mines, he also positioned Mali as not only an effective but an essential intermediary between this inland trade and the wider Islamic world. On a more ideological level, the anecdote also suggested that Mali was a holy outpost, a bastion on the edge of a heathen world from which Islam might spread and grow if it were more firmly connected to and regularly fed from Islam's geographical and spiritual center.

In orchestrating and undertaking the Hajj, Musa was not only looking to increase Mali's global profile; he was communicating with his subjects as well. His pilgrimage was an act of what Verena Krebs calls, in an East African context, "performative diplomacy," when transregional connections are made not solely for establishing ties with foreign powers but also to serve "a specific local agenda at home"—often to send a message about a leader's right and fitness to rule.[9] Musa became *mansa* only sixty years after the great Sundiata Keita founded the empire, and his succession had not been guaranteed due both to his bloodline—he was not a direct descendent from Sundiata Keita but rather from his brother Abu Bakr—and to ambiguous circumstances surrounding his rise to power. It was not precisely clear what happened to his predecessor, so Musa's reputation was haunted by the specter of treachery, and there is a possibility that he killed his mother or another royal matriarchal figure, which was a particularly serious offense in Mali.[10] The Hajj was an opportunity to legitimize his claims to leadership by broadcasting the extent of his influence and public support and by advertising his ability to grow and unite an empire.

One way that he appealed to his subjects through a more local register was by echoing the mythic tropes through which Sundiata Keita's rise to power was described in the epics sung by the *jeliw* (griots, or court bards).[11] Like Musa, Sundiata was a usurper, interrupting the usual patrilineal line of inheritance. But his usurpation is justified in his epic by the overriding forces of exceptionalism and destiny. Though a prophecy had dictated that Sundiata would someday be king, as the crippled son of the king of Mali's second wife, he was passed over when his father died in favor of his half-brother, the son of his father's first wife. Sundiata is sent into exile where he spends the next several years roaming around central West Africa, growing physically strong and collecting a critical mass of supporters from both inside Mali (a retinue of hunters, blacksmiths, and *jeliw* who declare their loyalty to him) and outside Mali (an army of allies from the surrounding twelve kingdoms).[12] He also amasses occult power by traveling through spiritually significant places and absorbing their potency.[13] Mansa Musa's own perambulations evoked these longstanding local beliefs about how specific geographical sites are imbued with power that can be harnessed by those who know how to use it. By identifying the holy places of Islam as the greatest source of such power, he manipulated what Gomez calls the "multiple and intertwining cultural signifier" of the spiritual journey.[14] Accompanied by his own extensive retinue of supporters, including *jeliw* to sing his praises, Musa enacted his own exceptional narrative and suggested that he, too, had a destiny to fulfill. And in growing the Mali Empire as Sundiata had done, he demonstrated that the fulfilment of this destiny would facilitate Mali's continuing rise to prominence.

Perhaps the least subtle example of how Musa's Hajj served as an instrument of geopolitical power and not merely as a religious or diplomatic display was the way it paved the way for him to incorporate Gao and Timbuktu into his empire. By the time Musa embarked on his return journey, stories of his wealth, piety, and martial strength had thoroughly spread through central West Africa. When he arrived on the doorsteps of Gao and Timbuktu in the flesh, neither city attempted any kind of resistance.[15] They may have been cowed by the sheer number of soldiers in the train as well as other signifiers of military might—horses and weapons. But the entourage's material riches must have also suggested the benefits of being attached to a central authority that could offer access to resources that neither city could accumulate on its own. The personal religious credibility Musa gained from the Hajj and the way it signified his intent to make his dominion part of the wider Islamic world were not insignificant factors in his success either. In the eyes of the two predominantly Muslim cities, these things enabled Musa, as a foreigner, to not only acquire but also maintain authority in the region, which he solidified through the building of mosques that he prayed in regularly, drawing attention to himself as a present and powerful but largely unobtrusive authority.[16] And both cities, Timbuktu in particular, eventually did pull in merchants from all over the world, growing into the cosmopolitan centers of trade and learning that Musa had envisioned.[17]

As an act of transregional diplomacy, Musa's Hajj failed on some key fronts. Traveling as a sovereign who bowed to no one but God, he refused to prostrate himself before the Mamluk sultan in Cairo, which may have had the opposite effect than intended. Descriptions of their interactions and the kinds of gifts the sultan gave Musa indicate that he considered Musa a man to be respected but not a peer.[18] For another, Musa had given away his gold so freely in Cairo on the way to the Holy Lands that he needed to resell some of his purchases on the return trip for half what he had paid for them, merchants feeling no prick of conscience for exploiting a ruler in whose country gold grew like plants.[19] Nevertheless, Musa's Hajj and the subsequent empire-building that it enabled were, in Gomez's words, the means by which "West Africa literally and figuratively enters the spatial and imaginary dimensions of Europe and the central Islamic lands."[20] In terms of the region's spatial dimensions, by the end of his reign, Mansa Musa had "realized a breathtaking political vision: the unification of the Niger, Senegal, and Gambia valleys, representing some forty to fifty million people, with the Niger valley as the realm's core."[21] When subsequent travel writers and geographers wrote about the Western Sudan, they maintained this unification, imagining the Land of the Blacks as a coherent geographical space presided over by a powerful ruler who controlled all the major trade arteries that linked Africa together and that, in particular, served as an intermediary between the continent's interior gold trade and the wider Islamic world.

It would be a mistake to assume that either the central Islamic states or Europe then imagined the Western Sudan as a mere outpost of the Muslim world. The way central West African rulers maintained a strong connection to more local worldviews in public performances of their sovereignty indelibly shaped the impressions of outsiders as well. For instance, when Ibn Battuta, a Berber scholar, writer, and explorer, visited Timbuktu and Gao in the 1350s during the reign of Musa's successor, Mansa Suleyman, he found the *jeliw*'s recitation of the lives and deeds of Mali's rulers at Islamic festivals to be strange and heretical.[22] Ibn Battuta also described another cultural practice of the Western Sudan with some trepidation—the earthen ablution—which dated back to the Empire of Ghana (750–1076) and would be repeated in both central West

African imperial theater and in European representations of the continent for hundreds of years. In Mali all the king's subjects, whether Muslim or not, were expected to kneel and sprinkle dust on their heads when they came into the *mansa*'s presence, humbling themselves to emphasize his spiritual and political elevation.[23] The sovereignty that these rulers dramatized and the symbolic registers through which they did so were considered to be uniquely African.

In sum, Musa's Hajj and the empire-building it facilitated are best understood not only as a historical event but as a carefully orchestrated and masterfully conducted performance. It was an exceptionally striking one such that people today who seek an example of Africa's historical sophistication and influence invariably point to it as an example of Africa's innovation and ambition. However, the performance's real power came not from its originality but from how it worked within a series of recognizable cultural expectations, symbols, and tropes. Musa's ability to identify and manipulate these cultural narratives had the immediate material effect of consolidating his power in Africa and strengthening Mali's place in trans-Saharan trade networks, and it also shaped how outsiders imagined and represented the region—its economic potential, its resources and culture, its geopolitical connection to the rest of Africa and to the Arab world, and its imperial clout.

A Fourteenth-Century Impression of the Land of the Blacks: The Catalan Atlas

Accounts of Musa's pilgrimage circulated through both oral and written reports that made journeys of their own. By the late fourteenth century, Musa's story had arrived in Europe, enshrined on a panel of the Catalan Atlas (fig. 2).[24] Presented as a gift to Charles V of France in 1375, the Atlas reflects a transition in the history of Western cartography between the symbol-laden *mappae mundi* of the Middle Ages, intended to organize and showcase various kinds of erudite knowledge about the world, and the portolan, a spatially accurate document used for navigation.[25] For instance, the Atlas features a compass rose and wind rose network, and the coasts of Europe, the Mediterranean, and North Africa are properly scaled and dense with names of port cities. The geographical information these regions offer is largely empirical, its underpinning grammar largely geometrical. But the parts of the world that had not yet been charted are filled in with richly colored drawings of historically significant people and legends describing who they are and what they have done.[26] The logic that governs the placement of the topographical features in these regions—cities,

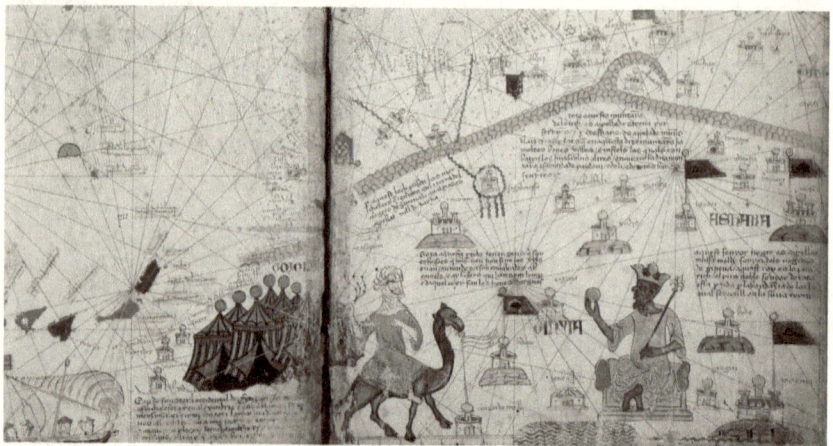

FIGURE 2. Travelers come to the *mansa* of Mali, from the nautical atlas known as the Catalan Atas, 1375, cartography credited to Abraham Cresques. (Bibliothèque nationale de France, MS Espagnol 30, panel 6)

mountains, rivers, and so on—is more literary than geometrical, its contours facilitating and facilitated by the way characters occupy or move through it.

Such is the case with central West Africa, which is spatially organized by and imbued with details from the narratives Mansa Musa projected about himself and his dominion. The clusters of carefully aligned place names along the North African coast give way to a tableau featuring two commanding figures. The first is a dark-skinned man with a gold-leaf crown on his head who is extending a gold nugget or coin out toward the second figure—a man on a camel traveling through the salt mining centers of Taghaza and Tacost through a pass in the Atlas Mountains whereby "the merchants . . . enter the land of the negroes." "This black Lord is called Musse Melly and is the sovereign of the land of the negroes," the legend beside the crowned man explains, his relative size and glittering adornment making visible his sovereign entitlement as clearly as the gold that the real Musa spread through Cairo.[27] And indeed, the text goes on to explain, "This king is the richest and noblest of all these lands due to the abundance of gold that is extracted from his lands." What constitutes "his lands" is demarcated by the polities he is seated between: "tenbuch" (Timbuktu) and "Geugeu" (Gao). To the southeast of Timbuktu is the "Ciutat de Mally"—the name by which Arabic geographers like Ibn Battuta referred to the empire's capital.[28] These place names are not situated according to their empirical locations but in relation to the man who subdued them and united them as part of the coherent entity, the Land of the Blacks, over which he rules. His throne aligns with and also towers over the buildings that denote them as urban centers, imbuing them with specific associations—gold, trade, and the seats of kings. In other words, Musa's Hajj and its reports not only inspired the inclusion of the *mansa* himself, as Evelyn Edson and Paul Freedman recognize; it is the justification for how Africa's spatial contours are mapped.[29]

The Atlas offers insight into how Europeans had situated such impressions of Africa's geography and trade networks into their global thinking. The bottom of Musa's throne rests against a sizeable lake with rivers extending from it east and west. The eastern river stretches the length of the continent and joins with the Nile. The western river disappears into the road beneath the Arab trader's feet, extending to the west coast, where a third figure approaches the continent in a ship: Jaume Ferrer, a Majorcan explorer who made an early attempt to sail down Africa's west coast. The writing next to the ship explains that it "departed for the River of Gold on the 10th of August of 1346, the feast of St. Lawrence." To illustrate this point, the ship appears to be in pursuit of a golden nugget or coin just off the coast—one that matches the gold in the *mansa*'s hand. The notion that Africa's east and west rivers might share a source predates Musa's pilgrimage, appearing for instance on Muhammad al-Idrisi's 1154 map of the world, but the Atlas demonstrates how they became inextricably intertwined in the European imagination, with the Senegal River (the "River of Gold" above) and Gambia River pinpointed as the most viable route through which Europeans could undercut the trans-Sahara trade and access Mali's resources for themselves.

At first glance, it may seem that the Europeans and the Arabs are the agents in the narrative the map tells and that Africa is the place waiting to be plundered, prefiguring later imperial representations of Africa as feminized and penetrable. Readings of the Africa portion of the Catalan Atlas have observed how the mapmakers depict the space as easily accessible despite the fact that it had not yet been charted.[30] For instance, Edson observes that the trade routes "extend the commercial use of the map" that is encoded in the sea charts that form the background of the Atlas into the interior of Africa."[31] This is perhaps even more true of the mouth of the river at which Jaume Ferrer's ship is poised, the legend beside it neglecting to mention that his expedition was never heard from again. Yet Musa and his gold are not simply an object of desire and consumption. The fact that he is stationary is not a mark of his passivity or of Africa's easy penetrability but a testament to the success of his pilgrimage in advertising who he was as a sovereign and who he would be as a trade partner. He remains comfortably seated, after all, his presence dominating sub-Saharan Africa, while the Arabs and the Europeans, lured by the gold in his hand, must undertake arduous and dangerous journeys in order to reach him.

As the Catalan Atlas tells it, Musa's vision for Mali has not only come to fruition, it has outlived him. He had been dead for forty years when the Catalan Atlas was made. The impression had such staying power because the optics of Mansa Musa's pilgrimage were striking, because it fueled European desires for a new source of gold, and because in geographical writing, old information was relied on in the absence of new. However, again, African impressions became deeply embedded in the geographical imagination not only through single, impressive events but because travelers and geographers sought and received confirmation of them. As the following sections show, Europe's impression of the Western Sudan was reified from two directions through the early modern period. Information continued to come over Atlas Mountains via the trans-Sahara trade from traders and travelers who made the trek into the Niger valley where the eventual rise of the Songhai Empire would inject new life into the way the wider world thought about Africa's riches and the sovereignty of its rulers. But as contact with the Atlantic coastal states that had been Ferrer's intended destination increased, brokers from what had been the western reaches of Musa's empire added their own details to the geographical narrative as well.

Brokers of the Senegambia and the Myth of the Silent Traders: Early Atlantic Contact Narratives

As one of the first European representations of sub-Saharan Africa, the Catalan Atlas illustrates not only the effect that Mansa Musa's pilgrimage and conquest narrative had on how the rest of the world imagined the interior of the continent; it also indicates that Europeans first imagined the continent from the inside out. If one were to look only at later maps of Africa with their increasingly blank interiors, one might conclude that the information Europeans gathered from coastal contact was the epistemological foundation from which they built their representations of the continent. But the opposite is actually the case. As Jaume Ferrer's ship indicates, firsthand explorations down Africa's west coast were not blind forays into the unknown but voyages motivated by a specific goal warranted by narrative accounts of the interior—to find an access point into Africa's gold and the trade cities of the Niger valley from its sub-Saharan rivers. To this end, once Atlantic contact did occur, European travelers asked coastal peoples about the continent's sub-Saharan kingdoms and rulers, about the location of its trade nexuses and gold mines, and about the waterways that might be a means of undercutting the dominance of the Barbary-controlled trans-Saharan routes.[32]

When Europeans first encountered the Wolof and Mandinka of the Senegambia region, they were encountering people who had existed on the fringe of the Mali Empire and were still connected to the Niger valley through trade, political alliances and conflicts, culture, and language. The Mandinka had a great deal of cultural and linguistic continuity with the interior states as a Mande-speaking people who had migrated from the Niger valley to settle along the Gambia. They facilitated much of the trade between the Niger valley and the coasts.[33] The Wolof of the Senegal valley were a coastal people who eventually established their own empire but were vassals of imperial Mali during the height of that empire's power. The information these groups offered about the interior reified European impressions about what might be found there and fueled their hopes that the continent's western rivers would be a viable way to tap into the continent's interior gold trade. Mandinkas in Portugal and Spain had told Prince Henry the Navigator, credited by early modern and eighteenth-century writers as the instigator of African exploration, that up the Gambia "there was gold in large quantities: and that the Christians who should go thither would become rich."[34] A Wolof prince, Bumi Jeleen, who travelled to Portugal in the late fifteenth century to ask João II to aid him in his efforts to claim the throne of the kingdom of Jolof, assured the Portuguese that an alliance with him would be to their benefit because the Senegal River was a pathway not only into the interior of the continent but all the way through to the Nile.

By fueling outstanding European impressions about Africa's gold trade and geography and by positioning himself and the territory over which he hoped to rule as a gateway into the interior, Bumi Jeleen exemplified how coastal Africans learned to identify European desires and use their privileged status as local informants in order to work their relationship with Europeans to their advantage. By contemporaneous accounts, Bumi Jeleen had the rhetorical savvy to pull off such a strategy. In the *Chronica del Rey João II*, which included a description of Bumi Jeleen's visit to Lisbon, Ruy de Pina described him as "a man of good speech and natural wisdom," who spoke words so fine they "did not appear as from the mouth of a black barbarian but of a Greek prince raised in Athens."[35] On the one hand, this description is a reminder that African impressions are not free from the racializing rhetoric that circulated and evolved simultaneously with the ideas about African imperialism, sovereignty, and geography that this chapter sketches out. On the other, it is also a testament to the extent to which Europeans embraced the exceptionalist discourse that African elites broadcast about themselves and the places from which they hailed. Bumi Jeleen's strategy worked, after all. Portugal did send aid, though his bid for the throne ultimately failed.

The early European contact narratives of the Senegambia region indicate that Mandinka brokers deployed similar strategies of appealing to European impressions about the interior. As travelers themselves, the Mandinka leveraged their specialized knowledge of African geography to establish and maintain the upper hand in trade relationships, which, in turn, reinforced how Europeans thought and wrote about the continent's political and economic situation and physical geography. Alvise Cadamosto, who wrote a detailed account of one of the first extended forays into the Senegambia in the mid-fifteenth century, is assured by both the Wolof and the Mandinka that if he travels far enough up the western rivers, he will find mountains of gold and reach the land of "the Emperor of Melli, the great Emperor of the Blacks."[36] As a result, Cadamosto attempted one of the first European voyages up the Gambia in the hopes of discovering both the gold and the seat of the *mansa*. In fact, the further he traveled inland, the more disappointed he was by how little gold he actually managed to acquire. "The rumour of it had been much greater," Cadamosto laments, "in the reports of the negroes."[37] Cadamosto's disappointment is illuminating in what it reveals about African expressions as they were deployed in Senegambian contact zones and about European attitudes toward the geographical knowledge they offered in the early days of the eyewitness account. On the one hand, it draws explicit attention to the fact that coastal brokers were self-consciously shaping the narrative of the interior, deploying "rumour" and "reports" to their advantage that very well may not have reflected reality. But Cadamosto's attempts to qualify such discourse were not enough to dispel the power it would have over subsequent travelers or the power it continued to have over the geographical record.

Diogo Gomes, for example, one of the next notable Europeans to attempt to sail up the Gambia, was not deterred by Cadamosto's experience, nor does his own eyewitness account corroborate it. Gomes writes about meeting a local Mandinka named "Bucker, who was acquainted with the whole country of the negroes."[38] "Finding him perfectly truthful," Gomes asks Bucker to take him to Cantor, a trade city, which Gomes is told attracted merchants from Timbuktu and Gao, "where I understood there was abundance of gold," and where trans-Saharan merchants came to trade for that gold.[39] When he questions the locals at Cantor about the roads that lead to this interior, he is told that the king of Gao is "lord of the mines" and that he "had before the door of his palace a mass of gold just as it was taken from the earth, so large that twenty men could scarcely move it, and that the king always fastened his horse to it," which was one of Mali's regional anecdotes that had circulated at least since the fourteenth century, as Ibn Khaldun recorded.[40] When Gomes inquired into the location of the gold mines, he was told that the gold came from the other side of Fouta Djallon, which pleased him because he was also told that all the rivers descending from the mountain run east to west, suggesting an easily navigable route from the coast to the interior.[41] Unlike Cadamosto's informants, Bucker is held up in Gomes's account as someone who is both knowledgeable and truthful, reliable because and not in spite of the fact that he is a well-traveled African with insider information.

Gomes's experience is unusual in that the Mandinka brokers gave him a relatively unembellished response to his question about the location of the gold mines. Cadamosto recorded the much more common response to this geographical inquiry, which became another key piece of how Europeans imagined the furthest reaches of the Land of the Blacks. When Cadamosto wondered what the sub-Saharan Africans did with all the salt that the Arab traders brought into the Western Sudan from Tagaza, he was told that the "blacks of Melli" carry the salt to the place where the gold is mined where they "pile it in rows, each marking his own." Then,

> having made these piles, the whole caravan retires half a day's journey. Then there come another race of blacks who do not wish to be seen or to speak. . . . Seeing the salt, they place a quantity of gold opposite each pile, and then turn back, leaving salt and gold. When they have gone, the negroes who own the salt return: if they are satisfied with the quantity of gold, they leave the salt and retire with the gold. Then the blacks of the gold return, and remove those piles which are without gold. By the other piles of salt they place more gold, if it pleases them, or else they leave the salt. In this way, by long and ancient custom, they carry on their trade without seeing or speaking to each other.[42]

Cadamosto was told these miners didn't want to be seen because their "lower lip, more than a span in width, hung down, huge and red, over the breast, displaying the inner part glistening like blood. The upper lip was as small as their own, This form of the lips displayed the gums and teeth, the latter they said, being bigger than their own: they had two large teeth on each side, and large black eyes. Their appearance is terrifying, and the gums exude blood, as do the lips."[43] Lest Cadamosto's reader find this story too incredible, he insists that he has heard it from multiple people who participate in the trade—"persons in whom faith can be placed."[44] He was furthermore told that the "Emperor of Melli" once tried to take one of these silent miners prisoner and force him to speak. But although they "spoke to this man in several negro languages . . . he would not reply, or speak at all, neither would he eat. He lived for four days and then died."[45] The gold miners were so angry about this kidnapping that three years passed before they would deal with the merchants of Mali at all, only re-instigating the trade when they grew desperate for salt again.

The silent trade never actually existed.[46] But the idea was captivating and pervasive enough that economists in the nineteenth and twentieth centuries cited silent trade as an important step in the evolution from local to global economies.[47] Its origin is not entirely clear. Herodotus includes a reference to a silent trade in his *Histories*.[48] However, medieval, early modern, and eighteenth-century travelers alike identify Mande-speaking traders who lived and worked the trade routes of the Senegambia and lower Niger as sources of the account, which was shared with Arabic-speaking travelers as well as European ones.[49] When the historian al-Umari asked a traveler to the Sahel in the fourteenth century about the source of the gold, the traveler replied that "he had heard some of the remote peoples of the Sudan do not show themselves. When the salt merchants come they put the salt down and then withdraw."[50] He also reports that the *mansa* cannot conquer these "uncouth infidels" because "the gold begins to decrease and then disappears, while it increases in the neighboring heathen countries," a different take on Mansa Musa's explanation above of why he did not simply conquer the place where the gold grows like plants. Ivor Wilks has suggested that the story may have specifically arisen out of contact between Mande-speaking traders and the Akan of the Gold Coast region (the third and farthest source of Mali's and Songhai's gold, which will be considered in the next chapter).[51] A branch of Mande-speaking traders called the Wangara did manage this trade, and the Akan were demonstrably different enough in culture and religion from the Wangara to be characterized through such extreme terms of difference. (The Akan called the Wangara "wild and bloody" as well.)[52]

Whatever the origin of the narrative, it became an instrumentalized discourse in the contact zone, a means through which the Mandinka maintained oversight of the different legs of the Western Sudan's interior trade. It tantalized, playing off European and Arabic expectations of Africa's economic potential, fueled as they were by displays of and rumors of Mali's gold. It continued to draw outside traders to the Gambia valley. But it also deterred; monstrousness aside, the Mandinka represented the terms of the gold trade as strange and elusive, just as Mansa Musa had done. Misstep and the trade would dry up completely, as al-Umari's account indicated. The story cast the Mandinka themselves as indispensable middlemen—willing and eager to establish economic relationships, apologetic about the limitations of what they could offer their guests—and it continued to be an effective and repeated strategy. In fact, Cadamosto cites the regularity with which the story was told to outsiders as evidence for its reliability. He makes clear that he is no credulous fool, stating in the opening of his text that he would rather "understate than to relate anything which exceeds the truth."53 But since the myth of the silent trader is "related by so many we can accept it," no matter how strange it may sound at first.

The story of the silent trade had an ongoing effect on evolving European geographical representations of the Western Sudan and of Africa more generally. It fed European stereotypes about Africa's monstrous interior, but it was emblematic of an epistemological monstrousness as much as anything, one that was rooted not in the interior traders' allegedly deformed visages but in their reluctance to be seen and their refusal, or perhaps inability, to speak. As it was described to Europeans, this threshold into the region where the gold was mined marked the limit not just of what could be seen but also of what could be said about the continent.

The Rise of Songhai: Sonni Ali, Askia Muhammad I, and Leo Africanus's *Description of Africa*

As European explorers began to glean more information about Africa from their explorations of the Atlantic coasts, accounts of the interior continued to enter the European literary record and geographical imagination from over the Sahara. Simultaneously, imperial performances in the Western Sudan continued to hearken back to the symbols and strategies established by Sundiata, Mansa Musa, and others, creating an internal African discourse of geography and sovereignty that also nurtured European impressions of the continent through the early modern period and into the eighteenth century. Most notable were the rulers who founded and expanded the Songhai Empire in the fifteenth and sixteenth centuries.

The beginnings of the Songhai Empire were established by Sonni Ali, who seized Timbuktu in 1468 and subsequently grew an empire that surpassed Mali in size. He established his rule through a ruthless campaign of conquest and maintained it by projecting an identity as a "magician-king" who hybridized symbolic Islamic practices with the traditional occultism of the Soninke people, leaning more heavily on the latter than the former.[54] It was the usurper of Sonni Ali's line, however, who brought Songhai to the height of its power and visibility, and he did so by resuscitating Mansa Musa's strategy of strengthening ties between West Africa and the wider Islamic world.[55] Askia Muhammad I also undertook the Hajj in part to legitimize a questionable ascension to the throne and to speak to both Islamic and non-Islamic subjects of his empire. Sonni Ali's claims to traditional occult power earned him a great deal of credibility with the empire's non-Muslim subjects. By contrast, according to Nehemia Levtzion, "Askia Muhammad, a usurper, was deprived of this vital power to manipulate the supernatural. The pilgrimage to Mecca bestowed on him the *baraka*, an emanating blessing, which was respected by both Muslims and non-Muslims."[56] Like Musa, then, Mohammad made his spiritual journey speak in more than one register in order to legitimize his rule, and he imitated Musa in other ways as well. He was not able to match the spectacle of Musa's pilgrimage, but he traveled with a retinue of about fifteen hundred soldiers and carried with him one ton of gold, two thirds of which he gave away in charitable acts.[57] He also traveled with representatives from across his domain, showcasing the variety of peoples and polities that were consolidated under the banner of Songhai.[58] How much this banner translated to actual geopolitical control in central West Africa is debatable—according to Bruce Hall, much of Mohammad I's "authority" over distant realms was "primarily religious and symbolic in nature."[59] But as Musa's Hajj had, it persuaded insiders of the *askia*'s right to power and outsiders of the extensive reach of his rule. The narrative projection of imperial Songhai, in other words, is as much a part of its legacy, if not more of its legacy, than the empire in fact.

Sonni Ali and Askia Muhammad I entered the European cultural consciousness through a source that would be disseminated more widely and excerpted more frequently through the early modern period than any other source on sub-Saharan Africa: Leo Africanus's *Description of Africa*.[60] A Berber born in Grenada and raised in Fez, Leo Africanus accompanied his uncle on a diplomatic mission across the Sahara around 1510. Captured by Spanish corsairs in his mid-twenties, he was brought to Italy where he converted to Christianity. His *Description*, completed in 1526, includes accounts of fifteen sub-Saharan states from Lake Chad to the Senegambia. As a text that has received a fair amount of attention in the wake of the postcolonial turn in literary studies, analyses of the *Description* have tended to focus on how Leo Africanus's subject position and the agendas of his editors and translators have biased his representation. Oumelbanine Zhiri rightly cautions against reading the *Description* as an empirical account of the Western Sudan given that it was "an attempt by an Arab-speaking author to describe the geography, the culture, the customs of North and West Africa, in a language, Italian, that he did not master, for readers who presumably knew next to nothing about the subject."[61] Subsequent editions in French, Latin, English, and Dutch each contain translation errors, elisions of information, cultural bias, and paratext written by editors toward political ends.[62] Pory's English translation has been singled out as particularly problematic because the lengthy editorial apparatus strives to transform Leo Africanus into a figure whose position as a "native informant" can legitimize Pory's Eurocentric, imperialist worldview.[63] And because Leo Africanus himself converted to Christianity and wrote for a Christian readership, he is interpreted by some as imperial figure himself whose text others Africa; his "description," in Kim Hall's words, functions as "an act connoting ownership and control" that enables readers to "become protected tourists, enjoying the wonders and promised wealth of Africa while safely distanced from its more ominous—and seductive—cultural practices."[64] Scholars like Jonathan Burton, Bernadette Andrea, and George Boulukos have revised this image of Leo Africanus as a mere tool of empire, reading him respectively as a hybrid figure engaged in postcolonial mimicry, a cultural amphibian who resisted Western assimilation through an outward-only dissimulation of Islam, and a merchant whose attention was primarily focused on whether a region would make a viable trade partner.[65] But they, too, read his representation of Africa primarily through the lens of his subjectivity.

Leo Africanus's fascinating and complex identity surely did shape the text, and analyses of his background productively complicate tidy assumptions about how global representations were produced and consumed. However, he, like other travel writers considered throughout this book, was also responding to and participating in the construction of an impression of Africa that was larger than his own take on the subject. Scholars generally accept that Leo Africanus did travel to Timbuktu, but it's also clear that he relied heavily on things he was told to write his account of most of sub-Saharan

Africa. He appears to have visited five states—Borno, Gaoga (not Gao, which is "Gago," but a state closer to Lake Chad), Timbuktu, Jenné, and Mali—"howbeit there are many more," he writes, "which although I saw not with mine owne eies, yet are they by the Negroes sufficiently known and frequented."[66] He made use of these local informants, one of whom was no less than "the kings brother, who is blacke in colour, but most beautiful in minde and conditions."[67] Others were "merchants which daily come from [the south] to the kingdome of Tombuto."[68] It is reasonable to assume that these sources would have been sharing not random information but coherent expressions consistent with how the dominant ruling and mercantile classes of the region imagined themselves and wanted others to imagine them as well. Leo Africanus observed things himself, spoke to locals about the places he couldn't travel to, and drew from his predecessors—al-Bakri, al-Idrisi, and the Atlantic sources above.[69] At the intersection of these influences, an impression arises that is consistent with Songhai's founding myths and projected imperial self-image, which is the narrative scaffolding through which the geographical category of the Land of the Blacks is articulated in the *Description*.[70]

A synopsis of Askia Mohammad's rise to power and pilgrimage is the frame story for Leo Africanus's account of fifteen kingdoms of this "Land of the Negroes," as the English translation deems it, comprising the majority of the proem that introduces the Western Sudan in general. The reader is told that the *askia*, who was once Sonni Ali's captain, overthrew his predecessor and seized his throne, and then "after having by warres for the space of fifteene yeeres conquered many large dominions, he then concluded a league with all nations, and went on pilgrimage to Mecca."[71] Once Leo Africanus establishes Songhai's ascendency as the key event that shaped the Western Sudan's modern political landscape, he then proceeds to describe each polity—its geographical situation, natural resources, trade goods, and architecture and the education level, religions, and manners of its inhabitants. The subnarrative running through most of these entries is Sonni Ali's and Mohammad I's reunification of the kingdoms along the Niger—some as tributaries and some as conquests—extending central west Africa's imperial reach once again to the west coast. The stories Leo Africanus was told about incorporation of these kingdoms into Songhai showcase the various arrangements these leaders had with the arteries of their empires. For instance, Gualata was once a main destination for Barbary traders, but as Timbuktu and Gao flourished under Sonni Ali's reign, trade was diverted away from Gualata: "In my time this region was conquered by the king of Tombuto, and the prince thereof fled into the deserts, whereof the king of Tombuto having intelligence, and fearing least the prince would returne with all the people of the deserts, graunted him peace, conditionally that he should pay a great yeerely tribute unto him, and so the said prince hath remained tributarie to the king of Tombuto untill this present."[72] The king of Guber meets a much more brutal fate. He was "slaine by *Izchia* the king of Tombuto, and his sonnes were gelt, and accounted among the number of the kings Eunuches. Afterward he sent governours hither who mightily oppressed and impoverished the people that were before rich."[73] Other territories of the Land of the Blacks merely have their judges appointed by the *askia* or have made alliances with the *askia*'s family via marriage. In contrast with much later representations of Africa that would represent it as a continent full of primitive, local chieftains constantly involved in petty wars, the political operations of the Land of the Blacks are represented as sophisticated diplomatic arrangements.

In the *Description*, Timbuktu is the hub for the *askia*'s imperial narrative (though it was never technically the capital). Mansa Musa's and Mansa Suleyman's fledgling aspirations for the city had come to fruition by the mid-sixteenth century: it is a place of trade, industry, and learning where the "inhabitants" are "exceeding rich," so much so that the king married his daughters into the merchant class.[74] The city houses the *askia*'s massive cavalry as well as his "magnificent and well furnished court." Like his Malian predecessors, Askia Mohammad also advertised his prestige and power by making it appear that he controlled an inexhaustible supply of wealth including "many plates and scepters of gold, some whereof weigh 1300 poundes." The *askias* maintained the practice of the earthen ablution as well: upon entering the king's court, "Whosoever will speake unto this king must first fall downe before his feete, & then taking up earth must sprinkle it upon his owne head & shoulders: which custom is normally observed by them that never saluted the king before, or come as ambassadors from other princes." Leo Africanus reports that, like Mansa Musa, Mohammad "so consumed his treasure, that he was constrained to borrow great summes of money of other princes," but the overall impression reinforced by his account of the Songhai Empire is that it's economically vibrant and politically complex. This is consistent with the impression Askia Mohammad strove to give and with preexisting impressions outsiders had of the Western Sudan at least since Mansa Musa's Hajj. In fact, historians have suggested that, like the epics, Leo Africanus inflated the conquest narrative, and if he did, it was likely because that was how the Western Sudan was presented to him by those he spoke with.⁷⁵

Songhai fell at the end of the sixteenth century. Muhammad I was overthrown by his son in 1528, but he and the rulers who followed were not able to maintain Muhammad I's expansive and complex political network. By 1591 the empire was unstable enough that Morocco successfully sacked its major urban centers. The European geographical tradition's continued reliance on Leo Africanus's text, however, meant that readers continued to imagine the Western Sudan as a coherent region under the control and influence of a sovereign they called the "King of Tombuto." The way his domains were portrayed in the *Description* had a formal influence on other kinds of geographical representation as early modern mapmakers—including Giacomo Gastaldi (1564), Abraham Ortelius (1570; fig. 3), and Willem Janszoon Blaeu (1635)—essentially put Leo Africanus's description of the Land of the Blacks (and therefore the

FIGURE 3. *Africae tabula nova*, Abraham Ortelius, cartographer, 1570. (Barry Lawrence Ruderman Map Collection, David Rumsey Map Center, Stanford Libraries)

Songhai conquest narrative) into a spatial format, dominating West Africa all the way up to the coasts.⁷⁶

As was the case with the Catalan Atlas, on these maps the Western Sudan is organized according to a literary cartography rather than a mathematical one, and the narrative it encapsulates transcended any individual text or translation of Leo Africanus's account. Although analyses of Pory's paratext offer insight into one way that British writers were thinking about Africa and appropriating it to expansionist ends, Pory's editorial apparatus does not, as Burton, Bartels, and Andrea have demonstrated, compromise the complexities of Leo Africanus's descriptions. And although the very first consumers of Leo Africanus's narrative in English would have encountered the narrative through Pory's frame, subsequent readers would have been more likely to have encountered it through one of the many texts that discarded Pory's frame in favor of their own, more interested in what Leo Africanus had to say himself than what Pory had to say about Leo Africanus or his text.⁷⁷

The king of Tombuto took on a mythic quality in the European imagination that also transcended Songhai's historical moment. The *askia* became a familiar character that animated sub-Saharan Africa just as the *mansa* had for earlier European representations. As just one example of his longevity, in John Evelyn's *Numismata* (1697), "Isaac *King of Tombut*" is included in a list of "Men of Names or Merit for something Extraordinary and Conspicuous" along the likes of the Medicis, Powhattan and Pocahontas, Moctezuma, and various kings of Europe.⁷⁸ Evelyn offers no explanation of who these people are because "it would be tedious but to Epitomize their several Exploits and Famous Atchievements [sic], which every body conversant in modern History, will call to mind upon the recital of their Names only."⁷⁹

The Land of the Blacks as a Literary Geography: Richard Zouche's *The Dove* and Shakespeare's *Othello*

Just as the Abyssinia-to-Sofala corridor became a coherent geographical unit in the British literary tradition, reiterated through recognizable tropes and topographical features, so, too, did the Land of the Blacks. Like *Paradise Lost*, *The Submarine Voyage*, and *The Fleece*, Richard Zouche's geographical poem *The Dove: Or Passages of Cosmography* (1613) assembles a map of Africa through the symbolic associations Europeans made with each diverse region. Egypt, for instance, is a place of pyramids and the Nile's floods. Abyssinia is the Land of Prester John and the home of the Nile's source. Libya is a place of deserts where, as Pliny had written, monsters bred around the watering holes.⁸⁰ The "Land of Negroes"—which is just west of Nubia and "extended to th'Atlanticke Maine"—is a place

> Wherein the Blacke-Prince keepes his residence,
> Attended by his jetty coloured traine:
> Who in their native beautie most delight,
> And in contempt doe paint the Divell white.⁸¹

Zouche's geographical vision emphasizes both the material wealth and the presumed sovereignty and civility of the Niger valley rather than representing it as a vast, howling, barbaric wilderness. And though Zouche's Land of the Blacks is a space of racial difference, it is not the space of "Pygmyes" and "headlesse" men "With eyes and mouth, like windowes, in their breasts" or of men with one eye in their foreheads that one might expect to find in Africa's interior. Those symbols are reserved for the southern tip of Africa—the region most harshly denigrated in European representations of the continent—and Libya. By contrast, the Land of the Blacks is the place of trade and empire that Europeans had grown predisposed to imagine it to be.

Zouche's Land of the Blacks is also situated within what by that point had become recognizable topographical parameters that took their cue from Mansa Musa and Askia Muhammed's purported imperial reach: Nubia and the Atlantic Ocean to the east and west; the Sahara—whose "sands want number"—and the "Sky-prop Atlas" Mountains to the north. On the other side of the Sahara and the Atlas Mountains is Barbary, and just past that are Italy, France, and Spain, their inclusion a reminder that more than a century after European nations had circumnavigated Africa and established fairly regular contact with Africa's coasts, it was still common to orient Europe in relation to sub-Saharan Africa through trans-Saharan connections. Zouche's heart of Africa, in other words, is actually one of the less geographically and epistemologically unstable regions of this part of the poem. His Land of the Blacks is governed by a set of geographical associations—both cultural and physical—that were considered by Europeans to be canonical knowledge about the continent even though no European eyewitness had ever been there and despite the fact that travelers like Leo Africanus who had been there offered only narrative reports and not navigational data. By the early seventeenth century the cycle of discursive reiteration had reached a point that the region was as recognizable through its "Blacke Prince" and his palaces and his envoys as Egypt was by the Nile flood and Abyssinia was by the Nile's headwaters and the kingdom of Prester John (and, as the next chapter addresses, these specific lines would be quoted in entries on the Land of the Blacks in seventeenth-century geography books).

Though not as explicitly articulated, this literary cartography structures Shakespeare's brief description of the continent in *Othello* (1603) as well. Explaining to the Duke of Venice that Desdemona's father would ask him again and again for the "story of [his] life" from boyhood to the present, Othello recounts that he was a soldier presumably from a young age since the only specific details he mentions are imbued with violence and adventure.[82] Britons believed that the North African potentates populated their armies with soldiers from the Land of the Blacks, who were considered to be the best calvarymen, and it was allegedly due to his retinue of sub-Saharan soldiers—ten thousand by some accounts—that Abu Marwan Abd al-Malik I was able to stop Sebastian I's invasion into Morocco in 1578.[83] Whether these soldiers were for hire or were enslaved isn't clear, but if Othello belonged to such a retinue, at some point, he was "taken by the insolent foe" and "sold into slavery." "Slavery" could mean many things in the early modern world, and the term is deployed a few different ways in the *Description*—a text that scholars accept that Shakespeare would have been familiar with—but the most frequent is in the context of those men and women who were "brought out of the Land of the Negroes."[84] In fact, this is the only category of slaves mentioned in the text specifically taken in battle and sold into North Africa and Europe via trans-Saharan trade routes, described in some detail in Leo Africanus's section on Borno.[85]

The topographical references in Othello's "travels' history" suggest this was his path as well, the "deserts idle" and the "rocks and hills whose heads touched heaven" evoking the Sahara and the Atlas Mountains, which are as high in some places as fourteen thousand feet and which Pory describes in his introduction to Leo Africanus's text as having "tops of incredible height rising out of the midst of sandy desertes" that "exalt themselves above the clouds."[86] For all early modern readers passingly familiar with geographical descriptions of Africa, these two features would have marked the inland boundary between North Africa and the Land of the Blacks and would have also evoked the trade routes that joined the two. "Rough quarries" existed along these routes—the source of the salt that was so coveted in exchange for the continent's gold—and "antres vast [caverns]" of various kinds peppered the Atlas Mountains as well as the Mountains of the Moon to the southeast. In fact, as chapter 4 details, some argued that the Nile burst out of one of these caverns, fed by an underground lake, and Abyssinia—as the land of its source and almost always imagined as much larger than it actually was—frequently marked the eastern border of the Land of the Blacks in literary representations of the continent.

For the modern reader these geographical signposts are easy to glide over in an eagerness to get to Othello's more exotic references further down—to the "Anthropophagi" and "men whose heads / Do grow beneath their shoulders," which critics have pointed to as evidence that Shakespeare was imagining Africa as a space of fantastical difference (more Mandeville than Leo Africanus) and which reiterates Othello's subject position in the play as ambiguous or even utterly other.[87] But these lines do not perform more imaginative or symbolic work than the ones that precede them. As Zouche's poem shows, by the early seventeenth century such monstrous exotics were not unquestionable emblems for all of sub-Saharan Africa but associated with specific regions. Nor are they the emblems of all of Africa in Othello's description of the continent. They—like Zouche's headless men and like the silent traders above—are evoked only at the fringe of Othello's world. The theater in which his life story plays out (of being a soldier, being captured in battle and sold into slavery, and acquiring his freedom) is an organized place, even though it had not been mathematically charted as Europe or the North African coast had been.

Thus, Othello's description of Africa is more orienting than it may first appear, though it is no straightforward map through which we can determine how he would have signified for a British audience. Occasionally, readers have made the case that Othello is best understood as a North African "Moor" rather than a sub-Saharan African, pointing as evidence for this to everything from parallels between Othello's and Leo Africanus's life stories, to analyses of what the word "Moor" would have meant to seventeenth-century Britons, to the perceived impossibility that Shakespeare could have imagined an actual Black African in such noble terms. In her overview of these arguments, Kim Hall justifiably makes the case that "Othello's blackness is symbolically crucial to the play," so much so that attempts to disassociate him from sub-Saharan Africa become, by a certain point, suspect in their refusal to engage with the historical and literary foundations of race.[88] As Hall ultimately shows, the question of "whether Othello should be associated more with North or sub-Saharan Africans" largely oversimplifies the way early modern Europeans conceived of blackness. It oversimplifies the way they conceived of Africa's geography as well. To understand the Sahara only as a "barrier" and not as a "bridge," to use Ghislaine Lydon's terms, is to misunderstand both the historical relationship between African regions and the symbolic role the Sahara played in European impressions of the continent.[89]

As the literary cartography of the Catalan Atlas and Leo Africanus's *Description* show, the Land of the Blacks was considered a distinct geographical region, but it was characterized and imagined not through its isolation from the rest of Africa but through its interconnectivity with the continent, including North Africa. It was populated by kings identified in the literature unambiguously as Black themselves—Mansa Musa is the "Black gentleman" on the Catalan Atlas; Askia Muhammad is "a Negro by birth" in the *Description*—who simultaneously laid claim to Islam but who also pitched their leadership strategies and imperial self-fashioning toward their non-Muslim subjects.[90] As a result, they were not understood by the rest of the Islamic world as belonging to the same realm as Muslims north of the Sahara, as evidenced by Ibn Battuta's skepticism over hybrid Islamic and local cultural practices, including the performances of the *jeliw* and the earthen ablution. European accounts, too, noted the hybridization of Islamic and non-Islamic religious and cultural practices of sub-Saharan Africa. In his introduction to Leo Africanus, Pory attempts to make sense of this, writing that there are two kinds of Muslim "Africans or Moores, properly so called." One type is the "white or tawnie Moores," and the other is composed of the "Negros or blacke Moores," a tidy binary for what Bartels and Boulukos point out is by no means a tidy matter in Leo Africanus's text.[91] But part of the reason the line between sub-Saharan Africans and North Africans was so hazy in both the *Description* and in European conceptions of the continent was because many religious and cultural systems coexisted in the metropolitan centers of the Western Sudan and because the narratives of sovereign entitlement that leaders of the region projected affected the strategies that outsiders used to make sense of its place in the broader Islamic world.

Emphasizing that there is a material context for the instability of the terms "moor" or "blackamoor" that is emblematic of (though not reducible to) historical African worlds does not stabilize the ambiguity of the terms in *Othello* itself or in the British literary tradition more generally.[92] Ultimately, the Land of the Blacks was a narrative object that was deployed to a range of purposes. But reading the play through broader impressions that Shakespeare and his audiences had of the region indicates that the geographical narrative *Othello* tells is more nuanced and less random than the fantastical and monstrous world of Africa pitted against the rational and reasonable world of Venice, North against sub-Saharan Africa, or even merely Black against white.[93] Shakespeare was working within a certain set of imaginative parameters that become visible in the larger context of European impressions of Africa, demonstrating that the reach of such impressions transcended discourse that was strictly geographical and showing how geographical discourse and its concerns permeated popular literature. The hunger that Brabantio and Desdemona express for Othello's account of his African travels—one asking him to tell it over and over again, the other coming "with a greedy ear" to "Devour up [his] discourse"—is a testament to its influence and appeal.

The literary geography of the Land of the Blacks would continue to structure the way writers put Africa into verse into the early Enlightenment. Consider the fact that once Archangel Michael and Adam loop from Abyssinia and Sofala around the Cape of Good Hope to West Africa, Milton doesn't mention the coastal states of Guinea at all but rather orients the region through "Niger flood to Atlas mount."[94] Heyrick's dolphin imagines the place "Where *Niger's* Streams the Parched Fields restore, / And spight of the Sun's dazling Light / On every Face writes the Night" before swimming through the western islands toward the place "Where groaning *Atlas* sinks beneath his Weight."[95] And even as the slave trade rather than the gold trade began to take over the associations Europeans had with the coasts, tying Africa more securely to the Atlantic, such ideas about the interior didn't fade. Dyer interrupts his tour of Africa to offer an aside that condemns the slave trade and gestures toward Caribbean plantations and markets. But his "Nigritian tracts," south of the place "Where lofty Atlas spreads his verdant feet, / While in the clouds his hoary shoulders bend," are full of gold dust that rolls with the rivers toward the coast.[96] The Senegal River, he tells us, shares a source in the middle of the continent with the Nile. It is only "what'er lies beyond that" that "ignorance o'ercasts / With her dark mantle."[97]

African Sovereignty in Europe's Imagination: Jean Bodin's *Six Bookes of a Commonweale* and Marin le Roy de Gomberville's *Polexander*

In part as a result of the political theater of the leaders first of Mali and then of Songhai, the emperor of the Land of the Blacks became a recurring character in European texts. One of the most influential nongeographical works in which the king of Tombut features is Jean Bodin's *Les Six livres de la République* (1576), translated into English by Richard Knolles as *The Six Bookes of a Commonweale* (1606)—a work that was foundational to early modern political discourse. A lawyer and political theorist, Bodin wrote and reasoned with an eye toward the sixteenth century's rapidly increasing knowledge about the world, looking to the governing strategies of non-European leaders as his evidentiary foundation for what he intended to be a universal account of sovereignty, descriptive in nature and free from judgment.[98] Broadly speaking, Bodin concluded that a true sovereign's power was absolute and perpetual—that is, the sovereign was subject to no one but God, and his power and position must last for life.[99] Relying on Leo Africanus's representations of Songhai, he counted the king of Tombut among the world's true sovereigns, a club to which a surprisingly small number of leaders belonged, but which also included the kings of England and France and, looking forward to the second half of this book, the emperor of Abyssinia.[100]

Bodin relied on Leo Africanus's description of the earthen ablution, for one, to make his case for including the *askia* among this list, which he characterizes not only as evidence that he holds absolute power over his people, who voluntarily submit to that power, but also as evidence that the *askia* understands the role that performance and comportment plays in constructing and maintaining this power. He writes that a wise prince should seldom show himself to his people and that when he does, he should "so prepare himselfe, as that he may unto all men seeme even in his face and countenance to carry with him a certaine state and majestie."[101] He names Tartary, Persia, and Turkey as places where princes have learned to successfully perform the power differentiation between themselves and their subjects, but "the kings of Affrike hold yet this majestie more."[102] This is apparent in Leo Africanus's *Description*, "where hee speaketh of the king of Tombut, before whome his subjects appeare not, but upon their knees, with dust upon their heads."[103] In fact, Bodin considers the kings "which dwell more into the hart of Afrike" to be more sovereign in behavior than those of North Africa because, despite the fact that they practice Islam, they don't "acknowledge any greater than themselves," while the leaders of North Africa answer to the Caliphs.[104] The earthen ablution, then, became an emblem even in Europe of how the leaders of the Western Sudan hybridized Islam with longer-standing local practices to project a unique form of royal entitlement to great political effect.

Throughout Bodin's text, the king of Tombut becomes a standard of leadership through which other examples of sovereignty are confirmed or refuted. Vassal kings who pay tribute to Songhai, for instance, are not sovereigns because someone else has power over them. By contrast, the king of Gaoga is sovereign.[105] Leo Africanus wrote that Gaoga was once stateless, but that the royal line of Gaoga began when a "Negro slave" from the region slew his merchant master; claimed his wealth, horses, and goods; and then returned home and took over, enslaving his enemies and selling them across the Sahara in exchange for more horses. He built up such an army this way that "he was accounted of all men as soveraigne K. Of Gaoga."[106] His descendants, men of "valour and high courage," have maintained their rule ever since, carrying on a robust trade with Cairo. Bodin repeats this story, citing it as a recent example of a polity transitioning from statelessness into a polity whose citizens consent to be governed.[107] He appears to have added a detail, though, that is not in Ramusio's Italian text (1550), Temporal's French translation (1556), or Pory's English translation (1600): that the founder of the Kingdom of Gaoga was inspired to greatness when he had "in his travell seene and noted the majestie of the king of Tombut: and thereupon conceiving a desire to make himselfe a king also in his owne countrie." If this is indeed Bodin's addition, it demonstrates the extent to which he held up the sovereignty of the *askia* as the standard by which all African rulers were measured. But it also demonstrates that it is not simply the king's geopolitical control or divine right that makes him such but the way he successfully performed his authority for the public. It is only after the man who would become king of Gaoga bears witness to the *askia*'s performance of his majesty, and sees the way his subjects respond with their own show of submission, that he understands what sovereignty is well enough that he can claim it for himself.

The *Six Bookes*, for all its significance to the trajectory of Western political thought, was a technical work of scholarship whose readership was niche. However, the leader of the Land of the Blacks became an emblem of absolute power in more popular forms of seventeenth-century literature as well. The "Emperour of Melly," for instance, is one of the characters in *Le Romant des Romans* (1626–29), a French romance by Gilbert Saulnier du Verdier that was translated into English as *The Love and Armes of the Greeke Princes* in 1640. The work stages an epic battle between the Greek princes and "Pagans" from Africa and Asia. Fighting on behalf of the pagans, the "Emperor of Melli" is able to rally "an hundred and thirteen Kings, Emperours, Caliphs, Soldans, and Soveraigne Princes, from whose valours great wonders were to be expected," from every kingdom in Africa to fight at his command.[108] William Walker's 1698 play *Victorious Love* is set in "Tombut," where the emperor, who is deep in unrequited love with a white princess of Senegal, describes himself as "I to whose Nod all Africa submits."[109] A play that appeared soon after Thomas Southerne's adaptation of *Oroonoko* (1695), it tells the story of an old and increasingly impotent king's tyrannical attempts to keep the princess from her true love, the king of Gualata.

The most widely read early modern romance that makes use of these tropes, however, was Marin le Roy de Gomberville's *Polexandre* (1632–37), translated into English as *Polexander* in 1647. *Polexander* was, as Edward Baron Turk observes, "a prototype for ensuing modern adventure novels," influential in both the French and the English prose tradition and extremely popular even though it was thousands of pages long and, in Thomas DiPiero's words, "the most torturous and labyrinthine narrative in all French literature."[110] Written in the years leading up to the *Fronde*—a time during which the French people sought to limit Louis XIV's power to increase taxation in his effort to fund a war with Spain—the text defends the notion, à la Bodin, that "the Power of Kings is a Power derived from above: and that the bonds which binde Subjects to their duties being made by the proper hand of heaven, cannot be broken without violating the divine Lawes as well as humane."[111] At the same time, DiPiero describes the text as "an aristocratic behest to Louis that he remain a strong monarch but that he recognize the contribution the aristocracy made to the construction and protection of the state."[112] Due to these royal and aristocratic overtones and allegories, scholars have pointed out, and rightly so, that Gomberville's Africans are mouthpieces for European political and cultural ideals.[113] But Gomberville, like Bodin, depended on and perpetuated what were presumed to be reliable geographical impressions of the Land of the Blacks to stage these ideals, and he uses the king of Tombut as the lens through which he examines the role that performance plays in constructing sovereignty.

Writing one of the first works of prose fiction to make use of a contemporary global setting, Gomberville deployed what Ellen R. Welch has identified as "prose cartography"—references to specific global landmarks, descriptions of how places are situated in relation to one another, the distances between them, and other physical attributes—to help his reader form a comprehensive geographical image of its settings.[114] In the case of Africa, such orienting details did not come from the charts of European navigators and explorers but from the impression that had arisen as Europeans married their expansionist desires with the political theater of the *mansa*, the *sunni*, the *askia*, the *negus*, and other high-ranking Africans like Bumi Jeleen. One of the main characters, Almanzor, is an articulate and courtly prince of "Senega" who has been passed over as heir in favor of the son of his father's second wife. The third volume of the novel positions Senega, which encompasses most of the Senegambia region, as the gateway to "all the lands washed by the River Niger," as did the maps, geographical texts, and poems cited above.[115] Senega's neighbors to the east are "Melley" and "Tombut." Over the course of the novel the king of Senega—Zabaim,

Almanzor's father and a pitiful and ineffectual figure—acquires various territories in the region, loses them to other kings and to rebellions, and claims them back again. These geopolitical interactions narrativize what Europeans knew about the break and conflicts between the Wolof Empire and the collection of territories in the Niger valley that fell under Mali's and then Songhai's banner. Throughout the text, the Portuguese, the princes of North Africa, and the Ottoman Turks visit these sub-Saharan kingdoms, sometimes traveling overland, as the Prince of Fez does, following the trans-Saharan trade routes to "Tombut," and sometimes by water, as "Vasquez de Gama, Generall of the of the Portugall Fleet" does as he seeks entre into the continent from the Atlantic side—another reminder that Atlantic contact with the continent supplemented rather than supplanted impressions that continued to enter the European geographical imagination via the Sahara.[116]

Though not a main character as such, the "King of Tombut" holds the center of this geographical space stable and functions as the figure through which Almanzor's royal destiny is portended and Gomberville's views on sovereignty are expressed. Almanzor first encounters "the untameable King of Tombut"—who has named himself "Indomptable, because he had never beene conquer'd"—when the king takes advantage of internal political instability in Senega to encroach on the kingdom's borders from the east and take Zabaim prisoner.[117] Still in exile and in disguise, Almanzor leads the charge against this invasion. As Almanzor and the King of Tombut come head-to-head, the latter "did as much as a man could doe who had term'd himselfe Indomptable. Yet his courage in this combat met not that successe it had found in some preceding."[118] Almanzor is victorious, demonstrating his "extraordinary valour." But instead of dispatching the mythic king, he "very generously treated him . . . and bearing apart in his affliction as well as in his paine, intreated him not onely to make it appeare on this occasion, that he was worthy of the title of Indomptable, but also to suspend all his resentments to give satisfaction to his word." Almanzor overcomes the king that Gomberville and his readers would have understood as the richest and most powerful king in Africa, which is a testament to Almanzor's martial prowess, and the mercy he shows him is a testament to his princely courtesy.

The truce is furthermore a recognition of the King of Tombut's divinely ordained right to his throne and a statement of the importance of maintaining the performance of such authority. Almanzor is determined to make it "appeare" that the king is still "worthy of the title of Indomptable," lest the office lose its power over the subjects and provoke a rebellion, which is precisely what happens to Zabaim, who has failed to maintain his image, in the very next section of the text. The narrative is one that validates the divine right of kings; however, encoded in Almanzor's gesture is a reminder that although kings are subject to no one but God, their rule is smooth because others, out of their own innate nobility of character, help maintain the integrity of the performance of their sovereignty. The King of Tombut, in turn, not only releases Zabaim, he comes to his aid when his people rebel, and with his army, they achieve a quick victory; Zabaim comports himself so courageously he "even made the King of Tombut admire him."[119] If *Polexander*'s vision of African kings upholding and respecting each other's absolute authority is, at core, a European aristocratic fantasy, it is one that Europeans looked to Africa to authorize. They considered the hold that African kings had over their subjects and the way they projected their "majestie" to be indicators of sovereignty's fundamental principles.[120] The strength of these African kings, the sizes of their palaces, the extent to which and speed at which they travel is exaggerated in *Polexander*. But so is everything in heroic romances—a genre that scholars now recognize was nevertheless engaged in meaningful ways with the global contexts in which romances were written and read.[121]

Bodin's characterization of the leadership of the Western Sudan fed and spread negative stereotypes of Africans even though he aspired to describe without passing judgment. An early proponent of climate theory, Bodin advanced a geographical system in the *Six Bookes* in which the people of the "south" were considered rash and duplicitous.[122] He extrapolated from Leo Africanus's descriptions of Songhai's military might and conquest that the base cultural and political character of African leaders was violent and despotic. The King of Tombut is likewise a qualified emblem in *Polexander*. His essential sovereignty is affirmed in volume 3, but he reappears in the fourth volume as a symbol of tyranny that Polexander (interpreted by some as a stand-in for Louis himself) vanquishes in another adaptation of the incorporation of Gualata ("Galatia") into Songhai.[123] It is not clear whether this is intended to be the same King of Tombut who was Almanzor's staunch ally, but regardless, the doubling indicates that African kings weren't necessarily presumed to be equivalent to European kings even if Europeans turned to them to validate a universal ideal. In fact, because of this dichotomy, they were useful characters for working through the question of how tyranny should be addressed by subjects who considered it their obligation to uphold the divine right of sovereigns through submission. However, the African king needed to be a persuasive sovereign and not simply a parody of one in order for this allegory to have any traction. Thus, neither Bodin or Gomberville necessarily held the *askia* or other African leader in esteem. But the efficacy of central West African leaders' self-displays of imperial power shaped the way these authors thought about Africa as a material place, and they also shaped the way they thought about the abstract concept of sovereignty itself, becoming a warrant for identifying the performance of rule and assent as a fundamental component of the acquisition and maintenance of sovereign power.

The Land of the Blacks in the Early Enlightenment Geographical Imagination: Richard Jobson's *The Golden Trade*

By the early seventeenth century, Portugal's supremacy in West Africa was beginning to wane and Britain had begun to establish political and economic ties to the Senegambia region. The slave trade grew as colonizers in the Caribbean sought an exploitable source of labor, but the primary objective of many of the voyages to the region was still to seek a way into the interior gold trade, and the Gambia and Senegal Rivers were still thought to be the most logical places to start. The purpose of Richard Jobson's voyage up the Gambia in the 1620s was to prove this connection, as the title of his travel narrative, published in 1623, makes clear: *The Golden Trade: or, A Discovery of the River Gambra, and the Golden Trade of the Aethiopians.*[124] Even though his voyage occurred more than 150 years after Cadamosto's and Gomes's, Jobson was motivated by the same information about Africa's interior empires and gold trade not because Europeans were clinging to an outdated fantasy but because this impression had been reiterated and affirmed through both internal African state-building and external diplomatic communications. The Mandinka continued to feature prominently in this cycle of discursive reiteration. Jobson's predecessor, George Thompson, had sent word to England that during his attempt to travel up the Gambia in search of the place "where the Moores of *Barbary* traded," he had received from "a blacke Merchant, called *Buckor Sano* . . . such intelligence of the trade hee lookt after, that such an extasie of joy possest him."[125] This "intelligence" was compelling and persuasive enough that when Jobson followed in Thompson's footsteps, he arrived in the Senegambia determined to find Buckor Sano specifically and work only with him.[126]

At their first meeting, Jobson is offered the same "intelligence" of the gold trade that filled Thompson with such ecstasy. Noticing that the blade of Buckor Sano's sword and a pair of bracelets his wife is wearing appear to be "brought in their beginnings, either from London, or some other part of this our native Country," Jobson asks the broker how he came by such far-flung artifacts.[127] Buckor Sano responds, "There were people used to come amongst them, whom they called *Arabecks*, who brought them these, and diverse other commodities . . . Tawny Moores [who] came in great companies together and with many Cammels."[128] The sword and the bracelets and their circuitous path—British in origin but ending up in West Africa through Eastern channels—not only emblemize the complex circulation and exchange of goods and ideas among Africa, Europe, and the Arab world, they also situate Buckor Sano at the crossroads of this trade, and they encouraged Jobson to inquire further. Jobson explains that Buckor Sano's

> relation made it certaine that these were the Moores of *Barbary*, the discovery of whose trade and trafficke, was the grounds of this our being so high in the river: we grew to question him, how neare those people came to the place we were now at, he answered, within 6 dayes journey there is a town called *Mumbarre*, unto which towne, the next Moone, these *Arabecks* will come: we askt againe, what commodities they brought with them, hee answered much salt and divers other things, we desired then to know what they exchange for, and carryed backe: he answered nothing but gold, and that they onely desire to have, and returned nothing else; wee questioned him farther, whether hee would undertake to carry any of us safe to see those *Arabecks*, and that we might return without danger.[129]

Throughout the whole exchange, Buckor Sano reveals enough to be persuasive and conceals enough to keep Jobson on a string. He drops specific details about the place Jobson wishes to go—the distance is six miles, the name of the town is Mumbarre (the Bure goldfields). The inland Africans trade only gold and want only salt. Yet Jobson is ultimately "hindred from understanding divers particulars," despite the fact that "*Buckor Sano* seemed very desirous to give [him] full satisfaction."[130] When pressed later, Buckor Sano ducks around his promise to take Jobson there with this story: the Arabs do not actually ever see the inland Africans who control this gold. The Mandinka don't see them either. Rather, they leave commodities—bracelets, beads, and, above all, salt—in piles at an agreed upon place and then "remaine away for a whole day."[131] The inland Africans then leave great quantities of gold in exchange for these goods, with each side giving and taking until both sides deem that an even trade has been made, and, thus, they "have a just manner of trading and never see one another."[132] This ceremony is not simply a social nicety—these inland Africans are allegedly "dangerous" and monstrous.

Buckor Sano explains to Jobson as others did to Cadamosto and Gomes that these people hide because their lower lips are swollen and putrid. They need the salt to preserve them.[133] Jobson affirms the likelihood of this explanation by reasoning that the people who bought his own salt in great quantities (exchanges brokered by Buckor Sano) had "for their owne occasions little or no use thereof, and being demanded what they doe with it, they doe not deny to tell us they carry it up further into the country, unto another people, to whom they do sell and vent the same."[134] Buckor Sano indicates that he will take Jobson to this place next time he visits, when they come back with replenished stores of salt.[135] Jobson departs from the region fully confident in "the certain knowledge we have gained in discovering the golden trade of the Moores in Barbary, which was," he reminds us, "the first incourager and beginning of this businesse."[136] He accepts or at least describes Buckor Sano's explanation as the truth.

Buckor Sano may have been particularly masterful at deploying these techniques to capture European interest—make a promise, establish a formal agreement, and then deflect on specifics—but they were obviously not unique to him, not even within Jobson's narrative itself. Jobson encounters different merchants who "belonged to a King further up in the Countrey," one of whom had also been friendly to George Thompson.[137] This man tells Jobson that he is from a place nine days up the river, "that there was a great store of gold, at that place, and that the Arabecks, which are the Moores of Barbary, came thither."[138] His interest piqued, Jobson asks if he will take them to that place: "He answered, yes, if wee were but past these bad people [Buckor Sano's people], pointing to our consorts ashore." Jobson tells the man that "they were a good people, and very loving to us." The man shakes his head, saying, "*immane, immane*, which signifies naught, or the thing they like not" and hastily departs. Jobson meets up with this man later at "Setico" [Sutukho], and he "had a full and large discourse, and received the intelligence which I will now recite: He told me that not farre from Jaye, there were a people who would not be seene, and that the salt was carryed unto them, and how the Arabecks, had all their gold from them, although they did never see them: demanding the cause, he made a signe unto his lippe, and could receive no farther answer."[139] Jobson writes, "We askt him, as we had done *Buckor Sano* and others, if they had a towne called *Tombutto*." This broker responds exactly as Buckor Sano did. He tells Jobson "that name they knew not," but assures him that "houses covered with gold" lie up the river, and he offers "many strong incouragements to invite us on."[140]

Jobson's belief in what Buckor Sano and this other merchant have to tell him about both the silent trade and the connection between the Gambia valley and the trade cities where the Arabs acquire their gold should not be chalked up to a simple credulousness. He, as did others, likely accepted this information as truth because of its consistency and the fact that it confirmed generally accepted knowledge about the interior, and, like the travel writers above, he hinges his own geographical authority on his local informants: "What doeth insewe of this discourse; is written from mee either as an eye witnesse," he writes, "or what I have received from the Country people, and none but such, as were of esteem, and as my confidence assures, would deliver no false thing."[141] The title page of Jobson's narrative reflects the extent to which such "eyewitness" accounts were marketed through the promise of insider information. It offers "A discovery of the River *Gambra*, and the Golden Trade of the *Aethiopians*," but it also promises an account of "The Commerce with a great blacke Merchant, called *Buckor Sano*, and his report of *the houses covered with Gold, and other strange* observations for the good of our owne countrey."

* * *

In tracking medieval and early modern European representations of Africa across a wide range of genres, two patterns emerge. One is an impression of the continent's interior that had been shaped in its essentials by the imperial performances of the ruling and economic elite of the Western Sudan. "The Land of the Blacks" in European writing was not simply an empty scene into which certain people and material objects were dropped; its spatial logic was organized around the ways that these Africans displayed their wealth and their sovereignty and the strategies they used to control their economic assets. They established the Niger valley and its cosmopolitan cities of trade and learning as the epicenter sub-Saharan Africa and presented it in such a way as to draw in commerce and diplomats from both Europe and the Islamic world and to spark Europe's literary imagination. Only at the internal fringes of these empires do European impressions of Africa begin to slip into monstrous silence, and even then, that margin is figured as a threshold of trade that is not an uninhabited, howling wilderness but unrepresentable because its inhabitants will not communicate.

The second pattern that emerges is a metanarrative of how this impression was formed. As Europeans encountered descriptions of the Western Sudan either through coastal peoples of the Senegambia who described the interior states of the Niger valley to which they had been at various times politically or culturally attached, or through written descriptions that continued to come out of the Western Sudan by way of the Sahara, they found that these descriptions affirmed impressions they already had of the region that were born from Mansa Musa's Hajj. Impressions were reiterated, in other words, not only because geographical texts tended to recycle the same information but because contact with the continent continued to produce anecdotes and accounts that squared with what they had heard before. Europeans did not reject this narrative evidence or even try to disguise its origins but blended it with burgeoning empirical practices, acknowledging their African informants and considering the information they offered as reliable and privileged enough to depend on not only in studies of the region but as a means of directing risky and expensive expeditions into the interior.

The next two chapters examine how both these patterns (the impression of the Western Sudan itself and the metanarrative of how impressions of Africa were formed) structured the geographical imaginations and texts of two writers of the long eighteenth century—Aphra Behn and Daniel Defoe. Even as Britain grew increasingly interested in and knowledgeable about Africa's coastal slave ports, the impressions of the Western Sudan sketched out in this chapter held sway over how both writers represented the continent. Although the extent to which either Behn or Defoe was self-consciously aware of their dependence on these impressions varies, both were interested in questions about geographical method and representation. Both use Africa as a backdrop to explore these questions, and both take up the fact that African sources comprised the majority of Europe's knowledge about the continent as a way to investigate the epistemological potential and pitfalls implicit in geography's growing commitment to the discourse of empiricism and the eyewitness account.

2

"A COUNTRY OF BLACKS SO CALLED"

The Romance of African Impressions in Aphra Behn's Oroonoko

In the first chapter of *Tropicopolitans*, Srinivas Aravamudan notes that literary critics have thoroughly plumbed Aphra Behn's *Oroonoko* for its insights into what lies ahead: realist novels, abolitionist discourses, colonial ideologies, and the professional female author, to name a few topics.[1] As Adam Sills has pointed out, this is true about *Oroonoko*'s geography as well, which critics analyze as an early narrative mapping of the Atlantic trade routes that would eventually so thoroughly structure how Britons thought about the world.[2] But in the seventeenth century, situating West Africa on the global stage through its Atlantic—and particularly through its transatlantic—connections was not a universal approach, and it did not replace the medieval and early modern geographical trend of representing parts of Africa from the inside out. Rather than looking at Behn's Africa as one of British literature's many starting places, this chapter contextualizes it first and foremost through what came before. I make the case that Behn's African world is grounded in longstanding impressions Europeans had of the Western Sudan or the Land of the Blacks, which geographers stretched in the seventeenth century to include the coastal states of Lower Guinea. These impressions more than any contemporaneous eyewitness account of coastal slave ports give Behn's Africa its character and shape.

This claim might at first appear overdetermined. After all, Behn gave her kingdom the name of a port on the Gold Coast from which a man is enslaved and carried across the Atlantic to a Caribbean plantation. All enslaved Africans in the Caribbean from the Gold Coast were referred to as "Coramantees," and they gained a reputation for being the most likely ethnic group to incite a rebellion, as Oroonoko ultimately does.[3] And "Coramantien" itself would have been in Behn's purview as more than a random name on a map. Until it was lost to the Dutch, Kormantin was Britain's most significant trade port in West Africa.[4] A strategically important holding in the Second Anglo-Dutch War, it was a major blow to the English when Engel de Ruyter successfully seized it in 1665. This was the same conflict in which England lost Suriname to the Dutch, an event that *Oroonoko*'s narrator laments, and the same war during which Behn worked as a spy for Charles II.[5] It is reasonable to assume that she would have been as well informed about what was happening on the coast of Africa as anywhere else in the theater of operations.

For these reasons, the few scholars who have made the case that Behn's Africa shares more than just a name and a Eurocentric set of associations with early modern African worlds have primarily looked for parallels between her Coramantien and descriptions of the coastal slave ports from late seventeenth- and early eighteenth-century travel writing and geographical texts. Katharine Rogers has noted enough ethnographic details that appear between *Oroonoko* and the eyewitness accounts that Behn likely would have read for scholars to conclude that she didn't, in Joanna Lipking's words, make up her Africa "of whole cloth."[6] Rising above the level of ethnographic details and painting a larger portrait of the novel's slave trade from the African side, Adam Beach sees a precedent for Oroonoko in descriptions of Atlantic creoles—the children of African women and European traders who often worked on behalf of both groups as translators and mediators—and he rightly argues that no one connected to the seventeenth-century Atlantic world would have found a coastal African who spoke fluent European languages an implausible character.[7] Yet, as the previous chapter shows, impressions of the Land of the Blacks literally determined the way Europeans approached the coasts, and, as Beach argues elsewhere, *Oroonoko*'s perhaps unwarranted centrality in Behn studies has tended to eclipse Behn's career-long interest in slavery in the Islamic world as seen in her plays.[8] She had more than one context for imagining Africa, as did her readers—a burgeoning transatlantic context and a longstanding trans-Saharan one.

Beach notes that this latter context is implicit in Behn's Africa, and George Boulukos has detailed some of the resonances between *Oroonoko* and Leo Africanus, but the extent to which geographical discourse is therefore driving Behn's representation of Africa is usually overlooked by critics in part because there is a general assumption that early Enlightenment Europeans held only fantastic ideas about the interior and in part because Behn's Coramantien, in contrast to her Surinam, is presented in the style of a romance rather than the style of an eyewitness account.[9] But as the previous chapter shows, the eyewitness account was not the only geographical discourse in circulation in the seventeenth century, and its epistemological supremacy was by no means guaranteed, especially when it came to representing Africa. Many of the strategies that geographers did rely on are not incompatible with the generic conventions of romance. In juxtaposing the empirical, protorealist world of Surinam with the discursive, romantic world of Coramantien, Behn is not setting up the factual against the fictional but bringing stylized versions of two accepted modes of representing place in conversation with one another. This juxtaposition, and what it can show about the nature of geography as a knowledge-making practice, depends not on Africa as fantasy space but on Africa as a place primarily "known" through the interpretation and synthesis of narrative accounts, many of them coming from Africans themselves. Following Sills, Laura Runge, Robert Markley, and Chi-ming Yang, who have all shown that geographical concerns are central to *Oroonoko*, I argue that the text demarcates the limits of Royal Society–style empiricism as a knowledge-making and narrative tool and that the African impression as a figure of thought—which was produced like the narrator's own account at the intersections of the seen, the heard, and the written—is the vehicle for this critique.[10]

The Influence of the Land of the Blacks on Early Enlightenment Accounts of the Gold Coast

Behn's use of the travel narrative as a frame for *Oroonoko* has long interested modern readers. The opening pages mimic the genre so well that some have concluded that it must be partially autobiographical—a text that offers evidence of and insight into Behn's own possible travels in Suirnam. "I was myself an eye-witness to a great part of what you will find here set down," *Oroonoko*'s female narrator states in the second paragraph, proceeding to describe Surinam in the mode called for in guides like Boyle's *General Heads*, which, as outlined in the introduction to this book, sought to turn travelers into trained eyewitnesses, fueled by the hope that if they learned to write, draw, or otherwise record what they saw, exactly as they saw it, they would be able to reproduce the world as it was.[11] She gives a brief account of the customs and governing systems of its native inhabitants and explains how the Europeans trade with them for all manner of "little rarities," the likes of which appear in early modern scientific collections.[12] She recounts the animals of the area, using the language of measurement and comparison suggestive of the Royal Society's early projects of taxonomy and speciation to describe them.[13] In Surinam there is, for instance, "a sort of monkey, as big as a rat or weasel, but of a marvelous and delicate shape" that "has face and hands like a human creature"; and a cat that is "a little beast in the form and fashion of a lion, as big as a kitten, but so exactly made in all parts like that noble beast, that it is it in miniature." There are "prodigious snakes, of which there are some three-score yards in length, as is the skin of one that may be seen at his Majesty's Antiquaries," which was the Royal Society's repository, lauded by fellows such as Thomas Sprat and John Wilkins as the space where "Ranks of all the *Species* of *Nature*" could be determined through observation.[14] In the opening pages of *Oroonoko*, animal, plant, and person alike are described as if already displayed in such a repository. This flattening out and freezing of a three-dimensional environment is partially a scientific practice and partially a stylistic effect. For such accounts to gain credibility in the late seventeenth century, their style needed to be "naked," as Boyle put it—untouched by flourishes and romanticized language—and Behn's narrator initially parrots this "discourse of fact."[15]

This naked discourse is haunted, however, by Behn's inclusion of a travel-writing trope that dramatizes rather than occludes the fact that the perspective of such eyewitnesses was limited and situated, not disembodied and universal, dependent on the also limited but epistemologically privileged perspective of cultural and geographical insiders. "What I could not be witness of," the narrator qualifies, "I received from the mouth of the chief actor in this history, the hero himself, who gave us the whole transactions of his youth."[16] Muddling matters further, the narrator explains that she has edited the text, "omit[ting] for brevity's sake a thousand little accidents of [Oroonoko's] life, which, however pleasant to us, where history is scarce and adventures are rare, yet might prove tedious and heavy to my reader in a world where he finds diversions for every minute, new and strange." As others have by this point amply shown, these latter statements trouble the first, calling the reliability and the utility of eyewitness testimony into question.[17] The stylistic shift from the opening description of Surinam to Behn's secondhand account of Coramantien is generally seen, in keeping with these readings, as a point of contrast rather than a point of continuity with the narrator's eyewitness claims—a space where the fictional, the ideological, and the antimimetic are valorized. Runge observes that because the Africa portion the text comes secondhand from Oroonoko, it is "in many ways resistant to the historical and ideological type of analysis which the descriptions of Surinam and London readily permit," though Runge agrees with Beach that we shouldn't be so hasty to assume that the Africa portion is therefore ahistorical.[18]

Considered in light of the African impression as an epistemological artifact, this setup is, in fact, historical in the sense that the majority of the information that Europeans had about Africa came from discursive sources—from African informants themselves, from other representations of Africa that also had their roots in African expressions, and from the cycle of discursive reiteration that continually linked the two. After all, the narrator's account of the relationship between the two halves of the narrative—"I was myself an eye-witness to a great part of what you will find here set down; and what I could not be witness of I received from the mouth of the chief actor in this history, the hero himself"—is not unique to *Oroonoko* but a convention that consciously stages a moment in which a person's account of their world becomes someone else's geographical knowledge. In addition to the examples cited in the introduction to this book, recall from the last chapter what Leo Africanus had to say about his section on the Land of the Blacks: "I my selfe saw fifteene kingdoms of the Negroes," he writes, "howbeit there are many more, which although I saw not with mine owne eies, yet are they by the Negroes sufficiently known and frequented."[19] Cadamosto, too, promises the reader that he has written down only what he has seen for himself or has been told to him by "persons in whom faith can be placed."[20] Jobson assures readers that "what doeth insewe of this discourse; is written from mee either as an eye witnesse, or what I have received from the Country people, and none but such, as were of esteem, and as my confidence assures, would deliver no false thing."[21] In echoing this trope, *Oroonoko*'s narrator is not, in other words, flagging a move from empirical travel writing to the world of fiction or even to the imaginatively provocative and critically compelling world of unrestrained discourse (at least in and of itself). She is flagging a move from one set of disciplinary practices to another—from Royal Society–style empiricism to a largely discursively grounded but nevertheless widely accepted geographical mode. The narrator's claims to have edited the text also situates the narrative squarely within this mode. It was the geographer's job, after all, to take a thousand little tedious details from a range of sources and synthesize them in such a way that made them digestible but still preserved the "Genius, Manners and Customs of People," the "great Actions" of their main protagonists, and the details that "strike the Imagination" that Herman Moll and John Green called for and that enabled geographical writing to both instruct and delight. Understanding how the Coramantien portion of the narrative might fit into Behn's geographical commentary requires not a different historical or analytical frame than London or Surinam per se but a broader understanding of what the production of geographical knowledge was presumed to entail—eyewitness accounting, yes, but also the citation and analysis of insider testimony and the synthesis and collation of both into a coherent work suitable for readerly consumption.

Coramantien is a coastal kingdom, which eyewitnesses could and did write about, but when Behn first introduces it, she attaches the setting as firmly to the geographical tradition of representing the interior world of the Western Sudan as to the coast. The narrator states that the African portion of the narrative is set in "Coramantien, a country of blacks so called."[22] It is unlikely that "so called" was intended to directly modify "blacks" in this sentence as some have suggested in the interest of examining how Europeans used language to establish blackness as a category of racial difference during this time.[23] Putting "so called" after place names was a convention that drew explicit attention to the act of organizing geographical knowledge through language. For example, John Ogilby's *Africa*—a translation of Olfert Dapper's Dutch text and a plausible reference text for *Oroonoko*'s more specific African details—introduces the continent as "AFRICA, so called from the Grecians."[24] Ceuta is "so called by both the *Spaniards* and *Portugals.*"[25] The Kingdom of Algiers is "so called from the Head City of the same name."[26] In Behn's usage of the phrase, the narrator is telling the reader that the African portion of her narrative is set in a country of blacks called Coramantien—a cue, just as the narrator's imitation of Royal Society–style eyewitness accounts is a cue, that this is a section not just about a geographical space but also about how geographical knowledge is made and communicated. Coramantien is populated by Blacks, but in making the tie to texts like Ogilby's so explicit, Behn also aligns her setting with their descriptions of the part of Africa that they and many others "call'd *Negro-Land*, or, *The Countrey of the Blacks*," which they, too, stretched to include the Gold Coast.[27]

Widening the referent in this passage from the racialized body to a geographical region of sub-Saharan Africa doesn't invalidate the notion that it offers significant insight into late seventeenth-century ideas about race, but the Land of the Blacks as a geographical category wasn't synonymous with the racialized body. In his introduction to the "Countrey of the Blacks," Ogilby observes that it is unclear what the name signifies, "perhaps derived from the colour of the Inhabitants" or perhaps derived from "the nature of the Soyl" or perhaps because the "*Niger* casts up a black or duskish Sediment, some Rocks appearing amidst in the River, which seem as if burnt."[28] It was inherited from the Arabic geographical tradition, Ogilby notes, not from European efforts to organize the world through visual taxonomies, and complexion wasn't what European geographers used to determine whether or not a place belonged to the Land of the Blacks. (It grew and shrank but even at its largest never included the majority of sub-Saharan Africa.) Rather, it was whether and how a place was connected economically, politically, or culturally to the interior states of the Niger valley, which in Ogilby's description is the well from which the geographical category of the Land of the Blacks and its people spring.

In both Ogilby's *Africa* and Peter Heylyn's *Cosmographie* (1652)—one of the best-selling geography books of the seventeenth century—the Land of the Blacks includes all of Guinea, its cutoff point being the Kingdom of Kongo, and it is clear from the organization of these texts that this was an effect of the still active tendency to imagine Africa from the Western Sudan out rather than from the coasts in.[29] In fact, the term "Guinea" may have originated from "Djenné"—a major trade center in the Western Sudan described by various Arabic sources.[30] Ogilby states that every kingdom of the Land of the Blacks will be given their "peculiar place, first beginning with the most In-land Countreys, or Centre of all these vast Dominions."[31] What follows is Leo Africanus's description of the Western Sudan with its emphases on urban centers, on the king of Tombut's conquests and sovereignty, on the nexuses of trans-Saharan and inter-African trade that line the Niger, and on the gold, goods, and enslaved peoples that moved through the region. Ogilby then details some of the countries of the interior Eastern Sudan, and only then does he move on to the Atlantic states, beginning with the Senegambia—the furthest historical reach of the empires of the Western Sudan—before finally moving south into a description of the Gold Coast. Heylyn opens his section on the Land of the Blacks by quoting the lines from Zouche's *The Dove* considered in the previous chapter, which describe the region through sovereign imagery of king, palace, and court: this is the part of Africa, he reminds us, "Wherein the *Black Prince* keeps his Residence, / Attended by his jetty coloured Train."[32] Heylyn follows the same spatial course as Ogilby in briefer entries—he doesn't offer as much extended detail on places like Gao and Timbuktu here—but he loops around to conclude his section on the Land of the Blacks with the story of Songhai's founding. He also speculates about the empire's potential future because the king of Tombuto is not only "affirmed to be the richest Prince in these parts of *Africk*," he also "possibly enough may in a short time bring all the rest under his command," including the kings of Mandinga, Guinea, Borneo, Gualata, and Gaoga.[33] In fact, he erroneously states that the king of Tombut seized his kingdom back from Morocco in 1589 "and being since that time in as eminent power, as ever in any times before."³⁴ Heylyn sees the Songhai conquest narrative and the "indomptable" nature of the *askia* as a living idea, too powerful to be ignored, not a story or character from a distant past.

Even books published about the Gold Coast in particular, like the anonymously compiled *Golden Coast, or a Description of Guinney* (1665), followed this pattern. Like Heylyn and Ogilby, the compiler considers "Guinney" as "part of that place they call *terra Nigritarum*, or the Land of the Negroes," and in the first pages he explains that "the People called *Nigrita*, give the Land its denomination; and the River *Niger*, that runs through there, gives them theirs."³⁵ Like Heylyn, he supplements this description with Zouche's lines on the Land of the Blacks from *The Dove*.³⁶ From this discursive geographical foundation, the compiler moves into various excerpts from eyewitness accounts of the Gold Coast, but even so, he chooses moments from those accounts that fit into canonical narratives about the interior states and trade. For instance, he includes an anecdote from Pieter de Marees's early seventeenth-century travel narrative about a set of merchants who come to the Gold Coast from "a hundred or two hundred miles from within the Land, bringing great store of Gold."³⁷ Akan brokers will bring these traders onto European ships, and if they don't speak Portuguese, the broker will tell the Europeans "to speak *Moorish* speech unto them, because their Merchant is one that dwells within the Land."³⁸ He then goes on to claim that all the gold traded on the coast comes from these inland countries where gold is bartered for salt, sold by "certain deformed *Negroes*, who will not be seen, and therefore it is left in the field, where the *Negroes* take it away, and leave as much Gold; the truest dealing men in the world."³⁹ Interestingly, Marees doesn't specifically identify these inland traders as coming from the interior Islamic states, nor does he explicitly connect them with the silent trade, only mentioning that the gold comes from inland and that the coastal brokers can't say from where.⁴⁰ It made sense to the compiler of the *Golden Coast*, though, to connect this eyewitness evidence with a narrative of the interior to which Europeans were still deeply committed.

As was the case with eyewitness accounts of the Senegambia, and as the compiler's interpretation of Marees shows, these commitments didn't float free of what was happening on the ground in terms of repeated contact with Africa. Often, travel writers were interpreting descriptions from locals of actual lines of communication and exchange between coastal and interior states. While Bambouk on the Senegal and Bure on the Upper Niger were two of the major sources of Mali's and Songhai's gold, the third major source came from the Akan-occupied territories of Lower Guinea—the threshold of trade that

Ivor Wilks speculates was the origin of the myth of the silent trader.⁴¹ This gold was carried north by a particular group of Mande-speaking traders, the Dyula or Wangara. The presence of these "Mandiguas" on the Gold Coast convinced the Portuguese that they had found a back door into the source of Timbuktu's and Gao's gold, and they began to dispatch expeditions into the interior from the Gold Coast as they had from the Senegambia. When Jean Barbot, who traveled to the Gold Coast twice between 1678 and 1682, asked the locals at Igwa about these "Mandinga," he was similarly told that the capital city of Songhai (Gao) was rich in gold that was carried to Timbuktu and that the Akan actually directed most of their trade toward the Niger states rather than toward Europeans on the coast.⁴² Trade with Europeans, in other words, was of secondary importance. Because of these economic links, Barbot, like the geographical compilers above, considered the Gold Coast to be the southern part of the Land of the Blacks, and he speculated that Gao was merely on the other side of Ashanti rather than over a thousand miles inland.⁴³ These narratives were affirmed, in other words, by earwitness accounts of the coastal states, so geographers had reason to maintain canonical impressions of what lay just beyond them.

Travelers like Barbot included plenty of empirical and ethnographic descriptions of the Gold Coast in their texts (either their own firsthand observations or borrowed from other eyewitness accounts) that didn't conform to medieval and early modern impressions of the Land of the Blacks as a place of kings and empires. The seeds were being simultaneously planted in these travelogues for what would become a vision of sub-Saharan Africa as universally uncivilized. In Barbot's estimation, commoners on the Gold Coast lived low, primitive lives, and elites, though elevated, are still described as uncouth and barbarous by European standards. But rather than taking these coastal encounters and assuming that the interior states must be more of the same—or, as later generations would come to believe, that Africans grew even more primitive the further one went into the interior—travelers speculated that the place "Wherein the Black Prince keeps his Residence, / Attended with his Jeaty-coloured train" was still just over the horizon.⁴⁴ After all, for the majority of travelers, contact with coastal polities was limited to the coastline itself. Unless they were part of a planned expedition like Jobson's or like the Portuguese attempts to reach the Niger states via the Gold Coast, many travelers had little firsthand experience of what lay even a dozen miles inland. And when geographers like Heylyn, Ogilby, and the compiler of the *Golden Coast* incorporated the information travelers brought back to Europe, they put it even more securely beneath the umbrella of the Land of the Blacks, making the connections between the Niger states and the coastal states appear seamless and making the substance of coastal encounters the tail rather than the head of descriptions of the continent. The way these geographers arranged these regions under one categorical heading indicates the firm grip the imperial history of the Western Sudan still had on how Europeans imagined the continent, even though both Mali and Songhai had fragmented. This categorical stretching also illustrates that, from a disciplinary standpoint, even as the production of empirical descriptions about the world became increasingly called for and increasingly available, geographers preserved canonically accepted, discursively substantiated knowledge about places as the core of their representations, adapting eyewitness accounts to fit them rather than altering them based on what eyewitnesses had to say about Africa and its peoples.

The Nonempirical Geographical Discourse of Behn's Coramantien

By identifying Coramantien as a "country of blacks, so called," Behn positions it within an African impression that did not have hard topographical boundaries in the European geographical imagination but did have certain entrenched associations, which had been shaped by African expressions about the Western Sudan and European attempts to confirm or refute them through increasing firsthand contact with the continent. As the above geographical descriptions indicate, readers still assumed the interior was populated with kingdoms or empires ruled by sovereigns who performed their majesty so successfully that their subjects, struck by their presence, fell down before their feet and sprinkled dust on their heads. These kingdoms were maintained through a combination of state-building and conquest, and the losers in military conflicts were sold into slavery. Their courts were luxurious because of their own unfettered access to the continent's riches but also due to their trade connections with North Africa and the Arab world.

How *Oroonoko* signals its proximity to this representational tradition—in particular, its literary cartography and its treatment of African sovereignty—is overlooked because such signals coexist comfortably with the aspects of the text that critics have identified as evidence that Behn's Coramantien should be understood as a strictly imaginative world. Other than the few exceptions described above, critics have overwhelmingly argued that Coramantien is best understood as an exotic elsewhere, a generic stage for a chivalric romance, or an allegory for Britain.[45] Yet as the previous chapter shows, texts as diverse as maps, eyewitness accounts, plays, and heroic romances drew from and fed back into shared impressions of the Western Sudan, operating as much closer cousins than they appear to be on the surface and inextricably tied to African worlds and worldviews, guided as they were by locally grown and widely circulated performances and narratives of imperial power. Given Polexander's wide circulation in both French and English and its many thematic similarities to Oroonoko, it's likely Behn would have read it or other romances like it. The clear resonances between Oroonoko and works like Othello also support rather than undercut the notion that she was drawing from and speaking back to an already established, culturally shared notion about Africa's interior. Thomas Southerne's stage adaptation of Oroonoko emphasizes its Atlantic connections: it is set entirely in the Caribbean, the African events are explained by the characters in retrospect, and Oroonoko is a prince of Angola.[46] But Walker's Victorious Love, which retells with a triumphant ending the Africa portion of the Oroonoko story, is explicitly set in Tombut and makes the Oroonoko figure the unfortunate king of Gualata, suggesting that for Behn's audience her narrative continued to resonate in both geographical directions.

Behn doesn't offer navigational coordinates, but Coramantien's location relative to other geographies is mapped through narrative cues consistent with the literary cartography of the Land of the Blacks. The Eastern commodities that fill the court connect it via the trans-Sahara trade to North Africa and the wider Islamic world, echoing how Leo Africanus described, for instance, the court at Gao. There, the king "hath a certain private palace wherein he maintaineth a great number of concubines and slaves, which are kept by eunuches"; and "it is a woonder to see what plentie of Merchandize is dayly brought hither, and how costly and sumptuous all things be."[47] Similarly, in Timbuktu "all the women . . . except maid-servants go with their faces covered," and "the king keepes a magnificent and well furnished court."[48] Between the trans-Saharan trade and trade with Europeans on the coast, broadly speaking all of the goods that Behn either names outright or alludes to would have been available in the Land of the Blacks in the seventeenth century, including the king's Turkish carpets, Onahal's pearl earrings, Oroonoko's battle pavilion and his clothing, which is so splendid that it makes him continually stand out among his fellows even after he is enslaved. Arabic and European geographers represented the Western Sudan as they did not only because African kings and merchants established and maintained these imperial and economic networks but because the political and imperial narratives they broadcast both to cultural insiders and to outsiders signified that their kingdoms were places of trade as well as conquest, part of the Islamic world but also uniquely African. This is not to suggest that Behn's oriental stylizing is therefore somehow a realistic representation of African worlds or that *Oroonoko* doesn't belong in the constellation of texts scholars have deemed oriental tales, but these continuities also don't mean that readers wouldn't have recognized her setting as African or connected it to outstanding impressions of the continent.

After all, Coramantien's attentions are primarily directed toward the interior of Africa while the Atlantic is a fringe locale. Inter-African warfare, for instance, and the inter-African slave trade it supported are more significant to Coramantien's operations than its economic relationships with Europeans. The narrator tells us that the Europeans "found" a robust slave market already in place in Coramantien due to the near constant military campaigns launched against its neighboring kingdoms. The Europeans are auxiliary to this economy in Behn's figuration, benefiting from but not driving the market (a point that Europeans would make to justify their participation in the slave trade through the eighteenth century). When the king gives the command that Imoinda and Onahal "should be both sold off as slaves to another country, either Christian, or heathen, it was no matter where," he doesn't have Atlantic slavery specifically in mind. Rather than crossing the Atlantic in a ship, they could have crossed the Sahara in a caravan and ended up in a different "Christian" land than the West Indies, such as Italy, or in a "heathen" land somewhere else in Africa or in the Ottoman Empire.[49] As was the case with *Othello, Polexander,* and the poetry considered in the previous chapter, Behn's literary cartography isn't arbitrary even though it is vague and imaginative—it is a stylized version of what arose when Europeans married their expansionist hopes for the continent with the ideas they had inherited from the political theater and empire-building strategies of the leaders of the Western Sudan.

The legacy of the king of Tombut permeates *Oroonoko*'s African setting as well. Early critics interpreted the text's use of African sovereignty, and the fact that her titular character is a "Royal Slave," purely as metaphors through which Behn dramatized the political turmoil surrounding the Glorious Revolution and the accompanying questions it raked up about the divine right of kings. A more recent trend has been to analyze how the text's Atlantic context concretizes Behn's investigations into this issue, enabling her to take sovereignty from the idealized realm of abstract political theory and test out its viability and limitations in a material and historical arena that was itself reassessing theories and practices of state formation and governance that had once been accepted as preordained.[50] However, like the former, this latter scholarship tends to implicitly or explicitly position Coramantien as the place where Behn establishes abstract, allegorical notions of kingship: the king of Coramantien is an archetype of a tyrannical, despotic, self-interested, and/or impotent sovereign, and Oroonoko is the embodiment of chivalric ideals and innate nobility. It is only in the transition to the New World, where Oroonoko becomes stripped of his rights and subject to indignity and abjection, that Behn moves the conversation from abstract theory to real-world application.[51]

Yet there was a precedent set by writers like Bodin, Gilbert Saulnier du Verdier, and Gomberville of using the king of Tombut and impressions of his domains as a sphere in which to explore these same questions (and which resulted in conflicting images of a king who was to be admired for his ability to so successfully perform his majesty and to be condemned for his tyranny). Critics like Eugenia Zuroski and Catherine Molineux have recognized the centrality of performance to Oroonoko's ability (or lack thereof) to compel and command throughout the text. His sovereignty is manifested when he is able to "strike reverend awe in his beholders" through the spectacle of his dress and person.[52] In fact, Molineux argues that the text's central epistemological and political concerns are driven by the ways in which sovereignty and assent are exposed as a performance and thus a fiction. "Chivalric virtues" are revealed to be "myopic beliefs" as Oroonoko's appearance increasingly fails to override self-interest and command the obedience of others as it ought.[53] For Bodin, too, the ability of the kings of Africa to perform their majesty was what gave them power over their subjects, and in *Polexander*, Almanzor's determination to uphold the King of Tombut's "indomptable" appearance validates the importance of such diplomatic theater in maintaining political stability and respecting divine as well as earthly law. In keeping with Molineux's line of reasoning, Behn has taken the dynamic Gomberville stages between Almanzor and the king of Tombut to its furthest unsettling conclusion. If Gomberville is suggesting that the aristocracy's willingness to play their part in upholding the performance through which a king signifies his sovereignty is foundational to the smooth running of a kingdom and keeping rebellious impulses in check, Behn transfigures such performances from the outward sign of an innate quality to a political principle wholly dependent on a subject's willingness to recognize its validity. For Molineux, it is "the availability of colonial experience and the historical particularity of imperial formations" that enables Behn to create "a new meditation on the uncertainty, indeed the illegibility, of appearance, formulated acutely around the question of whether a black prince could be a prince." This new meditation could just as well be in dialog not (or not only) with a static, idealized concept of sovereignty but with an old meditation supported by a different epistemological but still geographically located and historicized frame. After all, Bodin replied "yes" to the question of whether "a black prince could be a prince," not based on abstract theorizing but on an analysis of what he considered to be an adequately substantiated historical example of a real polity. Though the New World did indeed offer new terrain through which to explore these ideas, situating *Oroonoko* in a lineage of European texts that turned to African performances of sovereignty enables us to see that such investigations included Old World contact zones as well, mediated through the cycle of discursive reiteration that gave the Land of the Blacks its character and shape in the British imagination. Doing so also reminds us that early Enlightenment Europeans used geographical representations to reflect on larger social or political questions; they did not simply consume them as information.

To recap, Behn's Africa section doesn't look like her empirical description of Surinam not because it isn't informed by geographical discourse but because geographical descriptions of Africa were by and large not empirically constituted. Canonically accepted but discursively substantiated depictions of the Land of the Blacks were still at the core in large part because Europeans were still interested in the region for reasons ranging from the economic to the political. Descriptions of the coastal states were attached to this core like satellites, often shaped even by travelers themselves to be coherent with what came before. Behn's Africa is similarly organized by the long cycle of discursive accumulation through which Europeans were conditioned to imagine the continent. Mapping these relationships makes visible *Oroonoko*'s intellectual and imaginative debt to African worlds and worldviews. They made Behn's Africa possible—her text simply wouldn't have taken the form that it did without them. Although Behn was likely unaware of the depth of this debt, she harnesses the African impression as an epistemological artifact to signal her interest in nonempirical geographical discourse. Recognizing that Coramantien as a setting is constituted through this alternate method rather than categorizing it as an explicitly antigeographical space enables us to look back and see how the geographical task the eyewitness narrator undertakes in the portions of the text set in Surinam is far more complex than simply writing down what she sees as she sees it in the naked style of empirical fact.

African Romance and the Limitations of Royal Society–style Geographical Empiricism

Behn's reliance on the trappings of romance to narrate the Africa portion of *Oroonoko* is often seen as antithetical to any mode that a writer would use to represent a real geography. But—the fact that other writers also blended romance and geographical descriptions of Africa aside—the genre of romance and African impressions have more in common than they might appear to at first. Together they offer Behn a counterepistemology and mode of representation through which to examine the viability of the empiricism and naked style called for by members of the Royal Society as a means of producing and communicating knowledge about the world. In fact, paired they serve as a handy foil to Sprat's description of the relationship between knowing and writing in the *History of the Royal Society*, with which Behn was likely familiar.[54] Pursuing and communicating the "naked and uninterested Truth" required "a close, naked, natural way of speaking; positive expressions, clear senses; a native easiness."[55] According to Sprat, when reporting their findings, members of the Royal Society have learned to "reject all the amplifications, digressions, and swellings of style: to return back to the primitive purity, and shortness, when men deliver'd so many *things*, almost in an equal number of *words*." Adhering to these principles would not only ensure that the knowledge produced was grounded in empirical reality; it would ensure that this knowledge could move from place to place and from thinking subject to thinking subject in a way that was tidily transactional, with nothing important lost or superfluous added.

In *Oroonoko*'s opening pages, Behn's narrator initially seems to embrace such an attitude, her prose guided by "*Reason*" instead of by "its Slaves, *the Passions*" as she methodically works through her descriptions of Surinam's plant and animal populations.[56] When the narrator arrives at her description of Surinam's human inhabitants a few paragraphs later, though, Behn repurposes to ironic effect Sprat's romanticization of "Primitive purity" and "native easiness." The natives are themselves all "naked," and "if one lives among them, there is not to be seen an indecent action or glance; and being continually used to see one another so unadorned, so like our first parents before the fall, it seems as if they had no wishes, there being nothing to heighten curiosity, but all you can see, you see at once, and every moment see; and where there is no novelty, there can be no curiosity." The natives' nakedness is associated with truth, candor, innocence, virtue, and honesty, and these qualities are reflected, as Sprat idealized, in the way they use and understand language: they don't know the word for "liar," they are incapable of "fraud," and "they know no vice or cunning." When an English governor told them he would come see them on a particular day and then didn't arrive, they mourned him for dead because they believed "once a man's word was past, nothing but death could or should prevent him from keeping it."[57]

Yet the natives are emblems of prelapsarian naiveté, not characters with keen understanding of the world. Their disinterested gazes and purity of speech trap them in a timeless past and leave them with no means of coping with the world that is rapidly changing around them. "Nature" has been their teacher, but they understand nothing of "religion," "laws," or English governors who don't keep their word. "Curiosity" may be the impulse that leads people into vice and sin—and that leads the parents to fall—but there can also be no knowledge production if there is no curiosity. And while mistaking the surface for the whole story may allow one to blissfully ignore the world's more complex underpinnings, the misunderstanding between the natives and the governor suggests that a lack of knowledge about norms and laws, though it may give them "tranquility" in the short term, will not insure against the destruction of that tranquility in the future. Behn makes a parallel point in explicitly geographical terms later in the narrative. Oroonoko is enticed onto the boat of the treacherous captain who betrays him into slavery with "globes and maps, mathematical discourses and instruments."[58] Both Molineux and Sills observe that Oroonoko's fascination with these superficial representations of the world and the instruments that enable their production leads to his downfall "in such a way," as Sills puts it, "that the map and globe become symbolic of a whole way of *seeing* the world, one that is deeply suspect in Behn's estimation."[59]

The narrator's description of Surinam's natives similarly casts suspicion on the epistemological value of her own disinterested gaze and naked style. After all, her task is to freeze objects time and place through categorization and description so that "all you can see, you see at once, and every moment see." This was also what the Royal Society repository (to which the narrator donates an extensive collection of rare butterflies) was supposed to be—a "General Collection of all the Effects of Arts, and the Common, or Monstrous Works of Nature" organized according to Wilkins's handy "Universal Language," the literal purpose of which was to match things with their words.[60] Such organizational schemas may make knowledge tidily transactional, with nothing important lost or superfluous added, but their epistemological utility is otherwise somewhat dubious. Both this building of accumulated specimens and the narrator's catalogue of accumulated facts risk becoming a collection of curiosities that provokes no curiosity and that mistakes an understanding of appearances for an understanding of reality—an anxiety that is provoked in other subtle ways in this section: for instance, in addition to bringing back the collection of rare butterflies for the Royal Society's repository, the narrator also brings back a feathered costume made by the Amerindians that she donates to the "King's Theatre," which is then worn by an actress merely playing an Indian.[61]

As the setting changes from Surinam to Africa, the geographical mode shifts from the empirical description to the African impression: this is the part of the text that gains its character and shape from Oroonoko's testimony, the narrator's interpretation of it, and the way she edited an abundance of details down into the most striking and illustrative ones. The mode of narration also shifts from the eyewitness account to the romance, resulting in an "amphibious" form, as Corrinne Harol calls it, that enables Behn to bring seemingly contradictory ways of knowing and representing into conversation with one another, exploring their benefits and limitations and dramatizing their ironies.[62] When it comes to the text's geographical investigations, this amphibious form allows Behn to precisely invert the extended epistemological metaphor through which she—riffing off of Sprat—dramatized the limitations of Royal Society-style empiricism. Physical nakedness is replaced with layers that hide the body from the gaze like Imoinda's veil and the walls of the *otan*. Stylistic nakedness gives way to suggestion, implication, inuendo, and apophasis—the kinds of "specious *Tropes* and *Figures*" that Sprat fretted brought "mists and uncertainties . . . on our Knowledg."[63] In the hands of wise men, such tropes and figures can "represent *Truth* cloth'd with Bodies," and "bring *Knowledg* back again to our very senses, from whence it was first deriv'd to our understandings." But in the wrong hands, they "give the mind a motion too changeable, and bewitching, to consist with right practice." In *Oroonoko* both clothes and figurative language clothe in ways that encourage the roving of an envisioning mind rather than stabilizing or concretizing the understanding, and they do so by provoking the very erotic curiosity that nakedness in Surinam failed to incite. "It will be imagined," the narrator repeats throughout this section, coaxing the reader's fancy and passions, or "it is not to be imagined," inviting the reader to do just that, particularly in the text's most suggestive moments. What transpires between Oroonoko and Imoinda in the *otan* is not presented nakedly: "I believe he omitted saying nothing to this young maid that might persuade her to suffer him to seize her own, and take the rights of love; and I believe she was not long resisting those arms where she longed to be." "The satisfaction of these two young lovers" is "not to be imagined," and "it is impossible to express the transports [Oroonoko] suffered."[64] Rather, romance operates according to a striptease logic—the imagination is stimulated into action by what is hidden, desire and curiosity provoked by the act of undressing rather than by the state of being undressed, and satisfaction attained by active mental participation rather than passive consumption.

The fact that these extended metaphors run so parallel to one another, coupled with the fact that they follow a shift from the transferrable but unexciting representation produced by the eyewitness narrator to the diffuse and discursive but provocative representation of Africa, invites the reader to consider how romance might offer an alternate way to think about representing not imaginative geographies but real ones. As Campbell observes, there are many ways in which the romance as a genre works in opposition to the "scientific observational style" of *Oroonoko*'s opening pages. The latter is "antinarrative" in the sense that it seeks to freeze objects in time and place through categorization and description. The point of view the reader is asked to inhabit to inspect Surinam's native inhabitants maintains a strict separation between the observer and the observed. The former is plot-based and character driven, and we are asked to see the world through Oroonoko's eyes. But though this mode may be antiempirical, it is not antigeographical. Impressions of Africa's interior were likewise structured through characterization and action rather than frozen in place through either description or mathematical calculation—the Catalan Atlas, Leo Africanus's narrative, and the geographical space of the Land of the Blacks were organized around exceptional people and through the "great Actions" they performed. Such elements perhaps remained so central because the interior couldn't yet be mapped any other way, but thinking once again to Moll's preface to his *System of Geography*, events like wars and reigns of kings were considered by some to be "the most necessary Part of Geography" and the most interesting part as well.[65] Acquiring such knowledge did require one to think through the point of view of another and speculate about the imaginative world that unfolded. The reader of *Oroonoko* is put in the same position as the traveler, the geographer, and the reader of accounts of Africa's interior: each must be an active, curious interpreter of the text, not merely a passive consumer of it. Only then does the world of Coramantien emerge, and in contrast with Surinam presented as a curiosity cabinet that provokes no curiosity, flat and frozen in time and space so that "all you see, you see at once, and every moment see," it is a three-dimensional, layered, moving world. Imaginative depth perception is required to work through the descriptions given, which take the reader from the broad panorama of Africa's battlefields to the hidden spaces of the *otan* and back again. Such movement might "give the mind a motion . . . changeable, and bewitching," but it also exercises the intellectual faculties and results in a conceptualization of a place that is in some ways more authentic than the text's initial descriptions of Surinam because it is a theater for human action rather than a prelapsarian tableau.

The romantic mode doesn't need to be a perfect parallel for discursive geographical modes in order to invoke them; the narrator's first-person account is not a perfect parallel for empirical geographical modes either—subsequent events as they unfold in Surinam don't rigidly adhere to a realist logic or style. And in fact, once the narrative returns to Surinam, many of the representational and interpretive strategies that the Africa portion demands become an integral part of the text's geographical project. The narrator repeats several of the observational and narrational tasks from the opening pages but with different end results. She once again seeks out and offers a description of Surinam's native population, but instead of remaining frozen objects of the gaze, the natives gaze back, their curiosity and engagement prompted (tellingly) by the clothing of the narrator and her companions:

> By degrees they grew more bold, and from gazing upon us round, they touched us, laying their hands upon all the features of our faces, feeling our breasts and arms, taking up one petticoat, then wondering to see another, admiring our shoes and stockings, but more our garters, which we gave them, and they tied about their legs, being laced with silver lace at the ends, for they much esteem any shining things. In fine, we suffered them to survey us as they pleased, and we thought they would never have done admiring us.[66]

The charge in the feeling of the breasts, the lifting of the petticoats, and the fact that they desire the garters, not to mention that they get far enough up the leg to reach them as they "grow more bold," suggest that they won't long be "like our first parents before the fall," if they ever truly were. The desire for knowledge is provoked at last. Susan Scott Parrish points out that in seventeenth-century natural history writing in the Americas, "both people and things were curious and depended on each other to evince this quality," which dissolved rather than imposed a "division between the self and the world, between the investigator and the investigated."[67] The natives are now curious in both senses of the word, and so is the narrator. They begin to constitute each other just as the narrator's account and Oroonoko's account do, making the production of knowledge a joint project even in this empirical scenario.

Even the narrator's descriptions of the natural world begin to adhere to a logic that depends not on surface-level observations but on layers of discursive representations and imaginative association that dissolve categorical boundaries rather than instate them. Shortly before the scene with the now-curious natives, she offers once again a catalog of the plants and animals that populate Surinam. Much of what she names is already familiar to the reader, and so she can offer them in list form, "oranges, lemons, citrons, figs, nutmegs, and noble aromatics," words standing in for things in a straightforward manner.[68] However, near the end of the paragraph, she needs to describe something she presumes is not recognizable to the reader—"a little beast called an armadillo, a thing I can liken to nothing so well as a rhinoceros: it is all in white armour, so jointed that it moves as well in it as if it had nothing on."[69] Her strategy for transferring her empirical observation to the mind and understanding of the reader initially seems uncomplicated. It is one that she relied on earlier when she described the marmoset as a "sort of monkey" and explained that *cousheries* look exactly like lions only smaller, offering an empirical surrogate with which the reader is already familiar. The narrator's choice of the rhinoceros puts a peculiar spin on the strategy, though.

Unlike monkeys and lions, which had been staples in the menagerie in London for a long time, rhinos were only known in Europe through representations. Clara wouldn't make her famous tour of the continent and England and have her image immortalized and circulated by artists and engravers until the mid-eighteenth century.[70] Curiosity cabinets often contained the horns or sometimes even the heads of rhinos, yet the majority of people's mental pictures of rhinos—particularly the notion that their skin was jointed like armor—would have come from sources such as Albrecht Dürer's woodcut (1515), which was based on a written description and a sketch of a rhino in Lisbon that Dürer himself never saw in the flesh. The comparison of the armadillo to the rhino is a metaphor that requires quite a bit of adaptation on the part of the reader as well since armadillos and rhinos don't actually look alike. Their only similarity is their jointed armor, which in Dürer's woodcut is rigid plates, not at all fluid, and thus not in keeping with the imagery of the armadillo moving "as well in it as if it had nothing on." (The armadillo itself is, in this sense, also described as naked, but it is no more immediately comprehensible for all that.) It is not a representation of a fictional creature just as Behn's Arica is not a representation of a fictional place. But it similarly requires the reader to work through several layers—an act of undressing that may not ever result in a state of being undressed but that provokes curiosity and stimulates the imagination. If, as Aravamudan argues, accounts of collectible animals in *Oroonoko* "disclose a mixture of allegorical and realist modes," and if, as Robert Chibka argues, such descriptive "digressions" direct the reader back to the narrator's opening "disclaimer" that her eyewitness account is not strictly an eyewitness account, then Behn's armadillo is an example not of how the unfamiliar and far away are made knowable through empirical observation and the paralyzing, unprovocative discourse of fact but of how they are made knowable through the hybridization of a range of epistemological strategies and representational practices.[71] After all, immediately after describing the armadillo the narrator rather gives up on possibility that using empirical observation to match words with things will produce a stable representation of Surinam that can be imported intact and complete into the mind of her reader; she declares that "it were endless to give an account of all the divers wonderful and strange things that country affords."[72]

This inquiry into what Behn's armadillo looks like under its shell may also appear to be a digression from my argument that African impressions set the stage for the text's central epistemological questions. However, it is an example of how authorial engagements with African impressions ripple through their texts, not simply serving as backdrops or sources of illustrative detail but facilitating the text's central philosophical and literary inquiries. The way Behn combines romance and nonempirical geographical strategies to put pressure on Royal Society–style empiricism and the discourse of fact is only viable and visible if Coramantien evokes for the reader what they would have understood to be real African worlds. Africa is an advantageous setting for Behn to explore these issues because the European eyewitness was continually displaced there; to write about Africa with any effort toward veracity meant remediating other sources, which Behn's narrator demonstrates as she synthesizes the seen with the spoken and written. Her dependence on Oroonoko's testimony is a stand-in for a broader geographical phenomenon that Behn herself enacts as she represents Africa through indirect and mediated images that can be traced back to impressions of the Land of the Blacks. The result is not a specifically locatable or anthropologically recognizable West African polity, but it is nevertheless constituted through European attempts to make sense of the world by treating what Africans had to say and show about themselves as meaningful geographical evidence.

3

"A MEDIUM OF AN ENDLESS CORRESPONDENCE"

Rivers for Want of Empires in the African Impressions of Daniel Defoe's *Captain Singleton* and *Atlas Maritimus and Commercialis*

By the end of the seventeenth century, the slave trade had come to dominate Britain's interest in Africa, and much of the Royal African Company's energy was put into building forts on the coast and establishing political alliances with the locals in order to support that trade. But in the midst of heated political debates in the early eighteenth century over whether the Royal African Company should be allowed to maintain their monopoly over the slave trade or whether separate trading should be legalized and, if the latter, how such a trade should be regulated, there was a renewed interest in the exploration of Africa's interior.[1] By the 1710s, with a great deal of its power stripped away, the African Company was attempting to reinvent itself from an institution whose main purpose had been to supply the British colonies with slave labor into an institution whose main purpose would be, as one pamphlet put it, "penetrating into the Inland Parts where, beyond Controversy, are as Great Treasures of Gold as are found in Brazile, or in any other Parts of America."[2] By 1720 James Brydges, Duke of Chandos, had taken over as director of the Royal African Company with the express purpose, according to William Pettigrew, of transforming it into "a territorial entity and an agent of inland penetration and conquest, of gold mining, and of plantations."[3] In order to formulate this vision for the future of the company, Chandos revisited seventeenth-century travel narratives written during Britain's first concerted attempts to establish trade with the inland states where he would have encountered impressions not only of Africa's interior riches but also of the waterways that might be used to access and export gold and ivory and that might even be used to cross the continent entirely.[4]

As chapter 1 shows, such impressions arose from imperial state-building in the Western Sudan that predisposed Europeans to think about the Land of the Blacks as a geographical space, how that predisposition became blended with the Classical geographical theory that all of Africa's major rivers sprang from a single source in the middle of the continent, and how that connection was reinforced by Wolof and especially Mandinka descriptions of routes into the interior. To briefly recap, Europeans were initially drawn to the Senegambia region by the hope that its two rivers were branches of the Niger that could be navigated to the source of Mansa Musa's gold (as those who held that the Senegal, Gambia, and Niger were a single river believed) and perhaps even to the Christian Kingdom of Prester John (as those who held that the Niger and the Nile sprang from one source believed). In reality, the Gambia, Senegal, and Niger Rivers are distinct rivers fed by rainfall in the Guinea Highlands, which is roughly three thousand miles from the Nile. But Cadamosto's, Gomes's, and Jobson's accounts of their attempts to travel up the Gambia illustrate how Mandinka traders and guides strategically manipulated the hydrological notion that the Land of the Blacks was networked not only by political systems and trade routes but by these waterways in order to draw Europeans to them. Simultaneously, they deployed narratives about monstrous and silent inland miners, signifying the limits of what could be said or shown about the interior to maintain their roles as indispensable brokers between interior and coastal trade.

As people like Chandos pushed to make inland exploration and trade a priority again, these impressions garnered new interest, and it was in the midst of these political and geographical debates that Daniel Defoe published his various writings on Africa.[5] He defended the African Company's monopoly in the early decades of the eighteenth century, speaking out against separate trading and advocating for better support for the company's forts and settlements.[6] In later years he supported the company's efforts to rebrand itself as a vehicle for interior exploration, writing that inland trade would yield more profit than "the Commerce of both the *Indies.*"[7] He also had a lifelong interest in geography as a discipline. The astonishing variety of settings across Defoe's oeuvre, Srinivas Aravamudan points out, is a testament to how much he read on the subject.[8] Initially, critics dismissed Defoe's global descriptions as "mechanical" imitations, as Pat Rogers put it, "as if one can see Defoe poring over his maps and geography books at home" as he wrote.[9] More recently, though, scholars have moved beyond identifying how Defoe borrowed from geographical genres, emphasizing instead how he was in dialog with them.[10] Jess Edwards has made the case that Defoe took an active interest in reforming geography from a scholastic discipline into a scientific one geared toward utility and productivity, though he didn't intend to divest it of its potential to prompt reflection.[11] Despite the fact that Defoe appreciated geography as a form of practical knowledge that privileged experience over erudition, Anne Thell argues that Defoe could be frustrated by the limitations of the empirical eyewitness account and believed that the armchair geographer's or even the fiction writer's perspective could be more useful because by bringing together multiple points of view, such writers were able to create a fully immersive virtual world for the reader.[12] Jason Pearl demonstrates that moments in Defoe's fiction that "employ a prospective realism and anticipatory logic that universalized the familiar" cannot be taken at face value as fantasies about the infinite potential of uncharted lands because they are tempered by a subsequent disenchantment that reveals their impossibility in an increasingly globalized world.[13] Not simply mimicking geographical writing or instrumentalizing it in order to stage a colonial vision, then, Defoe saw himself as actively participating in conversations about the stakes and methods of global representation.

For all scholars interested in Defoe's geographical thinking, Bob Singleton's trek across Africa's interior is a particularly attractive object of analysis because it appears to enshrine a threshold where the factual gives way to the obviously fictional. Maximillian Novak writes that *Captain Singleton* was often found wanting because of this, "criticized sometimes for its lack of realism, sometimes for its lack of imagination."[14] But more recent readings have stressed that the ambiguity of this threshold is illuminating, offering insight into Defoe's use of and attitude toward realism, into how and why he manipulated both fact and imagination to suit economic and colonial agendas, into universal assumptions he made about human diversity, into how he theorized the relationship between the experiential and the abstract, and into what fiction could show about the world that more scientific or practical genres couldn't. Many of these arguments start from the assumption that the substance of early Enlightenment representations of Africa fell into two categories—what had been empirically and mathematically surveyed by European explorers (the coasts), and what was a product of the European speculative imagination (the interior). Critics tend to take for granted that in *Captain Singleton*, Defoe "inks in some of the blankest spaces on the map," in Knox-Shaw's words, without addressing the fact that the maps Defoe would have been familiar with, and that *Captain Singleton* directly references, were not blank.¹⁵ Those who do note that Defoe's Africa was not the Africa of eighteenth-century maps or geographical texts nevertheless indicate that Defoe had no compunctions about turning it into blank space himself so he could rewrite it as a "vast howling wilderness," dense with natural resources and sparsely populated by primitive natives, to suit his various agendas.¹⁶ This is the end result of Defoe's narrative, but this chapter makes the case that he arrived there not by sweeping the continent clean in a fell swoop but in subtle dialog with outstanding impressions of the Land of the Blacks, which he and his contemporaries still took very seriously.

I argue, as others have, that Defoe's Africa offers insight into both his expansionist fantasies and into how he imagined the relationship between empirically produced geographical knowledge and other forms of global representation. But I also argue that to advance that vision, he needed to rely on and strategically revise outstanding impressions of Africa's rivers, resources, and interior states, harnessing their illustrative potential but obfuscating their African origins. I demonstrate how two texts, *Captain Singleton* (1720) and the *Atlas Maritimus and Commercialis* (1728), maintain the geological and topographical ideas that those impressions of the continent popularized while simultaneously stripping away the cultural, economic, and political networks and institutions that had been the scaffold and warrant for those ideas. Since African informants and their networks were the only links that existed between outside eyewitnesses and knowledge of the continent past the coasts, in breaking those links, Defoe transforms substantiated ideas about the interior into speculative ones—a move that seems at odds with his geographical convictions even if it supported his political and economic aims. But I ultimately argue that he doesn't run those speculative ideas together with the scientifically mapped world, replacing one suspect discourse with another. He uses a variety of narrative strategies to maintain the space between speculative and scientific claims in both texts, creating an epistemological vacuum for European expeditions to fill and offering economic incentives for doing so.

Impressions of the Hydrography of the Land of the Blacks: The Single-River Theory

As chapter 1 shows, for centuries, impressions of the hydrography of the Land of the Blacks were inextricable from impressions of its trade nexuses, gold mines, and interior states. Medieval and early modern maps illustrate how tightly the two were bound. Muhammad al-Idrisi's 1154 *mappa mundi* depicted all the continent's major rivers springing from a single source, a choice that was based not only on Classical geographies but also on what he knew of the early medieval Ghana Empire—the regional predecessor of Mali and Songhai.[17] The Catalan Atlas (fig. 2) explicitly linked the single-source theory with narrative impressions of Mansa Musa's gold, and maps by Giacomo Gastaldi (1564), Abraham Ortelius (1570; fig. 3), and Willem Janszoon Blaeu (1635) reinvigorated it as they combined how Leo Africanus had oriented places like Gao and Timbuktu along the Niger with how Wolof and Mandinka brokers described the courses of the Senegal and Gambia Rivers. They each show the major western rivers as one, and the Niger and the Nile are drawn within centimeters of one another, flirting if not outright connecting.

By the early eighteenth century, when Chandos was attempting to rebuild the failing Royal African Company, the discursive geographical evidence that substantiated and reinforced these impressions still held a great deal of sway. For instance, Jean-Baptiste Labat—a Dominican missionary, botanist, and ethnographer who became an authority on Africa in the 1720s and 30s despite never having traveled there himself—was a committed advocate of the single-river theory, writing that if an explorer followed the Senegal or the Gambia, once those rivers turned into the Niger, he would pass the "Mines of Gold" and "the kingdoms of *Gago* and *Tombuto*" before arriving at a large lake that the locals called "*Maberia.*"[18] Labat cited the seventeenth century traveler André Brue and "the *Negroe* Merchants of the Kingdom of *Mandingoe*" as his evidence, deeming the Mandinka reliable on the grounds that they were better traveled than anyone else in the Land of the Blacks.[19] And when the Royal African Company hired Bartholomew Stibbs in 1720 to attempt just such a foray into the interior, he was given the same instructions that Jobson had been given one hundred years before—to "discover how far the *River Gambia* was navigable, and whether there were Gold Mines upon it."[20]

As Jobson's did, Stibbs's attempt failed. After a lengthy struggle through rocks and sand flats, Stibbs concluded that they had left too late into the dry season to make any appreciable progress up the river. Unlike Jobson, who remained optimistic that "houses covered in gold" could still be found up the river, Stibbs walked away from his expedition believing that the Gambia could not be connected into the Niger. He stated that he never heard the Gambia called by any other name, that "its Original or Head is nothing near so far in the Country, as by the Geographers has been represented," and that he "never heard the Natives mention any thing of Lakes."²¹ But rather than undermining the single-river theory, such reports sparked debates about how to weigh empirical evidence produced by explorers against the discursive evidence inherited from erudite traditions and reinforced by African informants. Depictions of African hydrography became flashpoints where writers and mapmakers made visible their own epistemological commitments and wrestled with their continuing dependence on African expressions.

While it might be tempting to assume that armchair geographers continued to advocate for the value of erudite traditions while travel writers advocated for prioritizing eyewitness accounts, this wasn't necessarily the case. Working as a clerk for the Royal African Company beginning in 1730, Francis Moore was the next British traveler to write extensively about the inland countries along the Gambia River. (In fact, Stibbs's journal was published for the first time as part of Moore's *Travels into the Inland Parts of Africa* [1738].) Unlike Stibbs, Moore remained committed to the single-river theory. He dismissed Stibbs's conclusion that the Gambia is not a branch of the Niger on the grounds that Stibbs was relying too heavily on his own observations and not giving enough credence to the word and expertise of his local guides, insisting that Stibbs had "been led into this Error from want of conversing with the Natives" and because he never learned the local names for places and thus couldn't ask the right questions.²² Stibbs had also failed to earn their trust. By contrast, Moore writes, "The *Joncoes* [merchants] that I myself have generally spoke to (knowing that I had no Intention to trade up that Way) told me, *That about a Month's Journey from* Joar *there are great Lakes, near which they pass.* And that is the general Opinion of the Country."²³ They were honest with him and not with Stibbs, he claims, because they knew Moore had no plan to undercut them, but since it was largely to the locals' advantage "to prevent the White Men going farther up the River," they also frequently "gave out such reports that would discourage them."²⁴

Moore's recognition that Africans manipulated geographical discourse to gain an advantage in their dealings with Europeans might at first appear to work against his insistence that insider knowledge was more reliable than the observations of an outsider. However, Moore trusts what the Mandinka told him about the hydrography of the Western Sudan because it also squared with a geographical narrative that had withstood both the test of time and close inspection by a critical mass of respected intellectuals. Moore considers Leo Africanus and Muhammad al-Idrisi—who both advocated for the single-river theory—to be more reliable than Stibbs on the grounds that they are "both *Africans*" and have thus "given a better Account of the Inland Parts of *Africa* than any other."²⁵ For this reason, Moore reprints what both have to say about the Gambia River, excerpting from Leo Africanus the entire section on how the trade caravans travel "through *Segelmassa*, to *Tombuto*, which was then the name of a powerful Kingdom, erected by one *Soni Heli Ischia* over the *Negroes* upon the River *Niger*."²⁶ Moore was not only a proponent of the single-river theory, he was a proponent of the single-source theory, making the case that the Nile sprang from the same lake as the Niger and citing other African evidence—what the Abyssinian traveler Gorgoryos told the Ethiopianist Hiob Ludolf about Abyssinian geography—as grounds for this belief.²⁷ Moore also quotes at length from Labat, whom he considers a more reliable source than Stibbs, even though Labat never traveled in Africa. Labat, Moore believed, was "a Person of Some Learning," whose views were backed up both by the word of the locals and by what geographers like Leo Africanus and al-Idrisi had to say, while Stibbs's conclusions from his personal experience were the mere "Conjectures" of one man.²⁸ If he is going to rely on someone who might be conjecturing anyway, Moore goes on to say, he will rely on the "learned Ludolf" and not on (by implication) an undereducated factotum.

Mapmakers were likewise reticent to throw out the single-river theory only on the word of a few eyewitnesses even as cartography grew into an increasingly empirical science. John Senex (1721), Jean-Baptiste Bourguignon d'Anville (1749; fig. 1), and Herman Moll (1710; fig. 4) each maintained some version this outstanding hydrography even as they dispensed with placing "elephants for want of towns."²⁹ D'Anville, like Moore, still considered Muhammad al-Idrisi and Leo Africanus to be the best authorities on the Land of the Blacks, and though parts of his map are only lightly illustrated and his rivers don't connect, they run horizontally toward one another, and the Gambia, Senegal, and Niger valleys are fairly well filled in with geopolitical boundaries and cities. Moll writes on the very center of his map of Africa "ETHOPIA this Country is wholly Unknown to the Europeans," but rivers and lakes, including "Niger Lake," cut through the very middle of "ET/HIOP/IA," "Euro/peans," and, most ironically, "unkn/own." The absence of knowledge denoted by the words is juxtaposed against the flagrant presence of the rivers, which blend seamlessly with the inlets and outlets around the coast. Impressions of Africa's interior rivers and the polities through which they flowed were still considered knowledge, even as mapmakers simultaneously recognized that such impressions had not been verified by European eyewitnesses. The role of the

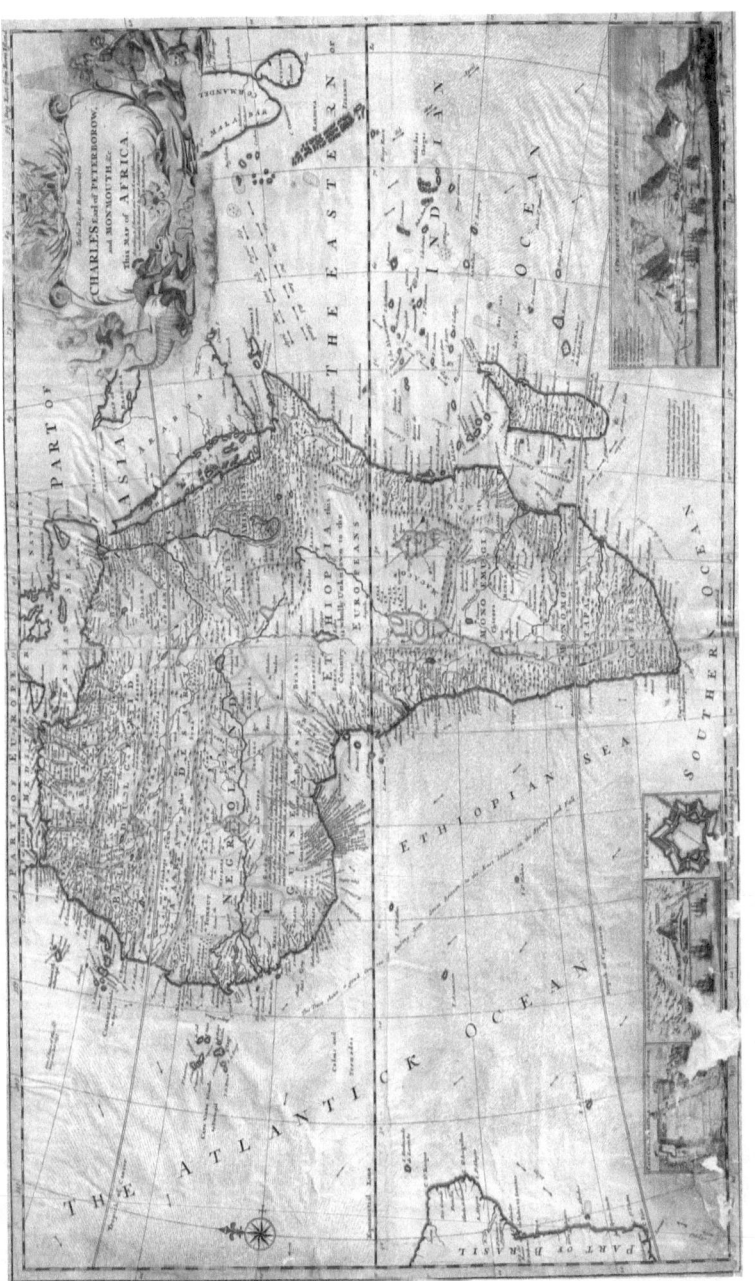

FIGURE 4. *To the right honourable Charles, Earl of Peterborow and Monmouth, etc.,* Herman Moll, cartographer, 1710. (University of Cape Town Libraries, Special Collections; maps scanned under the William and Yvonne Jacobson Digital Africana Program at UCT)

Mandinka in encouraging these impressions is memorialized on Moll's map as well—he breaks the syllables of the region he has attributed to the "Man/ dinga" in half with the words "Here are Gold mines."

Writers like Labat and Moore and cartographers like Senex, d'Anville, and Moll thus explicitly or implicitly validated the authority of both local informants and older sources that organized Africa's physical geography through African expressions of geopolitics and culture. They believed they had enough reason to maintain the single-river theory even while acknowledging that it wasn't an empirically proven fact. Still, frustration continued to grow in other quarters with geography's continued reliance on scholastic methods and the word of locals. In his footnotes on a compilation of some of the sources on the single-river debate, the editor of Astley's *New General Collection of Voyages and Travels* (likely John Green) is particularly scornful of what he saw as Jobson getting taken in by scheming brokers.[30] Defoe belonged in this camp as well, but as the above disagreements show, this stance wasn't as easy to defend as it first might appear to be, even well into the eighteenth century. Complicating matters, although Defoe was highly dubious of the reliability of secondhand sources in general and of African informants in particular, it suited his political and economic agendas to perpetuate the notion that the Senegal, Gambia, and Niger Rivers were one because it promised viable access to abundant commodities.

In what follows, I analyze how Defoe navigates this tension in the Africa portion of his pirate adventure novel *Captain Singleton* (1720) and in the *Atlas Maritimus and Commercialis*, which was planned in the early days of the African Company's renewed interest in interior exploration (1721) though it wasn't actually published until 1728.[31] Ostensibly, one is a work of fiction and the other is a work of fact, but as scholars of both texts have established, there is considerable bleed-over between the two both in content and in the narrative moves Defoe makes to create a compelling economic vision. Though *Captain Singleton* was published first, I begin with the *Atlas*, where the strategies that Defoe uses to both mobilize and undermine outstanding impressions of the Land of the Blacks are explicitly visible, which then throws into sharp relief how the same strategies are at work in a more understated though no less foundational way in *Captain Singleton*. In turn, an examination of the narrative techniques Defoe uses in *Captain Singleton*—which allows the coexistence of his image of the continent's interior riches, his criticism of the geographical methods that made such an image possible, and his valorization of empiricism—enables us see how Defoe deploys similar techniques in the *Atlas* to authorize imaginative speculation in a genre otherwise committed to representing the world as it was.

The Spatial Grammar of African Empires in the *Atlas Maritimus and Commercialis*

Of all the major texts considered in this study, the *Atlas*'s rhetoric about "Africa in General" most resembles the colonial rhetoric to come that would declare the continent as a whole to be essentially unsettled and uncivilized and thus fit for European conquest. It is the quarter of the world that "some are forward to call the worst," a designation that Defoe agrees is appropriate in the sense that "it is cultivated in the worst manner" and "inhabited by the worst People of any Country under the Sun."[32] Yet, Defoe argues, in its situation and commodities, it is actually the best, positioned in the middle of Europe, Asia, and the Americas and full of gold, copper, and ivory. Parts of the continent are suitable for planting, and even the hottest parts are inhabitable. Of particular value is the fact that "it is furnish'd with the greatest and most easily navigable Rivers," including the Niger, the Nile, the Congo, the Zaire, the Zambezi. These rivers "by their long Courses penetrate far into the Land: and were the Country bless'd with a People qualified for Business, that understood Trade, and furnish'd with a Genius for Improvement, they would be the Medium of an endless Correspondence." Read within the context of nineteenth-century colonial discourse, Defoe's treatment of Africa in the *Atlas* doesn't seem out of place, especially since Defoe himself is frequently pointed to as one of the harbingers of British colonial attitudes. But considered in the context of other representations of Africa published at the time, the fact that Defoe empties Africa of its cultural diversity and political complexity stands out since eighteenth-century readers were as likely to imagine it as a continent full of settled empires as they were to imagine it as the "vast howling Wilderness" that Singleton ultimately deems it.[33]

Particularly striking, given Defoe's interest in Africa's rivers and interior trade, is what he chooses to include and what he chooses to exclude in his representation of the Land of the Blacks. As most accounts of Africa do, the *Atlas* pinpoints the Senegal River as the boundary between North Africa and the Land of the Blacks, remarking as others did on how immediate the change in complexion was from white-faced Moors on one side of the river to "perfect Negroes" on the other.[34] Then, after declaring the Senegal a tributary of the

Niger, Defoe advances a version of the single-river theory and, more or less, the single-source theory as well. He describes the Niger as "rising in *Aethiopia*, and running from within a few leagues of the River *Nile*" from whence it "crosses the whole Continent of *Africa* from East to West, having perform'd a Course not less than 3700 Miles, perhaps the longest of any River in the World" except the Amazon.³⁵ In the Western Sudan, the Niger divides into "three mighty channels"—the Senegal, the Gambia, and the Rio Grande or Corubal River south of the Gambia. In keeping with his introductory statements about Africa's rivers in general, Defoe concludes that the Niger could be "the most noble River in the World for Navigation," and used to transport Africa's goods to the west coast, if only it ran through "a Country peopled by a trading and opulent Nation."³⁶

Any reader of Leo Africanus or the many other texts that represented the Western Sudan with the grain of how central West Africa's imperial states represented themselves would have thought of the Niger valley as already peopled by opulent trading nations given that the geopolitical reputation and economic sophistication of places like Gao, Djenné, and Timbuktu had been the grounds and the advertisement for investing in Africa's interior trade since the fourteenth century. However, according to the *Atlas*, no such people are to be found along the Niger. There is no mention of the former intellectual and economic capitals of the Mali and Songhai empires in Defoe's account of the Land of the Blacks. The *Atlas* claims, rather, that little is known about the region except what has been heard from the people who come to the coasts with goods to sell and about whom nothing specific or coherent can be concluded since they are so different from each other in language, dress, and behaviors.³⁷ "From all these Observations," Defoe concludes, "the Geographers have no knowledge of Particulars, so as to fill up the Spaces in the Charts and Maps, they satisfy themselves with telling us, that this Country, drawing a line from West to East of 16 to 1700 Miles, is the *Land of the Negroes*."³⁸ There is no indication that there was once political unity within this region or that there still was economic, linguistic, and cultural continuity within it even after the Mali and Songhai empires had dwindled. In fact, generally speaking, Defoe claims that African peoples have no formal economic communication with one another at all and that all meaningful trade in the continent is driven from the coasts by European supply and demand.³⁹

Defoe sketches out the few exceptions to this in a section at the very end of the Africa portion of the *Atlas*, less than a page long, titled "The Inland Trade of Africa." The inland trade is "scarce worth noticing" but necessary to mention since, despite his claims that the interior peoples have no communication with one another, Defoe must account somehow for how gold, ivory, and enslaved peoples make it from the interior either across the Sahara or to the coasts where the Europeans acquire them.[40] Thus, the trans-Sahara trade is mentioned briefly, but it is treated almost as if it is apocryphal: "They tell us that there is a yearly Caravan, or, according to some, a half-yearly one, from the Country properly call'd *Guinea*," Defoe writes, giving no clear indication of who "they" are. "They" also say that the caravan sets out from an unnamed "great *Negro* Town"—perhaps a gesture to Djenné or the city of Cantor whose bustling population and economic vitality Gomes wrote about in such specific terms based on Bucker's testimony. Defoe ultimately concedes that the trans-Sahara trade must exist, and even that North African merchants may travel as far as the Niger valley, but he positions North African and Jewish merchants as the orchestraters and overseers of the trade, treating sub-Saharan Africans, as he did in his short description of the Land of the Blacks, as disconnected entities merely providing, in a small-scale way, whatever commodities they have to offer to the next group over. He also takes pains to point out that he is basing this information not on what the ambiguous "they" have to say but on the testimony of "an English Merchant who lived in *Barbary*," whom he considers "a Good and Sufficient authority."[41] He avoids any mention of Leo Africanus's account or any of the other Arabic sources that organize the Land of the Blacks through either Mansa Musa's pilgrimage or the conquests of the Songhai Empire.

The silent trade that played such a central role in how people imagined and demarcated the boundaries of the Land of the Blacks is also mentioned briefly in "The Inland Trade of Africa," but it is detached both from the Mandinka traders who circulated the story and from the complex and extensive inter-African economic networks to which these traders were so central. Defoe simply describes how North Africans and sub-Saharan Africans exchange salt and gold without ever connecting personally. He never mentions that the inland miners *cannot* speak, nor does he suggest that there is anything monstrous about them.[42] This adoption and revision of the myth of the silent trade allows him to account for the fact that the gold moves all the way from "*Guinea* to the *Mediterranean* Sea" while simultaneously upholding his claim "that there is no Communication or Commerce between Country and Country in this Quarter of the World."[43] In the original descriptions of the silent trade, it was a system so finely tuned that a misstep could drive the silent traders away, as shown in the story of the *mansa* who captured one and tried to force him to speak, halting trade between Mali and the goldfields for three years. The delicacy of this relationship was part of how coastal brokers justified their refusal to show European traders the silent traders' location. By reimagining the silent trade as a lack of "communication" in general, Defoe transforms it into something so unsophisticated as to not count as "commerce." As opposed to the geographers and travelers in chapter 2 who imagined that opulent nations lay just over the horizon even if Africa's coastal peoples seemed primitive, Defoe suggests that since all technological advancements and complex economic arrangements were introduced to Africans by Europeans, it is more reasonable to assume that Africans grow more primitive the further one moves inland rather than less.

The result of these rhetorical maneuvers is an image of Africa's physical geography—its rivers and natural resources—that is consistent with outstanding impressions of Africa's interior and that took much of its shape, as the travel narratives and geographical texts in the previous section show, from African expressions. The *Atlas* enthusiastically endorses the idea that the Senegal, Gambia, and Niger Rivers join together and are the most viable pathway to the continent's interior gold (as opposed to traveling up from the Gold Coast or down across the Sahara, which is how the first two European visitors to Timbuktu who lived to tell about it eventually got there in the mid-nineteenth century). Waxing in a style both Edwards and Novak have described as the "geographic sublime," Defoe's geological descriptions of the continent's gold mirrors this hydrographic imagery.[44] A "Mass of Gold . . . of infinite Value" comprises the "very center" of the continent and is "for ever hid in the Deeps and Pits of the Rivers and driven down into the Ocean, as well as what remains in the Body of the Mountains, and of the Earth, which no Floods have ever been able to wash out."[45] If Africa ever had a giant earthquake, he speculates, "the subterranean Fires would melt the very Metal, and the fluid Body would run down from the Openings and Eruptions in liquid Streams." However, the people and the cultural narratives that had both scaffolded and justified these topographical notions have been excised. There is no mention of the Wolof and Mandinka brokers who encouraged the single-source theory or the narrative of Africa's literally endless supply of gold that Mansa Musa's pilgrimage broadcast and that subsequent accounts of the trans-Sahara trade affirmed.

In effect, Defoe relegates what at one time would have been the first things Europeans associated with Africa's inland trade—the sub-Saharan terminuses of the trans-Sahara trade and the points of contact for the silent trade—to the very end of the Africa section of the *Atlas,* and he frames them as relatively insignificant barriers to Europe settling Africa's interior. This is not simply the projection of an idle fantasy onto a blank space. In decoupling his representation of Africa's interior geography and geology from the narrative accounts that substantiated them, Defoe also erases the long-accepted rights and territorial claims of Africa's interior states, stripping them of their sovereignty. One reason why such an effort is advantageous to Defoe's vision is because it supports what would become a fairly standard justification for Africa's colonization down the road—that there was plenty of space and warrant for Europeans to make headway into the continent because Africans were not making proper use of it. Furthermore, in Defoe's vision for Africa, this interior full of innocent and potentially pliable natives who have not learned to "communicate" is symbolically juxtaposed against his representation of the brokers of the Gold Coast, whose control over coastal trade Defoe deeply resented. At the time of the *Atlas*'s publication, it was still the case that the Europeans had "not a Mark of Gold in the whole Trade, but what we must get of the *Negroes* by fair trading.... It is brought down from the Inland Countries by the *Negroes*, nor can we tell particularly from what Part of the Inland Countries it comes."[46] And unfortunately, the locals they are forced to negotiate with have, as a result of their interactions with Europeans, "been made meer Merchmen, wary and crafty as an Exchange-Alley Stock-Jobber," as Defoe wrote in the *Review*, and made "sharp, cunning, and knavish" as he puts it in the *Atlas*.[47] Defoe's expansionist imagery in the *Atlas* depends not only on the notion that gold and ivory will be ubiquitous and easily acquired but that, once Britain manages to push past these coastal controls, the inland Africans will not be an impediment to profit because they will be ignorant of how to drive a hard bargain. The Gold Coast is treated as separate from the Land of the Blacks in the *Atlas* the only part of the continent, Defoe argues, that can accurately be called "*Guinea*"— but it is nevertheless tied to the Land of the Blacks as it was in earlier sources through the gold itself, all of which, the *Atlas* says, is to be found around the Niger.[48] Europeans needed to devise some way to access what Defoe calls these "inland Frontiers" before they could start reaping the benefits of Africa's geography, which seemed so naturally formed for expansion and trade.[49]

As part of his efforts to separate the topography that African impressions offered from the cultural and discursive scaffolding that created and justified them, Defoe throws his hat in with those who sought to discredit African sources of geographical information. Despite the fact that the Africa portion of the *Atlas* opens with clear statements about the locations of Africa's rivers and the location of is gold, it also bemoans that Europeans have no firsthand knowledge "above 100 Miles from the Coast, except what is gather'd from the *Negroes* themselves; and they either so ignorant or so false and lying, that nothing can be depended upon which they give an Account of."[50] As stated above, the *Atlas* is clear about the fact that Europeans don't know where the gold comes from, and in a move that seems to undermine Defoe's earlier claim that the continent is full of navigable rivers, he specifically criticizes cartographers who have speculated too wildly about Africa's hydrography. They have from eyewitness accounts of the coasts "good Authority to begin a River or Stream," but they've been given no reliable account of "what Course they run, which part of the Country they pass thro', or what Nations inhabit their Banks and Borders; what Cities are situate[d] upon them, what Commerce or Navigation is manag'd by them at any considerable distance from the Coast."[51] He uses African impressions to show the viability and the payoff of a colonial project in narrative terms but undermines them as navigational tools, calling instead for more concerted and systematized forays into the interior. But in the process, he ironically recreates the very kind of representation of Africa he calls out in the *Atlas*—one that is not only wildly speculative but that is itself still dependent on the viability of African geographical discourse even as it works to excise African people and cultural institutions from the continent. Whether the narrative strategies outlined below are sufficient to save Defoe from accusations of sloppiness or hypocrisy, the *Atlas* retains the silhouette of the African worlds and worldviews it strives to erase.

Geological Speculation and Cartographic Critique in *Captain Singleton*

Captain Singleton was published the same year Chandos took over the African Company with the intention of turning its focus from coastal trade to interior exploration. As such, it has been frequently analyzed as an index of Defoe's ideas about and attitude toward global trade and colonization. Scholars have given particular attention to how the text stages a fantasy of British technological and cultural superiority and the infinite wealth and accumulation that could be available to British traders if they applied that superiority more effectively in Africa.[52] At the same time, each is sensitive to the fact that Singleton's trek across the interior is riddled with ideological ambiguity that resists being read as straightforward colonial propaganda. Are the text's contradictions indicative of an imperial agenda haunted by its own insecurities?[53] Is Defoe making a distinction between what expansion into Africa could look like and what it should look like?⁵⁴ Is he recognizing that a little piracy is a necessity for successful trade?⁵⁵ Are the text's inconsistencies merely a side effect of Defoe's sometimes slapdash writing?⁵⁶ Reading *Captain Singleton* through the *Atlas* and through outstanding impressions of the continent adds to this list of inquiries. The *Atlas*'s multiple geographical registers—the dependence on and revisions of outstanding African impressions; the criticism of those who represented Africa from speculative rather than empirical evidence while deploying those very same strategies—comprise the spatial grammar of the Africa portion of *Captain Singleton* as well, and to similar ironic effect. However, as a text that, in Aravamudan's words, "reminds the reader that all accounts are playing within an economy of self-justification in the eyes of others," *Captain Singleton* is more overtly reflexive in regards to this irony.⁵⁷

Defoe deploys several of the same expansionist ideas in *Captain Singleton* that he would later articulate even more explicitly in the *Atlas*: the closer Africans are to the European coastal trade, the less tractable and the more shrewd they are in their bargaining, while those who have not yet learned to be wary happily exchange valuable goods for mere trinkets.⁵⁸ The continent is emptied out of all organized government and commerce, and its inhabitants are described at times as "a Parcel of Creatures scarce human, or capable of being made sociable on any Account whastsoever."⁵⁹ Wheeler notes that *Captain Singleton*'s Africa seems to be written "in the spirit of sixteenth-century English commercial interests," looking in some ways more like an early modern account of Africa than an account of an early eighteenth-century traveler, so the exclusion of the continent's interior commercial infrastructure is all the more notable.⁶⁰ The inter-African trade that does exist is a relay trade between groups otherwise so disconnected from one another they must signify their intensions with a "friendship pole" that can be seen at a distance, and they communicate only through signs, which, Jason Farr has argued, Defoe presumed to have a pure quality to them, free, as they were, from the deceit of speech.⁶¹ As Defoe makes clear in the *Atlas*, these means of moving goods from place to place, with no actually "communication," cannot be understood as commerce. Thus, *Captain Singleton* like the *Atlas* suggests there is plenty of opportunity for people who "understood Trade" and who were "furnish'd with a Genius for Improvement" to take the continent in hand and no overly cunning locals to stop them.⁶²

The Black Prince—whom Singleton and his crew enslave to serve as their guide, along with several of his people to carry their baggage—is imbued with a kind of sovereignty, or at least ingenuity and nobleness of character, which, as Wheeler and Laura Brown have shown, offers clues into how Defoe thought about the intersections of various categories of human difference.[63] But he is a far cry from the *mansa, sonni, askia,* or *negus* of geographical accounts of the interior or even from the Swahili elites that Singleton and his crew would have been far more likely to run into on the coast of Mozambique. When the Black Prince discovers the first of the gold that Singleton and his crew will continually amass through their trek across the interior, he is ignorant of what it is, and thus he is also far removed from the various locals on Africa's southeast coast who told João dos Santos and Josiah Burchett stories about the ancient gold mines to be found up the eastern rivers.[64] He is, rather, one of the "Naked, Ignorant, and Blinded Natives" that the Defoe of the *Review* fantasizes might still be found in Africa—generous, good-natured, eager for trade, a more than competent navigator and guide (Singleton and his crew would have died several times over without him) but utterly without his own agenda.[65] The Black Prince has an attachment to his people, not to the land he inhabits, and he not only undertakes his role as slave and guide without complaint, he ensures that his subjects do so as well.

As was the case with the *Atlas*, even as Defoe empties Africa out of the peoples and institutions through which many Europeans still understood and imagined Africa, he maintains the physical geography such impressions enabled. As the marooned sailors travel across the interior of the continent from Mozambique to the Gold Coast, they pull so much gold from a network of rivers that it is no wonder that some critics have pegged the novel as pure propaganda for the Royal African Company. Even more so than in the *Atlas*, though, such geological fantasizing exists in an uneasy tension with *Captain Singleton's* simultaneous critique of geography's, and specifically cartography's, over-reliance on evidence that had not been confirmed by reliable European eyewitnesses and that had been far too influenced by what Europeans had been told by locals so "ignorant or so false and lying, that nothing can be depended upon which they give an Account of."[66]

Like the explorers of seventeenth- and early eighteenth-century travel narratives, Singleton and the sailors are tasked with figuring out the most efficient way to traverse Africa, with but little knowledge of what lies ahead other than bits of empirical data, hearsay, personal experience, and information from local guides. However, unlike their historical counterparts, who turned around when they reached the places where the Gambia or the Senegal Rivers were no longer navigable, Singleton and his crew push on. The entire continent sits between them and Europe, and the only way out is through. As the marooned sailors debate the best course to take, they consider, and then discard, the more conventional ways that Europeans circumnavigated Africa. They can't build a boat large enough to take them east to Goa or to sail south around the Cape. They fear that sailing north will result in being "killed by the wild *Arabs*, or taken and made Slaves of by the *Turks*."[67] This conversation sketches Africa's eastern coastline and lays out the size and scope of the task before the men. It also reminds the reader how little about Africa's interior had actually been documented and that the detailed travel accounts that Europeans did have only describe a tiny portion of the overall landmass. As Singleton puts it, "we were upon *a* Voyage and *no* Voyage, we were bound by *some* where and *no* where: for tho' we knew what we intended to do, we did really not know what we were doing."[68] By describing their trajectory as both "a Voyage" and "no Voyage," Singleton squeezes his account into the space between experiential travel and discursive knowledge about the interior, on the threshold where the map turns from a reliable tool of navigation to a highly speculative one. The starting place and the goal—the coasts—are clear, but the path that joins them is not.

The men try to decide how to accomplish the first step of turning their nonvoyage into a voyage—crossing the Mozambique Channel—and their debate reiterates the piecemeal nature of European knowledge about Africa's interior. The sailors first turn to the locals of Madagascar. As Singleton points out, their "Correspondence with the Natives was absolutely necessary," not only to ensure provisions and a place to stay while they gather their resources but also for information about how to proceed.[69] But when they ask their African hosts about the journey, their response is only that "there was a great Land of Lions beyond the sea." So, the men share the lore that they have each heard about the distance between the island and the mainland. "Some said it was 150 Leagues, others not above 100. One of our men that had a Map of the World shewed us by his Scale, that it was not above 80 Leagues. Some said there were Islands all the way to touch at; some say that there were no islands at all." At last, one of the locals speaks up again, "an old Man who was blind, and led about by a Boy," who tells them that the wind and sea will be in their favor if they hold off on departing for the mainland until the end of August.[70] The reliability of this information is highly dubious, offered as it is by a man to whom they can barely make themselves "intelligible," who is enfeebled, unable to see, and guided by someone too young to be knowledgeable about the world.

If local advice is a source to be extremely skeptical of in this exchange, the kinds of maps built on the testimony of such local informants (as the *Atlas* complains) are no more trustworthy, though the men believe in them. If they can agree on nothing else, Singleton says, "we all knew, if we could cross this Continent of Land, we might reach some of the great rivers that run into the Atlantick Ocean," a notion that would have been reflected in whatever map they are carrying with them, as even a cursory glance of the maps described above show.⁷¹ The Gunner, who is an "excellent mathematician," is the possessor of the maps, and Singleton refers to him as "our guide" throughout. The fact that the Gunner knows all about "the Sciences useful for Navigation, and particularly in the Geographical Part of Knowledge," is initially reassuring the same way that the grid lines and coordinates on a map imply that one could use it to actually orient oneself.⁷² But true to the scene in which the map is lumped in with other kinds of speculative discourse, neither the Gunner nor the map, for all that they wear the costume of rationality, turn out to be particularly dependable.

At one point, for instance, the Gunner is convinced that he's found the Nile, or at least the lake that the Nile comes out of:

> In three days march we came to a River, which we saw from the Hills, and which we called the Golden River, and we found it run Northward, which was the first Stream we had met with that did so; it run with a very rapid current, and our Gunner pulling out his Map, assured me that this was either the River *Nile*, or run into the great Lake; out of which the River *Nile* was said to take its Beginnings: and he brought out his Charts and Maps, which by his Instruction, I began to understand very well: and he told me, he would convince me of it, and indeed he seemed to make it so plain to me, that I was of the same Opinion.⁷³

Singleton, who thinks by this point that he "undertand[s maps] very well," has been seduced by the "plainness" of the maps and the Gunner's explanation of them. Yet, a few pages later, they encounter another river, one that's so big that they mistake it for the sea, and as Bob tells us, "My friend the Gunner, upon examining, said, that he believed he was mistaken before, and that this was the River *Nile*, but was still of the Mind, that we were before, that we should not think of a Voyage into *Egypt* that Way."⁷⁴ Shortly thereafter, the men have a discussion over what direction to turn next, which plots out the west coastline, just as their initial debate over how to get off of Madagascar plotted out the east. They are once again "bound by *some* where and *no* where." Though Singleton wants the crew to go straight north in hopes of finding the Niger, the Gunner advises the crew to continue northwest in search of a tributary that runs into the Niger, the Gambia, or the Senegal Rivers. This "good Advice" was "too rational not to be taken." After all, Singleton reminds us once more that the Gunner is "indeed our best Guide, tho'" it turns out "he happen'd to be mistaken at this time" yet again.[75] These moments caution that seemingly objective and "plain" geographical representations, and in particular ones that suggest that the interior of Africa is filled with connected waterways large enough to be navigable by boat, can mislead and deceive.

And yet, like the *Atlas*, the text simultaneously affirms the possibility of these river routes and reinforces the notion that gold is simply waiting to spring forth out of Africa's interior like water. The men literally pull gold nuggets from the river with ease: "We seldom took up a Handful of Sand," Singleton reports, "but we washed some little round Lumps as big as a Pin's Head, or sometimes as big as a Grapestone, into our hands."[76] They find ivory as well, a "prodigious Quantity of Teeth," "a hundred Ton of elephant's teeth."[77] "They were no Booty to us," Singleton laments, though the men "once thought to have built a large Canoe on purpose to have her loaded with Ivory." They decide against it because they don't yet know whether the path of rivers they are following will take them all the way through the continent. But once they find a village on the western side where they stay a few months with an English factor gone rogue, the English factor and several of the crew make two trips back into the interior and return with heaps of elephant tusks. Though it is unclear at times whether they will get the ivory all the way to the Dutch factory they are aiming for, Singleton reports that they ultimately do, via "the River, the Name of which I forgot, where we made rafts."[78] The fact that Singleton "forgot" the name of the river leaves open the possibility that any one of West Africa's major rivers or their tributaries could lead directly into the abundant interior and join up with the source of the Nile. Such a connection promises both an immediate profit through the direct acquisition of gold and ivory and the long-term potential for sustainable trade. Indeed, it may not even be necessary to name which one of the western rivers leads to this wealth because perhaps they are, as some geographers argued, all one and the same.

The notion of an inland threshold where Europeans might establish a new dynamic with the locals to replace the coastal relationships that had, in Defoe's estimation, gone so awry is also part of *Captain Singleton*'s Janus-like geographical narrative. The English factor who brings them to the ivory fields has been living with an African group positioned on the border between the European traffic of the coasts and the pure interior that Defoe dreams about in the *Review*. Like the threshold in which he has been dwelling, the factor is a liminal figure himself as Wheeler, Walmsley, and Backscheider argue, halfway between the civilized and the savage, his ability to speak English and his economic know-how in contrast with his nakedness and his "brown blackish" skin.[79] He found the Africans he currently resides with after being driven away from the coasts by aggressive locals, "sometimes . . . carry'd by Force, sometimes hurried by Fear" until "he had wandred beyond all Possibility of Return, and had taken up his Abode where we found him, where he was well received."[80] Unlike the Africans who bullied the factor farther and farther into the hinterland, these Africans are "not much acquainted with Things, being at the Distance of above 300 Miles from the Coast." These villagers mark the point at which Africa's inhabitants are no longer cunning—they trade in ivory but only cover a relay segment of 60 or 70 miles—and they also mark the entre into Africa's most abundant ivory and gold fields.[81] The factor informs Singleton not only about the location of this ivory but also suggests that he and the crew should wait until the "Land Floods," or the great rains that swell the rivers, after which the locals harvest the most gold. "[T]he Rage of the Floods always works down a great deal of gold out of the Hills," the factor argues, and if they tap into it before the locals can carry it to the English ships (or perhaps before the locals can get it at all) it would be to their great advantage.

Captain Singleton offers plenty of reason to be wary of this English factor, as it offers plenty of reason to be wary of maps and of African informants. He has taught the Africans he has been living with how to value their ivory for one, indicating that this threshold that could be exploited to Britain's gain won't last unless savvier men than the factor take charge of the situation. This brings an urgency to *Captain Singleton*'s economic vision that is lacking, for instance, in Defoe's brief scenes that trumpet Africa's trade potential in *Robinson Crusoe*, in which the west coast Africans are more akin to the Black Prince and his people than the shrewd Africans of the *Review*. In this way, the factor is aligned with the separate traders Defoe so decried (in fact, he became one briefly between leaving the company and fleeing into the interior), and his ability to use the rhetoric of limitless wealth to convince Singleton and his crew to go against their better long-term interests was something Defoe accused the separate traders of doing as well. The factor's own eye is so focused on accumulating wealth locally that he never manages to inject it into a global economy, and he nearly persuades Singleton and the crew to fall into the same trap.[82] Defoe is not merely staging a vision of the future of expansion in Africa in *Captain Singleton*, he is also staging a critique of how the situation has been, in his view, bungled in the past. Thus, the factor is an emblem of mishandled potential. But he is an emblem of potential nonetheless, and one that is dependent on a specific way of imagining Africa's interior resources and the waterways that might provide access to them.

Literary Mediators and Narrative Multiplicity: Defoe's Strategies of Geographical Speculation

As was the case with the *Atlas*, then, *Captain Singleton* advances two geographical ideas. One is a critique of cartographic representations of Africa. Their absurdity as navigational tools is thrown into sharp relief when Singleton and the crew actually try to use them as an itinerary. The other is a valorization of the geological narratives such maps afford, even though those narratives, in Defoe's estimation, require some heavy revision to remove the human impediments to European expansion in Africa. The result is a representation that still looks in some ways like the thing that the texts critique. In *Captain Singleton*, the fictional space of the novel in general and Singleton's paradoxical duplicity in particular enable Defoe to marry these two registers without needing to explain or account for how it is that they can coexist. Singleton tells the reader early and outright that thinking him "honest [would be] a very great mistake." By being honest about his dishonesty, performing his own version of the classic liar's paradox, Singleton designates his account as one that both deceives and tells the truth. Liminal figures like the factor, who can be a voice for Africa's investment potential and a cautionary tale rolled into one character, function in a similar way. The responsibility is on the reader, as is the case with much of Defoe's fiction, to make right judgments about the account. He or she can recognize that there might be real rewards for pushing inland without mistaking *Captain Singleton*'s golden rivers for anything other than an indulgence in the geographic sublime. Attaining those real rewards will require investing in real expeditions, not continuing to rely on geographical "knowledge" that promises a rich interior but that has, in five hundred years, gotten Europeans no closer to it.

Such competing representational strands are harder to reconcile in the *Atlas* since it is a genre that has a different kind of obligation to accuracy. At first, the text merely looks sloppy, written by the Defoe that Gary Scrimgeour saw as treating geographical representation as a means to a political end, rather than by the Defoe that Edwards, Thell, and Pearl have identified whose geographical thinking was sophisticated and engaged, or even by the Defoe that Rogers describes poring over his maps and geography books with such attention to detail.[83] But on closer investigation, Defoe offers some cues that indicate he understands his role as the narrator of a text like the *Atlas* differently than he does the roles of the mapmakers and geographers he endeavors to hold to account, suggesting that there is room in geographical writing for representations that deviate from the strictly empirical, as long as they are not mistaken for the empirical.

The preface to the *Atlas* makes a declaration about the text's narrative multiplicity: "It must be expected that our Style be various, according to the various Nature of the Subject. We must speak like a Geographer and Historian, when we are giving the Geographical and Historical Description of places, we must use the Terms of Art which have obtain'd among Merchants and Tradesmen, when we are treating of Commerce, and we must speak in the Language of the Seamen, when we are giving Directions for Sailing."[84] Perhaps for Defoe speaking in fictional terms—where contradictory ideas can coexist to different points and purposes—is not only licensed by but necessary for driving European expansion in Africa. Though perhaps not as paradoxical as Bob Singleton, the narrator of the *Atlas* does ask a similar kind of discernment from the reader when it comes to sorting out the moments when he is "committed to representing the world with 'pinpoint accuracy'" from his "digressions into what we might call speculative geographies . . . generally apologized for but enthusiastically indulged," as Edwards puts it.[85] The insertion of this narrator was, as Novak argues, likely intended to keep the reader interested in what might otherwise be dry description, but he also serves another function of signaling the movement between and holding the space between the text's factual discourse and its more imaginative moments.[86]

When the narrator refers to himself in the first person, he cues the reader that he is not speaking like a geographer or a historian but like a storyteller whose job it is to weave a narrative, offer compelling imagery, and spark the imagination. For instance, in the paragraph in which Defoe deploys the imagery of the rivers of gold literally spewing from the center of the continent, the precious metal driven to the surface by earthquakes or subterranean winds, he stuffs a qualification into the very last sentence that "neither of these things ever happens here, at least as I have heard." The first half of this qualification anchors the statement in probability, making it clear in retrospect that the preceding paragraph has deviated from empirical reality, but the second half leverages the possibility open again. Just because the narrator has never heard of it doesn't mean it might not still be the case.

The moment in the Africa portion of the *Atlas* in which the narrator indulges most notoriously in such blurring of fact and fiction is when he cites

Captain Singleton as if it were a real travel narrative—specifically the part where Singleton and the crew encounter the English factor, who is given a name, Mr. Freeman, who was an actual employee for the Royal African Company under Defoe's friend Dalby Thomas until he was dismissed in 1705 or 1706 for bad conduct.[87] After his dismissal the real Freeman remained a thorn in everyone's side—company, separate traders, and Africans alike—until his death in 1713, so it is surprising, as Furbank and Knox-Shaw both remark, that he is spoken of in relatively flattering terms in the *Atlas*, especially since *Captain Singleton* gives us plenty of reason to be wary of what he has to say or at least how he says it.[88] But like the piratical Bob Singleton, Freeman's in-between status affords him a kind of flexible authority in the *Atlas* that enables the narrator's use of fictional forms of geographical representation in what is otherwise expected to be a scientific genre. As he does in *Singleton*, the Freeman of the *Atlas* occupies the threshold between the part of Africa where the locals are overly cunning and the area where they are potentially pliable, three hundred miles inland, right between the two hundred and four hundred mile markers that the narrator of the *Atlas* demarcates elsewhere as the place where the gold first appears.[89] As an English speaker with a European sensibility, Freeman has the capacity to reliably describe the interior's economic potential, but he is a figure close enough to the ground to be a plausible replacement for the Africans who would otherwise be the only authority on the continent that far inland. He has attained the status of the native informant that the likes of Labat and Moore continued to privilege over European speculation or even eyewitnesses like Stibbs credited on the grounds that natives would know the place they lived better than a European traveler who had only seen a small part of their world.

Assigning Freeman this interstitial role allows the narrator to skirt the boundary between scientifically proven fact and discursive speculation in his accounting of Africa's interior resources. "What a Treasure must lie upon that Desart!" the narrator predicts based on Freeman's testimony, "and what prodigious Numbers of Elephants must be found upon those wild abandon'd Plains!"[90] He tells the story of how Freeman took Singleton and his crew "among the Rivers under the Mountains and Water-falls, after the Rains and Floods were ceas'd," where he "brought them to some Places, where they pick'd up in about two Months more, so much Gold, that they divided at last above 23 Poundweight a Man."[91] But the narrator adds two telling qualifications to this account. One regards what the men found in the interior. He claims that this story "is enough to shew, how both the Gold and the Ivory are found in this Country, and how inexhaustible a Store there is of both," and he deems the account "suitable to our present Description of the Country, and may I believe be depended upon for fact." As he did with his eruption of gold, though, he then backs off by adding that by "fact," "I mean so far as it relates to the Product and Customs of the place and of the People."[92] He recognizes that citing *Captain Singleton* as a factual account is fictional move, but he does so in a way that continues to empower its more tantalizing aspects. In fact, he directs the reader to *Captain Singleton* itself if they want to know more.[93] The second qualification the narrator puts on his account of these desert treasures regards how one would reach them. About the waterways the narrator adds: "As for the Course of the Rivers, their Beginnings, and what Countrys they run thro,' it cannot be expected *I* should be particular in them, no Discover having yet been made of the inland Countrys, nor any Account given of them, at least none that can be depended upon" (emphasis added).[94] The fact that geographers have not pinned down the specifics of the courses of Africa's rivers beyond what they've been told by local inhabitants leaves the narrator space to indulge in his imagined interior, and the fact that he is not held to the same standard of verisimilitude allows him to move more fluidly between empirically verified and discursively constructed impressions of the continent. If one finds the narrator a bit sly or even duplicitous in these moments—as they find Bob Singleton or Freeman—it is all the more motivation to invest in organized initiatives to fill in gaps in Europe's navigational knowledge. Only then can the narrator "speak like a Geographer and Historian," when he is "giving the Geographical and Historical Description of places."

Through Defoe's rhetorical strategizing in *Captain Singleton* and the *Atlas*, he was participating in a complex conversation not only about what Africa's interior looked like but also about how geographical knowledge of Africa was and should be produced. But the subtleties of this are only apparent when these texts are read in dialog with an impression of Africa that was not a "vast howling Wilderness" or a protoversion of Conrad's Africa but one populated with interior polities and trade. This impression needed to be revised in both content and form; Africans needed to be removed from both the space and the epistemological equation. Only then would there be room for Europeans to move in and transform Africa's rivers and resources to their advantage. These revisions are Defoe's task in these texts, which is distinct from the task of the cartographer. The two registers need not undercut each other as long as the reader is able—by following the narrator of the *Atlas*'s cues and by being wise to Singleton's paradoxical status—to understand the difference between a geographical representation meant to literally orient a traveler in space and one meant to enable a reader to imaginatively orient him- or herself in an anticipatory vision.

Defoe's case is a fitting example of how African expressions remained central to the spatial grammar of British impressions of the continent, even when writers attempted to excise them. Until explorers could produce actual eyewitness accounts of the interior—sidestepping, in theory at least, Africans as geographical authorities altogether—European texts would always be shaped by the discourses they had inherited. And such eyewitness accounts were still a long time coming. Efforts to send European explorers up the Gambia River, as Stibbs's journey shows, didn't succeed. They simply reinforced European dependence on African informants and guides. Defoe's scorn for the reliability and usefulness of the information those informants and guides provided was likewise not a universally adopted attitude. Labat's and Moore's narratives, which so stridently argue for the single-source theory and which stress the importance of relying on local evidence in the production of geographical knowledge, were published the same year as and a decade after the *Atlas*, respectively.

Defoe's efforts to take the inland African states out of the equation didn't catch on either. When the Association for Promoting the Discovery of the Interior Parts of Africa was founded in 1788, with the sole purpose of seriously attempting what Defoe calls for—empirical exploration of the interior of the continent—one of their major motivations for doing so was to at last discover the course of the Niger and the location of Timbuktu. Mungo Park, the first Briton who would have any appreciable success at this, wrote that his instructions from the African Association "were very plain and concise. I was directed, on my arrival in Africa 'to pass on to the river Niger, either by the way of Bambouk, or by such other route as should be found most convenient. That I should ascertain the course, and, if possible, the rise and termination of that river. That I should use my utmost exertions to visit the principal towns or cities in its neighborhood, particularly Tombuctoo.'"[95] He began his journey at the Gambia River, traveling under the protection of a Mandinka merchant caravan, whose knowledge he deemed necessary if he was to have any hope of achieving his aim.[96]

4

"WHERE THE NILE RISETH...
WHERE THE QUEEN OF SABA LIVED"

Impressions of Abyssinia, 1327–1759

In many of the texts considered in the previous chapters, Abyssinia is a haunting presence, a cornerstone, as Milton's *Paradise Lost* illustrates, of how Europeans thought about Africa in general. If one were to continue on the road shown in the third panel of the Catalan Atlas discussed in chapter 1 to the fourth panel, past the *mansa*'s domain, one would arrive at the "city of Nubia," marked by a flag and a note that "the king of Nubia is always at war with the Christians of Nubia who are under the dominion of the emperor of Ethiopia and the Land of Prester John." In 1486 an ambassador from Benin told the court of João II that "to the east of the kingdom of Tombut, there was among other Princes, one that was neither Mahometan nor Idolater, but who seemed to profess a religion nearly resembling the Christian."[1] This ruler had once sent three gifts to the Oba of Benin: "a kind of scepter, a helmet, and a latten cross." Abyssinia is not one of *Polexander*'s African settings, but references to the greatness of "the Emperor of Ethiopia" are laced throughout the text, serving, along with the king of Tombut, as an emblem against which other sovereigns are measured. The king of Benin, for instance, laments that his kingdom is not "as great as all the Empire of Ethiopia," and the king of Congo "hath always disputed with mighty Belul [for] the title of the Emperour of Ethiopia."[2] The fictional travel account of "S. Giacomo Baratti," which synthesized tidbits from several different texts on Abyssinia into a faux itinerary and was published in London in 1670, stretches the western border of Abyssinia all the way to "*Guangara* [Wangara]," where the Niger passes and where the traders never show themselves but simply lay down their goods for trade and then retreat into the woods.[3] And Defoe makes an exception for Abyssinia in his largely scornful account of African cultures, arguing that an alliance with Africa's Christians and the guardians of the source of the Nile could only be to Europe's advantage, bringing "ten times more Wealth into *Europe* by Trade, than all the Empires of *New Spain*."[4]

This chapter shows how European impressions of Abyssinia's influence and exceptionalism were set in motion and continued to be driven by Habesha expressions about their unique Christianity and Solomonic ties, which dictated the way Europeans thought not only about Abyssinia itself but also about other parts of the continent as they attempted to map the extent of the Queen of Sheba's domains and then the domains of the monarch they came to believe was the mythical Prester John.[5] The notion that Abyssinia not only housed but controlled the source of the Nile became the geological and symbolic backbone of these impressions. It was never a mere river in either Ethiopian or European worldviews; it was a conduit to Paradise, an emblem of geopolitical power, and, in Bruce's words, "a defiance to all travellers, and an opprobrium to geography."[6] As was the case with the Land of the Blacks, European impressions of Abyssinia morphed around the edges, but their core elements of religious and geographical exceptionalism were maintained because renewed contact with the continent continued to affirm them and because they had captured the European imagination to such an extent that even as eyewitness accounts tempered some of their more farfetched elements, it was not enough to exorcise them from the geographical tradition. They proliferated through genres as various as maps, ecclesiastical writings, travel narratives, and works of literature from the canonical (like Ludovico Ariosto's *Orlando Furioso* and Milton's *Paradise Lost*) to the popular (like periodical serials and mock travel narratives).

Abyssinia's Exceptional Christianity: The Solomonic Dynasty and the Land of Prester John

As briefly summarized in the introduction, the Habesha tell the story of the Biblical Queen of Sheba from a unique angle, as written in the *Kebra Nagast*. A queen of East Africa, Makeda commands a powerful commercial empire, controlling gold and silver mines and blessed with an abundance of camels, slaves, and merchants who trade along both land and sea routes on her behalf. As Solomon is preparing to build his temple, he makes contact with Tamrin, Makeda's head merchant, who brings him gold, sapphires, and pest-resistant timber. Tamrin carries stories of Solomon's wisdom, judgment, and successful government back to Makeda. A lover of wisdom and learning herself, Makeda decides to visit Solomon to see if these stories are true, and she arrives with a caravan of hundreds of camels loaded with precious gifts. Over the course of several conversations, Solomon persuades Makeda to worship the God of Israel and falls in love with her, and when she returns to Africa six months later, she is pregnant with his son, Menelik (also called David), who, when he comes of age, makes his own voyage to his father's land. When Menelik returns to Sheba, he brings the Ark of the Covenant with him, and Makeda cedes the throne to him, declaring that a woman shall never again be sovereign but that only the male descendants of Solomon will reign over Ethiopia.

This origin story of the Solomonic Dynasty does not simply drop the Biblical narrative of the Queen of Sheba and Solomon into an African setting. The *Kebra Nagast* changes the story in some key ways, including making Makeda rather than Solomon the central character and endowing her with wisdom equal to if not surpassing his. It also contains a prophecy that Ethiopia will someday rise up as the world's most powerful empire. In fact, the night Menelik is conceived, Solomon has a dream in which the sun that "shed exceedingly great splendour over Israel . . . suddenly withdrew itself, and it flew away to the country of Ethiopia, and it shone there with exceedingly great brightness for ever, for it willed to dwell there."[7] In this sense, in Ullendorff's words, the *Kebra Nagast* "is not merely a literary work . . . [;] it is the repository of Ethiopian national and religious feeling," a narrative of exceptionalism that would be used to justify political action within several evolutions of what would become the Ethiopian state.[8]

Though it's possible that versions of the *Kebra Nagast* date back at least to the sixth century CE, the earliest existent manuscripts date to the early fourteenth century when there was what Donald Crummey calls a "flowering of high culture" that served the strategic purpose of legitimizing a newly reestablished Solomonic dynasty.[9] Whether it is indeed the case that a Solomonic line ruled in the Ethiopian Highlands from the days of the Queen of Sheba through the early Medieval period, in the tenth century a different dynasty, the Zagwe Dynasty, came to power and lasted until Yekuno Amlak deposed the last Zagwe king in 1270. Tracing his own lineage to a pre-Zagwe king of Aksum, Yekuno Amlak authorized his takeover by claiming that he was reestablishing the Solomonic line that had been ordained by God to rule over Abyssinia. This reestablishment had a slow start. After Yekuno Amlak and his immediate successor's deaths, the dynasty went through five kings in five years.

But two of Yekuno Amlak's early fourteenth-century successors, Wedem Arad and Amda Seyon I, each amassed enough of a power base to begin substantially growing their empires, pushing back against Muslim expansion in East Africa and solidifying the relationship between the state and the Ethiopian Church.[10] The Solomonic narrative in the *Kebra Nagast*, which was also disseminated through psalters and church frescos, not only sanctioned these actions in and of themselves, it created an appearance of unification, spreading a shared sense of national and religious identity among disparate communities. These medieval kings cast themselves as Solomon as well, building churches and monasteries throughout the Highlands and sending out merchants and envoys to foreign lands to gather books, crosses, rich textiles, chalices, censers, and relics with which to furnish them. In fact, this internally pitched, aesthetic performance of sovereignty and right to rule, Verena Krebs argues, facilitated Abyssinia's first contact with Europe, initiating relationships that would only incidentally grow over time into political alliances.[11]

As was the case with the unity of the Songhai Empire, in some ways, this unification was more narrative than reality. Conversion to Christianity was forced in many communities, and even so, territories outside Abyssinia's core administrative regions remained both religiously and culturally heterogenous.[12] This would come back to haunt the Solomonic kings in the mid-sixteenth century during the Ethiopian-Adal War: when the Muslim sultanate began to seize once-Muslim regions of Abyssinia, many locals didn't put up much, if any, resistance.[13] The church also didn't submit easily to becoming a tool of the state and remained in and of itself an evolving institution.[14] But Europeans were exposed to the narrative of Christian exceptionalism and unity first, not the reality of the situation. As was the case with Mansa Musa I and Askia Muhammad I, Wedem Arad and Amda Seyon I and their successors like Zara Yaqob proclaimed their divinely ordained right to power to outsiders as well as to insiders. And as was the case with the sovereigns of the Western Sudan, pilgrimages were a dominant medium through which they did so. Following in Makeda and Menelik's footsteps, by the fourteenth century Ethiopian Christians were an established presence in Jerusalem, which became the first site of encounter between Europe and Ethiopia.[15] Habesha pilgrimages to Jerusalem, and eventually to Rome, were spiritual journeys, but they were also opportunities to gather relics for churches and monasteries and, eventually, to gain allies in the wider Christian world who might aid the Solomonic emperors in their increasing efforts to conquer the surrounding Islamic states, which not only stood between them and the Holy Lands but also kept them from establishing a port on the Red Sea—a necessary acquisition if Abyssinia was to become a contender on the global stage.[16]

Since reclaiming the Holy Lands and pushing against Muslim expansion in Africa and the East were also desired by many European nations, they were eager to make connections with these ambassadors in turn. As Matteo Salvadore puts it, though Abyssinians were the instigators of contact with the European Christian world, they found "fertile soil" for planting the idea of their Christian exceptionalism in the European geographical consciousness: "In the European mind, Ethiopians, their kingdom, and, in particular, their sovereign came to be associated with a variety of legendary figures, first and foremost that of Prester John."[17] Rumors of a wise and powerful Christian king who ruled over an empire of riches and marvels that was surrounded on all sides by Muslim and pagan nations began to spread through Europe in the twelfth century. Some believed he was a descendent of one of the three magi or possibly one of St. Thomas's converts from his proselytizing through Asia. All agreed that to reach his lands would be to discover a paradise on earth, and, perhaps more importantly, that an alliance with such a kingdom would lend a strategic advantage in the Christian world's quest to take back Jerusalem. The earliest narratives, like John Mandeville's *Travels*, speculated that Prester John's domains were in Syria or India, but as contact with the East increased, Europeans found no Christian kingdoms there. And the more that Europeans encountered Habesha pilgrims—first in Jerusalem and then in Rome and Iberia—the more reasonable it became to assume that the legendary kingdom might be found in Africa.

The possibility that Abyssinia and Prester John's kingdom were one and the same grew even more persuasive to Europeans as they were exposed to the details of the Solomonic Dynasty's origin story. At first this exposure came through the rhetoric of diplomacy. For instance, in the fifteenth century a contingent of Habesha monks from Jerusalem were asked to attend the Council of Florence as part of Pope Eugene IV's efforts to unite the Eastern Churches with the Church of Rome. The letter of invitation was addressed to "Presbyter John Emperor of Ethiopia," and the men who answered this call compared themselves to Sheba and the pope to Solomon in their own addresses as a form of political flattery.[18] By the beginning of the sixteenth century, first the Queen Regent Eleni and then Dawit II (better known as Lebna Dengel) sought an alliance with the King of Portugal once again with the hopes of launching a joint effort to take back the Holy Lands, or at least to create a safer thoroughfare through Muslim lands for pilgrims to travel between Africa and Jerusalem. In his correspondences, Lebna Dengel introduced himself as "the Beloved of God, the Pillar of Faith, of the Race of Judah, the Son of David, the Son of Solomon," who reigned over the land "of Goiam, where the Nile riseth . . . and of Sabaym, where the Queen of Saba lived."[19] A slightly later source reflecting on these letters lets this expression speak for itself as an account of the emperor's greatness, calling it "a sufficient Text for a more sufficient glosse, then we can give."[20]

When synopses of the *Kebra Nagast* itself began to circulate in Europe, this connection was reinforced. For instance, the account that Saga za Ab, Lebna Dengel's ambassador to Lisbon, wrote included a detailed summary of the *Kebra Nagast* from Sheba's journey through Menelik I's acquisition of the tablets of the Ark of the Covenant.[21] The notion that Abyssinia was the fabled kingdom of Prester John was an assumption that Europeans made about Africa and not, at first, something that medieval and early modern Habesha claimed for themselves. But the impression arose and gained traction because African expressions in the Abyssinian-European contact zone seemed to affirm it. And once the Habesha became aware that this connection had been made, they played into it, whether by intentionally manipulating a misassumption as they were later accused of doing or simply by accepting the Prester John legend as the European way of describing the unique lineage and Christian exceptionalism they believed and hoped to communicate about themselves. Álvares addressed Lebna Dengel as "Prete Ianni," and he never in the six years he lived there was given reason to doubt the appropriateness of the moniker. Saga za Ab also referred to Lebna Dengel as Prester John throughout his written account of Ethiopian Christian religious beliefs and customs. The Habesha seemed to understand that it was to their diplomatic advantage to at least uphold, if not exploit, this lens through which Europeans viewed their country. Doing so would not have been a stretch for Habesha ambassadors and dignitaries in any case since the Prester John legend was consistent with the Christian exceptionalism these people sought to project.

Early Modern Impressions of Abyssinia as the Source of the Nile: The Father of Waters and Ludovico Ariosto's *Orlando Furioso*

Abyssinians' expressions about themselves and their worlds didn't only shape impressions of ecclesiastical history and religious politics prior to extensive European contact with the region; they had a long-lasting impact on European representations—both scholarly and imaginative—of Africa's physical geography. As Salvadore argues, the Habesha pilgrims and dignitaries who traveled to Jerusalem, Italy, and Iberia were not simply spreading narratives about Ethiopian Christianity in the interest of establishing political and religious alliances with the wider Christian world; they were also "purveyors of geographical knowledge," offering European cartographers and cosmographers their first glimpses into the interior of the Horn of Africa.[22] For instance, in the early fourteenth century a priest in Genoa named Giovanni Mauro da Carignano encountered a group of monks on pilgrimage to the holy sites of southern Europe. Out of these conversations he produced a map containing an unprecedented amount of detail about "Terra Abaise," the land of the "Christiani Nigri."[23] In the mid-fifteenth century Pietro del Massaio's map of Africa would include Debre Damo, one of the three major *amba* (flat-topped mountain) fortresses that would so capture the European imagination.[24] And there still exists a European itinerary from the early fifteenth century that is essentially a travel guide for how to get from Jerusalem to the Ethiopian Highlands. It names the specific territories one would pass through and their local governors, and it even includes a list of common Amharic phrases and their Latin translations.[25] As a result of these interactions, geography books and maps filled Abyssinia, as they had the Land of the Blacks, with descriptive details that attained a canonical status before Europeans produced eyewitness accounts of Abyssinia's interior, let alone surveyed it.

By the fifteenth century the predominant geographical claim that governed European representations of Abyssinia was that the source of the Nile fell within its borders. When Abyssinians told Europeans this, they were not sharing mere topographical information; they were harnessing the cachet that came with possessing one of the world's most legendary rivers. Some of this symbolic power came from the river's religious associations. Medieval European Christians, Muslims, and Habesha alike theorized that the Nile was Gihon, one of the four rivers that flowed from Eden to water the world. In Ethiopia the source of the river Westerners now know as the Blue Nile was and is a pilgrimage site, its water believed to be holy enough to wash away sin and sickness.[26] Some of the symbolic power that came with laying claim to the source of the Nile was due to the river's long history and geological significance: its size and the fact that its tributaries connected and irrigated so much of Africa. Among the many groups who consider the Nile a life-giving river both spiritually and literally, Amharic speakers call it "Abay," which means "father" and "great." The Abay started appearing on European maps and in travel narratives as the "Father of Waters" by the sixteenth century.

When the monk Gorgoryos visited Ludolf in Germany, the imagery he used to describe the course of the Nile offers a glimpse into how the paternalistic greatness of the river was associated with both the paternalistic greatness of God and the *negusa nagast*: "As it flows along, it takes in all the Rivers great and small with several Torrents, as well Foreign as *Habessinian*, which by the general Tribute, acknowledge him their King; who having thus muster'd together all the Waters of *Ethiopia*, jocundly takes his leave, and proceeds on his Journey, like a *Hero*, according to the Command of his Creator, to drench the Fields of thirsty *Egypt*, and quench the drowth of Thousands."[27] Consistent with the Ethiopian practice of looking at the land as a sign of their blessings, and "retaining the flavor," in Belcher's words, of traditional Ethiopian poetry, which always has a surface "wax" meaning and an underlying "gold" meaning, this anecdote figures the Nile as an adventuring traveler but also as a monarch to whom both Habesha and foreigners pay tribute and whose path is divinely ordained.[28] Not simply a geographical description, then, Gorgoryos's words tell a story about Abyssinia's blessed authority, which Ludolf trusted and recorded, considering Gorgoryos an authority with insider information that surpassed in detail and accuracy what Europeans had managed to amass.[29]

The ideas Abyssinians projected to outsiders about their control over the Nile weren't always intended to be metaphorical. Gorgoryos's description of the Nile irrigating Egypt on command echoes another longstanding and less "jocund" claim that the Habesha made: that the *negusa nagast* could literally control the Nile's northward flow through a series of iron gates or mechanical engines. He had the power to either "quench the drowth of Thousands" or to starve his neighbors to the north into compliance if he so chose. This story was spread widely enough and believed well enough that it is recorded multiple times in Ethiopian, Arabic, and European texts across several centuries. There are Arabic accounts of two separate incidents in the eleventh century when famine in Egypt motivated the caliph to send emissaries to the *negusa nagast* to beg and bribe him to restore the floods, which he then supposedly did.[30] In the late fourteenth century, Dawit I was allegedly able to use the threat of diverting the Nile's flow to end a conflict with his Muslim neighbors. Europeans began to collect reports of these astonishing claims as early as the fourteenth century, and they took them at least somewhat seriously. Frustrated with his dealings with Egypt, Afonso de Albuquerque, the governor of Goa, even sent an envoy to investigate whether an alliance with Abyssinia might allow him to put pressure on Egypt from below to improve European access to the Red Sea.[31]

Habesha expressions about the Nile coupled with their projected image of religious and national exceptionalism began to change how Europeans mapped Africa. As maps discussed in earlier chapters show, the theory that the Nile took its source from a lake or several lakes in the center of the continent that were filled from springs beneath the Mountains of the Moon had been the predominant geographical view since the time of Ptolemy. As pilgrims told Europeans more and more about Abyssinia, and as Europeans were increasingly persuaded by their claims that the source of the Nile was in the domain of, and under the control of, the *negusa nagast*, they began to imagine that the country was large enough to cover Ptolemy's whole imagined course of the river. By the late fifteenth century, maps like Fra Mauro's *Planisfero* (1460) placed the Nile (labeled both "Nile" and "Gion") flowing through what were by then recognizable Abyssinian place names like Aksum, Amhara, and Simien and even hinted at the dramatic bend in the Abay as it circles Gojjam.[32] "Abassia" stretches nearly to the Cape of Good Hope, encompassing the Nile's several heads and placing Prester John's seat in the middle of the bottom third of the continent.

European interest in Abyssinia as a Biblical geography, as the Land of Prester John, and as the country that housed the source of the Nile spread beyond religious, political, and geographical texts and contexts. By the 1530s Ludovico Ariosto had combined these elements in his depiction of Abyssinia in the 33rd canto of *Orlando Furioso*.[33] Flying into Africa on a hippogriff in search of Orlando Furioso's lost wits, the English knight Astolfo flies down the Nile until he arrives in "Aethiopia" where the emperor

> . . . stead of sceptre, cross in hand does bear,
> Has people, cities, gold, in plenteous way,
> Thence, to where the red sea its head does rear;
> And does, as 'twere, our very faith obey,
> Which can deliver him from fate severe:
> In this place 'tis, if I do not mistake,
> With fire they the baptismal token make.[34]

The emperor's palaces are built of gold with colonnades inset with precious jewels of every color. In an aside, the speaker of the poem notes that this is the land from which Italy gets balm, musk, amber, and "those things . . . which, in our country, are of value great." This emperor is so powerful that

> 'Tis said, the Sultan, Egypt's Sovereign,
> As subject to this King, does tribute pay;

> Since he the Nile is able to restrain
> From its right course, and elsewhere cause it stray;
> And Cairo, thus afflicted, cause remain,
> With famine, and the parts that round it lay.

The emperor's people call him Senapus, which was glossed by one of Ariosto's contemporaries as "servant of the cross" and may have been a reference to Amda Seyon I's baptismal name, which also meant "servant of the cross."[35] But Europeans "call him Presto, or else Prester John." When Astolfo arrives at Senapus's palace, the emperor is in sorry condition. He has been blinded, and his dinner table is continually raided by harpies as punishment because in his youth, he had attempted to battle with God by bringing his troops to the source of the Nile, which descended into Abyssinia from "Paradise, the earthly sti'd, / Whereon once Eve and Adam did reside."[36]

Like Milton, Ariosto was an avid reader of geographical texts, and like Milton's *Paradise Lost*, his poem's aerial overview is not an imperial view from nowhere but an interface to a three-dimensional imaginative world. As was the case with the poetic renderings of the Sofala-Ophir impression, Ariosto borrowed specific details from the stories that African elites told about themselves and their country, which he blended to form a coherent setting. Some of these details he lifted directly: the detail that the *negusa nagast* could control the source of the Nile, the notion the Nile was Gihon, and the image of the emperor sitting on the throne holding a hand cross, which was part of the *negusa nagast*'s historical regalia and not simply a metaphor for his Christianity.[37] Others are more implied, extrapolated from the Ethiopia-Solomon connection, such as the palaces built of gold and jewels that seem echoes of Solomon's temple and the treatment of Abyssinia as a land of exotic exports. The geographical expansiveness invited by Abyssinia's claims to imperial greatness is also reflected in the poem. The top of the empire is at the Red Sea, where Abyssinia is positioned solidly on the sub-Saharan "side [of] the Nile" in "Nubia."[38] The bottom of the empire is all the way past the "Torrid Zone," where the Nile takes its source from the Mountains of the Moon.[39] In fact, Astolfo frees Senapus by chasing the harpies on his hippogriff while blowing a magical horn and driving them into the subterranean passages beneath these mountains. Abyssinia's sweeping and dramatic geography as Europeans imagined it is what gives this flight its spatial depth, and its Christianity and rich materiality give the canto its moral opportunity: Senapus offers to dedicate every gem in his palace to Astolfo and his progeny, but the knight tells him to dedicate his palaces, altars, and temples to God instead, "to whom they're due."⁴⁰ When Astolfo returns with a cure for Senapus's blindness, Senapus offers him a nearly infinite stream of soldiers to aid the Christians in the poem in pushing back against the expansion of Islam in Africa, dramatizing the shared vision that brought medieval and early modern Europeans and Ethiopians together.

Enduring Impressions in Early Modern Contact Narratives: Francisco Álvares's *Prester John of the Indies*

The earliest European contact narratives from Abyssinia, like the earliest contact narratives with the western reaches of the Land of the Blacks, altered these outstanding impressions in some ways but renewed them in others. What travelers saw and experienced bore out aspects of the Sheba narrative, increasingly persuaded them that the source of the Nile lay within Abyssinia's borders, and, at least at first, appeared to confirm that Abyssinia was indeed the Land of Prester John. When the earliest official embassy from Europe arrived there, of which Álvares was a part, they were heartened by the fact that the locals seemed to have been anticipating and then rejoiced at the arrival of their fellow Christians, suggesting to the embassy that their arrival had been preordained.⁴¹ The pomp with which Lebna Dengel surrounded himself seemed further evidence that they had arrived in the right place. When Álvares published his eyewitness account in 1540, he included a description of his first encounter with Lebna Dengel's itinerant capital city, which had tents enough to house twenty thousand people, elaborate archways, men decked out in silk and jewels, dignitaries sitting on daises, and even "four captive lions . . . bound with great chains."⁴² Once the embassy was allowed to finally see Lebna Dengel himself, they found a well-dressed, dignified young man wearing a crown and holding a hand cross. "In his presence and state," Álvares wrote, "he fully looks like the great lord that he is."⁴³ Conversations that Álvares had with the king about books and theology proved him to be a man of learning. Álvares writes that one night, Lebna Dengel and his courtiers "desired that I should tell them of books not seen by or known to them. Thus they kept questioning me . . . nor was I able to sit down, but only to lean upon a staff until the hours of vespers; and if these questions and answers had to be written down, two hands of paper would not suffice."⁴⁴ It would take five years before Álvares's embassy could leave Abyssinia, and once they did, their romantic beliefs about the country had palled. But Álvares's account maintains a commitment to the notion that

Lebna Dengel was "Prete Ianni" and treats European impressions of his land of exceptional Christianity as excessive but mostly correct.

Álvares's account upheld Makeda's story and Abyssinia's Solomonic connections in various ways as well. In a church in Aksum, he writes, "we found a very great chronicle written in the language of the country," which begins with how the Queen of Sheba heard about the "great and rich works which Solomon had begun in Jerusalem" and "determined to go and see them."[45] Preparing for the journey, "she loaded certain camels with gold to give for these works." The synopsis goes through Menelik's birth, his rearing in Jerusalem, his return to Abyssinia, and his reign. Álvares tells the story of "Queen Candace" next, also allegedly a resident of Aksum and the person, according to one legend, who brought Christianity to Ethiopia.[46] Kandake, like the Queen of Sheba, is not unique to Habesha narrative traditions, but she is another queen that Ethiopian Christians claimed as their own and developed their own stories about, including, according to Álvares, how she built the first version of the Church of Our Lady Mother of Zion, the home of the copy of the *Kebra Nagast* that Álvares saw and the alleged home of the Ark of the Covenant. Whether Kandake built the church or not—or whether, as is the more common story, Ethiopia was converted by a missionary named Frumentius in the fourth century—the Church of Our Lady Mother of Zion itself "constitutes an integral part of the legend of the queen of Sheba," as Tamrat writes, not only because it allegedly houses the Ark but also because Christianization was the next step in in the prophecy that dictated Ethiopia's religious destiny.

Álvares's characterizations of the aristocratic women he encountered are in keeping with this legacy of wise, pious, and politically influential African queens, in part because he was predisposed to think of them through Makeda's lens and in part because they, like other African elites, performed their public personas within this cultural and literary tradition. In the *Kebra Nagast*, Makeda hands the kingdom over to Menelik and declares that woman will never again rule Ethiopia, but she doesn't retreat into the private sphere. She retains political and cultural influence, with Menelik declaring in turn that he will still serve her in every way that she commands. The kinds of elite women that the early Portuguese travelers encountered similarly held a great deal of autonomy and political influence—even though they couldn't inherit the throne—and they were respected for their wisdom.[47] The night Lebna Dengel asked Álvares questions about Europe's books until he could barely stand, Eleni and Lebna Dengel's wife, Sabla Wangel, also participated in the interrogation. Eleni is not only well educated in Álvares's account, she is powerful and admired. She is the one, Álvares reminds the reader, who put Lebna Dengel on the throne, served as regent during his minority, and sent the first letter to Portugal that had started the diplomatic process that brought Álvares to Abyssinia.[48] When Eleni died during Álvares's time in Abyssinia, the courtiers told him "that since she had died all of them had died, great and small, and that while she lived, all were defended and protected; and she was father and mother of all."[49] In part because of Álvares's account, Eleni would become one queen in a line that Europeans would see as the inheritor of Makeda's character, bolstering the impression of elite Abyssinian women as intelligent, pious, admired by their people, and possessing a gift for international diplomacy.

Álvares's descriptions of Aksum's steles, churches, freestone palaces, waterworks, and decorative elements position Lebna Dengel as the cultural and political inheritor of the seat of Makeda's kingdom, just as Yekuno Amlak, Wedem Arad, Amda Seyon I, Zara Yaqob, and other emperors who sought to legitimize their right to the throne through their alleged Solomonic blood might have wished. He first introduces the town by telling the reader that it was "the city, chamber, and abode (as they say) of the Queen Saba" and the place she departed from to bring "camels laden with gold to Solomon when he was building the temple of Jerusalem."[50] The oldest ruins date back at least to this time, including a house full of stone chests that "they say . . . were the treasure chests of Queen Saba."[51] Of particular interest to Álvares were the elaborately carved stone steles in and around Aksum, the tallest of which was over one hundred feet and weighed hundreds of tons.[52] He writes that they were inscribed with an ancient language that the locals could no longer read, but which, "according to their appearance . . . must be Hebrew."[53] The Church of Our Lady Mother of Zion was also enormous, built at the center of two enclosures that were like the walls of a city and included, in addition to the church, two palaces and wells and fountains, all decorated with carvings of lions, dogs, and birds. One of the ruins within this enclosure, called "Ambazabete, which means house of lions," was the place where the Aksumite emperors' lions were kept, the forbearers of the four lions kept chained in Lebna Dengel's tent city. He saw twelve stone chairs around a giant tree, which according to his guides "belong to the twelve judges who at this time serve in the court of Prester John."[54] Everything Álvares was told about Aksum was pitched to create a sense of prophetic cultural and political continuity between Aksum as a site of Solomonic exceptionalism and ensuing Christianity and Lebna Dengel's royal authority. In fact, Álvares concludes, "It seemed to us that the Prester John had sent us here, in order that we should see these edifices, and we had rejoiced at seeing them, as they are much grander than what I write," indicating that Álvares's exposure to this legitimization narrative was orchestrated from the very top.

Though other eyewitness accounts of Abyssinia would be published within a hundred years that would say that Abyssinia was not the fabled Land of Prester John after all, Álvares's account remained an authoritative source, often mentioned in European geographical texts as the foundational authority on Abyssinia in the same paragraphs that cited Leo Africanus as the foundational authority on the Land of the Blacks.[55] His report, like those of other travelers to Africa, was made up of details he gathered "some by sight, and some others by the report of credible persons," as illustrated in his account of Aksum by his continual references to the things that "they say" about Makeda, Menelik, Candace, and the Prester.[56] In fact, in the early seventeenth century the missionary and scholar Pedro Páez attributed Álvares's continuing belief that Abyssinia was the Land of Prester John to the power and persuasiveness of these local informants.[57] Having lived in Abyssinia for twenty years and having made a particularly dedicated study of the local books and culture during that time, Páez argued that Álvares had mistaken an Ethiopian narrative trope in which hyperbolic amounts of material abundance is described as a symbol of God's favor—earthly riches signifying heavenly riches—as mimetic descriptions of the country.[58] Páez also noted more than once that if Álvares walked away with an inflated sense of Abyssinia's grandeur it was because the *negusa nagast* and other elites "wanted to show more splendour than they commonly do, since there were foreigners at their court."[59] They put on an excellent performance of feasts, dress, and imperial pomp that Álvares had taken as the norm rather than the exception. In other words, Álvares interpreted what he saw and what he heard through impressions of Abyssinia that he had arrived with—that it was the Land of Prester John as well as the land of the Queen of Sheba—and those impressions were confirmed by the political and diplomatic performances he witnessed, by the books that he encountered and what he was told about them, and by the architecture of Makeda's alleged royal seat.

Habesha Women from the Battlefield to the European Imagination: The *Itege* in Accounts of the Ethiopian-Adal War

The next wave of European eyewitness accounts of Abyssinia came from military reinforcements that Europe sent to Africa during the Ethiopian-Adal War. Around the time that Álvares arrived in Abyssinia, a Somali general from the Adal Sultinate named Ahmad ibn Ibrahim al-Ghazi (called Grahn by Ethiopians) began to amass a power base with the intention of conquering Abyssinia. Five years after Álvares's embassy left, Lebna Dengel lost a battle that opened the door for Grahn's troops to swarm into the Highlands, where they occupied some of its most materially and culturally rich regions, destroyed and looted churches and monasteries, killed priests and monks, and burned books. They converted local populations to Islam, some by force and some, who had never culturally assimilated into the Christian empire, willingly—a reminder that the Christian unity that medieval and early modern Solomonic rulers projected to Europe didn't necessarily reflect reality.[60] This occupation only lasted about ten years, but as Tamrat puts it, "The amount of destruction brought about in these years can only be estimated in terms of centuries."[61] Lebna Dengel wrote to the king of Portugal for aid, who sent a contingent of soldiers led by Cristóvão da Gama that arrived in Abyssinia in 1540, just after Lebna Dengel died at Debre Damo—one of the nearly impregnable fortresses built on the flat-topped, sheer-sided mountains that had fascinated Europeans ever since they had heard that the *negusa nagast* kept all the potential male claimants to the throne imprisoned in them to prevent usurpation and maintain the integrity of the Solomonic line.

According to Salvadore, this European "military intervention" had been "enabled by age-old discourses on the Prester," but it "ultimately disproved the very myth of the Prester—the African sovereign was barely capable of holding onto his kingdom, let alone march on Jerusalem."[62] Nevertheless, the accounts of Europeans who fought on behalf of the new *negusa nagast*—Galawdewos, the son of Lebna Dengel and Sabla Wangel—were still in dialog with outstanding impressions of Abyssinia, indicating that the legend continued to inform cultural representation even after it was no longer explicitly driving diplomatic relationships. João Bermudes, who had been a member of the same embassy as Álvares and had stayed behind when the others left, claimed in his account that a dying patriarch of the Ethiopian Church had appointed him his successor and that this appointment had been accepted by Lebna Dengel. Thus he too had a vested interest in continuing to write about Abyssinia as the Land of Prester John: maintaining the myth made his own spurious claims to authority more potent. Miguel de Castanhoso, a Spanish soldier under da Gama's command who published the most detailed European account of the conflict, also continued the tradition of referring to the emperor as the Prester. His repeated emphasis on the damage Grahn had done to Abyssinia's natural resources, buildings, and stores of accumulated wealth in every region through which they traveled signifies a great nation brought to its knees rather than one that was never great to begin with.

The treatment of Abyssinia's noblewomen in these accounts is in keeping with prior impressions as well. They represented Sabla Wangel as a woman of personal courage who refused to remain safely locked away as her country suffered. She had become Eleni's spiritual successor in Abyssinia, celebrated for her wisdom and for taking an active hand in political decisions on behalf of her son Galawdewos, as Eleni had done for Lebna Dengel. When da Gama's forces arrived, one of the first things they did was collect Sabla Wangel from Debre Damo, where she had taken refuge with her daughters, ladies in waiting, and servants; they knew that having her with them meant that they would be better received by the people who respected and obeyed her.[63] Álvares had written that the fortresses were grim and severe places. He never saw the inside of one himself, but he recounted an incident of a prince who escaped from one and fled to his mother the queen for aid because he and the other people on the *amba* were starving.[64] Castanhoso's description of the *amba* is no more hospitable, but it is so impregnable that Grahn's armies can't breach it: "It is squared and scarped for a height double that of the highest tower in Portugal, and it gets more precipitous near the top, until at the end it makes an umbrella all around, which looks artificial, and spreads out so far that it overhangs all the foot of the mountain, so that no one at the foot can hide from those above." A narrow, difficult foot path two-thirds of the way up ends at a locked gate. After that, anyone who would reach the summit has to be pulled up through a hole in the overhang in a basket.

When Sabla Wangel is told that it's time to leave her rocky retreat, she is elated despite the fact, Castanhoso alleges, that Grahn hoped to capture her in particular because he had heard she was so beautiful.[65] She "got ready immediately with all her women and servants, leaving on the mountain her second son and two very beautiful daughters."[66] The moment her feet hit the ground she was in danger, yet, Castanhoso writes, "When the Queen found herself away from the hill, she gave many thanks to God, weeping with pleasure for His great mercy in allowing her to leave that hill, where she had been imprisoned for so many years."[67] She remains in the thick of things through most of Castanhoso's account, "ready to share whatever fate befell us."[68] She is a commander and a spymaster, and she organizes reconnaissance missions.[69] After one particularly bloody battle, she and her women build a field hospital and begin binding up the wounded by tearing strips of their own clothing.[70] When da Gama is killed, she grieves for him as she would a son.[71] Bermudes described Sabla Wangel as more timid and fearful, and he was annoyed with what he considered her refusal to follow orders for her own good.⁷² He portrays himself throughout as the "father" to whom she turned to for advice.⁷³ But even there she is represented as pious and politically influential as well as fiercely protective of both her own people and the Portuguese soldiers, refusing to withdraw to safety unless there are mounts enough for all her women to accompany her and refusing to leave da Gama wounded on the battlefield. She is a constant presence at da Gama's side in Bathazar Telles's synopsis of the Ethiopian-Adal War, translated as part of *Travels of the Jesuits in Ethiopia* (1710)—through which English readers would have first encountered her—while Galawdewos, who remained sequestered on a different mountain for much of the conflict, appears in only the last two paragraphs.

Sabla Wangel was likely an intelligent and courageous person and a savvy stateswoman in her own right. But she, like Eleni, was also performing a diplomatic role within a particular set of expectations and allowances afforded by Abyssinia's tradition of women who ran the country through cultural influence and lateral forms of political power. In fact, Eleni set rather a precedent for this social role. Sabla Wangel was the first queen to be given the title *itege*, which ranked her above all other queens and designated her right to serve as regent over royal minorities.⁷⁴ But Eleni was the prototype of this figure such that, Margaux Herman finds, later *itege* were also called Eleni: "Like the ancient Roman personal names Caesar and Augustus, over time it became itself a title," which led to some confusion in European accounts of the two women.⁷⁵ The *itege* also became an archetype in European narratives. Though Castanhoso and Bermudes don't make suggestive connections between Sabla Wangel and Makeda as Álvares did with Eleni, subsequent writers would dovetail all of these figures. The result was an idea of elite Abyssinian women consistent with what emerges in their traditions: women who are uniquely able to maintain both feminine modesty and political power (to be both mother and father to the country) and who are symbols of piety and serve as "intermediaries with foreign rulers and dignitaries," as Herman describes them.⁷⁶

Ferñao Mendes Pinto, an explorer who wrote a fairly imaginative account of his travels in 1569, was one writer who created just such an *itege*. He left Portugal for India in 1537, but he describes stopping by Abyssinia on the way to deliver a letter to the Portuguese soldiers guarding a "Princess of *Tigremahon*, Mother to Prester John." The anecdote is almost certainly one of the parts of the narrative he made up or at least subjected to a great deal of literary license. The dates are wrong for this princess to be Lebna Dengel's birth mother or Eleni, whose deaths Álvares records, or Sabla Wangel, who was not yet "mother to Prester John" because Lebna Dengel didn't die until 1540, but the princess reads like a composite of all these women as Álvares, Castanhoso, and Bermudes described them, and she is endowed with some Makeda-like elements for good measure. She welcomes them into her "palace," where they find her at mass in her chapel. Pinto writes, "She received us with a smiling countenance, and to testifie how much she was pleased with our coming; Verily, said she, you cannot imagine how glad I am to see you, that are right Christians, for it hath been a thing which I have always as much desired, as a fair garden enameled with flowers doth the mornings dew, wherefore you are most welcome come, and may your entrance into my house be as propitious, as that of the vertuous Queen *Helena*'s was into blessed Jerusalem."[77] She then has them sit in a circle around her, questions them on matters of religion and politics, asks if any of them have ever made a pilgrimage to the Holy Lands, and wants to know the details of Portugal's holdings in India. She laments that the Christian princes of Europe have not yet succeeded in opening a path to Jerusalem. "She made us many other like demands," Pinto says, "to the which we answered the best we could for to content her; whereupon she dismissed us, and we returning to our lodging, continued there nine days, which we spent in waiting on this Princess, with whom we had much discourse on several subjects."[78] When it is time for them to depart, she bids them farewell, saying, "Truly . . . it grieves me that you will be gone so soon, but since there is no remedy, I wish your Voyage may be so prosperous, that at your arrival in the Indiaes you may be as well received by yours, as the Queen of *Sheba* was heretofore by King *Solomon* in the admirable Palace of his greatness."[79] She gives them 240 ducats as a parting gift, assigns them a guard of twenty soldiers to escort them to their ship, and includes "a rich present of divers Jewels of Gold and Stones" to the governor of the Indies.

This character embodies elements of both the historical women and the archetype of the ideal elite woman described above. She receives the Portuguese not only as a hostess but as a diplomat and scholar, pressing them on their progress in improving access to the Holy Lands—an issue that the real Eleni had called for in her 1509 letter to Manuel I. The "Queen Helena" Pinto's *itege* invokes is not a reference to this Eleni directly but to the mother of Constantine, who allegedly discovered the true cross on a pilgrimage to Jerusalem and who is an important figure in the Ethiopian ecclesiastical tradition, celebrated during the holiday of Meskel.[80] However, Eleni (who was born into a Muslim family and converted upon her marriage) took her name as a symbol of ideal Christian womanhood and in fact sent an alleged piece of the true cross on a silver ring to Manuel I with her letter, as ready to deploy the symbolism of her name for European Christians as she did with Ethiopian Christians.[81] Pinto's *itege*—with her interest in Jerusalem and appreciation for pilgrimage, her attachment to Constantine's mother and by association Eleni, her condescension to the Portuguese travelers, her education and propensity for debate, her piety, her riches, and her reference to Sheba and Solomon—is an idealized, romanticized figure. But she is also a product of the privileged place certain women occupied in history, in Habesha narrative traditions, and in European eyewitness accounts.

Images of Paradise in Early Modern Imaginative Accounts of Abyssinia: From Luis de Urreta's Pseudohistory to Milton's *Paradise Lost*

Though European attitudes toward Abyssinia may have shifted in the wake of the Ethiopian-Adal War, many different genres of cultural representations still treated it as a fabulously wealthy, expansive empire with a unique Christian identity traceable to Solomon and Makeda. One connection that kept these associations alive in the cultural imagination was Abyssinia's continuing claims to the source of the Nile. Sixteenth- and seventeenth-century European cartographers continued to portray Abyssinia as much bigger than it was and to label it as the Land of Prester John. Sebastian Münster (1544) maintained Ptolemy's topography and planted Prester John's kingdom between the Nile's two streams.[82] Giacomo Gastaldi (1564) positioned Gojjam and the Land of Prester John in the middle of the continent. On Mercator's (1569), Ortelius's (1570, fig. 3), and Blaeu's (1635) maps of Africa, the lakes and rivers are a bit more finessed, but their situations are still essentially Ptolemaic.[83] As a result, their Abyssinias encompass the modern-day equivalent of Eritrea, Ethiopia, Sudan, South Sudan, Democratic Republic of the Congo, and Zambia. That these cartographers would stretch Abyssinia's borders until it encompassed a fifth of the continent rather than move the source of the Nile speaks to how much sway Classical worldviews still had over African cartography, but it also indicates that cartographers took Abyssinian claims to imperial greatness seriously enough that it seemed reasonable—in the spirit of early modern geographical practices—to fit the two together in a way that lent equal credence to both. Each of these maps was produced before any European eyewitness had published an account of the source of the Abay, let alone taken its measurements, so these representations are contrived entirely through discourse.

Among all the stories about the Nile that these cartographers could have chosen to structure their maps—and there were as many as there were people who have lived on or dreamed about the Nile—the Ethiopian account of it kept rising to the top.

Another genre that kept these associations alive was imaginative or semi-imaginative accounts like Pinto's. The most notorious of these was Luis de Urreta's *Historia de la sagrada Orden de predicadores, en los remotos reynos de la Etiopia*, published in two volumes in 1610 and 1611. Urreta never traveled to Abyssinia himself, but he claimed the details for his "history" came from a Habesha monk named Juan de Baltasar who visited him in his home in Valencia. Baltasar had described Abyssinia to him as a lush utopia, full of treasure, palaces, books, and grand ceremonies. Urreta's pseudohistory represented the royal prison of "Amara"—where Juan de Baltasar claimed to work as a guard—as a paradise. In fact, he suggests that it was literally "Our Forefathers Paradise," and he claimed that a stream that flows through the amba's plain runs into the Nile.[84] The air is described as "wholesome and delectable," and the inhabitants live long lives and are never ill.[85] The top is full of churches that are "richly and cunningly wrought, the matter and the workmanship conspiring magnificence," and two temples are dedicated to Makeda and Candace.[86] There are thirty-four palaces, which are "spacious, sumptuous, and beautiful, where the Princes of the royall bloud have their abode with their families," and whose walls are filled with treasure. The palaces are allegedly filled with the books that the Queen of Sheba collected, a great number of which she received from Solomon, and this library has been cared for and added to by all the emperors since her reign.[87] Among those books are ancient records that document Makeda's visit to Solomon, and among the palace's treasures is a fragment of a tablet from the Ark of the Covenant.

The existence of Juan de Baltasar and the veracity of Urreta's account were almost immediately challenged. Though Purchas published Urreta's account of the Hill Amara with little commentary in his 1613 text, in the 1626 edition he claims he included it only as "a Comedie to delight our tyred Reader."[88] Indeed, read alongside a travel narrative like Álvares's or Castanhoso's, Urreta's account seems a pure fantasy. But when approached more like Ariosto's Abyssinia, similarities emerge that have deep ties to the stories the Habesha told about themselves, including the notion that paradise exists at the top of a mountain within Prester John's domain, that it is near the source of the Nile, that Abyssinia is filled with jeweled palaces, and that it is inhabited by exceptional Christians. And in other ways, it is not as different as it may first appear from Álvares's account of the ruins at Aksum, which was shaped by his hosts to encourage an impression of the kingdom that connected the Queen of Sheba to Ethiopia's conversion to Christianity to Lebna Dengel in one continuous line. The religious and political scaffoldings of Urreta's geographical description are dependent on these same associations. In other words, regardless of whether Juan de Baltasar was a real person or whether the account is realistic, Urreta's text is permeated with African discourse.

In fact, this was something that Urreta's most thorough detractor, Páez, stressed about Urreta's account. Páez's text had been commissioned specifically for the purpose of undermining Urreta's argument that the Dominicans had more right to establish a mission in Abyssinia than the Jesuits, though it turned into more of a history and ethnography.[89] Páez's refutation of Urreta is much more scornful than his treatment of Álvares, his fellow Jesuit, but his approach to correcting the two was the same. Instead of insisting that Urreta invented his description, he offered two other possibilities: Juan de Baltasar was telling stories about Abyssinia or Urreta misinterpreted what his informant had said. As Páez had with Álvares, he explained that Urreta's descriptions were stylistically consistent with the ideas the Habesha projected about themselves in order to make themselves seem, in Páez's estimation, grander than they actually were.[90] For instance, Páez stresses that Urreta got many of the names and dates of the reigns within the Solomonic dynasty wrong, but he doesn't deny that the Solomonic dynasty exists or dismiss its import to Abyssinian religious and political claims.[91] He takes Urreta to task for giving a faulty etymology of the term "Habesha" and for calling Makeda's son "Melilech" rather than "Menelik." He denies Urreta's statement that a fragment of the tablets from the Ark of the Covenant is held on Amba Geshen and that the fragment was given to Makeda by Solomon willingly. Menelik stole the Ark, the story goes, and it is held in Aksum, not on Amba Geshen. Regarding Urreta's description of the *amba* fortress, in particular, he only refutes that the palaces, churches, and treasure are on the mountain. He speculates that Juan de Baltasar was describing the whole region of Amhara to Urreta and that Urreta simply confused that with his "Hill Amara."[92]

After all, the same region that houses Amba Geshen also houses Aksum—which Páez reminds readers is "sumptuous"—as well as the monolithic stone churches of Lalibela, eleven multistory buildings cut thirty to fifty meters straight into the bedrock, which are unquestionably "richly and cunningly wrought."[93] Both Álvares and Castanhoso left descriptions of these churches, with Álvares going twice to see them and record all their details because he believed the world needed to know about their excellence.[94] Even Grahn left Lalibela intact. According to Castanhoso, when his army came to raid it, their horses foundered, which Grahn took as a sign that Allah "did not wish him to destroy such noble edifices."[95] If Juan de Baltasar was a real person, he could have easily described Aksum and Lalibela to Urreta in detail. If he was not, Urreta likely read others' accounts of both places. Either way, Habesha expressions are threaded through Urreta's narrative, even if it would have read more like a delightful comedy to a seventeenth-century reader than a plausible geographical representation.

Despite the best efforts of the likes of Purchas and Páez to disarm it, Urreta's pseudohistory proliferated. Mainstream geographical sources like Peter Heylyn's *Cosmographie* (1666) excerpted Urreta's description of Amara without comment. *The Late Travels of S. Giacomo Baratti*, another even more imaginative pseudohistory, features a narrator who claims to have entered Amba Geshen personally and seen its castles, fortifications, and books. In Giovanni Paolo Marana's *Letters Writ by a Turkish Spy* (1642–93), the Abyssinian strategy of confining heirs to a mountain of books and pleasantries is proposed as a solution to Ottoman problems of succession.[96] In *Paradise Lost*, Milton protests that Paradise is not to be found

> ... where Abassin kings their issue guard,
> Mount Amara, though this by some supposed
> True Paradise, under the Ethiop line
> By Nilus's head, enclosed with shining rock,
> A whole day's journey high ...[97]

Nevertheless, Milton scholars have noted similarities between early modern descriptions of Abyssinia's topography and Milton's Paradise. Particularly striking is Milton's description of the gate between earth and Paradise, which is at the end of a winding path that leads to "one entrance high; / The rest was craggy cliff, that overhung / Still as it rose, impossible to climb"—imagery that echoes Castanhoso's description of the way up Debre Damo.[98] As Evert Mordecai Clark argues, "Though Milton necessarily located his Garden of God 'wide remote' from Abyssinia, on the wings of memory and imagination and with the assistance of the compendia of Purchas and Heylyn he transported thither so much of Mount Amara that Mount Paradise, in its physical aspects, is decidedly more Abyssinian than Hebraic."[99] Clark offers a breakdown of all the textual resonances between *Paradise Lost* and two excerpts from Purchas and Heylyn. Both passages Clark identifies are borrowed from

Urreta. Even though on the surface Milton dismisses the long-held associations between Abyssinia and Paradise, such accounts seem to have made a profound impact on his spatial imagination, just as the Sofala-Ophir impression did.

The Enduring Imaginative Power of Makeda and Prester John in Early Enlightenment Literature

By the second half of the seventeenth century and into the eighteenth, those who wanted to move away from representing Abyssinia through some of its more fantastical associations found themselves continually needing to refute the notion that it was the Land of Prester John, which stubbornly lingered in the cultural imagination. This was in part because, as Jerónimo Lobo wrote in his refutation of the myth, the idea remained entirely "probable" given how Abyssinians presented, wrote about, and talked about themselves. The *negusa nagast* professed himself a Christian, carried a cross in his hand, and when he traveled, someone carried a processional cross at the head of his retinue. Furthermore, that the *negusa nagast* "was by ancient custom a Priest," Lobo writes, "is reported of him by tradition and their own Annals." Though some travelers to Abyssinia didn't find the country to be as full of books or riches as they expected, they offered the Ethiopian-Adal War as a partial explanation for this, noting correctly that Grahn's armies had destroyed and raided a great deal of the country's treasures and wealth.[100] And by the time Charles-Jacques Poncet published his travel narrative of Abyssinia (1703), the royal complexes of Gondar had been built, Lebna Dengal's moving tent capital replaced by a home base of elaborate stone palaces and churches. Poncet's account of Gondar and of Iyasu I's court breathed new life into older images, including descriptions of walking through twenty apartments to get from his rooms to the throne room; of Iyasu I's sumptuous, bejeweled couch and clothing and his "quick and piercing wit"; of elaborate ceremonies and retinues; and of island retreats and "charming palaces" built in the middle of Lake T'ana.[101]

As Barros's, Bruce's, and Afonso Mendes's acceptance of the Queen of Sheba story attests, it retained scholarly traction for much longer than the Prester John legend, with writers like Purchas, Telles, and Ludolf concluding that even if some of its details had been embellished, there was not enough evidence to refute it since it made just as much if not more sense than any other theory.[102] Furthermore, as was the case with the Prester John legend, those who did try to negate it also repeated it. Michael Geddes, for instance, opens his account "Of the Religions of the *Habassins*" in his *Church History of Ethiopia* (1696) with Makeda. He writes, "It is a constant Tradition among the *Habassins*, That the Queen of *Sheba* that went to Visit *Solomon*, was Empress of their Countrey, whose Name, they say, was *Maqueda*; and who, within a few weeks after she returned home, was delivered of a Son, Begat by *Solomon*, whom she Named *Menileher*."[103] He points out that upon this "Fable," the Abyssinians have "built a hundred more," and he deems them as "fitter for a Legend than a History." But the fact that he nevertheless makes this legend the starting place for of his own account demonstrates how foundational it remained to academic treatments of the country. Nearly every account of the Solomonic dynasty in European texts begins with her and traces the line from her crowning of Menelik to the present emperors of Abyssinia.

Both Prester John and Makeda remained staples in literary representations of Abyssinia, circulating in popular publications marketed toward a broad-based audience. In the *History of Little Goody Two-Shoes* (1765), for instance, Tom Two-Shoes washes up on the shore of East Africa where he "met with a strange book . . . which gave him some Account of Prester John's Country" to the north, which he then sets out to find, attended by a tame lion that follows him like a dog.[104] George Lyttelton wrote a humorous periodical essay (1775) about how "that great emperor, Lord of the Mountains of the Moon; and, except one, the highest potentate upon earth, the most illustrious Prester John of Abyssinia" is guarded by a band of thirty chained lions.[105] Thomas Berington's *News from the Dead* (1715–16), another periodical publication, tells a story in which "*Maqueda*" visits the narrator, Mercury, asking him to clear her name on earth because "some have entertain'd the Opinion of me, that I came to *Solomon* . . . to have a Bastard by him."[106] In a monologue that captures not simply plot points but a great deal of Makeda's characterization from the *Kebra Nagast*, she explains,

> I was always a Lover of Wisdom, and much given to Studies and Observations: I had heard great Things of *Solomon's* wonderful Wisdom and Knowledge. . . . I concluded, that to converse personally with one of so wonderful a Genius . . . could not but be an extraordinary Improvement to me. I took some Time beforehand, to collect all the curious Questions and difficult Points I could think of, which I desired to be satisfied in, and compos'd some Enigma's in Verse, to make Trial of his penetrating Wit.

Mercury tells her that this has all been confirmed by scripture. But he informs her that the fact she had "a Son by him" is "a Thing very currently believ'd by all *Ethiopia*. The great Emperor call'd *Prester John*, does yet boast of it, and will not suffer it to be doubted, but that he has the Honour to be descended from you and *Solomon*." He cites details from the *Kebra Nagast* as evidence of this, telling Maqueda, "Most of the Historians that write of Ethiopia, speak of it as a current Truth. They tell us, that one *Tamerin*, a Merchant, that traffick'd to *Jerusalem*, gave you Account of the Wonders of *Solomon's* Reign, of his Wisdom and Worship of one true God; That you came with such Pomp and Retinue, as rais'd great Wonder in *Jerusalem* itself."[107] He cites Páez as his source for this information, who "brought, not many Years since, these particular Accounts from *Ethiopia*." Maqueda affirms the truth of this narrative, only denying that she gave birth to Menelik out of wedlock. Rather, maintaining Makeda's sovereign autonomy, she says that she married Solomon on the condition that she be allowed to return to her own kingdom, where she then passed the crown on to her son.[108] As these texts demonstrate, the Prester John legend and the African Sheba story were not relegated to a few esoteric church histories but circulated through publications consumed by a wide range of readers—including, in the case of *Little Goody Two-Shoes*, young children—who would have had varying levels of formal education in religion or geography. That these African details are preserved with such precision is indicative of the interest they garnered.

Cartographic representations that stretched Abyssinia to accommodate Classical ideas about the source of the Nile persisted as well. Lobo bemoaned the fact that "people so biggotted to antiquity" still did not "pay any regard to the relations of travellers who have been upon this spot," even though "the evidence of their eyes can confute all that the ancients have written."[109] By the early eighteenth century, even as knowledge about Abyssinia's true geopolitical borders increased, John Green was still chiding mapmakers who drew the Nile "with 7 mouths" and placed its head "below *Abyssinia*."[110] Even so, his issue was not with Abyssinia's claims to house the source of the Nile but with cartographers' need to cling to the Ptolemaic view. Following Green's lead, cartographers like Guillaume Delisle (1722) scotched Ptolemy's lake but still fit the Nile entirely within Abyssinia's borders.[111] Mapmakers began to adjust their maps to account for increasing knowledge about Abyssinia's contours, in other words, but many still accepted Abyssinia's claims to the source above all other claims.[112] It was considered by many a settled matter, despite the fact that no European had traveled the entire course of the Abay and only a handful of early modern Jesuits had ever seen the source. Even then—as Bruce would later say about those Jesuits and as others would say about Bruce—they only had the word of their local guides that they were standing at *the* source.

* * *

Well into the eighteenth century, Europeans thought of Abyssinia as a land of exceptional Christianity with Solomonic ties, a land that had historically been, even if it wasn't at present, an expansive empire that covered much of Africa and even crossed the Red Sea into Asia. That presumed historical greatness coupled with the fact that Abyssinia was believed to be the country that housed the source of the Nile meant that impressions of Abyssinia's geography in particular exerted a great deal of influence over impressions of Africa's geography in general. These associations weren't European fantasies projected onto Africa, although Europeans had their own motivations for continuing to believe and perpetuate them. They were the result of the Habesha projecting national and religious narratives both internally, as an act of empire-building, and externally, making declarations to the wider world about Abyssinia's place in it.

Even though by the eighteenth century there were more eyewitness accounts published by Europeans about Abyssinia than there were eyewitness accounts about the Land of the Blacks, representations of the country were still guided by these impressions. What the Habesha had to say and show about themselves remained central to representations of the country because their narratives were compelling, because the question of whether or not Sheba had indeed been located in Africa was considered historically and theologically significant, because the Nile had not been charted by Europeans even if its presumed source had technically been seen by Europeans, and because even "eyewitness" accounts of Africa were still mostly earwitness accounts. As such, impressions of Abyssinia, like impressions of the Land of the Blacks, were sites of argumentation and contemplation over the role that discursive evidence and scholastic methods should play in the production of geographical knowledge.

The next two chapters show how Samuel Johnson and James Bruce, respectively, engaged with these impressions of Abyssinia and these epistemological questions. Both men were scornful of people who wrote about or bought too credulously into fabulous accounts of Abyssinia (and, in the end, each accused the other of doing just that). However, both were also fascinated by local, discursively grounded perspectives on the country's history and geography. And even as men who emphasized reason over fancy, both saw a place for these local perspectives in the production of knowledge about the country and suggested that the consequences of disregarding them were just as detrimental as accepting too credulously the fantastical things they had to offer.

5

"BETWEEN THE INLAND COUNTRIES OF AFRICK AND THE PORTS OF THE RED SEA"

African Impressions amid Fact and Fancy in Samuel Johnson's *Rasselas*

In an article in a 1774 issue of *the London Magazine* about James Bruce's travels in Abyssinia, James Boswell introduces his subject by noting that "Abyssinia has become an object of interest and pleasing attention in Europe, since the publication of Mr. Samuel Johnson's tale, called *Rasselas Prince of Abyssinia*." He goes on to describe the generic balance of *Rasselas* as "a work in which that eminent writer has displayed a rich fund of moral instruction, embellished with oriental imagery, and rendered interesting by a well conducted story, in the tissue of which several real facts concerning that country are interwoven." In sorting out the relationship between such "oriental imagery" and "real facts concerning the country," critics have tended to emphasize the former rather than the latter as the stronger influence on Johnson's text, although they haven't always agreed with Boswell that he used either successfully. In his May 1759 review of *Rasselas*, Owen Ruffhead complained that not only did Johnson do a poor job at "cloth[ing]" his narrative in an "agreeable garb" of orientalism, but any moral lesson the tale has to offer can be "acquire[d] without going to Ethiopia to learn it."[1]

Modern readers frequently agree with Ruffhead. Some note that *Rasselas* doesn't quite meet the criteria for an oriental tale and many consider the text's engagement with Ethiopian history, culture, and geography to be a mere means to an end.[2] Johnson's Abyssinian "facts" seem to amount to little more than the novel's foundational plot point (the internment of the royal heirs) and a few specific details scattered throughout that he drew from the travel accounts and geographical texts available to him, his most immediate sources being his own translation of Joachim Le Grand's French version of Jerónimo Lobo's *Voyage to Abyssinia* (1735) and Le Grand's accompanying dissertations.³ These scattered details are overshadowed by Johnson's invocations of more literary or pseudo-historical representations of Abyssinia, which are themselves considered to be only passing engagements with the country (in particular, *Paradise Lost*) or outright fabrications (the Urreta-esque texts that describe the prisons as a paradise).⁴ Scholars have thus concluded, as Gwin Kolb does, that Johnson "prefer[ed] fancy to fact in *Rasselas*" or, as Srinivas Aravamudan does, that Johnson "could not, or chose not to, render the particularities of East and North Africa, instead crossing Turks with Arabs."⁵

The evidence that is most often cited to justify dividing empirical fact so strictly from imaginative fancy in readings of *Rasselas*—and for attributing everything that looks like a fact to sources like Lobo and Ludolf and everything that doesn't to sources like Milton and Urreta—comes from Johnson's preface to Lobo's travel narrative, in which he praises Lobo because "he appears by his modest and unaffected narration to have described things as he saw them, to have copied nature from the life, and to have consulted his senses, not his imagination."⁶ The geographical attitude captured in this preface is that of a man who preferred descriptions derived from observation that did not rely on allegory or analogy, that were written in a straightforward style, and that confirmed universal truths about man.⁷ That *Rasselas* recreates the kinds of geographical representations Johnson decried rather than those he praised has led scholars to conclude that he believed geography and literature had wholly separate obligations or that he stages the Happy Valley as an absurdity—a realm of unfettered imagination that is then regulated as the characters gain firsthand experience of the world and learn to rely on their reason.⁸ To support this latter point, Edward Tomarken argues that Abyssinia is meant to signify simultaneously a paradise and an actual location in the material world. In his analysis of the text's enigmatic ending, he suggests that once the travelers supplant their naïve longing for a paradise on earth by acquiring a more sound "interpretive procedure" for understanding the world—one that the reader acquires along with them—they return not to the Happy Valley where they started but to the Abyssinia of the travel narratives that Johnson read and translated.⁹ Still, Tomarken's reading traces how "the text unfolds as a literary form that reaches out beyond the bounds of the literary," not how the extraliterary might unfold into the text; thus Abyssinia as "a location . . . of actual events recounted in history books" is a concept or analogy in *Rasselas* rather than something that shaped its contours.¹⁰ Curley gestures toward how Abyssinia's history, as well as stories about its Solomonic ties, shaped *Rasselas*'s themes and characters, but he ultimately concludes that it is mere scaffolding for general principles and archetypes, since "particularity would have interfered with the summary moral design of the tale."[11]

One limitation of suggesting that empirical facts about Abyssinia in *Rasselas* are meant to signify material reality and that everything else is meant to signify not just a departure from reality but a dangerously delusional one is that this view neglects a third arena—geographical knowledge that Johnson thought important but that couldn't be divined through empiricism or the senses. In this chapter I argue that Johnson's Abyssinia acquired much of its character and shape from early Enlightenment debates about Abyssinia's ancient past and Biblical ties. These were still topics of serious inquiry for travelers and geographers and were considered as necessary to a comprehensive account of the country as descriptions of its observable topographical situation, system of government, and cultural norms. Johnson's interest in this category of geographical knowledge and his interest in the epistemological and narrative strategies required to produce it have been overlooked because the details and conventions that signal it appear in texts like Urreta's and Milton's. However, they also appear in Lobo, Le Grand, and Ludolf. As the previous chapter shows, these texts all drew from and fed back into a shared impression of Abyssinia as a vast and mighty empire that extended deep into Africa, was ruled by monarchs who loved books and learning, and was connected via trade networks and pilgrimage routes to the wider world. This way of writing about Abyssinia was very different from an eyewitness account—what critics tend to think of when they imagine a "factual" source for *Rasselas*—but it was not considered by early Enlightenment thinkers and writers to be "fancy."

To make this case, I rely on and diverge from Wendy Laura Belcher's intervention into the question of how Ethiopian realities are "interwoven" into *Rasselas*'s "tissue." Belcher invaluably interrupts the fact-fiction binary through which readers generally approach *Rasselas*'s Abyssinian setting by shifting the focus from the empirical details that appear in both *Rasselas* and Johnson's source texts to more abstract connections that were forged between them as African discourse moved from contact zones into contact narratives into Johnson's imagination.[12] As a result of this discursive possession, Belcher argues, *Rasselas* features women whose intellectual faculties and political savvy are equal to any man's; a melancholic, intellectually inclined man who "goes on a journey with a friend, and has a devoted sister who is his equal partner"; an Abyssinian scholar born in the Highlands near the Nile who takes on a young man as his pupil; and a man who believes he can control the source of the Nile.[13] These characters voice Habasha attitudes toward asceticism and self-denial, and *Rasselas*'s setting is structured from their geographical point of view—the source of the Nile is the point of origin for the story (rather than the destination, as one might expect of a European text), and the destination is Egypt rather than Europe, which barely features in the text at all.[14] By redefining what counts as a distinctly African detail, Belcher has changed the terms under which scholars can say Johnson's text was shaped by the African world it purports to represent. However, her focus on how Johnson was unwittingly possessed by African discourse somewhat obscures or at least can't account for the fact that Johnson was both interested and invested in the question of what role local points of view should play in the production of global knowledge.[15]

The source texts for *Rasselas* that Belcher and others have identified, including Lobo, Ludolf, and Le Grand, explicitly wrestle with the question of how African discourse should be weighed against empirical observation and erudition in geographical accounts. As I will show, Johnson's translations of Le Grand's dissertations suggest that he was not only aware of these quandaries, he was troubled by them as well. Although Johnson did champion consulting one's senses and relying on one's own experience to revise what one might have learned through books or armchair speculation, he also demonstrated an acute sensitivity to the constraints of empiricism as a method, of the eyewitness as a figure, and of narrative as a mediating device.[16] Johnson's engagement with the African impression as a figure of thought suggests that he ultimately considered an accurate geographical description to be one that is not simply correct but distinct—that captures the unique character of a place—and a useful geographical description to be one that prompts reflection. To meet these goals, both writers and readers need to rely on their imaginations as well as their reason and senses to generate a coherent and defined though never stable spatial image out of the movement among a variety of local and global points of view.

African Expressions as Distinct Ideas in Johnson's Translations of Le Grand's Dissertations on Abyssinia

For such an avid and lifelong consumer of travel narratives and other geographical texts, Johnson's attitude toward the genres could be surprisingly ambivalent.[17] "Few books disappoint their readers more than the narrations of travellers," Johnson wrote in *Idler* 97.[18] We sit down to read them with the hopes that they will "enlarge our knowledge and rectify our opinions," but all we find are "such general accounts as leave no distinct idea behind them, or such minute enumerations as few can read with either profit or delight." This is in part because travelers themselves don't spend enough time learning about the places they're reporting on. They simply survey them quickly, jot down some sweeping observations, and depart. Or, conversely, they write in painful detail about the topography, architecture, antiquities, or superficial beauties of a place but fail to synthesize any of those minutiae into anything useful.[19] Either way, they "bring home" no "incidents" or "reflections" to their readers nor offer any "distinct idea" of the place—a sense of its unique, local character. As such, Johnson told Boswell, he often simply skipped over great chunks of travel narratives and geographical texts because they offered nothing to advance the intellect.[20]

In a reversal of Johnson's praise of Lobo, *Idler* 97 disparages travel writers who only consult their senses and not their imaginations, though the type of "imagination" called for here is not the faculty that leads impressionable minds astray but the faculty by which one combines ideas to form novel concepts, as Johnson describes in *Idler* 44 and in the *Dictionary*.[21] Johnson certainly championed consulting one's senses and relying on one's own experience to revise what one might have learned through books or armchair speculation. And he was curious about expeditions like those of James Cook and Joseph Banks, the purpose of which was to scientifically quantify as much of the world as possible.[22] But in Ian Donaldson's words, he could also be disdainful of the value of "mere observation," which, as *Idler* 97 shows, yielded only a generic overview or a catalogue of facts.[23] Observations don't become useful until they are framed in such a way as to give the traveler and the reader something to reflect on—an idea unique enough to either change or reconfirm their prior beliefs—which is a process that requires intellectual heavy lifting from the traveler in situ, the traveler as writer, and the reader. Johnson was also sensible of the fact that a great deal of what there was to know about a place couldn't be learned from observation at all. Even the "most diligent and sagacious Traveller" will struggle to "obtain any Knowledge of the History, Government, or Religion of a People, without Skill in their Language" and from "conversing with those who might best inform him."[24] Complicating matters further, locals are not mere objects of observation and representation but subjects who might refuse to be "communicative and sincere" and who might bar travelers "from the View of those Places which most excite their Curiosity."

Thus, for a traveler writer to create a distinct idea of a place for their reader, they ideally needed to employ a range of representational strategies, not simply write down what they saw as they saw it. Johnson faced firsthand the complexities involved in transforming "*travel* into *travel narrative*," to borrow Anne Thell's words, when writing his *Voyage to the Western Islands of Scotland*, and analyses of the resultant text have revealed how seriously Johnson took his multifaceted theory of what geographical representation was supposed to accomplish.[25] One of his own narrative strategies was to shuttle the reader through a range of points of view at a range of scales, some distant, sweeping, and expansive, and some narrow and particular, some observations Johnson's own and some borrowed from others.[26] At times he plays the scientific observer; elsewhere he represents himself more as the passive recipient of the scene laid out before him.[27] He doesn't trumpet sensory perception over all other ways of acquiring knowledge about a place, particularly since he is interested in Scotland's history and people, not just its scenery. (In *Idler* 97 he puts generic landscapes in the same category as superficial descriptions.) In fact, he legitimately entertains local accounts of the second sight as a means of investigating the limitations of sensory perception, expressing the belief that specific locations could act upon the mind through some pathway other than the senses.[28] Thell, Poovey, Mack, and Taylor have all described how he at times adopts the point of view of the Highlanders, closing the gap, as Mack puts it, between "two registers of experience: that of the observer and that of the observed."[29] Because both are limited, both are necessary for generating in narrative what is unattainable in reality. And it is, of course, imagination that enables Johnson and his reader to shift among and synthesize these many scales and perspectives.[30] As Boswell describes it, Johnson's intellectual strength came from the fact that he "united a most logical head with a most fertile imagination," which enabled him to "reason close or wide, as he saw best for the moment," and in the *Journey*, he asks the same of his readers.[31]

Recognizing how nuanced Johnson thinking was about the role of observation and experience in travel and geographical writing enables us to return to *Rasselas*'s representation of Abyssinia with fresh eyes and see how the text might be engaging a wide definition of geographical knowledge and not simply imitating or diverging from eyewitness accounts. Like Johnson's travel narrative, *Rasselas*'s setting is assembled through a range of spatial and temporal scopes, from the unbounded to the constrained, and through a range of points of view, from the distant and disembodied to the local and subjective. In titling his book *The History of Rasselas, Prince of Abissinia*, Johnson flags it as a story that is as much about a place as it is about a person, and the text's opening pages bear this out. Chapter 1 is not a description of Rasselas himself, who doesn't appear in any substantive way until the second chapter, but rather a "Description of a palace in a valley" and a description of a valley in a nation and a nation in a continent—layers of abstraction that call to mind geographical texts that move from distant descriptions of continents in general to nations to cities to sites of local interest.[32] The imagery that Johnson uses to move the reader through these layers of abstraction, however, is ineluctably local and breaks out of the tidy categories that European geographical texts use to organize their accounts.

As the segue into *Rasselas*'s opening setting states: "Rasselas was the fourth son of the mighty emperour, in whose dominions the Father of waters begins his course; whose bounty pours down the streams of plenty, and scatters over half the world the harvests of Egypt."[33] The Nile is the central topographical image of Johnson's initial description of the country, but it is not called the "Nile"; it is called the "Father of waters"—what Lobo and others gave as the literal translation of the "Abay."[34] In designating the river this way, Johnson is not merely swapping a Western label for an Abyssinian one. In the description of the Nile that Gorgoryos gave to Ludolf discussed in the previous chapter, the name "Father of Waters" was a metaphor for the way the river gave life to "the Fields of thirsty *Egypt*" and was also an allegory of the centrality of the emperor himself to East African geopolitics: "As it flows along, it takes in all the Rivers great and small with several Torrents, as well Foreign as *Habessinian*, which by the general Tribute, acknowledge him their King."[35] In *Rasselas*, too, the power of the "mighty emperour" is inextricably linked to the Father of Waters. Moving like the river itself, Johnson's description doubles into one image the emperor's geopolitical power ("whose dominions") and the Nile's riches ("whose bounty") and disperses the influence of both far beyond their immediate contexts: the source flows not simply into Egypt but into the crops that Egypt grows and thus into the "half the world" fed by the harvest. This doubling, along with the syntax of the sentence, initially sets up the reader to assume that it is the emperor's dominion and bounty or the Nile's course that "scatters over half the world," recalling the maps that stretched both Abyssinia and the Nile deep into the south and the west of Africa. The end of the sentence reveals that it is the harvest that scatters, but the harvest not only takes its substance from the "bounty" of the emperor/Nile, the bounty is also the grammatical subject that does the scattering, and tracing the chain of cause and effect back to its source reveals the emperor as the prime mover of the whole works. Thus, the narrative that the Habesha circulated that the emperor could literally stop the river's flow into Egypt and pitch Egypt into famine if he deemed it necessary is suggested by these lines as well, which is invoked more explicitly later, Belcher argues, in the astronomer's delusion that he is responsible for monitoring the Nile's annual inundation.[36] What seems like straightforward geographical description—a named nation, Abyssinia, positioned in relation to another named nation, Egypt, along an axis, the Nile, that is in theory a stable control point—turns out to be anything but straightforward because it is simultaneously constructed from an African point of view that is literary and cultural rather than empirical. The setting gains its shape and character from the interplay among the pieces, which results in a graspable geographical idea but not one with fixed boundaries despite the fact that erecting both spatial and epistemological boundaries is ostensibly geography's raison d'être.

This setting is thus not the seventeenth-century Abyssinia of Lobo's eyewitness account either in content or in terms of the prioritization of empirical knowledge that Johnson praised him for. In contrast to Johnson's expansive empire described above and maps that continued to represent Abyssinia as covering as much as a quarter of the continent, Lobo describes an atrophied empire and a monarchy in shambles. Throughout the sixteenth and into the seventeenth centuries, Jesuits continued to send missionaries into Abyssinia in hopes of converting the emperor to Catholicism. Pedro Páez, who resided in Abyssinia from 1603 until his death in 1622, had some success at doing so but with disastrous results in the long run. Za Dengel embraced Catholicism shortly after he took the throne in 1603, leading to a rebellion led by an aristocracy who was either committed to Ethiopian Christianity or uninterested in ceding power to foreigners, or both, which resulted in Za Dengel's death on the battlefield less than a year later. Just prior to his own death, Páez converted Susenyos I, and Lobo arrived shortly after, accompanying Páez's replacement, Afonso Mendes. Despite Susenyos I's apparent sincerity in his adoption of Catholicism, however, much of Lobo's account of his time in Abyssinia is about the resistance the Jesuits faced from the aristocracy (the noblewomen were a particular thorn in his side), who violently rebelled against Susenyos's attempts to make Catholicism the state religion as they had against Za Dengel's and who ultimately forced Susenyos to abdicate.[37] His son and successor, Fasilides, whom Lobo portrayed as a power-hungry usurper, expelled the Jesuits from Abyssinia entirely.[38] Between the devastation that Grahn had wrought on the country and these decades of civil unrest, Abyssinia had been reduced, according to Lobo, to an area "not much bigger than all Spain," now comprised "but of five kingdoms and six provinces."[39] But impressions of the "mighty emperour" of Abyssinia and his vast "dominions" had not disappeared from geographical discourse—they remained an important part of the "distinct idea" of the country. Even as geographers and travel writers began to temper their impressions of Abyssinia's contemporary geographical boundaries, they continued to affirm its historical expansiveness, its territorial reach in Africa, and its economic and ecclesiastical connections to the Holy Lands. Though it may have been only the size of Spain during Lobo's years there, at one time "the empire of Abyssinia hath been one of the largest which history gives us an account of, it extended formerly from the Red-Sea to the kingdom of Congo, and from Egypt to the Indian Sea."[40] Discussions of the extent of the Aksumite Empire, the Queen of Sheba's domains and provenance, and the connections between Abyssinia and Solomonic Jerusalem were still crucial elements of most detailed writings on Abyssinia.

Several of Le Grand's dissertations that accompany his translation of Lobo dwell on these topics at length, including one on the location of Ophir and one on the location of the capital of Sheba. These two dissertations contain descriptions of Abyssinian history and geography that surface in Johnson's Happy Valley in a variety of ways, but they also contain a metadiscourse about the different kinds of evidence that geographers and historians depended on, with Le Grand offering his opinions on how they should be weighed, including local testimony. He examines in depth the African-given evidence for locating Ophir in southeast Africa, and he takes on the question of whether Abyssinians' own claims that the Queen of Sheba hailed from their country are defensible, excerpting in the process a summary and analysis of the historical viability of the *Kebra Nagast* written by Afonso Mendes (Pedro Páez's successor and Lobo's direct superior). The subtle exclusions, inclusions, and shifts in emphasis of Johnson's translations of these dissertations offer insights of their own. They don't provide a window into his thoughts on the location of Ophir or whether the Queen of Sheba was really Abyssinian, but they do suggest he was thinking about these topics carefully and weighing the value of different kinds of geographical evidence and methodologies along with Le Grand.[41] Johnson stated in the introduction to a *Voyage to Abyssinia* that his translation of Lobo's text is more of an "epitome"; he cut fairly liberally from it and from Le Grand's account of what happened after Lobo's own narration ends, including only what he thought would be "useful" or "entertaining" to the reader.[42] But he noted that "an exact translation has been attempted" of the dissertations. He only occasionally paraphrased quotes or condensed descriptions, suggesting he not only paid particularly close attention to those moments in the original text but was also executing a particularly self-conscious judgment when he made changes.

For instance, Le Grand opens his account of the location of Ophir by taking issue with the majority of scholars who have tried to pin down Ophir's location, writing that they depend on sophistry to make their case, that they are "more occupied with displaying their erudition than in seeking the truth," and, as such, "they have built systems according to their fancy, they have supported them with various quotations, and with vague and weak reasonings; which almost always happens when one ventures to assume uncertain facts" (translation mine).[43] Johnson's translation, Joel J. Gold notes, shifts the "force and balance" of this critique, framing it in particularly scathing terms and heaping scorn on the scholars themselves, not just their methods: "All the learned men who have undertaken to treat of this subject have been in more care to make a pompous display of their own erudition, than a discovery of the truth. They have advanced imaginary systems to shew how well they could defend them, and have ransack'd their memories for quotations and their invention for arguments, to support the greatest uncertainties."[44]

Le Grand goes on to list some of their conclusions, citing Benito Arias Montano's infamous parsing of "Parvaim" into "Peru" and noting that others have located Ophir in Saint Domingo, Malacca, or Ceylon. Johnson truncated the already brief attention given to these theories, excising several lines about the manuscripts and maps that espouse them.[45] The critique implicit in the two alterations is characteristic of Johnson's attitudes toward knowledge and learning expressed elsewhere. The learned men here are indulging in imagination of the worst kind and—unlike, for instance, the astronomer in *Rasselas* who falls into similar errors unwittingly—are doing so willfully for the sake of inflating their egos. Johnson was tempted by such impulses himself. Creating imaginary systems to see how well he could defend them was a game for him.[46] In conversation, he apparently derived pleasure from drawing on his massive store of knowledge and quick mind to support ideas merely to see if he could. That he actively suppressed those tendencies in his writing lest he make "errour permanent and pernicious" may account for the level contempt for the scholars themselves that comes through in his translations of Le Grand, and it also suggests a reason for his exclusion of the direct citations of their texts. That he might perpetuate in writing what he perceived to be errors perhaps gave Johnson pause even in a work of translation.

By contrast, both Le Grand and Johnson give the Sofala-Ophir theory its detailed due. Le Grand observes that if the scholars above (Johnson derisively refers to them as "great men" here) had only read João dos Santos's account, they would see that the case for locating Ophir in Sofala is significantly better substantiated.⁴⁷ Le Grand walks through the evidence I describe in the introduction to this book, highlighting the contributions of local informants to the theory, including "the ancient tradition of the country" that the ruins of Great Zimbabwe "are the remains of the magazines of the Queen of Sheba, who, 'tis said, receiv'd all her gold from the mines in this mountain"; "the testimony of the Abyssins who are firmly persuaded that this celebrated queen was of their country"; and the alternate claims of the Swahili that "these magazines were erected by Solomon" himself.⁴⁸ Belcher observes that in his dissertation on Ludolf, Le Grand is hostile to Ludolf's reliance on Gorgoryos's testimony about Ethiopian Christianity, deploying citations of European authorities in an effort to contain and correct what Gorgoryos had to say because it ran counter to Le Grand's own political and religious vision.⁴⁹ Some of this same dismissiveness of the way Abyssinians talked about their own worlds surfaces again in his consideration of the location of Sheba discussed below. However, in the Ophir debate, Le Grand finds the local testimony of Africans themselves a far more credible body of evidence than theorizing about etymologies, using Classical sources to calculate distances, and citing surface-level similarities between the Biblical description of Ophir and what travelers saw in places like Peru and Ceylon.

    Whether Johnson is persuaded that Ophir was in southeast Africa isn't indicated one way or another, but he allows the explanation its full real estate and makes no qualifying comments about it. He likely would have viewed the fieldwork performed by travelers like Santos to be a viable method of inquiry. Johnson took much the same approach to his own historical investigations in Scotland. He was no naïve consumer of what the locals had to say about themselves. In the *Journey* he expresses frustration with the Highlanders' manipulation of the stories they told of Scotland's past, particularly when his different informants contradicted one another, and he was attuned to the fact that by nature of their subject position locals can't objectively observe their own geographies and culture.⁵⁰ But as Mack argues, his solution was not to reject local knowledge and prize the perspective of the eyewitness but to seek epistemological equilibrium between them.⁵¹ I would add that this involved bridging not only two points of view, that of the observer and that of the observed, but many viewpoints, since he received more than one local take on things. And in general he approved of the cycle of discursive accumulation, writing that one should first learn "the intellectual treasures which the diligence of former ages has accumulated" and then "increase them by his own collections," which is precisely what Santos and the others who contributed to the Sofala-Ophir impression endeavored to do.[52] The kind of epistemological approach that produced the Sofala-Ophir impression, in other words, is reasonable and defensible even if does not and couldn't result in objective knowledge.

When Le Grand moves on from the Sofala-Ophir impression to an account of scholastic attempts to pin down the location of Tarshish (another city from which Solomon acquired goods), both his and Johnson's contempt returns: Le Grand observes that these scholars rely on Strabo, Pliny, and Heliodorus— "quoted with great solemnity," Johnson mockingly adds—in order to display their learning rather than to excavate the truth.[53] "Each party exert their utmost abilities to support their sentiments by a great number of authorities," Le Grand notes, to which Johnson adds as his own aside: "In my opinion to very little purpose."[54] The issue at hand for Johnson here is not that these scholars study the ancients, which Johnson thought worthwhile up to a point.[55] But he cautioned against getting caught up in the "inexhaustible amusements" offered by "the fictions of antiquity" and advocated instead for acquiring knowledge oneself by taking advantage of modern methods.[56] The Sofala-Ophir impression, the evidence for it, and the methods used to interpret that evidence seem all the more reasonable with these censures positioned on either side of it, and it is the local testimony that makes the difference. Advocates of the Sofala-Ophir impression relied on mathematical, Classical, and scriptural evidence to support their theory as well, and Le Grand's dissertation includes these details, but they become persuasive only when anchored to what Africans had to say about them. Their testimony is concrete information that has stood up to repeat testing, and it is set in sharp contrast to "imaginary systems" built primarily from sources far removed from the locations in question and linked by an irresponsible application of rationalist methods.

The question of the role that local testimony should play in the production of geographical knowledge is brought even more to the fore in Le Grand's dissertation on the historical location of Sheba's capital, introduced by Le Grand himself and subtly manipulated by Johnson. The dissertation's aim is to lay out the cases for its two most plausible locations, Abyssinia and Yemen. Though Le Grand was convinced that Ophir was in southeast Africa and found the interplay between local testimony and travelers' reports plausible and dependable, he is suspicious of Abyssinian claims that the Queen of Sheba resided in Abyssinia even though the Abyssinians "are persuaded that this celebrated princess reigned amongst them, and shew to this day the ruins of her palace [Aksum]," and even though "their opinion is supported by those who have travelled into Abyssinia."[57] He doesn't consider the Abyssinians themselves knowledgeable about the subject; he calls them too "uncivilized" to be "acquainted with the controversies which divide the learned world into parties." Meanwhile, "most learned interpreters have almost universally agreed to place her in that part of Arabia-the-Happy, known now by the name of Yemen."[58] Johnson puts more weight on the Abyssinians' claims than Le Grand does, adding a transition into this sentence that states that these learned interpreters have agreed to this, "however firmly this notion may be established in Africa." In doing so, he carries over his condemnation of the learned world and their parties from the preceding dissertation into this one and reasserts as a viable alternative the local view on the question that Le Grand temporarily downgraded.[59] For Johnson, the fact that the Abyssinians held onto a very deep, local worldview unshifted by outside theories would have likely increased the worth of what they had to say. Belcher argues that his motivations for translating Lobo and Le Grand in the first place stemmed from his interest in "primitive Christianity," which he believed offered insight into a faith that had been twisted out of shape by modern interpretations of scripture and by the party divides of the European world.[60]

By adding a transition that puts the interpretations of learned Europeans and longstanding African beliefs about their own worlds directly in conversation with one another, Johnson emphasizes that the subsequent debate concerns which is more reliable: local testimony expressed on the ground or European evidence that comes from scholastic sources, particularly if the two conflict. The primary source that Le Grand offers in favor of locating the Queen of Sheba's capital in Abyssinia is Afonso Mendes's *Expeditionis Aethiopicae*, in which Mendes summarizes and then defends the *Kebra Nagast* as a viable historical source for his position. In fact, Le Grand excerpts this entire portion of Mendes's narrative since it captured so precisely Abyssinia's own "particular interest in maintaining that the Queen of Sheba was of their country, for they affirm that their kings are descendants in a right line from her and Solomon."[61] Mendes is skeptical of Abyssinia's claims to house the Ark of the Covenant, but he otherwise sees nothing objectionable in the account the *Kebra Nagast* gives of Makeda herself, her journey to see Solomon, their marriage and her giving birth to his son, and Menelik's traveling back and forth between Abyssinia and Jerusalem, concluding that "though many fables may be detected in the traditions of the Abyssins, it will not be reasonable to conclude that there is nothing true in their history."[62] In addition to the *Kebra Nagast*, Mendes drew from

Páez's writings on and translations of Ethiopian texts and from his own twelve years in Abyssinia to offer evidence that the Habesha version of the story was not only reasonable but probable, citing the grandness of Abyssinia's retinues, the large number of camels that are bred there, the fact that Abyssinia had significantly more gold than Arabia (brought up from its mines in Sofala, he theorized), the fact that their royal line has passed unbroken from father to son, Hebraic retentions in both Abyssinian culture and Christianity, and the ruins of Aksum.[63]

Johnson translated the Mendes excerpt with minimal changes. He inserts a criticism of Mendes at only one point. When Mendes begins to speculate about whether the writers of the scripture would have considered Abyssinia a "Kingdom of the South" relative to Jerusalem, Johnson comments that Mendes is grabbing at anything that will support his argument and that there is nothing in the texts he cites that confirms one way or another what direction Sheba lay.[64] This says more, though, about his disapproval of relying on imaginary systems to support one's argument than about Le Grand's reliance on local testimony. He also cuts a lengthy marginal note from Le Grand running alongside the Mendes excerpt that attempted to correct and qualify Mendes's account by reinterpreting his evidence in a way that supports locating Sheba in Arabia instead of Abyssinia. The marginal note tempered Mendes's claims about the size of Abyssinia and the extent of its gold and challenged Abyssinia's account of the unbroken nature of the Solomonic dynasty by suggesting that Abyssinian elites simply put whoever best suited their agendas on the throne and that the bloodline had also been highly diluted because the crown could pass to illegitimate children.[65] Of these points only the last is incorporated in some form in Johnson's translation. He inserts a sentence a few paragraphs later acknowledging that Mendes is mistaken that the crown always passes to the first-born son, but he excludes Le Grand's remarks about bastards and puppet kings, affording the Abyssinians and their governing system a level of dignity that Le Grand does not.[66]

Despite Le Grand's inclination to locate Sheba in Yemen—or at least his resistance to locating it in Abyssinia—his account of that justification is much briefer and contains no local testimony except the remark that "the Arabs show ruins of the palace of Sheba in their own country with equal confidence; nor would it be less dangerous in Arabia, to affirm that Sheba was Abyssinia, than in Abyssinia, to maintain that it was Arabia."[67] Samuel Bochart's *Geographia Sacra* (1651) is his authoritative source, but, in contrast to the several pages he excerpted directly from Mendes, he only offers a few paragraphs summarizing the Classical sources and quoting passages of scripture that Bochart cites. Johnson shifted this balance even further, cutting these summaries and Biblical quotes.[68] The effect of Johnson's changes to Le Grand's dissertation on the location of the capital of Sheba is consistent with Johnson's tendency throughout the whole of *Voyage to Abyssinia*, as both Belcher and Gold note, not only to prioritize African worldviews by minimizing digressions that move too far into European intellectual or political concerns but also to defend Africans by stripping or neutralizing Lobo and Le Grand's negative commentary and by introducing words, asides, and transitions that make clear his disapproval of the Europeans' behaviors and attitudes toward Abyssinian peoples and knowledge.[69] In particular, Johnson's implicit defense of the *Kebra Nagast* as a source of knowledge if not a source of truth is at least partially explained by his respect for literacy and books.[70] Part of his frustration with gleaning testimony from the Scottish Highlanders, as Poovey explains, was a lack of written records that preserve cultural memory.[71]

Overall, the effect of Le Grand's presentation of the two cases for Sheba's location is curious because although he seeks in some ways to discredit or at least temper Abyssinian testimony, he implicitly recognizes the preponderance of evidence in favor of their case, justifying Johnson's added transition about how "firmly this notion" was "established in Africa." That he excerpts Mendes directly means—as Belcher notes about Le Grand's treatment of Gorgoryos—that he has enshrined a remarkable amount of African discourse into his account regardless of whether he found it persuasive.[72] In the end he actually validates the case in a sense, citing another common theory that Abyssinia and southern Yemen were once "one empire," and thus concluding that "these opinions, so contrary in appearance, may be made consistent without great difficulty."[73] He advocates for the Arabian claim in the sense that he argues the Abyssinians originated from Yemen and not the other way around, but academically it remains an open question of whether the Queen of Sheba had her seat on the African side or the Arabian side of the Red Sea. And formally, Makeda's empire dominates the dissertation not only in terms of length but also in making Abyssinia's "Sheba" a fully fleshed out place, animated with characters and a plot, giving it much more imaginative grip than Le Grand's passing remarks about Asia. It offers a "distinct idea" of Abyssinia, whereas the case for locating Sheba in Yemen offers virtually no distinct idea about Yemen itself, and it adheres to Johnson's preference that history and geography be written through events, which made the subjects more pleasurable to learn and their content easier to remember.[74]

Ultimately, Le Grand's dissertations would have been one of several ways that Johnson was exposed to impressions of Abyssinia's ancient past and Biblical ties. That they are simultaneously about how to weigh African expressions among other kinds of evidence makes it reasonable to conclude that these inquiries would have been inextricable for Johnson just as they were for each of his source texts. His translation choices don't indicate that he believed these arguments, but they do indicate that as he closely engaged with their content, he was also thinking about their form and considering in particular the role that local testimony or points of view should play in the production of geographical and historical knowledge. They furthermore suggest he found these local points of view worthy of serious consideration or at least that he did not put them in the same category as the other kinds of nonempirical evidence of which he could be so critical.

Abyssinia Close and Wide: Perspectival Multiplicity and Johnson's Happy Valley

The distinct ideas of Abyssinia that arose from Le Grand's dissertations carry over into *Rasselas*. This wider view of Abyssinia's geography governs, for instance, many of the details of Imlac's history, in which Abyssinia is situated at the center of a great network of material and intellectual exchange. Imlac's father is "a wealthy merchant, who traded between the inland countries of Africk and the ports of the Red Sea."[75] This image situates Abyssinia at the center of a trade world that includes not only Sofala to the south, Egypt to the north, and Arabia and the East Indies to the east, but also the country's western borders, which were presumed to extend all the way to the "kingdom of Congo," as Lobo said, and to Timbuktu. (In fact, as chapter 3 shows, Ludolf was one of the people who argued, based on Gorgoryos's testimony, that the Niger was a western branch of the Nile.)[76] The Nile itself features prominently at the center of Imlac's geographical account as it did the center of *Rasselas*'s initial description of the country: Imlac's family—the node through which all this trade passes—hails from Gojjam, "at no great distance from the fountain of the Nile."[77] Imlac himself opted to travel east not in hope of accumulating riches via these routes as his father had but in search of knowledge.[78] His travels bring him through India, Persia, Arabia, and Palestine, and then back to Abyssinia.

The ease with which Imlac is able to make this voyage recalls not only the ancient days when merchants like the wise Tamrin traveled the world trading on Makeda's behalf but the era before Adal and other Islamic nations cut off

Abyssinia's access to the Holy Lands and essentially halted what Le Grand calls the Abyssinian "Addict[ion] to pilgrimages."[79] Jerusalem is a contact zone in *Rasselas* between Abyssinians and Europeans, as it had been in the fourteenth and fifteenth centuries. There, Imlac learns about the martial and naval prowess of European nations that rulers like Eleni would later bank on when they asked for aid in reopening the route to the Holy Lands. He also learns about Europe's questionable taste for "plant[ing] colonies" and "giv[ing] laws to" other nations' "natural princes," an anticolonial sentiment Johnson expressed in other writings on Africa in which he criticized Europe for building "forts upon ground to which they had no right."[80] However, *Rasselas* is not a book about Europe. If Europe has a role to play in marking the geographical scope of Imlac's journey and in orienting Abyssinia in its global context, it is only to signal the fringe of a world that extends far beyond Africa but that still puts an African nation at the center not simply of the narrative but of the routes through which the world's material and intellectual riches circulated.

Likewise, the Happy Valley is full of architectural marvels, books, spices, gold, and other treasures—the kinds of sumptuous material goods that the Queen of Sheba supplied to and brought home from Jerusalem. If Álvares's informants were to be believed, Aksum was her capital city, with its palaces, fountains, and the Church of Our Lady Mother of Zion. The church "has a large enclosure, and it is also surrounded by another large enclosure, like the wall of a large town or city. Within this enclosure are handsome habitations of terraced buildings," including "two palaces" and "a large ruin, built in a square, which in other times was a house, and it has at each angle large stone pillars, squared and wrought."[81] This church houses the copy of the *Kebra Nagast* that Álvares encountered, and according to the excerpt from Mendes quoted in Le Grand's dissertation, the Ark of the Covenant and one of its tablets is "still preserved in the Church of Axuma, the chief of the Abyssinian churches." Telles writes that the priests jealously guard these, always keeping them "close and concealed."[82]

The main palace of the Happy Valley is likewise "divided into many squares or courts," and it is "so large as to be fully known to none but some ancient officers who successively inherited the secrets of the place." It was "built as if suspicion herself had dictated the plan."[83] These ancient officers guard the places "in which a long race of monarchs had reposited their treasure," which is enclosed in the palace's marble columns, "never to be removed but in the utmost exigencies of the kingdom." They also "record their accumulations in a book which was itself concealed in a tower not entered but by the emperor, attended by the prince who stood next in succession."⁸⁴ The "accumulations" recorded in the book refer to material wealth, but the *Kebra Nagast* was also a book of accumulations of a different kind, so important to Abyssinians, as Le Grand noted, because they "maintain that the Queen of Sheba was of their country, for they affirm that their kings are descendants in a right line from her and Solomon."⁸⁵ The Aksum-like space of the palace, the cherished book, the treasure that is locked up tight and guarded "from century to century," and the "long race of monarchs" described in this passage depend on and reiterate Abyssinia's claims to this lineage.

These details about the Happy Valley serve no purpose to the plot and are never revisited. None of the characters reflect on them the way they do other aspects of the Happy Valley like its animals, greenery, artisans, and entertainments, and at no other point in *Rasselas* is such a distinct idea of a place given without serving some obvious purpose, like the description of the pyramids. They only set the scene. But since that is their essential function, they invite the reader to consider what setting such a scene entails. Giving the distinct idea of a place requires the traveler, geographer, or historian—or the poet, for that matter—to picture it at a range of scales and from a range of perspectives and to find the right words to recreate that three-dimensionality. As Imlac says, the poet "must be conversant with all that is awfully vast and elegantly little" and utilize his skills to produce representations that are neither so tiresomely detailed that they "number the streaks of the tulip" nor so generic that lack the "prominent and striking features, as recal the original to every mind."⁸⁶ Such "prominent striking features" have similar characteristics to the "distinct idea" that Johnson sought in travel writing—they are generalized, but they lose their illustrative function if they are too generalized. And, indeed, Imlac states that he has brought this kind of attention to "every country [he has] surveyed," the descriptions of which he recounts for Rasselas just prior to this "dissertation upon poetry."⁸⁷ Johnson likewise brings this level of attention to the setting of *Rasselas*: he takes the reader from the limitless borders of Abyssinia's empire to the inside of a locked box in "a palace in a valley," and he places the narrative's events in an extensive history by contextualizing them through Abyssinia's "long race of monarchs" (in fact, the first edition of *Rasselas* called them a "long race of successive monarchs"), the continuity of which was preserved by placing the heirs in royal prisons.⁸⁸ The task Johnson sets for himself in *Rasselas*'s opening pages is that of the poet but also that of the geographer and the historian: to put parameters around the potentially boundless arenas of space and time in order to produce a microcosm of reality upon which the reader can reflect for the purpose of advancing the intellect. But Johnson doesn't model any tidy or even systematized method for completing this task—for instance, endorse a list of steps one could follow in order to guarantee the production of accurate and useful knowledge. He continually sets the reader up to confront the fact that no stable point of view will enable one to fully compass a place. The text's geographical descriptions demand a near constant nimbleness of thought.

Johnson's description of the geological contours of the Happy Valley is an example of this. Within the narrative's internal logic, nothing in the text seems to be so emblematic of an observable and thus knowable world as the physicality of the Happy Valley, particularly if, as Michael Karounos suggests, Johnson used different typography to distinguish the "Happy Valley" as a "location in space" from the *"happy valley"* as a generalized concept.[89] In fact, the Happy Valley's insistent materiality is fundamental to the novel's foundational plot point. Without it, Rasselas would not be trapped. As Johnson describes it,

> The place, which the wisdom or policy of antiquity had destined for the residence of the Abissinian princes, was a spacious valley in the kingdom of Amhara, surrounded on every side by mountains of which the summits overhang the middle part. The only passage by which it could be entered, was a cavern that passed under a rock, of which it has long been disputed whether it was the work of nature or of human industry. The outlet of the cavern was concealed by a thick wood, and the mouth which opened into the valley was closed with gates of iron, forged by the artificers of ancient days, so massy that no man could, without the help of engines, open or shut them.[90]

Furthermore, if the Happy Valley were not an observable and knowable spatial materiality, Rasselas would never have been able to escape it, at least not by the methods he uses, which are frequently understood as central to the text's epistemological commentary.[91] It is not until Rasselas begins to experientially and empirically engage with the physical landscape—examining every inch of the "bars of nature" that surround him, clambering through every nook and cranny of the mountains, caves, and trees, and tracing the course of the river to see how it escapes—that his eventual solution is set in motion.[92] Because he put the work into fully investigating the Happy Valley, when he and Imlac later observe a coney burrowing through the prominence, the solution seems immediately clear: they, too, dig a hole through the overhang and thus solve at least one problem that the Happy Valley presents.

However, as Oscar Kenshur has argued, what the reader of *Rasselas* is asked to grapple with epistemologically is not always the same as what the characters are asked to confront.[93] Though it may be oversimplifying the matter to claim that *Rasselas*'s "empiricist program" is frequently "at odds with" its "mode of narration" (since Johnson's attitude toward the role that narration and imagination played in the production of empirical knowledge was complex), Rasselas and the reader are not performing the same intellectual task in these scenes. As Rasselas surveys the material form of the Happy Valley, the reader is surveying a description of it and assembling a mental picture of a place they have never been. And what emerges from this interpretive work is a composite of different eyewitness descriptions of Ethiopia's royal prisons that maps back over nothing that can be found anywhere in the physical world. It is a place that can only exist in the imagination. Most accounts of the royal prisons that circulated in European literature situate them on top of an *amba*, which is inaccessible not only due to its completely sheer sides but also because it can be crowned by an overhang like a mushroom or an umbrella, as reported in Castanhoso's description of Debre Damo and adopted by writers like Urreta for his Hill Amara and Milton for his gate to Paradise. As Sabla Wangel's descent showed, the only way up or down was via a guarded hole tunneled through the rock. Álvares was the one person who reported that the royal prison was in a valley between two mountains closed up with a gate, but he makes no mention of overhangs.

Others have noted that Johnson combined these features of different accounts of the royal prisons into one space—essentially turning Debre Damo inside out so the "summits overhang the middle part."[94] But little consideration has been given to how challenging if not impossible it is to picture the result of this combination all at once. Had Johnson simply adopted Álvares's valley and given it a gate on each end, that would be one thing. But the Happy Valley has only one entrance dug through a cavern. Where it originates is never explained, and it is difficult to find a logical place for it in the exterior landscape. The valley is not only fully enclosed; Johnson has it fully ringed by an inward-projecting lip. Contra Tomarken's remark that the Happy Valley is "subject to the laws of geography," it has no existent corollary.[95] A cirque might have an overhang on its backwall, but not even the most impressive is surrounded on every side, and craters and calderas have no overhangs. Critics who have attempted to redescribe the Happy Valley in different physical terms than Johnson did, or even to draw a diagram of it in an effort to remove for their readers some of the imaginative work that Johnson forced on his own, inevitably end up reiterating the point at hand. Such efforts appeal, as Johnson does, to the reader's ability to draw from a storehouse of geological images and recombine them to picture what is being redescribed.[96] Thus, the place in the text that seems the most material, measurable, and empirically knowable for the characters turns out for the reader to be, of all the text's settings, the least connectable to anything in the world. As such, the Abyssinian "real fact" that seems like Johnson's most overt and straightforward empirical borrowing from travel writing turns out to require a great deal of imaginative work from the reader. Without it, the Happy Valley doesn't exist. Physical contours of a place can be mapped and measured, and Johnson called for travelers to do just that. But that only results in knowledge about those physical contours—it doesn't offer a stable or comprehensive truth about the geography of which they are only a part, the circumscription of which could vary enormously depending on whether one is reasoning narrow and wide and whether they are approaching geographical space as a mere container for human life or something that is constructed from it.

Knowing the Nile: Reflections on Uncircumscribable Geographies

If distinct ideas of places are meant to foster reflection, the reflection that *Rasselas*'s representation of Abyssinia provokes is reflexive, cautioning the reader that no single, stable point of view offers complete knowledge of the world. Scholars have recognized that the impossibility of reasoning narrow and wide, of grasping all at once "all that is vast and elegantly little," is one of the text's central concerns, as is the epistemological overwhelm that results from trying to hold too much in one's head simultaneously without a stable frame to hold it in place.[97] Returning for a moment to Imlac's dissertation on poetry: as his account of what a poet must know grows and grows, he enters into such an "enthusiastic fit" that Rasselas panics and halts him, crying out, "Enough!" and adding, "Thou hast convinced me, that no human being can ever be a poet."[98] In terms of the text's geographical commentaries, Johnson stages these concerns through recurrent images of the Nile, which—as an object that both provoked a desire for geographical knowledge and insistently eluded it—serves as the central and unifying symbol in Johnson's articulation of various characters' epistemological aspirations and foibles.

Most obvious is the role the Nile plays in illustrating the astronomer's delusions that he can control the weather, which, as Belcher has argued, he specifically manipulates in order to regulate the Nile's flow and inundation.[99] The cause of the inundation of the Nile was, along with the location of its source, one of the Western world's geographical obsessions. The astronomer has come up with an answer, but, like the learned men Johnson was so hostile toward in his translation of Le Grand's dissertation, it is substantiated entirely through an imaginary system, arising not from time spent observing the Nile itself but from forty years of studying "the motions and appearances of the celestial bodies" and "draw[ing] out his soul in endless calculations."[100] As he tells Imlac, at first he simply entertained the question of whether he could control the Nile, but the notion entirely took him over. He "sat days and nights in an imaginary dominion, pouring upon this country and that the showers of fertility" until one day he decided to attempt to "raise the Nile to an inundation."[101] The rain he commanded does fall, and from this loosest of correlations he begins to believe that his imaginary system accurately reflects reality. Though the astronomer himself does not have the ostentatious arrogance of the learned men who are inventing imaginary systems to show how erudite they are and then supporting them for the fun of it, his inquiries have similarly led him to radically overestimate both his power and his understanding. His theory explains nothing about the Nile; it is only a monument to the ease with which people can persuade themselves of the truth and viability of their theories even when their application to the world results in an absurd conclusion. Because the astronomer is not an object of contempt, Johnson's staging of where his thinking went wrong isn't a negative comment on abstract or erudite knowledge itself. The astronomer attributes his integrity, which is not in doubt, to the acquisition of this knowledge, and Imlac says that he "always found new cause for admiration in the profundity of [the astronomer's] mind. His comprehension is vast, his memory capacious and retentive, his discourse is methodical, and his expression clear."[102] But, as Nekayah and Pekuah ultimately bring him to realize, his error is that he has "passed [his] time in study without experience; in the attainment of sciences which can, for the most part, be but remotely useful to mankind."[103] More direct observation of and engagement with the world around him eventually allow him to regulate his thinking.

Yet the text doesn't necessarily offer more empirical, observer-dependent methods for producing practical geographical knowledge as sound alternatives to the astronomer's imaginary system, as illustrated most dramatically through the global fantasy of *Rasselas*'s would-be aviator. In an effort to muster Rasselas's enthusiasm for his flying machine, the aviator trumpets the benefits of viewing the world from the widest and most encompassing angle possible:

You, Sir, whose curiosity is so extensive, will easily conceive with what pleasure a philosopher, furnished with wings, and hovering in the sky, would see the earth, and all its inhabitants, rolling beneath him, and presenting to him successively, by its diurnal motion, all the countries within the same parallel. How must it amuse the pendent spectator to see the moving scene of land and ocean, cities and deserts! To survey with equal security the marts of trade, and the fields of battle; mountains infested by barbarians, and fruitful regions gladdened by plenty, and lulled by peace! How easily shall we then trace the Nile through all his passage; pass over to distant regions, and examine the face of nature from one extremity of the earth to the other![104]

It is not by happenstance that the Nile is both the orientation point for and the climactic image of this fantasy. It remained one of global exploration's event horizons. Even if some believed that the source had, indeed, been seen by travelers like Páez and Lobo, its course had not been charted. Cartographers still used written and oral evidence to place it on maps. A view from above, the aviator suggests, would enable one to objectively determine the Nile's course once and for all, erasing uncertainty and eradicating the need to work through multiple existent and contextually dependent narratives about the river in order to grasp it oneself or map it for others. The pendant spectator's description mirrors what maps were increasingly called on to be, or so thought geographers like John Green, who contended that "the Eye will learn more in one Hour by Observation, than the Ear will benefit in a day by discourse."[105] One could sate one's curiosity about the world "easily," "from one extremity of the earth to the other," at a glance without ever leaving one's study.

The geographical goal toward which the aviator strives stands in stark opposition to the text's initial representation of the Nile, in which the river was made intelligible through its symbolic relationship to Abyssinia and its mighty emperor. To attain his epistemological goal, the pendent spectator doesn't need to bother with such local points of view. But the text is doubtful of both the plausibility and the value of this goal. If the aviator's non sequitur that humans can fly even though they are not birds because they can swim even though they are not fish doesn't clue the reader into this, the fact that his wings don't hold him even for a moment does. "In an instant" he "dropped into the lake," his hypothetical perspective on the world impossible to attain let alone sustain.[106] And if he were able to sustain it and reproduce it through a map or a purely empirical description, such texts, Johnson once told Boswell, are not so much "read" as "consulted," their content gleaned rather than contemplated.[107] Thus, they are useful in a practical sense but not particularly useful in terms of what Johnson expected geographical discourse and travel writing to offer readers in the interest of advancing their intellect.

Even if one could attain the aviator's altitude and thus acquire a snapshot of the earth's vastness, one would lose sight of all the variety that comprises it. Realistically, to see the entirety of the Nile, one would also need to be too high to see "with equal security the marts of trade, and the fields of battle; mountains infested by barbarians, and fruitful regions gladdened by plenty, and lulled by peace." In contrast to the aviator's fantasy that one could "easily . . . trace the Nile through all his passage" if he could only arrive at the right vantage point, Nekayah describes the epistemological overwhelm inherent in the fact that, as she says later, "No man can, at the same time, fill his cup from the source and from the mouth of the Nile."[108] Following their respective investigations into whether public or domestic life is happier, Rasselas and Nekayah compare notes "in a private summer-house on the banks of the Nile."[109] The setting asks the reader to imagine the river not from above but through the subject position of the characters and frames their subsequent conversation through the epistemological and representational instability the Nile has raked up. At one point, Rasselas accuses Nekayah of arriving at a formal fallacy in her comparison of marriage and celibacy—she suggests that each is worse than the other.[110] In explaining herself, Nekayah resuscitates the aviator's fantasy of objectivity and reiterates its impossibility:

> To the mind, as to the eye, it is difficult to compare with exactness objects vast in their extent and various in their parts. Where we see or conceive the whole at once we readily note the discriminations and decide the preference: but of two systems of which neither can be surveyed by any human being in its full compass of magnitude and multiplicity of complication, where is the wonder, that judging of the whole by parts, I am alternately affected by one and the other as either presses on my memory or fancy?[111]

As Nekayah observes, something as vast and various as "the earth, and all its inhabitants" that the aviator longs to simultaneously view could never be "surveyed by any human being in its full compass of magnitude and multiplicity of complication."

As part of Nekayah's struggle with this issue, Johnson addresses the limitations of the highly situated, local geographical perspective that the reader has implicitly been inhabiting, viewing the world through Nekayah's eyes. Frustrated by her inability to gain any insight into what it means to live a happy life, Nekayah attempts to command the Nile to reveal a sure truth to her, just as the aviator attempted to fix its course from above. Nekayah "cast her eyes upon the river that flowed before her. 'Answer,' said she, 'great father of waters, thou that rollest thy floods through eighty nations, to the invocations of the daughter of thy native king. Tell me if thou waterest, through all thy course, a single habitation from which thou dost not hear the murmurs of complaint?'"[112] For Neyakah, in this moment at least, the Nile is not a geological feature that can been seen from above, its contours mapped in the way the aviator dreams. It is the "father of waters," the emblem of her own father's power, a symbol of the expansiveness of Abyssinia, a great uniter but also a river that passes through various "habitations." She gains her identity from it as the daughter of the emperor, and she hopes it will respond to her "invocations" just as it allegedly does her father's. But Nekayah doesn't have any more success at extracting knowledge out of the river than the aviator did. She and Rasselas give up on the conversation once Imlac arrives and coaxes them out to see the pyramids.

Throughout this literary survey on the Nile, any given epistemological frame or point of view breaks when the characters push it too far. The text concedes that each has its merits, but only as a temporary container to hold what is otherwise a liquid idea, as reiterated by *Rasselas*'s frustrating and enigmatic ending. The penultimate chapter seems to offer a notion in which the characters can rest secure: that one should turn one's attentions to the "choice of eternity" rather than the "choice of life," as Nekayah expresses.[113] However, if this is indeed what one should do, it is not what Nekayah or any of the other characters actually do. By the last chapter—"the conclusion, in which nothing is concluded"—Nekayah, Pekuah, and Rasselas are fantasizing once again about their "various schemes of happiness," all of which involve limiting the scope of their fields of knowledge and experience in some way or another. They themselves are bound by the inundation of the Nile that has risen around their house, but their fantasies are free to spin out into imaginary systems. Pekuah desires to retreat into a monastery to contemplate a pious life, "fixed in some variable state." Nekayah resolves to "found a college of learned women" and produce "models of prudence, and patterns of piety." Rasselas "desire[s] a little kingdom in which he might administer justice in his own person, and see all the parts of government with his own eyes." Tellingly, however, "he could never fix the limits of his dominion, and was always adding to the number of his subjects."[114] Thus, the imagery of the text comes full circle—a kingdom and a river that will not stay in their bounds. The travelers "resolved, when the inundation should cease, to return to Abissinia," but it is left entirely open whether they do so. As the symbol throughout the text of the impossibility of attaining epistemological stability, the inundations of the Nile will never cease. The only indication as to the course their futures will take is Imlac's and the astronomer's understanding that they will continue to be "driven along the stream of life." Hence, "the conclusion" eludes the characters and the readers, narratively and epistemologically.

Yet it would be a mistake to walk away from *Rasselas* with a pessimistic or futile view of either the writing or the study of other times and places. Through narrative and imagination, Johnson succeeds in creating a distinct idea of Abyssinia and the Nile, and these efforts offer the reader something on which to reflect. The Nile is an intelligible artifact in *Rasselas* that serves an orienting function for the reader. It has no definite topographical contours, but it has meaningful associations. It enables the reader to compass the text's Abyssinian setting even though that setting itself essentially has no boundaries, its "bounty pour[ing] down the streams of plenty, and scatter[ing] over half the world." Attaining a sense of the vastness and the variety of the world requires synthesizing many perspectives from varying angles and at varying levels of depth (from locked boxes to half the world) and then endeavoring to imagine the way everything fits together. This can be highly frustrating, as Rasselas and Nekayah learn, but it can be delightful as well, enabling the reader to develop the kind of detailed yet comprehensive sense of a place that for Johnson made geographical texts worth writing and reading. Johnson may have felt acutely the limitations of human perception and of the human mind to grasp fully or simultaneously all that is "awfully vast and elegantly little," and he fretted about representing the world for others in a way that might perpetuate pernicious factual or moral errors, but he also found satisfaction in uniting his logical head with his fertile imagination and picturing the world anew.

No other setting would have lent itself so well to facilitating this intellectual exercise. Johnson depends on Abyssinia's long history and expansive geography and the fact that local points of view were accessible through their unique textual tradition as well as through the accounts of travel writers who had confirmed those local points of view over time. His knowledge of the country enabled him to create a world that was distant enough from Europe to prompt comparison, fleshed out enough to give readers something to reflect on, and material enough to keep his imaginative investigations tied to the real debates about historiography and geographical method that underpin his source texts. A vaguely oriental setting would not have allowed him to do this and neither would a utopia or a setting that was simply supposed to be Europe relocated. Impressions of Abyssinia and the expressions that comprise them—the "several real facts concerning the country" that are "interwoven" into "the tissue" of the story—are crucial to *Rasselas*, not simply on an aesthetic level, though they serve that purpose as well, but in how they undergird the articulation of some of the narrative's most central themes and aims.

6

"DESCENDED FROM THE QUEEN OF SABA"

African Women as Geographical Authorities in James Bruce's *Travels to Discover the Source of the Nile*

In 1769 James Bruce arrived in northeast Africa with the intent of discovering the source of the Nile. Though it took him until 1790 to publish his five-volume account of the journey, stories of his exploits circulated almost immediately upon his return to Europe.[1] Bruce was at first hailed for having performed invaluable services on behalf of science and navigation, particularly on the continent, where figures like the Comte de Buffon praised his attention to detail and the wealth of drawings, specimens, and geographical data he brought back with him. However, public opinion quickly degenerated. The London literati were skeptical of Bruce's claims that he effortlessly ingratiated himself into the court at Gondar due to his vast medical knowledge and his knack for acquiring Ethiopian languages. Some, including Samuel Johnson, took particular umbrage with Bruce's report of how Abyssinian military officers would cut steaks from the rumps of live cattle and then stitch the cattle back up again and send them out to pasture. Particularly galling to Bruce were those who pointed out that Bruce hadn't discovered the source of the Nile at all—that Pedro Páez and Jerónimo Lobo had been there more than a hundred years before him.[2] Horace Walpole circulated an oft-repeated anecdote that captures the skepticism and ridicule to which Bruce was subject: during a dinner party, one of the guests asked Bruce if he saw any musical instruments in Abyssinia. "Musical instruments," said Bruce, and paused—"Yes I think I remember one lyre." The dinner guest then leaned to his neighbor and whispered, "I am sure there is one less since he came out of the country."[3] Bruce thus earned his reputation as the Abyssinian Liar, and his account became a test case for what it means to tell the truth about the world.[4]

Once Bruce finally began to write his narrative in the late 1780s, he was fueled at least in part by defensive indignation. He leaned heavily on his status as a traveler and eyewitness to ratify his knowledge and was not hesitant to call out his detractors for being mere armchair geographers. When informed of the scorn people showed for his account of the cow butchering, Bruce recounted, "I asked the reason of this disbelief and was answered, that people who had never been out of their own country, and others well acquainted with the manners of the world, for they had travelled as far as France, had agreed the thing was impossible, and therefore it was so." This was likely a jab at Johnson, who was still considered by many to be an authority on Abyssinia even though he had never been there.[5] Of all the travelers considered in this book, Bruce is the closest to Mary Louise Pratt's seeing man. He transformed himself into what Nigel Leask calls "a mobile recording machine even when this was rendered difficult by both his cultural disguise and the rigours of transporting delicate instruments over rough terrain."[6] He carried a range of instruments for measuring, calculating, and encoding the interior of Africa, including quadrants, telescopes, barometers and thermometers, and parallactic instruments, and he was particularly fond of his camera obscura, the artificial eye that enabled him to capture the landscape with such precision. Brash, brave, and manly (his self-aggrandizement didn't endear him to his critics either), Bruce also set the tone for many travelers to come—the Livingstones, Stanleys, Burtons, and Spekes—who would portray themselves or be portrayed as simultaneously intimate with their African hosts and guides and vastly superior to them in intellect and civility.[7] Leask reads Bruce's reliance on his claims to empiricism, his self-characterization as a both a gentleman and a manly adventurer, his fervent rejection of what previous travelers had to say, and the sheer length of his narrative as the primary means through which Bruce attempted to wrest back credibility—strategies that Leask argues ultimately backfired.[8]

Leask's thorough examination of the treatment of the literary record of Bruce's reception is a persuasive account of why the *Travels* failed to gain credibility among a certain demographic, and his point is well taken that these responses shed a great deal of light on public expectations regarding travel writing at the end of the eighteenth century; however, approaching the question of what Bruce's narrative sought to do in and of itself through the lens of its failures risks obscuring the presence, the sophistication, and the efficacy of some of the other epistemological strategies at work in his text. Similarly, the tendency to draw the conclusion from what high profile, largely literary figures had to say that the *Travels* was read as a romance rather than a serious work of scholarship conflates the way the narrative was talked about with how it was actually used.[9] It did fuel the romantic imaginations of writers like Frances Burney, Hugh Blair, Samuel Coleridge, William Wordsworth, Felicia Hemans, Anna Letitia Barbauld, Walter Scott, and Charles Lamb.[10] However, it has also been cited as a source of valuable information by geographers, historians, ethnomusicologists, anthropologists, theologians, botanists, and linguists from its first publication to the present.[11] Debates about Bruce's credibility and suspicion over his methods did not negate the massive influence the *Travels* had over what academics and popular readers alike believed to be true about Abyssinia.

This chapter focuses not on how Bruce packaged himself as an eyewitness traveler dominating the landscape with his camera obscura and his pen but on how he depended on both European and African erudite traditions to fully flesh out his Abyssinian world—a dependence that he emphasized rather than tried to obscure. As Bruce's Ophir argument illustrates, he considered himself a man of the study, not simply a man of the field, with large portions of the *Travels* dedicated to documenting Abyssinia's history and to the translation of the Royal Chronicles out of Ge'ez. This scholarly foundation was necessary, in Bruce's estimation, for writing a reliable travel account. Mere eyewitnesses, like Lobo and like Charles-Jacques Poncet, misunderstood what they saw because they were "ignorant of the history of this country," though Poncet was to be forgiven, in Bruce's opinion, because "he did not pretend to be a scholar."[12] By contrast, Bruce admired Páez for his academic bent and in particular for the fact that he, like Bruce himself, had taken the time to learn to read Ge'ez, "in which he arrived at a degree of knowledge superior to that of the natives themselves."[13] He is at times critical of Páez's missionary efforts, but as an authority on Abyssinia, Bruce considered him categorically different from Lobo. If Lobo's travel account was "a heap of fables," Páez's was "closely written in a plain style" and full of useful information.[14] Páez himself is never accused of falsely claiming to have reached the source of the Nile. Bruce theorizes that Athanasius Kircher, a Jesuit living in Rome who first published Páez's description of the source, made up the account and simply attributed it to Páez.[15] In fact, Bruce cites Páez's "genius" and thorough knowledge of the country as evidence that Kircher's attribution was implausible: Páez's account would have been more accurate, and he would have left a detailed map instead of a description so vague it could be of any river.¹⁶ Bruce judged that Páez's knowledge of Ethiopian languages and history and the close relationships he built with Abyssinia's elites endowed him with credibility that a mere eyewitness shouldn't be afforded. Bruce packaged himself in a similar light, citing both his knowledge of Ethiopian languages and literature and the intimacy of his ties with his hosts as evidence of the quality of his insider information about the country.

Bruce cites the relationships he built with the Abyssinian noblewomen of the court at Gondar as the primary reason that he was able to overcome the suspicion that the Habesha had developed of Western Europeans, or "Franks" as they called them, in the wake of the disaster of Susenyos I's conversion the century before: "Being in the prime of life, of no ungracious figure, having an accidental knack, which is not a trifle, of putting on the dress, and speaking the language easily and gracefully, I cultivated with the utmost assiduity the friendship of the fair sex, by the most modest, respectful distant attendance, and obsequiousness in public, abating just as much of that in private as suited their humor and inclinations. I soon acquired a great support of these at court."¹⁷ Though the suggestion here is that he made headway with these women through his ability to charm and perhaps even seduce them, his subsequent characterizations of the two women with whom he built the closest relationships—Empress Mentewab, the *itege* who had been regent for both a son and grandson, and her daughter Woyzero Aster Iyasu, a powerful noblewoman—are not reducible to exotic or sexualized stereotypes in his account.¹⁸ In particular, Mentewab was nearly sixty, and Bruce portrays her as shrewd, pious, and more than a little intimidating. They are fleshed out, complex figures, and this chapter argues that they function in Bruce's text as both natural extensions of the impressions that many Europeans already had of Abyssinian noblewomen and touchstones through which Bruce reiterates that both his literal access to the source of the Nile and his intellectual access to local culture and history were facilitated by elite insiders who wielded significant political and symbolic power. If his account of Abyssinia is different from others, he suggests, it is in part because his connections with these women offered an inroad into locations and ideas that the Franks—the Catholic missionaries and diplomats that preceded him—never attained. Though these women are mobilized to a particular rhetorical end in Bruce's account, to read them only as an invention of his text or, in Aster's case, only as an eroticized object, doesn't do justice to their complexity as literary or historical figures who had the capacity to shape not only Bruce's impressions of them but also the way he and his many readers thought about Abyssinian culture, history, and even the Nile itself.

Mentewab's Self-Fashioning and Bruce's Annals of the Solomonic Dynasty

As is the case with most patriarchal societies, even ones with as robust a history of life-writing as Ethiopia, detailed narratives about historical Ethiopian women are much scarcer than detailed narratives about historical Ethiopian men. Mentewab is an exceptional case.[19] Not only do records of her life and reign exist, there are clear indications that she shaped those records herself through her management of her public image. Named *itege* by Emperor Bakaffa in the early eighteenth century, Mentewab had been regent during the minorities of Iyasu II and Iyoas I and had thus been one of Abyssinia's central ruling figures for thirty years at the time of Bruce's arrival in the capital city of Gondar.[20] This power had been by no means guaranteed: although she was a favorite and a mother of Bakaffa's children, she was not his wife.[21] So, like other queens such as Eleni who needed to fend off suspicion of her origins in order to legitimize her right to power, she symbolically positioned herself within a constellation of women idealized in Habesha culture and history—Makeda; Helena, mother of Constantine; Eleni; and the Virgin Mary—summoning in particular their earthly significance as mothers of great men and their symbolic significance as mothers of the nation, the cross, and the word made flesh.

Mentewab staged a coronation ceremony for herself, for instance, allegedly at the insistence of her seven-year-old son, during which Iyasu II submitted to her authority, declaring that Mentewab's power was sanctioned because without her as his literal mother or his regent, his own divinely ordained reign would not exist.[22] The performance echoed the moment in the *Kebra Nagast* in which Menelik is made king: Makeda declares that only men can sit on the throne, but in turn he tells her he will be her slave in everything she commands of him.[23] She is the head and Menelik is merely the foot. The chronicler who recorded the ceremony notes that Mentewab was also dressed and positioned like the royal bride in Psalm 45. An allegory for the Virgin Mary, the Psalm describes the new queen as adorned in "gold of Ophir" and prophesizes that her sons will become "princes throughout the land."[24] In the context of the coronation, the restaging of the Psalm would have implied Makeda as well, who, as the mother of the Solomonic Dynasty, is the Old Testament prefiguration of the mother of Christ in Ethiopian Orthodox typology.²⁵ The two are twinned, for instance, throughout the *Kebra Nagast*, linked by the same repeated mother-son imagery that Mentewab sought to stage between herself and Iyasu.²⁶ During the ceremony, dignitaries also likened her to Helena, mother of Constantine—another spiritually significant mother-son couple—which was a strategy that Eleni had also used to garner acceptance by adopting her name and sending an alleged piece of the cross with her emissary to Portugal.²⁷ If, as Margaux Herman argues, Eleni was the prototype for the *itege* and that others adopted her name as a title, this move on Mentewab's part may have served the additional purpose of positioning her not only within a mythological lineage but within a historical one as well.²⁸

Portraits painted during Mentewab's reign reiterated and built on this symbolic display of her right to the title of *itege* and the political power it afforded. One of the most striking depicts her discoursing with Iyasu, surrounded by six other members of their family who also assumed power when she became regent and through whom she exercised her government (fig. 5). Of the eight figures, Mentewab is the largest and most elaborately dressed, crowned in a unique rayed diadem that makes it appear as if there is an aureole behind her head of the sort that would appear on paintings of the Virgin Mary. (This became part of her signature look in her portraits, though there is no indication she wore anything like it in real life.)²⁹ She is sitting across from Iyasu, their position mimicking, according to Bosc-Tiessé's analysis, the "divine mother-son couple" of Christ and Mary and the "royal mother-son couple" of Helen and Constantine as they appear in contemporaneous paintings.³⁰ The portrait is unusual for the time because, even though it relies on this religious imagery, it stages a contemporary, secular event, and thus the portrait also reveals Mentewab's interest in writing herself into the historical record—she is portrayed as an active governor, not merely a figurehead. In fact, she utilized her son's chronicle to a similar purpose. Her courtship and relationship with Bakaffa appear there rather than in Bakaffa's own chronicle, constructed after the fact in service to the narrative Mentewab hoped to circulate about her own lineage.³¹ Ultimately, she managed her image successfully enough through these means that she went from Bakaffa's unmarried consort to one of the most influential queens in the history of the Solomonic dynasty. She was, as Makeda and Eleni were, considered to be like a father and a mother to the country.³²

Just before Bruce arrived in Gondar, Mentewab's star fell. In 1769 her grandson Iyoas I was assassinated by Ras Mikael Sehul, the governor of Tigre, who largely owed his own rise to Mentewab's favor and who, to complicate matters,

FIGURE 5. Portrait of Mentewab (right) and Iyasu II (left), from the *Acts of St. George*. (British Library, MS Or. 715, f. 134r; used with permission)

was also related to Mentewab by marriage—his son was married to one of her daughters, and he ultimately married another of her daughters himself, Woyzero Aster Iyasu. Mikael Sehul put his own preferred heirs on the throne, ushering in the *Zemene Mesafint* or "Era of the Princes"—a century during which regional governors maintained control over the majority of the country and the Solomonic emperors were reduced to puppets with little influence outside

Gondar. Mentewab retired to her palace and never formally returned to court life. Nevertheless, she still had considerable influence there through people who remained devoted to her. By winning her support, Bruce gained insider knowledge into history and court intrigue as well as access to places and spaces that a Frank would never be invited to enter. When he recounts the story of her personal history and their relationship, she authorizes his presence in Abyssinia, and he upholds her illustriousness, positioning her as the culminating figure of a lineage of powerful, intelligent Abyssinian queens stretching back to the Queen of Sheba in his "annals of the country"—which is a translation of the Royal Chronicles interspersed with details from Portuguese travel narratives and Bruce's running commentary on both.

Makeda's story is the literal and literary foundation of Bruce's account just as she was the literal and literary foundation of the Solomonic dynasty. He introduces her in the first volume of his narrative, in his defense of why Ophir was located in East Africa. He extends her domain as far south as Sofala. He also extends her domain across the Red Sea, but he insists that the Arabian Peninsula is the periphery of her empire, not its center, which was unequivocally in Africa.[33] He makes a "promise to the reader" that he will return to her extraordinary story—"the dignity of the expedition itself . . . merits that it should be treated in a place by itself"—and indeed he does return to it as "the foundation of the monarchy of Abyssinia." In his synopsis of the *Kebra Nagast*, he emphasizes that Makeda was "a person of learning," and that her reason for traveling to Solomon was to see "whether Solomon was really the learned man he was said to be" by testing him with "allegories, or parables."[34] Despite the fact that she clearly proved herself Solomon's match and that she was a successful head of state, Bruce ends his introduction to her with an account how she passed her crown to Menelik, declaring that a woman would never again rule over Abyssinia.

Bruce brings up Makeda's prohibition on women becoming heads of state several times through the subsequent "list of kings of the race of Solomon, descended from the queen of Saba," which takes up the end of volume 1 and all of volume 2 of the *Travels*.[35] But each time he does so, the prohibition is paired with descriptions of the forms of covert or lateral power that women have wielded throughout Abyssinia's history as tutors to young princes, as agents of resistance to invasions, as models of piety and builders of churches, and as mothers who strategize on behalf of their sons.[36] He makes clear, in other words, a range of ways that women were the head in history when the men were only the foot. In particular, he emphasizes the importance of the *itege*, writing that "though it be true that all women are excluded from the Abyssinian throne, yet it is as true that there is a law, or custom, as strictly observed as the other, that the queen upon whose head the king shall have put the crown in his life-time . . . that woman is regent of the kingdom, and guardian of every minor king, as long as she shall live."[37] Bruce observes that this is not a rare occurrence: throughout the "Abyssinian annals . . . very frequent minorities happen," and he details several of them.[38] He resists the impulse seen in texts like Pinto's to over-romanticize these women, but his representations still work within the recognizable archetype as she appears in Álvares and Castanhoso. He doesn't, for example, write flatteringly about all of Eleni's political decisions, and he criticizes what he sees as her imprudent ambition, but he also defends her initial reluctance to go to war with Adal, arguing that "the princess, perfectly informed of the interests of both nations, seems, in her whole conduct, to have acted upon the most judicious and sensible principles."[39] When war became inevitable due to an increased Turkish presence in the region, Bruce remarks that she should have stepped down and put an experienced warrior on the throne instead of a child (Lebna Dengal). He claims that "the empress Helena saw this distinctly" but that her "love of reigning" led her to appoint a king on whose behalf she could rule even though, in Bruce's opinion, women were not suited to be generals.[40] Nevertheless, she manages to devise a solution to the country's troubles by instigating the alliance with the Portuguese. Bruce is no more or less critical of her than he is any of her male counterparts, and she is, on the whole, represented as intelligent and actively involved, making strategic decisions from a place of keen understanding.

Bruce also notes how these women drew their symbolic power from the ones who came before, assuming layers of identity that denote their exceptionalism. When Galawdewos comes to power, he is young, but he has "graceful and affable manners" and is "expert in all warlike exercises, and brave beyond his years." "The princess, to whom he was indebted for his education," Bruce writes, "was Sabel Wenghel, celebrated in Abyssinian history for wisdom and courage equal to Helena herself."[41] In fact, Bruce writes that she is sometimes called "Helena" in Abyssinian texts. She continued to advise Galawdewos well into his majority, and, as chapter 5 shows, was a major player in the Ethiopian-Adal War.[42] Bruce includes one of her notable deeds that is left out of Castanhoso's and Bermudes's accounts—she negotiated with Grahn's widow, Bati del Wambara, for the release of Galawdewos's brother and heir, Menas, who had been taken captive in the early days of the conflict and who succeeded Galawdewos after his death.[43] In Bruce's account, noblewomen are key pieces in the machinery of history and politics, exercising various forms of influence, some institutionally sanctioned and some through more covert or behind-the-scenes channels.

Thus, by the time Bruce arrives at the recent past in his recounting of the "Abyssinian annals," he has been describing throughout what it means for a woman to be *itege*, the title by which he always refers to Mentewab. The *itege* has state-sanctioned power. She has insider information. She is well-educated and intelligent. Sometimes she is the person pulling the strings even when it appears that she is not. She is realistic—a Pinto-like *itege* would not serve Bruce's aims—but she is still tied through ceremony and symbolism to a privileged archetype. Once Mentewab is finally introduced into Bruce's history of the Solomonic dynasty, she embodies all these qualities, and she becomes a main character of Bruce's version of the next three chronicles, beginning with Bakaffa's. Bruce doesn't reveal exactly who she is at first. It seems that she is just another queen, though the tone of the chronicle in which Bruce claims she first appears is unusual. This is because, according to Bruce, Bakaffa was so "silent, secret, and unfathomable in his designs," not to mention so ruthless, that the royal historiographers were reluctant to write anything down during his life for fear of retribution. They were also afraid to write anything down since—as will be explained—he once faked his own death, leading to "a general belief prevailing in Abyssinia that he is alive to this day, and will appear again in all his terrors."[44] Because of this, there is no complete account of the king's reign: "Only a few anecdotes are preserved, some of them very odd ones."

Bruce doesn't relate all of these anecdotes, a reminder that his "annals" are not direct translations but a collation of what he has determined are the most important and illuminating details of each reign. Regarding Bakaffa's chronicle, he says, "I shall only, for the present, choose such of those as lead me to the subject I have in hand," which, on the face of things, is the progression of power from one Solomonic king to the next.[45] The chronicle begins with Bakaffa traveling the countryside in disguise. He runs across a priest divining the future from pieces of straw thrown into a stream. When he asks the priest what knowledge he was seeking, the priest tells him that "he was trying whether the king would have a son, and who should govern the kingdom after him." The divination revealed "that he should have a son; but that a Welleta Georgis should govern the kingdom after him for thirty years, though that Welleta Georgis should be neither his son nor any descendant of his." This prophecy, and the implication that the Solomonic dynasty would be interrupted, throws Bakaffa into a panic. He begins to imprison and execute anyone named "Welleta Georgis" who was in any position to ever make a claim to the throne. He continues to travel in disguise, looking for Welleta Georgis as well as assessing the state of his kingdom when no one is putting on a performance for the king.

During one of these investigations, he is seized by a fever and is carried to the home of a local landowner, where he is cared for as a stranger. He recovers due to the "kind assistance and unwearied diligence of the beautiful daughter of the house," a woman who is described as "gentle, mild, and affable," as having "great understanding and prudence beyond her age," and as "the darling not only of her own family but of all the neighborhood."[46] Her name is "Berhan Magrass, the Glory of Grace," and she makes such an impression on the king that once he has recovered his health and returned to the palace, he summons her to Gondar, reveals his true identity, and (in Bruce's version of the story) marries her.[47] Within a year a son is born, and as a result, Bakaffa's obsession with ferreting out Welleta Georgis returns, so Bakaffa devises a stratagem. First, he "directed that the queen should be crowned, a ceremony that carries great consequences along with it when solemnized properly, as at that time she is made regent, or Iteghè, in all minorities that may happen afterward."[48] Then he fakes a mortal illness hoping that Welleta Georgis will show himself once the rumor is circulated that the king has died. In the midst of this scheme, the *itege* overhears Bakaffa discussing the prophecy with one of his advisors for the first time. Bruce writes that as she listened,

> The Iteghé all this time was lost in silence. She desired the king to repeat to her the whole circumstances of the prophecy, which he distinctly did. "I wish," says she laughing, "this Welleta Georgis may not be now nearer us than we imagine; perhaps in the palace." "In the palace!" says the king, with great emotion. "I doubt so," says the queen; "suppose it should be me your own wife; for Welleta Georgis was the name given to me in baptism; and your late coronation of me, should a minority happen in the person of your son, or even a grandson, undoubtedly leaves me regent of the kingdom by your own intentions when you made me Iteghé."[49]

His fears assuaged, not only does Bakaffa end his obsessive search for Welleta Georgis, he ends his reign of terror in general. He returns from the "dead," appears to his people dressed all in white, forgives those who celebrated his assumed death, and states that the rest of his reign will be a reign of peace, justice, and mercy, and allegedly it is, though Bakaffa's ruthlessness lingers in people's memories. This coupled with the fact that Bakaffa faked his death once is why, as Bruce states in the beginning, people still fear that he will return someday and resume his old ways.[50]

In general, Bruce takes the tone of a historian in his retelling of the chronicles, noting what he considered to be flaws as well as strengths in his subjects' characters. By telling this chronicle in a fairy-tale-like form, Bruce endows its *itege* with all the best aspects of the archetype, which testify to her personal qualities but also situate her in a constellation of other remarkable women that Bruce has mentioned—Makeda, Eleni, Sabla Wangel, the mother of Constantine, the Virgin Mary. She is so beautiful, wise, intelligent, and good that she impresses a Solomonic king until he falls in love with her. Her handling of her volatile and paranoid consort, which essentially reforms his reign from one that sought stability through violence to one that sought stability through peace, is a testament to her quick understanding and diplomatic savvy. Her power and influence have been sanctioned both by divine will (the prophecy) and by rule of law (when she is designated *itege* by the king). Though Bruce is generally scornful of the Abyssinian obsession with prophecy and the interpretation of dreams, this one he validates, however wryly, pointing out that "to the credit of the prophet, she continued to regent full thirty years; till the folly and ambition of her own family gave her a master that put an end to all her influence, except what she enjoyed from exemplary piety, and the most extensive works of charity and mercy."[51]

With this allusion to contemporary events, Bruce anchors the chronicle back in the real world and reveals that this *itege* has not two but three identities. The woman in the story, Bruce writes, was none other than "my great patroness while at Gondar, and from her I received constant protection in the most disastrous times."[52] She is also, it turns out, the source of much of what Bruce has just related about her, which she told him often, he says, "among several anecdotes of that singular reign."[53] As coauthor of Bruce's account of her integration at court and rise to power, she worked within the same symbolic economy as her coronation ceremony, her portrait, and her own rewriting of the Royal Chronicles of her son and grandson. The result takes quite a bit of liberty with Bakaffa's chronicle given that in the original, Mentewab is not actually mentioned at all.[54] In telling her stories to Bruce, she has continued her practice of rewriting history in her favor.

This doesn't mean that Bruce wrote down what she said word for word, despite his claim that it was his general practice to do so, or that he didn't add his own spin on the details.[55] However, her version of the story would have worked in Bruce's favor. The line between the world of the past that Bruce has been describing and the present is seamless in his account, with the slow reveal of Mentewab's identity as the transition point. By claiming her as his patroness and informant, he coopts not only her personal authority but also the symbolic power of the narrative history into which she has been situated—the very strategy that women like Eleni and Mentewab used to authorize their right to serve as regent. Bruce's translations of Iyasu II's and Iyoas I's chronicles are likewise as much accounts of how Mentewab amassed family resources around her—who were the agents of her government as represented in her portrait—as they are the histories of those two kings. After her son and grandson reach their majorities, Mentewab recedes into the background in their chronicles, but she surfaces from time to time as a reminder that she is still one of the main people, if not the main person, moving the chess pieces around the board.

The first meeting Bruce describes between himself and Mentewab indicates that although she is no longer actively involved in court life, she still embodies the nobility, intelligence, piety, education, and pride of the woman in the chronicles. Already off on the wrong foot with her that day for scorning the notion that divine intercession by a living saint will cure one of her sons-in-law of the smallpox, Bruce prostrates himself before her. Rather than welcoming him with open arms, "she received that token of respect without offering to excuse or to decline it."[56] She remains deadpan, and they converse about different sites in Jerusalem associated with Christ's death and ascension, "with the situations of which she was perfectly well acquainted." They debate whether Bruce's Protestantism or Mentewab's Orthodox Christianity is closer to Catholicism, a conversation that she turns into a challenge to Bruce over his skepticism that a miracle might cure her family of the smallpox, observing that a Christian must surely believe in Christ's miracles. Bruce concedes that point but counters that he cannot believe stories like the one of the "saint, who, being sick and hungry, caused a brace of partridges, ready-roasted, to fly upon his plate that he might eat them."[57] Realizing that he has read the Synaxarium, which tells the lives of the Ethiopian Christian saints, Mentewab smiles for the first time and simply reminds him that all things are possible through God. Bruce, who is well aware that he may have made another misstep, is relieved that the conversation ends there, but it turns out that he has won her trust. When the living saint fails to cure her son-in-law, Mentewab asks Bruce to come stay in her palace and look after her sick grandchildren—the turning point in the narrative that ensures Bruce's integration into court circles.[58]

Posterity has identified Bruce's eventual success in curing several of Mentewab's family members of smallpox as the reason why she welcomed him into her home and became his patroness, and indeed, Bruce does cite his medical skills as one of the things that enabled his passage through and survival in hostile lands.[59] But Mentewab has seen no evidence of this yet when she asks him to come stay at Kuskuam. He had to pass a much more complicated test than simply performing her and her family a service. He needed to hold his footing in debate and prove his worth through his knowledge of Abyssinia's books, culture, and religious traditions. Mentewab's grandson Aylo, who was present during this conversation and who is also one of Bruce's most steadfast allies throughout the *Travels*, remarks at a later point that it is precisely Bruce's ability to quickly grasp "the customs of the country," and his willingness to abide by them, that has kept him alive.[60] In one of the many moments throughout the narrative when he denies the accusation that he is a Frank, he does so by denying that he is a Catholic, but he also does so by pointing out that he has not conducted himself as an outsider: "I conform in every shape to the laws, religion, and customs of Abyssinia," he emphasizes, and the priest to whom he is speaking agrees, promising him that, for this reason, "whatever your faith is I would defend you myself."[61] Mentewab presides over this conversation. In fact, it happens as part of Bruce's final leave-taking on his last night in Gondar, his interactions with her ending where they began, with a tacit affirmation that his understanding of Abyssinian history and culture was endorsed by those who knew it best.

In the chronology of Bruce's narrative, then, Mentewab—whose social position and personal character have been validated by a literary foundation laid out in Abyssinia's own books—has in turn validated Bruce's understanding of the country. She is not Bruce's textual invention. The similarities across various representations of her indicate that he was responding to and endeavoring to capture those consistencies, not to mention the fact that his account of her life before he met her was taken from translations of Habesha accounts as well as from what she had to say about herself. But Bruce does capitalize on her social position, public persona, and her own words to send a message about the depth of his understanding to a readership who would have already had a sense of what it meant to earn the favor and protection of an *itege*. Lest the reader doubt the veracity of Mentewab's reported speech, Bruce states that he wrote these conversations down word for word and thus "can assure the reader these speeches and conversations were absolutely real, and not the fabrication of after-hours."[62] His citation of Mentewab's authority as a means of establishing his own ethos is an elaborate version of the deferral to the native informant deployed in all early Enlightenment African travelogues, functioning as a cue to consider the text as a collaborative artifact.

Woyzero Aster Iyasu and the Cultural Power of Abyssinian Court Women

As indicated by Mentewab's determination to write herself into Ethiopia's political history and not simply its mythology, Bruce's aristocratic women had genuine clout in the political and social worlds that he needed to navigate to reach the source of the Nile and make it out of the country alive. Even though Mentewab has retired from court life, the citizens of Gondar still "flock to see her" when she goes abroad, and she "inspires" "enthusiasm" in "all sorts of people."[63] If Bruce invokes Mentewab's symbolic power to endorse his understanding of Abyssinian history and culture, he trades on more tangible forms of power to explain how he was able to gain access to certain spaces and places where no Frank had ever been allowed to go. Aster Iyasu has influence with the two most significant men in Abyssinia—the governor of Tigre and the emperor.

It took Bruce several years to reach the source of the Nile following his arrival in Gondar not because the terrain was impenetrable or because the location was a mystery to the locals but because the events that instigated the Era of the Princes caused conflicts across territories, and the people whose aid Bruce needed fell on all sides of these conflicts. Though Ras Mikael Sehul, the governor of Tigre, had long been Mentewab's ally and was eventually married to Aster, his orchestration of Iyoas I's assassination ended all goodwill between the two. Mikael had put Tekle Haymanot II in place and thus had a great deal of pull with the emperor, so it was important for Bruce to remain in Mikael's favor. However, Mikael was at odds with Fasil, the governor of Damot (and Iyoas I's cousin), whose domain Bruce needed to travel through to make it to the southern edge of Lake T'ana. To complicate matters even further, when Mikael and Tekle Haymanot were forced to leave Gondar to stop a series of rebellions in Tigre, a second emperor (Susenyos II) was briefly appointed, who was lukewarmly and somewhat inconsistently supported by Mentewab and Fasil. All these alliances shifted with alarming rapidity whenever and however it suited the principal players. Bruce's task, as he tells it, was to establish friendly relationships with each of these factions so that he could move through their respective territories without getting killed. "I wish you would tell me," Tekle Haymanot apparently once said to him, "how you reconcile all these people to you."⁶⁴ One of the primary reasons he was able to do so, the narrative makes clear, was because Mentewab and Aster were the connective tissue of these political networks. By earning their trust and favor, he gained information, introductions, and safe passage across regions in conflict in a way that would never have been possible if he had focused his attentions only on those who held immediate and visible power. Throughout the *Travels*, Bruce highlights his ability to use his quick wits, not to mention his prowess at manly pursuits like shooting and riding, to manipulate powerful Abyssinian men, whether friend, enemy, or some sliding combination of the two. But he doesn't disguise the fact that none of that would have been possible without Mentewab and Aster serving as his patronesses.

As the various noblewomen who surface in Bruce's translations of the chronicles indicate, elite women were able to exert influence even when they had not, like the *itege*, been granted institutionalized power. They kept their names and their property upon marrying, and they were able to divorce their husbands and establish new alliances as it suited them and their various goals and agendas.⁶⁵ This was in part because they married outside the royal family and thus usually outranked their husbands, giving them, Belcher argues, "a strong sense of their own value and rights."⁶⁶ In Bruce's account, Aster Iyasu was one of these women.⁶⁷ Though she was Mentewab's daughter and Iyoas's step-aunt, after her previous husband is killed in a conflict between Mikael Sehul and Fasil, she marries Mikael Sehul, proposing the arrangement to him herself, because it put her in a position to avenge her first husband's death.⁶⁸ Bruce describes Aster as having "the courage and decision of a Roman matron" when she walked to Mikael Sehul's tent, accompanied by Aylo. She knelt before him even though she was "his superior." Aylo explained to Mikael that "her resolution was to give him instantly her hand" in order to attain her political objective.⁶⁹ The first Bruce ever hears of Aster is a rumor on his way into Abyssinia that she succeeded in capturing the man who assassinated her first husband and has ordered him flayed alive (a common capital punishment for a constitutional criminal, not necessarily an indication that she was particularly vengeful). After meeting her personally, Bruce assures the reader that Aster is "kind and humane" and so charming that Mikael Sehul immediately agreed to marry her and Tekle Haymanot "contracted a decided tenderness for her."⁷⁰ In fact, "it was impossible to see Ozoro Esther, and hear her speak," Bruce mentions elsewhere, "without being attached to her for ever after."⁷¹

Bruce writes that "next to her mother," Aster was "the greatest friend I had in Abyssinia, and one who had the most frequent opportunities of being so."[72] In his narrative he is often dining with Aster, or socializing with her in her apartment, when he learns important political news. She ensures that Bruce is received kindly by Mikael because of his thoughtful attention to her and to her children.[73] This gives Bruce some leeway with Mikael, ruthless and decisive though he is. For instance, when Bruce gets into a fistfight with a courtier that Mikael had an outstanding quarrel with, Mikael uses the incident as an excuse to secretly imprison the man. When Bruce goes to Mikael to intercede on the man's behalf, asking him to set the man at liberty, the governor feigns ignorance of the man's whereabouts. "At liberty?" Mikael asks. "Where is he?" "In your house," Bruce replies. "Somewhere in irons." At this, Mikael owns up to his feint, grumbling, "This is Esther's intelligence . . . these women tell you all their secrets."[74] Such secrets and such citations of their origins enable Bruce to talk himself out of otherwise sticky situations as he makes his way through an ever-shifting political landscape in his journey across Abyssinia's physical landscape. In another illustrative example, while traveling through Fasil's territory, Fasil grows violent at one point and accuses Bruce of feeding him false intelligence that Mikael's troops have taken a strategically important mountain. Bruce explains "how the news had come to the Iteghé—who had brought the intelligence [to Bruce]—how it had come from the Ras to Ozoro Esther."[75] Mentewab and Aster are Bruce's insurance that his information is reliable, and they are the link by which intelligence passes from one side of the political drama to the other. His mention of them assuages Fasil, who redirects his temper from Bruce to Mikael.

Because Bruce wins the acceptance of Mentewab and Aster, he suggests, he wins the acceptance of all. They call him "Yagoube," and they joke that his last name means he is descended from one of their own kings, Brus.[76] He was thus of the line of Solomon and perhaps, Tekle Haymanot would say, even "heir to the crown" himself.[77] And Aster and her family defend Bruce against those who accuse him of not belonging in such inner circles. One day he enters Aster's apartment and finds her with Abba Salama, a high-ranking priest with whom Bruce comes to heads several times throughout the *Travels* and who, according to Bruce, despises him for no other reason than that he assumes Bruce is a Frank.[78] Abba Salama expresses the opinion to Aster that Franks should not be allowed to "remain at liberty in the country and meddle in affairs" and that Bruce should be prohibited from traveling to the source of the Nile. Bruce, who has already by this point arrived at the source of the Nile and returned to Gondar again, writes, "I interrupted him by a laugh, and by saying, If it is me, father, you mean by the word Frank, I have, without your advice, gone where I intended, and returned in safety." Bruce is denying that he is a Catholic, but he is also denying the charge of outsider implicit in the word "Frank," refusing to identify with the designation the way one would refuse to identify with an insult. It is not only Bruce who rejects the charge. Aster's son, who happens to walk in just at this moment, is enraged that Abba Salama would insult "Yagoube" by accusing him of being a Frank on top of all the other ways that he tried to inhibit Bruce's passage through the country, a litany of which he then relates to his mother. Aster observes that none of Abba Salama's attempts succeeded because "God . . . saw the integrity of [Bruce's] heart, and that his hands were clean."[79] Abba Salama is furious that they have sided with Bruce against him and threatens to excommunicate Aster's son, but the young man is unintimidated. He invites Bruce to come ride horses with him and promises, "When I have put a good man upon each of them we shall together hunt your enemies to Sennaar."[80] They depart together, leaving, "Abba Salama dying with fear, as Ozoro Esther told [Bruce] afterwards." Bruce's recounting of this incident emphasizes his status as an accepted insider as well as the social agency of the faction he has chosen to ally himself with. The person who ostensibly has the most overt power in the room—both political and ecclesiastical—in fact turns out to have the least because Aster and her family refuse to acknowledge it.

A similar incident plays out in even more dramatic form when Bruce meets the emperor who Tekle Haymanot's detractors put on the throne during his and Mikael's absence from Gondar. Bruce has largely remained at Kuskuam and avoided the court during this time, but when Susenyos finally orders Bruce to attend to him, Bruce finds him unintelligent and lacking in royal dignity, and throughout their interaction implies that he understands his place in the court better than Susenyos understands his own.[81] When Susenyos chides Bruce for not coming to see him sooner and not lavishing the praise and attention on him that he believes Bruce lavished on Tekle Haymanot, Bruce replies that he did not have the intimate relationship with the king that Susenyos imagines, which would run counter to the custom of the country.[82] Susenyos grows angry that Bruce has called Tekle Haymanot "the king," accusing him of being "a Frank, a dog, a liar, and a slave." Bruce says that Mentewab will attest to his honesty.[83] When Susenyos spits at Bruce, one of Susenyos's advisors intervenes, chiding the king for mistreating "Yagoube" who is "a friend, not only to the king, but to us all: the whole people love him."[84] This defender turns out to be one of Mentewab's nephews, who reassures Bruce that he need not worry about Susenyos's ire. Bruce reports what transpired to Mentewab, who councils him to "stay near Ozoro Esther, as in her service, and go no more to the palace," once more rallying around him, though both Mentewab and her nephew are ostensibly Susenyos's supporters.[85]

Bruce harnesses Mentewab and Aster's discursive and symbolic power for his own ends and transforms them into characters as it suits him. In these examples, Aster in particular comes across as devoted to the point of ridiculousness, though Bruce's readers found her dynamic and fascinating overall: Samuel Coleridge immortalized her as the "Abyssinian maid" in *Kubla Khan*, playing on her dulcimer and "Singing of Mount Abora"; and Hugh Blair once confessed to Bruce, "You make me absolutely in love with your great favorite, Ozoro Esther."[86] The *Travels* is not a documentary record of the way Mentewab and Aster thought and lived. However, attending to the consistencies between Bruce's account, the symbolic and cultural means by which Habesha women in general wielded their power, and what Ethiopian sources propose about these women in particular suggests that they drove Bruce's perceptions and were the cultural brokers through which he navigated the country.

The Nile Is Unsettled: Mentewab's Melancholy at the Source

One of the more unexpected places Mentewab's influence surfaces is in Bruce's description of the object of his explorations. Of all the aspersions leveled at Bruce by his critics, the one that stung him the most were the accusations that the Portuguese missionaries had made it to the source of the Nile first or, worse, that Bruce had never made it to the source at all. In response, Bruce emphasized in his introduction that its location had eluded men no less determined than Alexander the Great, Julius Caesar, and Cambyses. When it had come to finding the source of the Nile, Bruce wrote, "Even conquerors at the head of immense armies, who first discovered and then subdued great parts of the world, were forced to lower their tone."[87] After such a set-up, one would expect that Bruce would narrate his actual arrival at the source with all the imperial exultation he could muster. The so-called discovery of Lake Victoria, which is the presumed source of the White Nile, is often imagined this way. Perhaps nothing captures the colonial attitudes of the mid-nineteenth-century expeditions into Africa's interior like the telegram that John Hanning Speke sent from Khartoum to London after he saw and named Ripon Falls: "The Nile is ours," he wrote. "The Nile is settled." Possession ("ours") coupled with scientific certainty ("settled") portends both British settlements and the settling of an uncivilized place.

This was not Bruce's approach. In fact, despite his narrative's triumphalist introduction, Bruce's enthusiasm for his search waxes and wanes throughout in proportion to his hosts' skepticism over it or encouragement of it. During one of the rare moments when Fasil and Tekle Haymanot are on good terms, the emperor expands Fasil's domains to include the source of the Nile, and, seeing an opportunity to make headway toward his goal, Bruce asks the emperor if he will grant him a favor. The emperor says he will on the condition that Bruce not "relapse into [his] usual despondency, and talk of going home."[88] Bruce asks for his permission to travel unmolested through Fasil's new territories and requests that the emperor command Fasil to take him to the source of the Nile "without fee or reward, and without excuse or evasion." Tekle Haymanot is amused at the ease of the request. "Tell Fasil I do give the village of Geesh, and those fountains he is so fond of, to Yagoube and his posterity forever," he instructs two of Fasil's messengers. "It will be easily guessed," Bruce writes, "this rendered the conversation a chearful one."[89] Though it's clear that Tekle Haymanot doesn't take Bruce's aspirations very seriously, as Bruce remarks elsewhere, this is because the Abyssinians "knew nothing of the prejudice of ages in favor of the attempt I was engaged in."[90] His "despondency" is momentarily abated by the emperor's goodwill and good humor.

His conversations with Mentewab about his search for the source of the Nile, on the other hand, are never cheerful ones, and her skepticism of the value of his mission affects Bruce much more deeply. According to Bruce, she "treated the intention of going to the source of the Nile as a fantastical folly, unworthy of any man of sense or understanding."[91] She says to him, "See . . . how every day our life punishes us with proofs of the perverseness and contradiction of human nature; you are come from Jerusalem, through vile Turkish governments, and hot, unwholesome climates, to see a river and a bog, no part of which you can carry away were it ever so valuable, and of which you have in your own country a thousand larger, better, and cleaner."[92] Chapter 4 outlines several of the methods that Habesha elites used to harness the symbolic power of the fact that the source of the Nile was housed within Abyssinia's borders, which dovetailed with European impressions of the mythical river and altered the way Europeans imagined the country's very topography, so it may seem odd that Mentewab would speak of the river in such dismissive and negative terms. Mentewab is indeed offering a counterdiscourse to the Christian exceptionalism inherent in associating the Nile with Gihon and the geopolitical power implicit in the rumor that the emperor was able to control its northward flow, but it is one that was also very much a part of Habesha ways of understanding the world—the importance of rejecting earthly ambition and goals and striving for a purified life in preparation for death.

As Mentewab chides Bruce for turning away from Jerusalem to chase after a fantastical folly, she states her wish for her remaining years, hearkening back to the very first conversation with her that Bruce relates, when she asked him about the Holy Sepulcher, Calvary, and the Mount of Olives: "I . . . the mother of kings who have sat upon the throne of this country more than thirty years, have for my only wish, night and day, that, after giving up every thing in the world, I could be conveyed to the church of the Holy Sepulchre in Jerusalem, and beg alms for my subsistence all my life after, if I could only be buried in the street within sight of the gate of that temple where our blessed Saviour once lay."[93] Though the turn from worldly concerns to spiritual ones at the end of one's life is a common refrain in most Christian cultures, it was lived out in a formalized way by some Ethiopian Christian women. If they were past the procreative age, they could leave behind the worldly life and devote themselves to God.[94] They could more frequently take communion in the Ethiopian Church, which was reserved for only the most pure of heart and body.[95] It was not uncommon for older women to live a monastic or ascetic life to strive for this purity, which did not necessitate sequestering oneself away but did require a shift in attitude and conduct.[96] Aster, too, in one of her final meetings with Bruce, announces her intention to die in Jerusalem and be buried in the Holy Sepulcher.[97] Not simply using Mentewab to ventriloquize his own melancholy, Bruce's report of Mentewab's turn toward thoughts of the afterlife is consistent with how she appears in the Royal Chronicles, which, according to Crummey, portray her twice as "devoid of worldly ambition and inclined to seek refuge in a monastery."[98] Facing the folly of her own ambition, having outlived both her son and her grandson, Mentewab is in an appropriate frame of mind to caution Bruce that whatever he discovers here, in this life, he can't take it with him when he goes.[99]

Bruce leaves Mentewab "very much affected with the disposition I had found her in," but by reminding himself of the august nature of his goal, "which had baffled the courage and perseverance of the bravest men in all ages," he is able to "chas[e] away all those gloomy apprehensions which I imbibed from the appearance and discourse of the queen."[100] Once Bruce finally does arrive at his destination, though, his reaction more resembles Mentewab's than Speke's. He writes that

> the place itself where I stood, the object of my vain-glory, suggested what depressed my short-lived triumphs. I was but a few minutes arrived at the sources of the Nile, through numberless dangers and sufferings, the least of which would have overwhelmed me but for the continual goodness and protection of Providence; I was, however, but then half through my journey, and all those dangers which I had already passed, awaited me again on my return. I found a despondency gaining ground fast upon me, and blasting the crown of laurels I had too rashly woven for myself.[101]

"Come triumph with your Don Quixote," he tells his one of his companions, Strates, deeming himself the man who has confused giants for windmills, romance for reality. The whole incident descends into a farcical display during which Bruce tries to trick Strates into lifting a coconut husk cup full of river water to various public figures and harasses him over his enthusiasm or reticence to do so. Strates grows so animated that the locals ask their guide, Woldo, what is wrong with the man. Woldo tells them that he has been bitten by a mad dog.[102] Thus, Bruce quips, "I was very well pleased . . . with this turn Woldo gave the action . . . which discovered a connection, believed to subsist at this day, between the river and its ancient governor the dog-star," whose rising, some Classical sources claimed, caused the inundation of the Nile in Egypt.

Reflecting on his arrival at the source seventeen years later, Bruce recalls the despondency more than the humor. He calls his journey "a violent effort of a distempered fancy":[103]

> I was, at that very moment, in possession of what had, for many years, been the principal object of my ambition and wishes: indifference, which, from the usual infirmity of human nature, follows, at least for a time, complete enjoyment, had taken place of it. The marsh, and the fountains, upon comparison with the rise of many of our rivers, became now a trifling object in my sight. I remember that magnificent scene in my own native country, where the Tweed, Clyde and Annan, rise, one hill; three rivers, as I now thought, not inferior to the Nile in beauty.[104]

Second only to the steak incident, this is the passage in the *Travels* most written about, in part because it is so unexpected and seemingly out of character. It has been read as evidence of Bruce's homesickness, of his frustration at not receiving the accolades he thought his due, and of his Scottish pride.[105] Taken in the context of Mentewab's reflections above, however, one wonders whether the sentiment expressed here is Bruce's alone. What she called a "fantastical folly" Bruce calls a "distempered fancy." She insists that the rivers in his own country must be "larger, better, and cleaner," and, indeed, Bruce reflects in this moment on the rivers of his homeland. Rather than joy, he feels indifference, confronting the "the perverseness and contradiction of human nature" that Mentewab predicted he would experience, and he is once again "affected with the disposition [he] had found her in" then: "Grief or despondency now rolled upon me like a torrent," he writes.[106] All that Bruce will bring back to Britain is a memory infused with Mentewab's melancholy and her reflection on the afterlife. The only thing that abates his grief is the same thing that abated hers—remembering that "another Guide, more powerful than my own courage, health, or understanding, if any of these can be called man's own, had uniformly protected me in all that tedious half; I found my confidence not abated, that still the same Guide was able to conduct me to my now wished for home."

Written at the end of his own life, after having withdrawn from the world in his own way by retreating to his estate in Scotland, Bruce's account of his search for the Nile is not settled or settling. Because his narrative is called *Travels to Discover the Source of the Nile*, one might be surprised to see his continual references throughout volume 3 to "sources"—it turns out that he describes three fountains that come up out of a marsh and gradually converge into a single flow. As the river moves through the marsh, it "receives many small contributions from springs that rise in the banks on each side of it."[107] It has to travel a fair distance, and be fed by several tributaries along the way, before it "becomes a considerable stream."[108] Bruce's skeptical reviewer complained that, in the end, Bruce's map makes the Nile look "like the hydra, to have many heads," and did not "prove any one of them in particular to be the head of the Nile," just as he complained of Bruce's reliance on African expressions for his account of Abyssinia's culture and history.[109] The multiplicity of Bruce's geographical conclusion is a fitting metaphor for the *Travels*, though. As a source itself—of Abyssinian history, biography, and geography—it, too, gained a coherent though never stable form only due to the Habesha tributaries who fed into it.

CODA

By the time James Bruce's *Travels to Discover the Source of the Nile* was published in 1790, it was, in some ways, a vestige of a bygone era of African travel and travel writing. In part, Bruce struggled to establish trust with his audience because sensibilities and expectations had changed in the seventeen years it took him to actually publish his account. In other ways, Bruce's journey was a harbinger for the model of African exploration to come. It was partially Joseph Banks's correspondences with Bruce following Bruce's return to Britain that inspired Banks to found the Association for Promoting the Discovery of the Interior Parts of Africa in 1788, which raised money for expeditions solely devoted to the systematic, empirical mapping of the interior of the continent. The epistemological, stylistic, and generic scaffolding that had been such a key part of the accumulation and circulation of African impressions in the early Enlightenment began to evolve along with the standardization of methods for determining longitude, the adoption of the chronometer in land surveys, the development of effective treatments for malaria, and the steamboat. Exploration and colonization of the continent became a real possibility rather than an expansionist fantasy. The first eyewitness accounts of places like Timbuktu dealt a blow to many geographical ideas that Europeans had harbored about the interior. As René Caillié, the first European to see Timbuktu and live to tell about it, wrote in 1830: "I had formed a totally different idea of the grandeur and wealth of Timbuctoo. The city presented, at first view, nothing but a mass of ill looking houses."[1]

Writers and readers began to take a different attitude toward African expressions as geographical evidence. For instance, Henry Salt's *Voyage to*

Abyssinia (1814)—the purpose of which was, in part, to verify and correct Bruce's account—takes issue with Bruce's impressionistic recounting of the Royal Chronicles. Once Salt arrives at his own history of the Abyssinian royal line, he declares that he is limiting himself only to "such particular events" that are "mentioned in the native annals" that are *also* "confirmed by the writings of contemporary authors of other nations."[2] It is only from this "concurrent testimony" that the details of the Abyssinians' take on themselves "may be considered as established historical facts." He contends that "to wade further into the obscure materials of these chronicles would be trespassing on the patience of my reader, more especially after what has already been attempted by Mr. Bruce."[3] He likewise scorns Bruce's case for why Ophir was in southeast Africa, arguing that the information about the inland towers and gold mines "rests entirely on a story received from the Moors."[4] He denies that the region's non-Muslim inhabitants confirm these stories, reiterating that something should be admitted into the geographical or historical record only if it can be corroborated by multiple external sources that agree with one another.

Of course, Salt himself relied on African informants. He turned to an Abyssinian he calls "Doster Esther" to help him determine the veracity of Bruce's account—"a learned man, looked up to with much respect by the country" who resided in Gondar and visited with Bruce often.[5] Doster Esther remembered Bruce fondly, spoke of him kindly, confirmed that he had endeared himself to Mentewab and Aster, and told Salt that when Bruce left Abyssinia, he "left behind him 'a great name.'"[6] But Doster Esther denied that Bruce had as good a command of the language as he claimed and asserted that he often used a translator; he said Bruce was not actually present at several battles or events he professed to have born witness to; and—most damning in Salt's eyes—he confirmed that Bruce had actually been accompanied to the source of the Nile by an Italian artist in his party named Luigi Balugani, of whom he makes no mention in his account of his arrival.[7] Salt endeavors to meticulously confirm these correctives, too, through "accounts from many different quarters, which all tended in the strongest manner to corroborate the statements of Doster Esther." Salt concludes that the man "may have been mistaken upon some few immaterial points of his narrative, but upon the whole I have reason to think it extremely correct."[8] The "testimony of the natives" is still useful to Salt, in other words, but the "native" perspective is not privileged as it had been in earlier travel narratives for what it might reveal about Africa that couldn't be known any other way.[9] Throughout the early Enlightenment, African testimony had been challenged and corroboration had been desired. But the necessity of relying on what Africans had to say and show about themselves, coupled with an approach to geographical representation that tended to conserve rather than overthrow outstanding impressions, meant that African expressions had also enjoyed a special status in geographical literature, even in texts written by authors who ardently wished it might be otherwise. Salt treats African expressions as only one point of "data" (Salt's word) that offers no more insight into the matter than any other point of data.[10] In fact, they must be interrogated all the more carefully for their implicit biases.

As a result of these shifting attitudes, early Enlightenment impressions of Africa permuted in the nineteenth century. Salt wasn't convinced by Bruce's argument that Sofala had been Ophir, but many others invested in colonial expansion in southeastern Africa resuscitated the idea in a new form, especially after the German explorer Karl Mauch "discovered" Great Zimbabwe in 1871. Mauch speculated that the ruins were the Queen of Sheba's palace, and, as Timothy Alborn puts it, as a result, "archaeologists, adventure novelists, company promoters, and journalists all jumped on the Ophir bandwagon and rode it into the new century."[11] The explorer, painter, and cartographer Thomas Baines drew a meticulous map of southeast Africa's rivers and mountain ranges in which he labeled Great Zimbabwe the "Supposed Realm of the Queen of Sheba."[12] Robert White, Baines's friend and the editor of his posthumously published *Golden Regions of South East Africa* (1877), enthusiastically supported this conclusion, writing that "the memory of the Queen of Sheba is still preserved amongst the Arabs of Sofala, as well as among the Habesh of Gondar in their scandalous chronicles."[13] He cited everyone from Milton to "no less a personage than the author of the Koran" as evidence that "the situation of Ophir is undoubtedly in favour of South Eastern Africa." Now that Europeans could examine the ruins for themselves, however, these local accounts became of secondary importance to what could be divined through empirical analysis—deemed scandalous chronicles rather than historical records. In fact, the likes of H. Rider Haggard popularized the theory that Great Zimbabwe had been built by Phoenicians on the grounds that sub-Saharan Africans lacked the technical sophistication for such a project. Haggard claimed that these Phoenicians were conquered by Zulu "savages" who "stamped out whatever civilization, Christian or Mohammedan, still flickered in Monomotapa so completely that even native tradition is silent concerning it, and once more oblivion covered the land and its story."[14] In Haggard's estimation, there was nothing to be gained by asking the Zulu for information that would be better attained and better understood by European archaeologists.

King Solomon's Mines (1888), Haggard's novel in which three Englishmen follow a treasure map in search of diamonds and wind up discovering a lost city, memorializes the death of the era when European explorers gathered impressions about the interior from rumor, hearsay, and the scantest of geographical evidence, turning such practices into the inciting incident of an action-adventure story. Allan Quatermain's interest in locating the mines is first sparked by "a tradition of the natives" who say that far inland there lay "a ruined city . . . believed to be the Ophir of the Bible" and by the claims of an old "witch doctor" that King Solomon's diamonds were mined just beyond that.[15] When he acquires a vague map to these mines, which one of the first Portuguese explorers in East Africa drew in his own blood as his final act before he died, Quatermain chooses to follow both rumors and map in search of adventure and riches, even though, as he tells his companions, "I do not think it probable that we can come out of it alive."[16] Haggard harnesses the epistemological instability of the past to set up the plot that will unfold, but it's clear that such instability is a vestige of a bygone era. Quatermain is writing a retrospective "history" of his adventure, so the reader already knows he will indeed come out of it alive, and by the time he does, he has grown "pretty sick of adventure."[17] The "ruined city" that Quatermain learned about from a "tradition of the natives" has since been confirmed as "Ophir" by "learned men."[18] The geographical insecurity raked up by *King Solomon's Mines* stays safely in the realm of both the imagination and the past. Haggard, writing after Park, Speke, Burton, Stanley, and Livingstone, can afford to be dismissive about the impression as a source of otherwise unknowable geographical information.

Nevertheless, these changes don't foreclose the discursive significance of or the power of the African impressions this book has described or of the African expressions that shaped them—they merely alter the terms under which that significance and power would need to be located and understood. In an essay on "The Real King Solomon's Mines," Haggard claims that when he wrote his novel, he had not yet heard of much less seen the ruins of Great Zimbabwe and had no idea that "the ancients had carried on a vast gold-mining enterprise in the part of Africa where it stands."[19] He says instead that those details as they appear in *King Solomon's Mines* were "the fruit of imagination, conceived, I suppose, from chance words spoken long ago that lay dormant in the mind; of that imagination which in some occult way so often seems to throw a shadow of the truth." On the one hand, this claim seems highly dubious. Haggard was familiar with Baines's work, and it hardly seems possible that he could have lived in Natal for seven years and never heard of the sensationalized archaeological digs being conducted just to the north. On the other hand, it is clear that "chance words spoken long ago"—what the Swahili, Lemba, and others told Portuguese traders about what lay up the Zambezi River; what Pedro Páez, James Bruce, and others read in Ethiopian books; what geographers like Barros made of this evidence; how writers like Milton remediated it—left their mark in *King Solomon's Mines* as surely as Mauch's excavation did. African impressions changed in shape, but they never disappeared.

NOTES

INTRODUCTION

1. For an account of this "age of the world picture," see Heidegger, *Question Concerning Technology*, 129, 132; Gregory, *Geographical Imaginations*, 15–16, 21–22; Jay, *Force Fields*, 115. For an overview of the role of scientific categorization in this, see Foucault, *Order of Things*, xiii; Pratt, *Imperial Eyes*, 15–36; Lamb, *Preserving the Self*, 76–113.
2. Said, *Orientalism*; Said, *Culture and Imperialism*, xii, 11.
3. Spivak, *Critique of Postcolonial Reason*, 334; Chakrabarty, *Provincializing Europe*, 43–46.
4. Said, *Orientalism*, 18; Foucault, *Order of Things*, 264–68; Pratt, *Imperial Eyes*, 8–9; Chakrabarty, *Provincializing Europe*, 7.
5. McLeod, *Geography of Empire*, 8.
6. Mudimbe, *Invention of Africa*, 8–9; Miller, *Blank Darkness*, 14–21.
7. Mbembe, *On the Postcolony*, 2.
8. Hegel, *Philosophy of History*, 99.
9. Conrad, *Heart of Darkness*, 8.
10. Masolo, *African Philosophy*, 3–6; Jordan, *White over Black*, 3–43; Hammond and Jablow, *Africa that Never Was*; Kim Hall, *Things of Darkness*, 25–61; McClintock, *Imperial Leather*, 21–24; Stiebel, *Imagining Africa*, 11–36.
11. Miller, *Blank Darkness*, 5.
12. Foundational work in this area includes Hulme, *Colonial Encounters*; Ferguson, *Subject to Others*; Pratt, *Imperial Eyes*; McLeod, *Geography of Empire*; Brown, *Ends of Empire*; Nussbaum, *Torrid Zones*. For more recent work on what postcolonial methodologies continue to bring to the study of early Enlightenment literature, see Kaul, *Eighteenth-Century British Literature*. As he articulates, the neocolonial can still quite easily masquerade as the postcolonial while simultaneously deploying the same tried and true intellectual and cultural strategies of imperial control that existed at least since the eighteenth century; this offers ample reason why postcolonial approaches remain relevant and important to the study of historical literatures (2–3).
13. Wheeler, *Complexion of Race*; Wahrman, *Making of the Modern Self*; Orr, *Empire on the English Stage*; Wilson, *Island Race*; Nussbaum, *Limits of the Human*;

Nussbaum, *Global Eighteenth Century*; Festa and Carey, *Postcolonial Enlightenment*, 23; Aravamudan, *Enlightenment Orientalism*, 2–3.

14. Festa, *Sentimental Figures of Empire*; Molineux, *Faces of Perfect Ebony*.
15. Lamb, *Preserving the Self*; Sudan, *Fair Exotics*, 1; Colley, *Captives*, 313; Vitkus, *Turning Turk*; Kugler, *Sway of the Ottoman Empire*, 35–54.
16. Ballaster, *Fabulous Orients*; Yang, *Performing China*; Aravamudan, *Enlightenment Orientalism*; Zuroski, *Taste for China*.
17. O'Quinn, *Engaging the Ottoman Empire*, 2–3; Colley, *Captives*, 18–19; Markley, *Far East*, 12; Porter, *Chinese Taste*, 38–39; Kugler, *Sway of the Ottoman Empire*, 1–2; Vitkus, *Turning Turk*, 78.
18. Táíwò, *How Colonialism Preempted Modernity*, 1; see also Parry, "Problems in Current Theories," 34.
19. Belcher, "Consuming Subjects," 213; Markley, *Far East*, 1; Porter, *Chinese Taste*, 1–7; Sudan, *Alchemy of Empire*, 27–28.
20. McLeod, *Geography of Empire*, 12–16; Lamb, *Preserving the Self*, 83–113.
21. For the influence of indigenous knowledges and technologies, see Sudan, *Alchemy of Empire*; Parrish, *American Curiosity*; Chaplin, *Subject Matter*. For European dependence on local translators, guides, and cultural brokers, see Lisa Brooks, *Our Beloved Kin*; Cohen, *Networked Wilderness*; Heywood and Thornton, *Central Africans, Atlantic Creoles*; Cassander Smith, *Black Africans*.
22. For a range of approaches to the problem of the archive in early modern and eighteenth-century studies, see Jehlen, "History before the Fact," 677–92; Aljoe, *Creole Testimonies*; Joseph, *Reading the East India Company*, 1–32; Mallipeddi, *Spectacular Suffering*, 12–18; Johnson and Molineux, "Putting Europe in Its Place," 62–99; Gikandi, *Slavery and the Culture of Taste*, 10, 69; Mbembe, *Critique of Black Reason*, 129, 2; Hartman, "Venus in Two Acts," 3.
23. Joseph, *Reading the East India Company*, 27; Cassander Smith, *Black Africans*, 2, 24.
24. See, for example, Diana Taylor, *Archive and the Repertoire*; Glover, *Paper Sovereigns*, 6; Cohen, *Networked Wilderness*, 1–2; Mallipeddi, *Spectacular Suffering*, 15; Sudan, *Alchemy of Empire*, 2; Lisa Brooks, *Our Beloved Kin*, 1–16.
25. Aravamudan, *Tropicopolitans*, 4; Mallipeddi, *Spectacular Suffering*, 5–6; Joseph, *Reading the East India Company*, 11–15, 26; Belcher, *Abyssinia's Samuel Johnson*.
26. Said, *Culture and Imperialism*, 32, 51, 67. Contrapuntal reading was a heuristic rather than a fully theorized concept throughout Said's scholarship, and, as such, he offered slightly different accounts of it as suited his purposes. But in his now-iconic reading of *Mansfield Park*, he described contrapuntal reading this way: "In practical terms, 'contrapuntal reading,' as I have called it means

reading a text with an understanding of what is involved when an author shows, for instance, that a colonial sugar plantation is seen as important to the process of maintaining a particular style of life in England" (66).

27. Wheeler, *Complexion of Race*, 94–107; Boulukos, *Grateful Slave*, 38–74; Beach, "Behn's *Oroonoko*," 215–33; Bartels, "*Othello* and Africa," 45–64; Bartels, *Speaking of the Moor*, 45–48.
28. Boulukos, *Grateful Slave*, 47, 52–53; Bartels, "*Othello* and Africa," 58, 47.
29. On Hegel's ghost, see Táíwò, "Exorcising Hegel's Ghost," 3. Scholars who have looked at European-African contact zones in particular include Thornton, *Africa and Africans*; Northrup, *Africa's Discovery of Europe*; Sparks, *Where the Negroes Are Masters*; Bennett, *African Kings*. For studies that situate Africa in terms of its eastern geopolitical relationships, see Aplers, *East Africa and the Indian Ocean*; Krebs, *Medieval Ethiopian Kingship*; Salvadore, *African Prester John*. Historians who have focused on Africa's connections to the wider Islamic world include Gomez, *African Dominion*; Bruce Hall, *History of Race*; Lydon, *On Trans-Saharan Trails*; Fauvelle, *Golden Rhinoceros*.
30. Fromont, *Art of Conversion*; Bennett, *African Kings*; Salvadore, *African Prester John*; Gomez, *African Dominion*.
31. Belcher, *Abyssinia's Samuel Johnson*, 18.
32. See, for instance, Gates, *Signifying Monkey*; Cartwright, *Reading Africa into American Literature*; Sobel, *World They Made Together*; M'Baye, *Trickster Comes West*; Sweet, *Domingos Álvares*; Carney, *Black Rice*.
33. Scholars who have written about how discourse about Africa itself, not only discourse about the African body, became part of European discourses about human difference include Kim Hall, *Things of Darkness*; Bartels, *Speaking of the Moor*; Nussbaum, *Torrid Zones*; Aravamudan, *Tropicopolitans*, 4; Boloukos, *Grateful Slave*, 38–74; Wheeler, *Complexion of Race*, 91–136, 264–68.
34. On the limitations of approaching global Blackness primarily through a "Middle Passage epistemology," see Wright, *Physics of Blackness*.
35. Hartman, "Venus in Two Acts," 3.
36. Morris, introduction to *Can the Subaltern Speak?*, 8.
37. Bruce Hall, *History of Race*, 21.
38. Spear, *Oxford Encyclopedia of African Historiography*; Curtin, *Africa Remembered*, 3–4.
39. Mudimbe, *Invention of Africa*, x; Chakrabarty, *Provincializing Europe*; Masolo, *African Philosophy*, 1–45.
40. Mbembe, *On the Postcolony*, 3; Táíwò, "Looking Back," 60.
41. Certeau, *Practice of Everyday Life*; Bourdieu, *Distinction: A Social Critique of the Judgement of Taste*, 170.
42. Diana Taylor, *Archive and the Repertoire*, 3.

NOTES TO PAGES 16–22

43. Theologians debated how to translate the Hebrew word "thukkijm," with some suggesting peacocks and others suggesting parrots, parakeets, ostriches, and apes. Le Grand, "Dissertations," 221.
44. Purchas, *Purchas His Pilgrimes* (1625), 1:25; Shalev, "Sacred Geography," 71.
45. Purchas, *Purchas His Pilgrimes* (1625), 1:34.
46. Abraham Ortelius, *Geographia Sacra*, 1606. LUNA: Folger Digital Image Collection, *Folger Shakespeare Library*, accessed April 12, 2022, https://luna.folger.edu/luna/servlet/detail/FOLGERCM1~6~6~791536~150477:Theatrum-orbis-terrarum-Abrahami-Or.
47. Ullendorff, *Ethiopia and the Bible*, 74–75.
48. Scott Carroll, "Solomonic Legend," 233–47.
49. Quoted in le Roux, "In Search of the Origin," 34. See also Purchas, *Purchas His Pilgrimes* (1625), 1:28.
50. Purchas, *Purchas His Pilgrimes* (1625), 1:28.
51. Romm, "Biblical History," 42.
52. Le Roux, "Kohenim Travelling South," 71–78; le Roux, "In Search of the Origin," 24–50.
53. Purchas, *Purchas His Pilgrimes* (1625), 1:28.
54. Burchett, *Complete History*, 9.
55. Carroll, "Solomonic Legend," 241. For Barros's connection to Saga za Ab, see Davis, "Background to the Zaga ZaAb Embassy," 255n102.
56. Bruce, *Travels*, 1:445.
57. Yewbrey, "John Dee's 'Brytish Impire,'" 247–76; Boon, *Other Tribes, Other Scribes*, 154–77; Purchas, *Purchas His Pilgrimes* (1625), 1:4.
58. Yewbrey, "John Dee's 'Brytish Impire,'" 275.
59. Livingstone, *Putting Science in Its Place*, 148.
60. Carey, "Inquires, Heads, and Directions," 26, 46; Pearl, *Utopian Geographies*, 32–33.
61. Lamb, *Preserving the Self*, 76–113; Campbell, *Wonder and Science*, 6–7; Park and Daston, *Wonders and the Order of Nature*, 328–31.
62. Pratt, *Imperial Eyes*, 9.
63. Ogborn and Withers, "Travel, Trade, and Empire," 20; Withers, *Placing the Enlightenment*, 98; Livingstone, *Putting Science in Its Place*, 81.
64. Livingstone, *Putting Science in Its Place*, 21.
65. Pratt, *Imperial Eyes*, 51, 67–83. I have cited Pratt directly because *Imperial Eyes* is frequently cited in service to such arguments; however, Pratt herself suggests that such blatant silencing doesn't begin until the last quarter of the eighteenth century (48).
66. Carey, "Problem of Credibility," 524–47; Leask, *Curiosity and the Aesthetics*, 54–101; Chico, *Experimental Imagination*, 44–75.

67. Courtney Weiss Smith, *Empiricist Devotions*, 20; Parrish, *American Curiosity*, 59; Zuroski, *Taste for China*, 11; Schmidgen, *Exquisite Mixture*, 149; Broglio, *Technologies of the Picturesque*, 21–22.
68. Thell, *Minds in Motion*, 3.
69. Purchas, *Purchas His Pilgrimes* (1625), 2:1026–27.
70. Leo Africanus, *Geographical Historie*, 5.
71. Barbot, "Description of the Coasts," 13.
72. William Smith, *New Voyage to Guinea*, 77.
73. Newton, *Thoughts upon the African Slave Trade*, 40, 4.
74. Parrish, *American Curiosity*, 246.
75. Spivak, *Critique of Postcolonial Reason*, 5–6; Greenblatt, *Shakespearean Negotiations*, 35–36.
76. Cassander Smith, *Black Africans*, 2, 24; Jehlen, "History before the Fact," 677–92; Aljoe, *Creole Testimonies*, 15–16; Joseph, *Reading the East India Company*, 25.
77. Aljoe, *Creole Testimonies*, 16. Embedded slave narratives are perhaps best characterized not as travel narratives but as traveling narratives since they were written by settlers in the Caribbean, but they were written for readers in England who wanted to know what was happening in a distant place and thus serve a similar function of making a faraway world intelligible (12–13).
78. Aljoe, *Creole Testimonies*, 21; Hartman, *Lose Your Mother*, 11.
79. Glover, *Paper Sovereigns*, 20–21.
80. Aljoe, *Creole Testimonies*, 13, 59–60.
81. Lisa Brooks, *Our Beloved Kin*, 12; Diana Taylor, *Archive and the Repertoire*, 33.
82. Pratt, *Imperial Eyes*, 43; Gregory, *Geographical Imaginations*, 23; Kim Hall, *Things of Darkness*, 29.
83. Mayhew, *Enlightenment Geography*, 28.
84. Latour, *Science in Action*, 23; see also Livingstone, *Putting Science in Its Place*, 100; Carey, "Inquiries, Heads, and Directions," 40; and McKeon, *Secret History of Domesticity*, xix. As Livingstone and Withers emphasize, this wasn't actually possible, but the presumption is that the intent was there. Livingstone, *Putting Science in Its Place*, 81; Withers, *Placing the Enlightenment*, 96–97.
85. Latour, *Science in Action*, 216–23.
86. Ibid., 219–21.
87. Daston, "Description by Omission," 13.
88. For an explanation of how Enlightenment geographers imagined the methods and aims of geography as a specifically defined discipline, see Mayhew, *Enlightenment Geography*, 23–48. For a broader consideration of what Charles Withers calls "geography as a discourse," meaning the way geographical ideas permeated and shaped Enlightenment thought and knowledge beyond strict

disciplinary boundaries, see Withers, *Placing the Enlightenment*, 12–14. My use of the term "geography" falls somewhere in between. It refers to a self-consciously epistemological practice, but it includes efforts by geographers in the narrow sense, travel writers, cartographers, and authors of imaginative literature who saw themselves participating in an academic conversation.

89. Kroupa, "Humanists and Travellers," 794.
90. Green, *Construction of Maps and Globes*, 171.
91. Ibid., 191, 155.
92. Ibid., 132, 174, 135.
93. Ibid., 170, 191.
94. Carey, "Problem of Credibility," 532.
95. Moll, *System of Geography*, preface.
96. On the variety of people who read such texts, including women and children, see Withers, *Placing the Enlightenment*, 167–68.
97. *New General Collection*, v.
98. Ibid., vi.
99. Barker, *African Link*, 4; Markley, *Far East*, 3; Pearl, *Utopian Geographies*, 34.
100. Harley, *New Nature of Maps*, 105.
101. Ibid., 113. For overviews of scholarship on this topic, see Sills, "Eighteenth-Century Cartographic Studies," 981–1002; and Edwards, "How to Read," 1–58. For accounts of the complex production of maps and how they exist at the intersection of science and aesthetics, see Schmidt, *Inventing Exoticism*; Sutton, *Early Modern Dutch Prints of Africa*; Klein, *Maps and the Writing of Space*.
102. Harley, *New Nature of Maps*, 39, 44.
103. Siobhan Carroll, *Empire of Air and Water*, 1–5; Hiatt, "Blank Spaces on the Earth," 245; Furtado, "Evolving Ideas," 212.
104. Jean Baptiste Bourguignon d'Anville, cartographer, *Afrique publiée sous les auspices de Monseigneur le Duc d'Orléans Prémier Prince du Sang*, 1749, Maps of Africa: An Online Exhibit, Stanford University, accessed April 12, 2022, https://purl.stanford.edu/pz676cy6968.
105. Haguet, "J.-B. d'Anville as Armchair Mapmaker," 92.
106. Ibid.
107. Jean Baptiste Bourguignon d'Anville, cartographer, *Carte de L'Ethiopie Orientale situee sur La Mer des Indes Entre le Cap Guarasouin, & le Cap de Bonne Esperance*, 1727, Bibliothèque nationale de France, accessed April 12, 2022, https://gallica.bnf.fr/ark:/12148/btv1b53036684k.
108. Jean Baptiste Bourguignon d'Anville and Solomon Boulton, cartographers, *Africa, Performed by the Sr. D'Anville under the Patronage of the Duke of Orleans*, 1755, Maps of Africa, Stanford University, https://purl.stanford.edu/gk907by1720.

109. Jean Baptiste Bourguignon d'Anville and Solomon Boulton, cartographers, *Africa: With all its states, kingdoms, republics, regions, islands, & ca.*, 1772. Maps of Africa, Stanford University, https://purl.stanford.edu/nd857rh9142.
110. See Schmidt, *Inventing Exoticism*; Sutton, *Early Modern Dutch Prints*; Klein, *Maps and the Writing of Space*.
111. "So geographers in Afric maps / With savage pictures fill their gaps, / And o'er inhabitable downs / Place elephants for want of towns," Jonathan Swift, "On Poetry," 104.
112. *Monthly Review*, 290.
113. McCleod, *Geography of Empire*; Pearl, *Utopian Geographies*; Thell, *Minds in Motion*.
114. Milton, *Paradise Lost*, 619, book 11, lines 396–400.
115. McCleod, *Geography of Empire*, 139.
116. Ibid., 134.
117. Qtd. in Saur, *Milton, Toleration, and Nationhood*, 115.
118. Heyrick, *Miscellany Poems*, 60–61.
119. Joseph Hall, "Sea-Floor Property," 641.
120. Dyer, *Fleece*, 132, book IV, lines 245–49.
121. Ibid., 132–33, book IV, lines 254–62.
122. Chico, "From Fleece to Fleets," 102.
123. Belcher, *Abyssinia's Samuel Johnson*, 209; Said, *Culture and Imperialism*, 52; Brown, *Cultural Fables of Modernity*, 2.
124. Tally, *Topophrenia*, 2.
125. Gregory, *Geographical Imaginations*, 203–5; Nussbaum, introduction to *Global Eighteenth Century*, 6–7; Withers, *Placing the Enlightenment*, 12–14; Livingstone, *Putting Science in Its Place*, 3; Ogborn, *Spaces of Modernity*, 20.

1. "WHEREIN THE BLACKE-PRINCE KEEPES HIS RESIDENCE, ATTENDED BY HIS JETTY COLOURED TRAINE"

1. Fauvelle, *Golden Rhinoceros*, 195–96.
2. Gomez, *African Dominion*, 106; Hopkins and Levtzion, *Corpus of Early Arabic Sources*, 334–35.
3. Gomez, *African Dominion*, 121; Hopkins and Levtzion, *Corpus of Early Arabic Sources*, 271, 358, 335; Fauvelle, *Golden Rhinoceros*, 196.
4. Gomez, *African Dominion*, 113.
5. Bennett, *African Kings*, 34.
6. Ibid., 34, 35.
7. Gomez, *African Dominion*, 108.
8. Ibid., 107–8.
9. Krebs, *Medieval Ethiopian Kingship*, 139.

10. Gomez, *African Dominion*, 110–11.
11. Fourteenth-century Arabic accounts of the Western Sudan appear to confirm that *jeliw* sang praise songs or panegyrics about Sundiata at the time of Mansa Musa's pilgrimage. See Wilks, "History of the *Sunjata* Epic," 47. Scholars disagree on when the Sundiata epic took its modern form, but the part of the story considered here—Sundiata's imperial conquests—are confirmed by Ibn Khaldun. Wilks, "History of the *Sunjata* Epic," 48; Levtzion, "Western Maghrib," 377–78.
12. John William Johnson, "Dichotomy of Power," 16–17; Wilks, "History of the *Sunjata* Epic," 28, 49.
13. John William Johnson, "Dichotomy of Power," 14; Gomez, *African Dominion*, 97.
14. Gomez, *African Dominion*, 97; Levtzion, "Western Maghrib," 393.
15. Gomez, *African Dominion*, 123–24.
16. Ibid., 123–25.
17. Ibid., 125.
18. Ibid., 115–17.
19. Ibid., 120–21.
20. Ibid., 92.
21. Ibid., 123.
22. Levtzion, "Western Maghrib," 390–91.
23. Ibid., 391.
24. The map was likely the joint work of two Jewish cartographers from Majorca known as "Cresques, son of Abraham" and "Yehuda, son of Cresques." Fauvelle, *Golden Rhinoceros*, 192.
25. Edson, *World Map*, 79; Estow, "Mapping Central Europe," 2n3.
26. On the written texts and genres that shaped the Catalan Atlas, see Edson, *World Map*, 74–79.
27. Translations are from "Catalan Atlas Legends," *The Cresques Project*, edited by Juan Ceva, last modified August 21, 2021, https://www.cresquesproject.net/.
28. It is unclear to modern scholars exactly where this capital was located. Hopkins and Levtzion, *Corpus of Early Arabic Sources*, 414n5. For an overview of the possibilities, see David Conrad, "Town Called Dakajalan," 355–77.
29. Edson, *World Map*, 83; Freedman, *Out of the East*, 194–95.
30. Estow, "Mapping Central Europe," 6; Edson, *World Map*, 83.
31. Edson, *World Map*, 83.
32. Crone, introduction to *Voyages of Cadamosto*, xix.
33. George Brooks, *Landlords and Strangers*, 59–77.
34. Cadamosto, *Voyages of Cadamosto*, 52.
35. Quoted in Goodwin, *Africa in Europe*, 134.

36. Cadamosto, *Voyages of Cadamosto*, 67.
37. Ibid., 68.
38. Gomes, "Voyages," 92.
39. Ibid., 93.
40. Fauvelle, *Golden Rhinoceros*, 197.
41. Gomes, "Voyages," 93–94.
42. Cadamosto, *Voyages of Cadamosto*, 22–23.
43. Ibid., 24.
44. Ibid., 23.
45. Ibid., 24.
46. Farias, "Silent Trade," 9; Garrard, "Myth and Metrology," 443; Sundström, *Trade of Guinea*, 22–31.
47. Dolfsma and Spithoven, "Silent Trade," 517–26.
48. Historically, there has been some debate over whether Herodotus's silent trade is the same practice referenced in accounts of West Africa. E. W. Bovill proposed in the 1920s that Herodotus was writing about the westernmost point of the trans-Sahara trade, which was controlled by the Wangara. "Silent Trade of the Wangara," 27–38. However, Timothy Garrard points out that "Herodotus does not mention West Africa; he speaks only of Libya and the Pillars of Hercules, both north of the Sahara." "Myth and Metrology," 444. P. F. de Moraes Farias breaks the history of the story of silent trading into two strands—a Classical strand based in Northern Africa that can be traced to Herodotus and a West African version in which the Wangara played "the role of middlemen between the gold producers and the Arabs and Moors or Europeans." "Silent Trade," 9.
49. See Farias, "Silent Trade," 11; Garrard, *Akan Weights and the Gold Trade*, 43. About Mansa Musa's gold, Gomez observes that the Mande were "responsible for perpetuating myths regarding its source." *African Dominion*, 121, 108n53.
50. See Hopkins and Levtzion, *Corpus of Early Arabic Sources*, 317, 273, 252.
51. Wilks, "Wangara, Akan and Portuguese," 342.
52. Barbot, "Description of the Coasts," 168.
53. Cadamosto, *Voyages of Cadamosto*, 1.
54. Levtzion, "Western Maghrib," 428; Bruce Hall, "Arguing Sovereignty," para. 26.
55. Gomez, *African Dominion*, 231; Levtzion, "Western Maghrib," 389.
56. Levtzion, "Western Maghrib," 428.
57. Gomez, *African Dominion*, 232.
58. Ibid., 234.
59. Bruce Hall, "Arguing Sovereignty," para. 38.

60. Zhiri, "Leo Africanus and the Limits," 176.
61. Ibid., 175.
62. Kim Hall, *Things of Darkness*, 25–61; Black, "Leo Africanus's 'Descrittione dell'Africa,'" 262–72. For a modern critical English translation, see Hunwick, *Timbuktu and the Songhay Empire*, 272–91.
63. Kim Hall, *Things of Darkness*, 29–31; Andrea, "Assimilation or Dissimulation?," 9; Bartels, *Speaking of the Moor*, 140, 149–50.
64. Miller, *Blank Darkness*, 16; Kim Hall, *Things of Darkness*, 29–30. Christopher Wise has observed that despite this eventual Christian readership, Leo Africanus himself had not yet converted at the time of the actual journey and was traveling on behalf of a Moroccan pasha, and, as such, he "is a historical composite of the opportunistic invader from the north," and his narrative is the record of a "scouting trip" for what would become the Arab Muslim and then eventual European Christian takeover of the Western Sudan. "Leo Africanus," 141, 156.
65. Andrea, "Assimilation or Dissimulation?," 18–19; Boulukos, *Grateful Slave*, 45.
66. Leo Africanus, *Geographical Historie*, 2. The Pory translation mistakenly says he visited fifteen kingdoms, but a more recent analysis indicates that he only visited five. Fisher, "Leo Africanus and the Songhay Conquest," 93.
67. Leo Africanus, *Geographical Historie*, 289.
68. Ibid., 2.
69. Hunwick, *Timbuktu and the Songhay Empire*, 272.
70. Because the history of Imperial Songhai is one of the most thorough locally written histories of early modern Africa, there is a robust set of external sources against which to compare the *Description*. Gomez, *African Dominion*, 170.
71. Leo Africanus, *Geographical Historie*, 285.
72. Ibid., 285–86.
73. Ibid., 290.
74. Ibid., 288.
75. Fisher, "Leo Africanus and the Songhay Conquest," 87.
76. Giacomo Gastaldi, cartographer, *Il disegno della geografia moderna de tutta la parte dell'Africa*, 1564, Library of Congress, https://www.loc.gov/item/2021668433; Abraham Ortelius, cartographer, *Africae tabula nova*, 1570, Barry Lawrence Ruderman Map Collection, Stanford University, http://purl.stanford.edu/cm885mn6792; Willem Janszoon Blaeu, cartographer, *Africae novo descriptio*, 1635, Ruderman Map Collection, Stanford University, http://purl.stanford.edu/jg200yj8932.
77. Though Pory's biases certainly come through his translation in general, his translation of the geographical narrative this chapter focuses on is not substantively different from Hunwick's modern critical translation.

78. Evelyn, *Numismata*, 268–69. It is possible that Evelyn is referring to Ishaq I or II, but it seems more likely that he is anglicizing "Izchia," the first king of "Tombutum, who managed his affairs so well," that he conquered the rest of the Western Sudan. Heylyn, *Cosmographie*, 57.
79. Evelyn, *Numismata*, 269.
80. Pliny, *Historie of the World*, 23.
81. Zouche, *The Dove*, 21.
82. Shakespeare, *Othello*, 2129, act 1, scene 3, lines 127–49.
83. Defoe, *Atlas Maritimus and Commercialis*, 267.
84. For evidence that Shakespeare read Pory's translation of the *Description*, see Whitney, "Did Shakespeare Know Leo Africanus?," 470–83.
85. Leo Africanus, *Geographical Historie*, 293.
86. Pory, introduction to *Geographical Historie of Africa*, 3.
87. Emily Bartels, for instance, argues Othello's origin story is "set in an exotic elsewhere." *Speaking of the Moor*, 170. Bernhard Klein identifies the geography sketched out here as "a monstrous periphery beyond the civilized world." "*Oroonoko* and Mapping," 32. Jordan finds continuity between the Classical and then European notion that Africa was the home of monstrous hybrids and the cause of Othello's hypersexuality. *White over Black*, 37.
88. Kim Hall, "*Othello* and the Problem of Blackness," 358.
89. Lydon, *On Trans-Saharan Trails*, 102.
90. Leo Africanus, *Geographical Historie*, 285.
91. Pory, introduction to *Geographical Historie of Africa*, 6; Bartels, *Speaking of the Moor*, 150; Boulukos, *Grateful Slave*, 42–44.
92. For instance, Kim Hall, "*Othello* and the Problem of Blackness," 359–67; Bartels, *Speaking of the Moor*; Aravamudan, *Tropicopolitans*, 2–9.
93. For arguments that Shakespeare was exposed to other forms of African discourse via Atlantic contact, see Arndt, "Trans*textuality in Shakespeare's *Othello*," 393–429; Mafe, "From Ògún to Othello," 46–61; and Balogun, "Ajubaba," 18–25.
94. Milton, *Paradise Lost*, 620, book 11, line 402.
95. Heyrick, *Miscellany Poems*, 60–61.
96. Dyer, *Fleece*, 64, 130, book IV, line 163; book II, lines 368–69; book IV, lines 209–10.
97. Ibid., 131, book IV, lines 22–24.
98. McRae, introduction to *Six Bookes*, A24, A19–A20; Heller, "Bodin on Slavery," 53–65.
99. McRae, introduction to *Six Bookes*, A15.
100. Bodin, *Six Bookes*, 222.
101. Ibid., 506.

102. Ibid., 507.
103. Ibid.
104. Ibid., 147.
105. The location of Leo Africanus's "Gaoga" is not entirely clear. It is distinct from "Gago" [Gao], but it is one of only two kingdoms that he describes in the Land of the Blacks that is not either conquered by or a vassal of the *askia*, the other being Borno. It's possible both were provinces of the Kanem-Bornu Empire.
106. Leo Africanus, *General Historie*, 294.
107. Bodin, *Six Bookes*, 47–48.
108. Duverdier, *Love and Armes*, 146, 154–55.
109. Walker, *Victorious Love*, 20.
110. Turk, *Baroque Fiction-Making*, 12; DiPiero, *Dangerous Truths*, 105.
111. Gomberville, *Polexander*, 3:68.
112. DiPiero, *Dangerous Truths*, 108.
113. Bertaud, "Afrique et Africains dans *Polexandre*," 94–96.
114. Welch, *Taste for the Foreign*, 33–34.
115. Gomberville, *Polexander*, 3:36.
116. Ibid., 3:69–70, 3:63.
117. Ibid., 3:64, 3:65.
118. Ibid., 3:66.
119. Ibid., 3:67.
120. Bodin, *Six Bookes*, 507.
121. See, for instance, Welch, *Taste for the Foreign*, 32–33; Aravamudan, *Enlightenment Orientalism*, 33–40; Emily Kugler, *Sway of the Ottoman Empire*, 93–95.
122. Jordan, *White over Black*, 593.
123. Gomberville, *Polexander*, 4:246–56.
124. Jobson's account has garnered particular interest from scholars for the way it bridges early modern and eighteenth-century attitudes toward race and slavery. He makes it clear to brokers who offer him slaves that he is there to acquire gold and that "neither did we buy or sell one another, or any that had our own shapes." Jobson, *Golden Trade*, 88–89. However, even as he expressed this sentiment, British participation in the transatlantic slave trade was beginning to expand. See Guasco, "Agents of Empire," 47–49; Morgan, *Reckoning with Slavery*, 116; Jordan, *White over Black*, 60–61; Mark, "Portuguese" Style, 24–25; Hair, "Attitudes to Africans," 43–68; Boulukos, *Grateful Slave*, 50–51.
125. Jobson, *Golden Trade*, 7.
126. Ibid., 85. For an up-to-date account of Thompson's and Jobson's expeditions, see Svalastog, *Mastering the Worst Trades*, 45–85.

127. Jobson, *Golden Trade*, 92.
128. Ibid., 92.
129. Ibid., 93.
130. Ibid.
131. Ibid., 102.
132. Ibid., 103.
133. Ibid.
134. Ibid.
135. Ibid., 104–5.
136. Ibid., 161.
137. Ibid., 100.
138. Ibid., 101.
139. Ibid.
140. Ibid., 102.
141. Ibid., 8.

2. "A COUNTRY OF BLACKS SO CALLED"

1. Aravamudan, *Tropicopolitans*, 29.
2. Sills, "Surveying the Map of Slavery," 317–18.
3. Handler, "Slave Revolts and Conspiracies," 15.
4. Crouch, *English Acquisitions in Guinea*, 31.
5. Behn, *Oroonoko*, 51.
6. Katharine Rogers, "Fact and Fiction," 1–14; Lipking "Confusing Matters," 171; Lipking, "At London and Paris," 267.
7. Beach, "Behn's Oroonoko," 215–33.
8. Beach, "Global Slavery, Old World Bondage," 418.
9. Beach, "Behn's Oroonoko," 225; Boulukos, *Grateful Slave*, 52–53.
10. Runge, "Constructing Place in *Oroonoko*," 20; Sills, "Surveying the Map of Slavery," 314–40; Markley, "Global Analogies," 188–212; Yang, "Asia out of Place," 236–37.
11. Livingstone, *Putting Science in Its Place*, 148. On Behn's interest in scientific empiricism in general, see Gevirtz, "Behn and the Scientific Self," 85–100; Hayden, "As Far as a Woman" 123–42; Campbell, *Wonder and Science*, 257; Coppola, *Theater of Experiment*, 63–83.
12. Behn, *Oroonoko*, 9.
13. Ibid., 10.
14. Sprat, *History of the Royal Society*, 251; Pearl, *Utopian Geographies*, 68.
15. Boyle, *New Experiments Physico-mechanical*, 485; Hayden, "As Far as a Woman" 126; Campbell, *Wonder and Science*, 267, 277.
16. Behn, *Oroonoko*, 9.

17. Chibka, "Oh! Do Not Fear," 510–37; Paxman, "Oral and Literate Discourse," 88; Gruber, "Dead Girls Do It Better," 99; Starr, "Objects, Imaginings, and Facts," 510; Dickson, "Truth, Wonder, and Exemplarity," 579.
18. Runge, "Constructing Place in *Oroonoko*," 24.
19. Leo Africanus, *Geographical Historie*, 2.
20. Cadamosto, *Voyages*, 24.
21. Jobson, *Golden Trade*, 8.
22. Behn, *Oroonoko*, 13.
23. Gallagher, *Nobody's Story*, 77; Nussbaum, "Between 'Oriental,'" 137–66.
24. Ogilby, *Africa*, 2.
25. Ibid., 198.
26. Ibid., 205.
27. Ibid., 315.
28. Ibid.
29. Heylyn, *Cosmographie*, 58; Ogilby, *Africa*, 9.
30. Hunwick, *Timbuktu and the Songhay Empire*, 273. The term "Ginyih" also appears on the Catalan Atlas (fig. 2) in prominent lettering near Mansa Musa's gold nugget.
31. Ogilby, *Africa*, 316.
32. Heylyn, *Cosmographie*, 53.
33. Ibid., 57.
34. Ibid., 58.
35. *Golden Coast*, 3.
36. Ibid., 4.
37. Ibid., 59.
38. Ibid., 59. The translation in Purchas is a little clearer on this point. The broker asks the European *not* to speak the Moorish speech to them because they want to cheat the merchant. Purchas, *Purchas His Pilgrimes* (1625), 2:938.
39. *Golden Coast*, 67.
40. Marees, *Description and Historical Account*, 48–49.
41. Fage, "Upper and Lower Guinea," 472; Wilks, "Wangara, Akan and Portuguese," 336–39.
42. Barbot, "Description of the Coasts," 168, 189.
43. Ibid., 3.
44. *Golden Coast*, 3.
45. On chivalric romance, see Brown, *Ends of Empire*, 37–38; Lipking, "Confusing Matters," 260–65; Rivero, "Aphra Behn's *Oroonoko*," 451–52; Aravamudan, *Tropicopolitans*, 30; Kroll, "Tales of Love and Gallantry," 582–601. On the oriental tale, see Nussbaum, "Between 'Oriental,'" 154–55; Yang, "Asia out

of Place," 236; Campbell, *Wonder and Science*, 262; Kroll, "Tales of Love and Gallantry," 593; Kugler, *Sway of the Ottoman Empire*, 148–49. On the court as an allegory for Britain, see Guffey, "Aphra Behn's *Oroonoko*," 3–41; Brown, *Ends of Empire*, 37; Pacheco, "Royalism and Honor," 492; Gallagher, *Nobody's Story*, 93; Kroll, "Tales of Love and Gallantry," 583–601; Visconi, "Degenerate Race," 677–91.

46. Southerne, *Oroonoko*, 14, 25.
47. Leo Africanus, *Geographical Historie*, 289.
48. Ibid., 287–88.
49. Behn, *Oroonoko*, 31.
50. Molineux, "False Gifts/Exotic Fictions," 457; Katharine Rogers, "Fact and Fiction," 10; Lipking, "Confusing Matters," 260; Griffin, "Dismembering the Sovereign," 107–33; and Iwanisziw, "Behn's Novel Investment," 75–98.
51. Beach is an exception to this, making the case that the text's seemingly chivalric inter-African slave trade is deconstructed in Africa itself as Behn ties it explicitly to New World slavery. "Behn's *Oroonoko*," 223–25.
52. Behn, *Oroonoko*, 35.
53. Molineux, "False Gifts/Exotic Fictions," 457.
54. Bratach, "Following the Intrigue," 211–13.
55. Sprat, *History of the Royal Society*, 26, 112.
56. Ibid., 112.
57. Behn, *Oroonoko*, 11.
58. Ibid., 36–37.
59. Molineux, "False Gifts/Exotic Fictions," 468; Sills, "Surveying the Map of Slavery," 320–21.
60. Sprat, *History of the Royal Society*, 251–52.
61. Behn, *Oroonoko*, 10.
62. Harol, "Passion of *Oroonoko*," 453.
63. Sprat, *History of the Royal Society*, 112.
64. Behn, *Oroonoko*, 29.
65. Moll, *System of Geography*, preface.
66. Behn, *Oroonoko*, 57.
67. Parrish, *American Curiosity*, 38.
68. Behn, *Oroonoko*, 51.
69. Ibid.
70. Ridley, *Clara's Grand Tour*.
71. Aravamudan, *Tropicopolitans*, 40; Chibka, "Oh! Do Not Fear," 518.
72. Behn, *Oroonoko*, 51.

3. "A MEDIUM OF AN ENDLESS CORRESPONDENCE"

1. Pettigrew, *Freedom's Debt*, 162–63.
2. *Proposal for Settling the Trade*.
3. Pettigrew, *Freedom's Debt*, 165, 166.
4. Ibid., 170.
5. On Defoe's connections to the Royal African Company, See Kiern, "Defoe and the Royal African Company," 243–47; Knox-Shaw, "Defoe and the Politics," 938. See also Scrimgeour, "Problem of Realism," 21–22; Wheeler, *Complexion of Race*, 136; Novak, *Daniel Defoe*, 361.
6. For a detailed account of these writings, see Mitsein and Powell, "Defoe, Africa, and the Levant."
7. Defoe, *History of the Principal Discoveries*, 302.
8. Aravamudan, "Defoe, Commerce, and Empire," 45. See also Backsheider, *Daniel Defoe*, 441–42, 449.
9. Pat Rogers, "Speaking within Compass," 113. See also Scrimgeour, "Problem of Realism," 37; Baker, "Geography of Daniel Defoe," 263.
10. Pearl, *Utopian Geographies*, 75–114; Thell, *Minds in Motion*, 111–52.
11. Edwards, "Defoe the Geographer," 180–81.
12. Thell, *Minds in Motion*, 116, 113.
13. Pearl, *Utopian Geographies*, 22, 76–77, 108–9.
14. Novak, *Daniel Defoe*, 584.
15. Knox-Shaw, "Defoe and the Politics," 937; Scrimgeour, "Problem of Realism," 22; Novak, *Daniel Defoe*, 584; Turley, "Piracy, Identity, and Desire," 200; Wear, "No Dishonour," 579–80; Markley, *Far East*, 211; Pearl, *Utopian Geographies*, 114; Thell, *Minds in Motion*, 121.
16. Defoe, *Captain Singleton*, 129, 159; Boulukos, *Grateful Slave*, 40, 53–54; Wheeler, *Complexion of Race*, 107–8, 113–14; Powell, introduction to *Captain Singleton*, 25–33; Cole, "Guns, Ivory, and Elephant Graveyards," 38–43.
17. Muhammad al-Idrisi, *Tabula Rogeriana*, 1553 [1152], Digital Bodleian, Bodleian Libraries, University of Oxford, accessed April 13, 2022, https://digital.bodleian.ox.ac.uk/objects/ced0d8bd-1019-4af2-9086-e411115f1507.
18. Quoted in Francis Moore, *Travels into the Inland*, 228.
19. Ibid.
20. Ibid., vi–vii.
21. Ibid., 224.
22. Ibid., 225.
23. Ibid., 226.
24. Ibid., 200n1.

25. Ibid., viii. The fact that neither was what we would now consider strictly African indicates the extent to which Moore is mobilizing the category of the cultural insider here.
26. Ibid., ix.
27. Ibid., 20, ix.
28. Ibid., 229.
29. John Senex, cartographer, *A New Map of Africa from the Latest Observations*, 1721, Ruderman Map Collection, Stanford University, accessed April 13, 2022, http://purl.stanford.edu/pc274xk1527; Jean Baptiste Bourguignon d'Anville, cartographer, *Afrique publiée*, 1749, Maps of Africa, https://purl.stanford.edu/pz676cy6968; Herman Moll, cartographer, *To the right honourable Charles, Earl of Peterborow and Monmouth, etc.*, 1710, Maps of Africa, Stanford University, accessed April 13, 2022, https://purl.stanford.edu/bq814vd7327.
30. *New General Collection of Voyages and Travels*, 2:189nc.
31. Edwards, "Defoe and the *Atlas*," 141. There is no consensus among Defoe scholars on whether Defoe is the author-compiler of all of the *Atlas* or parts of the *Atlas*, or whether the author-compiler simply borrowed extensively from Defoe's writings on Africa. Backscheider (*Daniel Defoe*, 468, 471–73) and Novak (*Daniel Defoe*, 687–88) argue he is the author, and Edwards makes a case for why it is highly probable that he is. Furbank and Owens have suggested there is reason to be skeptical that he was the sole or even the main compiler of the text (*Critical Bibliography of Daniel Defoe*, 276–79). I proceed from the assumption that he was the author-compiler of at least the Africa portion of the text. The *Atlas* not only borrows word-for-word from works like Defoe's *Tour*, *Review*, and *General History*, it quotes his poetry and includes a scene from *Captain Singleton*. Furthermore, as Edwards points out, when "the distinctive, critical voice of the compiler dominates . . . it sounds very like the voice that we have come to think of as Defoe's" ("Defoe and the *Atlas*," 144). Finally, given the wealth of other, much more canonical and frequently recycled sources that existed about Africa at the time of the *Atlas*'s publication, it is unusual that the author-compiler would rely so heavily on Defoe's works. It seems more reasonable, at least based on the evidence currently available, to assume that Defoe had a heavy hand in its creation than to come up with equally conjectural reasons as to why he didn't.
32. Defoe, *Atlas Maritimus*, 236.
33. Defoe, *Captain Singleton*, 129. See also Boulukos, *Grateful Slave*, 53–54; Wheeler, *Complexion of Race*, 107–9; Powell, introduction to *Captain Singleton*, 25–33. Each observe that anyone passingly familiar with nonfiction representations of Africa would have perceived Defoe's imaginative license

in texts like *Captain Singleton* and *Robinson Crusoe* when he portrayed the continent's coasts as sparsely populated by primitive natives.

34. Defoe, *Atlas Maritimus*, 246–47.
35. Ibid., 246.
36. Ibid.
37. Ibid., 247.
38. Ibid.
39. Ibid., 263, 276.
40. Ibid., 276.
41. Ibid.
42. Ibid.
43. Ibid.
44. Edwards, "Defoe and the *Atlas*," 164; Novak, *Daniel Defoe*, 687.
45. Defoe, *Atlas Maritimus*, 250.
46. Ibid., 270.
47. Defoe, *Defoe's Review*, 21:570, 19 February 1712; Defoe, *Atlas Maritimus*, 270.
48. Defoe, *Atlas Maritimus*, 249–50.
49. Ibid., 251.
50. Ibid., 252.
51. Ibid., 253.
52. Turley, "Piracy, Identity, and Desire," 200; Wheeler, *Complexion of Race*, 108, 109; Newman, "Property, History, and Identity," 567; Wear, "No Dishonour," 588; Zuroski, *Taste for China*, 105–21; Cole, "Guns, Ivory, and Elephant Graveyards," 38–50.
53. Walmsley, "African Artisan," 363; Loar, *Political Magic*, 107.
54. Lee, "Mercantile Gentility," 301; Mitsein and Powell, "Defoe, Africa, and the Levant."
55. Wear, "No Dishonour," 574; Aravamudan, *Tropicopolitans*, 102.
56. Scrimgeour, "Problem of Realism," 37.
57. Aravamudan, *Tropicopolitans*, 80.
58. Defoe, *Captain Singleton*, 168, 79, and passim.
59. Ibid., 72.
60. Wheeler, *Complexion of Race*, 109–10.
61. Defoe, *Captain Singleton*, 78; Farr, "Colonizing Gestures," 551.
62. Defoe, *Atlas Maritimus*, 236.
63. Wheeler, *Complexion of Race*, 126–29; Brown, "Defoe's 'Black Prince,'" 153–69.
64. Defoe, *Captain Singleton*, 142.
65. Defoe, *Defoe's Review*, 21:570, 19 February 1712.
66. Defoe, *Atlas Maritimus*, 252.

67. Defoe, *Captain Singleton*, 80.
68. Ibid., 82–83.
69. Ibid., 86.
70. Ibid.
71. Ibid., 100.
72. Ibid., 107.
73. Ibid., 141.
74. Ibid., 152.
75. Ibid., 159.
76. Ibid., 143.
77. Ibid., 164.
78. Ibid., 177.
79. Walmsley, "African Artisan," 359; Backscheider, *Daniel Defoe*, 475. Wheeler notes that as soon as the Englishman is shaved and dressed, "no hybridity of behavior or appearance lingers" but he still possesses "'native' knowledge" of the land. *Complexion of Race*, 124.
80. Defoe, *Captain Singleton*, 170.
81. Ibid., 169.
82. Lee, "Mercantile Gentility," 308. See also Walmsley, "African Artisan," 360; and Mitsein and Powell, "Defoe, Africa, and the Levant."
83. Scrimgeour, "Problem of Realism," 37.
84. Defoe, *Atlas Maritimus*, ii–iii.
85. Edwards, "Defoe and the *Atlas*," 151, 148.
86. Novak, *Daniel Defoe*, 688.
87. Backscheider, *Daniel Defoe*, 475.
88. See Furbank, "Naked White Man"; Knox-Shaw, *Explorer in English Fiction*, 64.
89. Defoe, *Atlas Maritimus*, 250.
90. Ibid., 253.
91. Ibid.
92. Ibid.
93. Ibid.
94. Ibid.
95. Mungo Park, *Travels in the Interior*, 1:9.
96. Ibid., 1:13.

4. "WHERE THE NILE RISETH ... WHERE THE QUEEN OF SABA LIVED"

1. Johnson, *Johnson on Demand*, 451.
2. Gomberville, *Polexander*, 3:38, 3:77. Though "Ethiopia" is still used as a general or poetic term for Africa at this time, "Belul" specifies the *negusa nagast*. In attempts to align the nation with the fabled Christian kingdom of folklore,

"Belul Gian" was given as one etymology of "Prester John." See d'Avity, *Estates, Empires, and Principallities*, 1082.
3. *Late Travels of S. Giacomo Baratti*, 212–14.
4. Defoe, *History of the Principal Discoveries*, 7–8. See also Defoe, *Atlas Maritimus*, 274.
5. "Ethiopia," as Moll's map shows (1710; fig. 5 in this work), could be used generically to refer to sub-Saharan Africa during this time, but as the above quotes show the term was increasingly used to denote the part of Africa that Europeans more frequently called "Abyssinia," from the Ge'ez word "Habesha," which is how the Christians of the Ethiopian Highlands referred to themselves. I generally use the word "Abyssinia" to refer to the nation ruled over by the *negusa nagast*, but I use "Ethiopia" at times to refer to institutions or ideas still relevant to Ethiopia today.
6. Bruce, *Travels*, 1:vi.
7. Budge, *Queen of Sheba*, 35.
8. Ullendorff, *Ethiopia and the Bible*, 75.
9. Crummey, *Land and Society*, 20.
10. Tamrat, *Church and State*, 106.
11. Krebs, *Medieval Ethiopian Kingship*, 6–7, 139, 265. Pushing back on the scholarly narrative that medieval Ethiopian sovereigns were invested first and foremost in a military alliance with Europe, Krebs argues that their interest in the wider Christian world remained tied up in the acquisition of relics until Eleni's diplomatic outreach in the early sixteenth century (90, 143, 187).
12. Tamrat, *Church and State*, 297.
13. Ibid., 299.
14. Crummey, *Land and Society*, 25.
15. O'Mahony, "Between Islam and Christendom," 147; Salvadore, "Ethiopian Age," 599.
16. Krebs, *Medieval Ethiopian Kingship*, 39; O'Mahony, "Between Islam and Christendom," 147.
17. Salvadore, *African Prester John*, 4.
18. Ibid., 58.
19. Geddes, *Church History of Ethiopia*, 50–51.
20. Purchas, *Purchas His Pilgrimes* (1625), 2:738.
21. Geddes, *Church History of Ethiopia*, 93–95.
22. Salvadore, "Ethiopian Age," 593–94.
23. Salvadore, *African Prester John*, 1.
24. Pankhurst, "Early Contact," 400.
25. Salvadore, *African Prester John*, 26–27.
26. Oestigaard and Firew, *Source of the Blue Nile*, 35–36.

27. Ludolf, *New History of Ethiopia*, 37.
28. Belcher, *Abyssinia's Samuel Johnson*, 215, 111, 116.
29. Ibid., 117.
30. Oestigaard and Firew, *Source of the Blue Nile*, 37–38.
31. Pankhurst, "Ethiopia's Alleged Control," 32.
32. Clapham, "European Mapping of Ethiopia," 294.
33. For other examples of the Land of Prester John in Italian literature, see Cavallo, *World beyond Europe*, 185.
34. Ariosto, *Orlando Furioso*, 183.
35. Van Donzel, "Legend of the Blue Nile," 124.
36. Ariosto, *Orlando Furioso*, 184.
37. Álvares, *Narrative of the Portuguese Embassy*, 203.
38. Ariosto, *Orlando Furioso*, 183.
39. Ibid., 187.
40. Ibid., 185.
41. Salvadore, *African Prester John*, 142–43.
42. Álvares, *Narrative of the Portuguese Embassy*, 167.
43. Ibid., 203.
44. Ibid., 226.
45. Ibid., 78.
46. Ibid., 80.
47. Belcher, "Sisters Debating the Jesuits," 123–24.
48. Álvares, *Narrative of the Portuguese Embassy*, 143, 391.
49. Ibid., 330.
50. Ibid., 78.
51. Ibid., 84.
52. Ibid., 82.
53. Ibid., 83.
54. Ibid., 82.
55. Bodin, *Six Bookes*, 507; Green, *Construction of Maps and Globes*, 191.
56. Purchas, *Purchas His Pilgrimes* (1625), 2:1027.
57. Páez, *Páez's History*, 144.
58. Haile, "Works of Ras Səm'on," 7.
59. Páez, *Páez's History*, 161, 267.
60. Tamrat, *Church and State*, 297.
61. Ibid., 301.
62. Salvadore, *African Prester John*, 184.
63. Castanhoso, "Castanhoso," 10.
64. Purchas, *Purchas His Pilgrimes* (1625), 2:1066.
65. Castanhoso, "Castanhoso," 15–16.

66. Ibid., 14.
67. Ibid.
68. Ibid., 64.
69. Ibid., 22, 24, 32, 51, 72.
70. Ibid., 47.
71. Ibid., 72.
72. Bermudez, "Bermudez," 156–59.
73. Ibid., 158, 197.
74. Herman, "Towards a History," 383.
75. Ibid., 389.
76. Ibid., 386–87.
77. Pinto, *Voyages and Adventures*, 6.
78. Ibid.
79. Ibid.
80. Haile, *Ethiopian Orthodox*, 207.
81. Herman, "Towards a History," 389.
82. Sebastian Münster, cartographer, *Map of Africa* from *Cosmographia*, 1578 [1544], Maps of Africa, Stanford University, accessed April 13, 2022, https://purl.stanford.edu/cx466kj4658.
83. Abraham Ortelius, cartographer, *Africae tabula nova*, 1570, Ruderman Map Collection, Stanford University, accessed April 13, 2022, http://purl.stanford.edu/cm885mn6792; Gerhard Mercator, cartographer, *Africa*, 1595 [1569], Maps of Africa, Stanford University, accessed April 13, 2022, https://purl.stanford.edu/qd912wh8072; Willem Janszoon Blaeu, cartographer, *Africae novo descriptio*, 1635, Ruderman Map Collection, Stanford University, accessed April 13, 2022, http://purl.stanford.edu/jg200yj8932.
84. Purchas, *Purchas His Pilgrimage* (1613), 565, 566.
85. Ibid., 566.
86. Ibid.
87. Ibid. 567.
88. Purchas, *Purchas His Pilgrimage* (1626), 749.
89. Boavida et al., introduction to *Páez's History*, 12.
90. Páez, *Páez's History*, 62.
91. Ibid., 76.
92. Ibid., 121.
93. Ibid., 208.
94. Castanhoso, "Castanhoso," 96; Álvares, *Narrative of the Portuguese Embassy*, 130.
95. Castanhoso, "Castanhoso," 96.
96. *Late Travels of S. Giacomo Baratti*, 15, 33–35; Marana, *Letters Writ*, 144–45.

97. Milton, *Paradise Lost*, 236–37, book IV, lines 280–84.
98. Ibid., 253, lines 546–48.
99. Clark, "Milton's Abyssinian Paradise," 144.
100. Páez, *Páez's History*, 129.
101. Poncet, *Voyage to Aethiopia*, 71, 79.
102. Ludolf, *New History of Ethiopia*, 162.
103. Geddes, *Church History*, 8.
104. *History of Little Goody Two-Shoes*, 145.
105. Lyttelton, *Works*, 737.
106. Berington, *News from the Dead*, 77. For the periodical life of *News from the Dead*, see Powell, *Performing Authorship*, 199–203.
107. Berington, *News from the Dead*, 77–78.
108. Ibid., 82.
109. Lobo, *Voyage to Abyssinia*, 87.
110. Green, *Construction of Maps and Globes*, 140.
111. Guillaume de l'Isle, cartographer, *Carte D'Afrique Dressée pour l'usage du Roy*, 1722, Maps of Africa, Stanford University, accessed April 13, 2022, https://purl.stanford.edu/zr331tm8568.
112. As stated in the introduction, d'Anville is an exception to this, but his solution is to maintain the Ptolemaic lakes and mark the river by its Ethiopian name, Abay, or the Father of Waters, so his map is nevertheless bound up in this impression.

5. "BETWEEN THE INLAND COUNTRIES OF AFRICK AND THE PORTS OF THE RED SEA"

1. Ruffhead, Review of *Rasselas*, 167.
2. James Watt observes that "*Rasselas* makes almost no concession to any readerly demand for Oriental exoticism." "What Mankind Has Lost," 25. Christopher Brooks points out that in Pekuah's tale of captivity by an Arab despot, he uncharacteristically never poses any threat to Pekuah's virtue. "Nekayah's Courage and Female Wisdom," 56.
3. See Leyburn, "No Romantick Absurdities," 1059–67; John Robert Moore, "*Rasselas* and the Early Travelers," 36–41; Kolb, "'Paradise' in Abyssinia," 10–16; Lockhart, "Fourth Son," 516–28; van Wyk Smith, "Father Lobo," 5–16.
4. On Johnson's invocation and revision of Milton's Abyssinia, see Rees, *Johnson's Milton*, 58–81. Lockhart has detailed the overlaps between *Rasselas* and Urreta's text in depth, arguing that Johnson would have read it directly and not simply encountered it through its English epitomes in Purchas and Heylyn. "Fourth Son," 523.
5. Kolb, "'Paradise' in Abyssinia," 11; Aravamudan, *Tropicopolitans*, 203.

6. Johnson, *Voyage*, 3.
7. Mayhew, *Landscape, Literature*, 214–15.
8. For the first, see Kolb, "'Paradise' in Abyssinia," 16; Mayhew, *Landscape, Literature*, 169, 199, 212; Leyburn, "No Romantick Absurdities," 1067; Aravamudan, *Tropicopolitans*, 204; Sudan, *Fair Exotics*, 25–26. These critics make the case that this departure is an explicit signal that the text's primary aim is not to represent an earthly geography but to direct the reader's attentions to the hereafter, to philosophize about human universals, to stage a moral vision unfettered by the rules of travel writing, or to stage ideas of British nationalism at the expense and containment of an exotic other. For the latter, see Tomarken, *Johnson, Rasselas, and the Choice of Criticism*, 102–3; Potkay, *Passion for Happiness*, 48–52; Rees, *Utopian Imagination*, 254; Curley, *Samuel Johnson*, 158–60, 163.
9. Tomarken, *Johnson, Rasselas, and the Choice*, 24, 37, 68, 102–3. Curley likewise argues that Johnson's geographical citations in *Rasselas* "add authenticity to its moral lessons." *Samuel Johnson*, 158.
10. Tomarken, *Johnson, Rasselas, and the Choice*, 37, 68.
11. Curley, *Samuel Johnson*, 169.
12. Belcher, *Abyssinia's Samuel Johnson*, 229.
13. Ibid., 230–31, 234, 217–18.
14. Ibid., 238–42, 226–28.
15. Following this line of reasoning qualifies but doesn't negate Belcher's account of how African expressions are at work in the text. The African presences in *Rasselas* that Belcher points to that are historically specific—in particular, how the text is permeated by the actions and attitudes of people that Lobo encountered—are not explained by Johnson's interest in local testimony as a necessary ingredient of geographical representation. Suggesting that Johnson was self-consciously attentive to African discourse as discourse in *Rasselas* also doesn't undermine Belcher's theory that Johnson struggled on some level to excise this discourse. People can be sanguine when they intellectually entertain a certain idea and react very differently when the substance of that idea affects them on a personal level, a point that *Rasselas* itself frequently illustrates.
16. See, in particular, Poovey, *History of the Modern Fact*, 249–57; Mack, "Limits of the Senses," 279–94; Thell, *Minds in Motion*, 189–226; David Francis Taylor, "Johnson's Textual Landscape," 66–75.
17. Curley, *Samuel Johnson*, 1–4. For a meticulous overview of the prefaces, reviews, and essays in which Johnson expresses views on travel writing and geography, see Mayhew, *Landscape, Literature*, 213–61.
18. Johnson, *Idler* no. 97, Saturday, 23 February 1790, 298.

19. Ibid., 298–300. In Johnson's review of Patrick Browne's *Civil and Natural History of Jamaica* (1756), he criticized Browne not for "omission" in his descriptions but for "unnecessary diligence." Johnson, *Johnson on Demand*, 347.
20. Donaldson, "Samuel Johnson and the Art," 779–80.
21. Johnson, *Idler* no. 44, Saturday, 17 February 1759, 137–39.
22. Donaldson, "Samuel Johnson and the Art," 779.
23. Ibid., 781.
24. Johnson, "Essay on the Description," 320.
25. Thell, *Minds in Motion*, 201.
26. Hickey, "'Extensive Views' in Johnson's *Journey*," 540–43; McKendry, "Haphazard Journey of a Mind," 14–19.
27. Mack, "Limits of the Senses," 291; Poovey, *History of the Modern Fact*, 253; David Francis Taylor, "Johnson's Textual Landscape," 75; Thell, *Minds in Motion*, 209; McKendry, "Haphazard Journey of a Mind," 18.
28. On the second sight, see Duncan, "Pathos of Abstraction," 38–56; Mack, "Limits of the Senses," 289–91; Thell, *Minds in Motion*, 211–13; and David Francis Taylor, "Johnson's Textual Landscape," 75.
29. Mack, "Limits of the Senses," 291; Poovey, *History of the Modern Fact*, 253; Thell, *Minds in Motion*, 213; David Francis Taylor, "Johnson's Textual Landscape," 75.
30. Perkins, "Regulating Reality," 37–38; Damrosch, *Fictions of Reality*, 39; Thell, *Minds in Motion*, 203–5; Taylor, "Johnson's Textual Landscape," 75.
31. Boswell, *Life of Johnson*, 1402.
32. Johnson, *Rasselas*, 7.
33. Ibid.
34. Lobo, "Voyage to Abyssinia," 81.
35. Ludolf, *New History of Ethiopia*, 37.
36. Belcher, *Abyssinia's Samuel Johnson*, 217.
37. Belcher, "Sisters Debating the Jesuits," 121–66.
38. Lobo, "Voyage to Abyssinia," 96.
39. Ibid., 63, 42.
40. Ibid., 42.
41. Both Belcher and Joel J. Gold see Johnson's exclusions, inclusions, and shifts in emphasis as evidence that he is in dialog or even debate with Lobo/Le Grand's ideas and not simply translating them. Belcher, *Abyssinia's Samuel Johnson*, 58–61; Gold, introduction to *Voyage to Abyssinia*, l–lvi.
42. Johnson, *Voyage to Abyssinia*, 6.
43. "Tous les Sçavans qui ont parlé des flottes de Salomon, ont été aussi occupez à étaler leur érudition, qu'à chercher la verité. Ils ont bâti des systêmes à leur fantaisie, ils les ont appuyéz de diverses citations, & de raisonnemens vagues & peu

solides; ce qui arrive presque toûjours lorsqu'on veut supposer des faits incertains." Le Grand, "Sixie'me Dissertation," 259.

44. Gold, introduction to *Voyage to Abyssinia*, 218n2; Le Grand, "Dissertations," 218.
45. Gold, introduction to *Voyage to Abyssinia*, 218n3.
46. Boswell, *Life of Johnson*, 1402.
47. Le Grand, "Dissertations," 220.
48. Ibid., 219–22.
49. Belcher, *Abyssinia's Samuel Johnson*, 58.
50. Mack, "Limits of the Senses," 291.
51. Ibid.
52. Johnson, *Rambler* no. 154, Saturday, 7 September 1751, 3:55.
53. Le Grand, "Dissertations," 222; Gold, introduction to *Voyage to Abyssinia*, 222n4.
54. Le Grand, "Dissertations," 222; Gold, introduction to *Voyage to Abyssinia*, 222n3.
55. Johnson, *Rambler* no. 154, 3:54–59.
56. Johnson, *Idler* no. 66, Saturday, 21 July 1759, 205–7.
57. Le Grand, "Dissertations," 225.
58. Ibid.
59. Gold, introduction to *Voyage to Abyssinia*, 225n1.
60. Belcher, *Abyssinia's Samuel Johnson*, 70–74.
61. Le Grand, "Dissertations," 226.
62. Ibid., 227.
63. Ibid., 228–29.
64. Ibid., 228. Gold identifies this paragraph as Johnson's interpretation of a quote from Isaiah that Le Grand added as a marginal note. Introduction to *Voyage to Abyssinia*, 228n7.
65. Le Grand, "Septie'me Dissertation," 269.
66. Gold, introduction to *Voyage to Abyssinia*, 230nn4–5.
67. Le Grand, "Dissertations," 225, 231.
68. Ibid., 232.
69. Belcher, *Abyssinia's Samuel Johnson*, 59–60, 89–95; Gold, introduction to *Voyage to Abyssinia*, l–lvi, and throughout various footnotes tracking Johnson's changes.
70. Belcher, *Abyssinia's Samuel Johnson*, 74.
71. Poovey, *History of the Modern Fact*, 255–56.
72. Belcher, *Abyssinia's Samuel Johnson*, 58.
73. Le Grand, "Dissertations," 232.
74. Curley, *Samuel Johnson*, 159.

75. Johnson, *Rasselas*, 31.
76. Ludolf, *New History of Ethiopia*, 39–40.
77. Johnson, *Rasselas*, 31.
78. Ibid., 34.
79. Le Grand, "Dissertations," 207.
80. Johnson, *Rasselas*, 47; Johnson, introduction to *The World Displayed*, in *Johnson on Demand*, 445.
81. Álvares, *Narrative of the Portuguese Embassy*, 81.
82. Ibid.; Le Grand, "Dissertations," 227; Tellez, *Travels of the Jesuits*, 73.
83. Johnson, *Rasselas*, 10–11.
84. Ibid., 11.
85. Le Grand, "Dissertations," 226.
86. Johnson, *Rasselas*, 42, 43, 44.
87. Ibid., 43, 35–38.
88. Lobo, "Voyage to Abyssinia," 40; Le Grand, "Dissertations," 210–13. For more on Johnson's relationship to history and to the historians of his day, see Davies, "Dr. Johnson on History," 1–21; Tomarken, "Perspectivism," 262–90; Lock, "Johnson's View of History," 159–80; Insalaco, "Thinking of Italy," 99–113; Brownley, "Johnson and the Writing," 97–109.
89. Korounos, "*Rasselas* and the Riddle," 40.
90. Johnson, *Rasselas*, 8.
91. Potkay, *Passion for Happiness*, 51; Rees, *Utopian Imagination*.
92. Johnson, *Rasselas*, 21.
93. Kenshur, *Dilemmas of Enlightenment*, 204.
94. Kolb, introduction to *Rasselas and Other Tales*, xvi–xxxi; Lockhart, "Fourth Son," 521; Karounos, "*Rasselas* and the Riddle," 42.
95. Tomarken, *Johnson, Rasselas, and the Choice*, 41.
96. Lockhart, "Fourth Son," 521; Karounos, "*Rasselas* and the Riddle," 42–44.
97. Others who have considered the ways that *Rasselas* provokes a sense of epistemological instability in its readers and not only in its characters include Potkay, *Passion for Happiness*, 209; Hudson, "'Open' and 'Enclosed' Readings," 47–48; Kenshur, *Dilemmas of Enlightenment*, 199–203; Folkenflik, "'Rasselas' and the Closed Field," 337–38; Ballaster, "Eastern Tale," 120; Parker, "Skepticism of Johnson's *Rasselas*," 134–36; Curley, *Samuel Johnson*, 156.
98. Johnson, *Rasselas*, 45, 46. Though scholars once interpreted Imlac as the voice of Johnson's own attitudes toward poetry, critics have noted that although Imlac may begin espousing a view that sounds very much like ones that Johnson expressed elsewhere, he ends up self-aggrandizing the task in a way that Johnson would have rejected. Weinbrot, "The Reader, the General," 82–85.

99. Belcher, *Abyssinia's Samuel Johnson*, 217–18.
100. Johnson, *Rasselas*, 142.
101. Ibid., 146.
102. Ibid., 144, 142.
103. Ibid., 161.
104. Ibid., 25–26.
105. Green, *Construction of Maps and Globes*, 154.
106. Johnson, *Rasselas*, 28.
107. Boswell, *Life of Johnson*, 393.
108. Johnson, *Rasselas*, 110.
109. Ibid., 92–93.
110. Ibid., 104.
111. Ibid., 105.
112. Ibid., 93.
113. Ibid., 175.
114. Ibid., 176.

6. "DESCENDED FROM THE QUEEN OF SABA"

1. According to Richard Sher, once Bruce finally did publish his narrative, two thousand copies of the first edition were printed, and the text quickly became a bestseller. Sher speculates that "if Bruce had lived longer, he might well have earned more money from his Travels than any other eighteenth-century author received for a single book." *Enlightenment and the Book*, 242–43.
2. Reid, *Traveller Extraordinary*, 137–38.
3. Quoted in Leask, *Curiosity and the Aesthetics*, 58.
4. Withers, "Travel and Trust," 47–54; Leask, *Curiosity and the Aesthetics*, 54–101.
5. Bruce, *Travels*, 3:144.
6. Leask, *Curiosity and the Aesthetics*, 70.
7. Critics who have read Bruce as a link in the chain in Britain's conquest of Africa include Haddad, "Florence Nightingale," 53–69; and Christoph Bode, "Ad Fontes!," 70.
8. Leask, *Curiosity and the Aesthetics*, 94–95.
9. Perkins, "Regulating Reality," 46. Malvern van Wyk Smith has similarly observed that problems arise when scholars rely on edited and augmented travel narratives as stand-ins for the original text. "Would the Real James Bruce," 59–83.
10. Bredin, *Pale Abyssinian*, 259; Leask, "*Kubla Khan* and Orientalism," 1–21; Liu, "Wordsworth," 505; Bode, "Ad Fontes!," 63–78; Leask, *Curiosity and the Aesthetics*, 70.

11. Ullendorff, "James Bruce," 128–43; Moorefield, "James Bruce: Ethnomusicologist," 493–514; Hulton et al., *Luigi Balugani's Drawings*.
12. Bruce, *Travels*, 3:132, 2:478.
13. Ibid., 2:244, 2:345.
14. Ibid., 3:616.
15. Ibid., 3:615–16.
16. Ibid., 3:616–20.
17. Ibid., 1:xxii–lxxiii.
18. On Bruce's sexualization of Ethiopian women, see Leask, *Curiosity and the Aesthetics*, 83–92; and Carnochan, *Golden Legends*, 16–52.
19. Crummey, *Land and Society*, 94.
20. Ibid.
21. Ibid., 99.
22. Bosc-Tiessé, "How Beautiful She Is!," 298.
23. Budge, *Queen of Sheba*, 125–27.
24. Bosc-Tiessé, "How Beautiful She Is!," 298.
25. Spencer, "Matrifocal Retentions."
26. Ibid.
27. Bosc-Tiessé, "How Beautiful She Is!," 298.
28. Herman, "Towards a History," 389.
29. Bosc-Tiessé, "How Beautiful She Is!," 314.
30. Ibid., 310.
31. Ibid., 295.
32. Crummey, *Land and Society*, 95.
33. Bruce, *Travels*, 1:445, 1:473–74.
34. Ibid., 1:474–76.
35. Ibid., 1:472, 1:446.
36. Ibid., 2:174, 2:188, 2:531, 2:241.
37. Ibid., 1:507.
38. Ibid., 2:114, 2:531, 2:78, 1:15.
39. Ibid., 2:125.
40. Bruce, *Travels*, 2:130.
41. Ibid., 2:174.
42. Ibid., 2:195.
43. Ibid., 2:199–200.
44. Ibid., 2:596–97.
45. Ibid., 2:597.
46. Ibid., 2:598.
47. Ibid., 2:599.
48. Bruce, *Travels*, 2:601.

49. Ibid., 2:606–7.
50. Ibid., 2:603.
51. Ibid., 2:607.
52. Ibid.
53. Ibid.
54. Bosc-Tiessé, "How Beautiful She Is!," 295.
55. Bruce, *Travels*, 1:lxvi.
56. Ibid., 3:207.
57. Ibid., 3:208.
58. Ibid., 3:209.
59. Pankhurst, "Medical Activities," 256–76.
60. Bruce, *Travels*, 4:5.
61. Ibid., 4:266–67.
62. Ibid., 1:lxvi.
63. Ibid., 4:242.
64. Ibid., 4:243.
65. Herman, "Towards a History," 382.
66. Belcher, "Sisters Debating the Jesuits," 123–24.
67. I say "in Bruce's account" because, unlike Mentewab's case, details of Aster's life are scant outside of what Bruce had to say about her. He is the source of the claim that she and Mikael Sehul were married, for instance, though another of Mentewab's daughters was definitively married to Mikael Sehul's son. Crummey, *Land and Society*, 98.
68. Bruce, *Travels*, 2:698–700.
69. Ibid., 2:698.
70. Ibid., 3:286, 2:699, 3:545.
71. Ibid., 2:665.
72. Ibid., 2:612.
73. Ibid., 4:53.
74. Ibid., 3:240.
75. Bruce, *Travels*, 3:523.
76. Ibid., 2:481–82.
77. Ibid., 2:482.
78. Ibid., 4:37.
79. Ibid., 4:38.
80. Ibid.
81. Ibid., 4:46–47.
82. Bruce, *Travels*, 4:48.
83. Ibid., 4:49.
84. Ibid.

85. Ibid., 4:50.
86. Leask, "*Kubla Khan* and Orientalism," 16. Blair qtd. in Bredin, *Pale Abyssinian*, 259.
87. Bruce, *Travels*, 1:vi, 1:i.
88. Ibid., 3:472.
89. Ibid., 3:473.
90. Ibid., 3:377.
91. Ibid.
92. Ibid., 3:378.
93. Ibid.
94. Hannig, "Pure and the Pious," 307.
95. Boylston, *Stranger at the Feast*, 5, 43, 52.
96. Belcher, introduction to *Life and Struggles*, 15, 13.
97. Bruce, *Travels*, 4:294.
98. Crummey, *Land and Society*, 95.
99. Bruce, *Travels*, 3:378.
100. Ibid., 3:379–80.
101. Ibid., 3:598.
102. Ibid., 3:602.
103. Ibid., 3:641.
104. Ibid., 3:640.
105. Critics who have analyzed or remarked on the peculiarity of this passage include Leask, "*Kubla Khan* and Orientalism," 16; Liu, "Wordsworth," 505; Bode, "Ad Fontes!," 69; Carnochan, *Golden Legends*, 26; Crawford, *Scotland's Books*, 378.
106. Bruce, *Travels*, 3:641.
107. Ibid., 3:642.
108. Ibid., 3:645.
109. *Monthly Review*, 435.

CODA

1. Caillié, *Travels through Central Africa*, 49.
2. Salt, *Voyage to Abyssinia*, 475.
3. Ibid.
4. Ibid., 101.
5. Ibid., 334.
6. Ibid., 337.
7. Ibid., 338.
8. Ibid.
9. Ibid., 258.

10. Ibid., 338.
11. Alborn, "King Solomon's Gold," 499.
12. Stiebel, "Creating a Landscape of Africa," 125.
13. White, preface, vi.
14. Quoted in Stiebel, "Creating a Landscape of Africa," 128.
15. Haggard, *King Solomon's Mines*, 15.
16. Ibid., 29.
17. Ibid., 1.
18. Ibid., 14.
19. Haggard, "Real King Solomon's Mines," 146.

BIBLIOGRAPHY

Alborn, Timothy. "King Solomon's Gold: Ophir in an Age of Empire." *Journal of Victorian Culture* 20, no. 4 (2015): 491–508.

Aljoe, Nicole. *Creole Testimonies: Slave Narratives from the British West Indies, 1709–1838*. London: Palgrave, 2012.

Alvarez [Álvares], Francisco. *Narrative of the Portuguese Embassy to Abyssinia during the Years 1520–1527*. Translated and edited by Lord Stanley of Alderley. London: Hakluyt Society, 1881.

Andrea, Bernadette. "Assimilation or Dissimulation? Leo Africanus's 'Geographical Historie of Africa' and the Parable of Amphibia." *ARIEL* 32, no. 3 (2001): 7–29.

Aplers, Edward A. *East Africa and the Indian Ocean*. Princeton, NJ: Markus Wiener, 2009.

Aravamudan, Srinivas. "Defoe, Commerce, and Empire." In *Cambridge Companion to Daniel Defoe*, edited by John Richetti, 45–63. Cambridge: Cambridge University Press, 2008.

———. *Enlightenment Orientalism: Resisting the Rise of the Novel*. Chicago: University of Chicago Press, 2012.

———. *Tropicopolitans: Colonialism and Agency, 1688–1804*. Durham, NC: Duke University Press, 1999.

Ariosto, Ludovico. *Orlando Furioso, by Ludovico Ariosto*. Translated by William Huggins. Vol. 2. London: Printed for James Rivington and James Fletcher, 1757.

Arndt, Susan. "Trans*textuality in William Shakespeare's *Othello*: Italian, West African, and English Encounters." *Anglia* 136, no. 3 (2018): 393–429.

Backsheider, Paula R. *Daniel Defoe: His Life*. Baltimore: Johns Hopkins University Press, 1989.

Baker, J. N. L. "The Geography of Daniel Defoe." *Scottish Geographical Magazine* 47, no. 5 (1931): 257–69.

Ballaster, Ros. "The Eastern Tale and the Candid Reader: *Tristram Shandy, Candide, Rasselas*." *Revue de la Société d'études anglo-américaines des XVIIe et XVIIIe siècles* 67 (2010): 109–25.

———. *Fabulous Orients: Fictions of the East in England 1662–1785*. Oxford: Oxford University Press, 2005.

Balogun, Lekan. "Ajubaba: Shakespeare and Yoruba Goddess." *International Journal of Comparative Literature and Translation Studies* 1, no. 3 (2013): 18–25.

Barbot, John [Jean]. "A Description of the Coasts of North and South-Guinea." In *A Collection of Voyages and Travels*. Vol. 5. London: Printed for Awnsham and John Churchill, 1732.

Barker, Anthony. *The African Link: British Attitudes to the Negro in the Era of the Atlantic Slave Trade, 1550–1807.* London: Frank Cass, 1978.

Bartels, Emily C. "*Othello* and Africa: Postcolonialism Reconsidered." *William and Mary Quarterly* 54, no. 1 (1997): 45–64.

———. *Speaking of the Moor: From Alcazar to Othello.* Philadelphia: University of Pennsylvania Press, 2008.

Beach, Adam R. "Behn's *Oroonoko*, the Gold Coast, and Slavery in the Early-Modern Atlantic World." *Studies in Eighteenth-Century Culture* 39 (2010): 215–33.

———. "Global Slavery, Old World Bondage, and Aphra Behn's *Abdelazer*." *Eighteenth Century* 53, no. 4 (2012): 413–31.

Behn, Aphra. *Oroonoko*. Edited by Janet Todd. New York: Penguin, 2003.

Belcher, Wendy Laura. *Abyssinia's Samuel Johnson: Ethiopian Thought in the Making of an English Author.* Oxford: Oxford University Press, 2012.

———. "Consuming Subjects: Theorizing New Models of Agency for Literary Criticism in African Studies." *Comparative Literature Studies* 46, no. 2 (2009): 213–32.

———. Introduction to *The Life and Struggles of Our Mother Walatta Petros*, edited and translated by Belcher and Michael Kleiner, 1–48. Princeton, NJ: Princeton University Press, 2016.

———. "Sisters Debating the Jesuits." *Northeast African Studies* 13, no. 1 (2013): 121–66.

Bennett, Herman L. *African Kings and Black Slaves: Sovereignty and Dispossession in the Early Modern Atlantic.* Philadelphia: University of Pennsylvania Press, 2018.

Berington, Thomas. *News from the Dead: or, the Monthly Packet of True Intelligence from the Other Worlds.* London: Printed by J. Morphew, 1757.

Bermudez [Bermudes], João. "Bermudez." In *The Portuguese Expedition to Abyssinia*, translated and edited by R. S. Whiteway, 127–258. London: Hakluyt Society, 1902.

Bertaud, Madeleine. "Afrique et Africains dans *Polexandre*." In *L'Afrique au XVIIe siècle: Mythes et réalités*, edited by Alia Baccar Bournaz, 93–104. Tübingen: Gunter Narr Verlag, 2003.

Black, Crofton. "Leo Africanus's 'Descrittione dell'Africa' and Its Sixteenth-Century Translations." *Journal of the Warburg and Courtauld Institutes* 65 (2002): 262–72.

Boavida, Isabel, Hervé Pennec, and Manuel João Ramos. Introduction to *Pedro Páez's History of Ethiopia, 1622*, 1–53. Edited by Isabel Boavida, Hervé Pennec, and Manuel João Ramos. Translated by Christopher J. Tribe. 2 vols. Farnham: Hakluyt Society, 2011.

Bode, Christoph. "Ad Fontes! Remarks on the Temporalization of Space in Hemans (1829), Bruce (1790), and Barbauld (1812)." *Romanticism* 10, no. 1 (2004): 63–78.

Bodin, Jean. *The Six Bookes of a Commonweale*. Edited by Kenneth Douglas McRae. Translated by Richard Knolles. Cambridge, MA: Harvard University Press, 1964.

Boon, James A. *Other Tribes, Other Scribes: Symbolic Anthropology in the Comparative Study of Cultures, Histories, Religions, and Texts*. Cambridge: Cambridge University Press, 1982.

Bosc-Tiessé, Claire. "'How Beautiful She Is!' in her Mirror: Polysemic Images and Reflections of Power of an Eighteenth-Century Ethiopian Queen." Translated by Jonathan Good. *Journal of Early Modern History* 8, no. 3–4 (2004): 294–315.

Boswell, James. *Life of Johnson*. Edited by R. W. Chapman. Oxford: Oxford University Press, 1998.

Boulukos, George. *The Grateful Slave: The Emergence of Race in Eighteenth-century British and American Culture*. Cambridge: Cambridge University Press, 2008.

Bourdieu, Pierre. *Distinction: A Social Critique of the Judgement of Taste*. 1984. Translated by Richard Nice. London: Routledge, 2010.

Bovill, E. W. "The Silent Trade of the Wangara of Africa." *Journal of the Royal African Society* 29, no. 113 (1929): 27–38.

Boyle, Robert. *New Experiments Physico-mechanical, Touching the Air*. 3rd ed. London: Printed by Miles Flesher, 1682.

Boylston, Tom. *The Stranger at the Feast: Prohibition and Mediation in an Ethiopian Orthodox Christian Community*. Oakland: University of California Press, 2018.

Bratach, Anne. "Following the Intrigue: Aphra Behn, Genre, and Restoration Science." *Journal of Narrative Technique* 26, no. 3 (1996): 209–27.

Bredin, Miles. *The Pale Abyssinian: The Life of James Bruce*. New York: Harper Collins, 2000.

Broglio, Ron. *Technologies of the Picturesque: British Art, Poetry, and Instruments 1750–1830*. Lewisburg, PA: Bucknell University Press, 2008.

Brooks, Christopher. "Nekayah's Courage and Female Wisdom." *CLA Journal* 36, no. 1 (1992): 52–72.

Brooks, George. *Landlords and Strangers: Ecology, Society, and Trade in Western Africa, 1000–1630*. Boulder, CO: Westview Press, 1993.

Brooks, Lisa. *Our Beloved Kin: A New History of King Philip's War*. New Haven, CT: Yale University Press, 2019.

Brown, Laura. *Cultural Fables of Modernity: Literature and Culture in the Eighteenth Century*. Ithaca, NY: Cornell University Press, 2001.

———. "Defoe's 'Black Prince': Elitism, Capitalism, and Cultural Difference." In *Defoe's Footprints: Essays in Honor of Maximillian E. Novak*, edited by Robert M. Maniquis and Carl Fisher, 153–69. Toronto: University of Toronto Press, 2009.

———. *Ends of Empire: Women and Ideology in Early Eighteenth-Century English Literature*. Ithaca, NY: Cornell University Press, 1993.

Brownley, Martine Watson. "Samuel Johnson and the Writing of History." In *Johnson after 200 Years*, edited by Paul J. Korshin, 97–109. Philadelphia: University of Pennsylvania Press, 1986.

Bruce, James. *Travels to Discover the Source of the Nile*. 5 vols. London: Printed by J. Ruthven, 1790.

Budge, E. A. Wallis. *The Queen of Sheba and her Only Son Menyelek*. London: Medici Society, 1922.

Burchett, Josiah. *A Complete History of the Most Remarkable Transactions at Sea*. London: Printed by W. B., 1720.

Cadamosto, Alvise. *The Voyages of Cadamosto*. Edited and translated by G. R. Crone. London: Hakluyt Society, 1967.

Caillié, René. *Travels through Central Africa to Timbuctoo*. Vol. 2. London: Printed by G. Schulze, 1830.

Campbell, Mary Baine. *Wonder and Science: Imagining Worlds in Early Modern Europe*. Ithaca, NY: Cornell University Press, 1999.

Carey, Daniel. "Inquires, Heads, and Directions: Orienting Early Modern Travel." In *Travel Narratives, the New Science, and Literary Discourse, 1569–1750*, edited by Judy A. Hayden, 25–52. Farnham: Ashgate, 2012.

———. "The Problem of Credibility in Early Modern Travel." *Renaissance Studies* 33, no. 4 (2019): 524–47.

Carney, Judith. *Black Rice: The African Origins of Rice Cultivation in the Americas*. Cambridge, MA: Harvard University Press, 2001.

Carnochan, W. B. *Golden Legends: Images of Abyssinia, Samuel Johnson to Bob Marley*. Stanford, CA: Stanford General Books, 2008.

Carroll, Scott T. "Solomonic Legend: The Muslims and the Great Zimbabwe." *International Journal of African Historical Studies* 21, no. 2 (1988): 233–47.

Carroll, Siobhan. *An Empire of Air and Water: Uncolonizable Space in the British Imagination, 1750–1850*. Philadelphia: University of Pennsylvania Press, 2015.

Cartwright, Keith. *Reading Africa into American Literature: Epics, Fables, and Gothic Tales*. Lexington: University of Kentucky Press, 2002.

Castanhoso, Miguel de. "Castanhoso," in *The Portuguese Expedition to Abyssinia*, edited and translated by R. S. Whiteway, 3–104. London: Hakluyt Society, 1902.

Cavallo, Jo Ann. *The World beyond Europe in the Romance Epics of Boiardo and Ariosto*. Toronto: University of Toronto Press, 2013.

Certeau, Michel de. *The Practice of Everyday Life*. Translated by Steven F. Rendall. Berkeley: University of California Press, 1984.

Chakrabarty, Dipesh. *Provincializing Europe: Postcolonial Thought and Historical Difference*. Princeton, NJ: Princeton University Press, 2000.

Chaplin, Joyce E. *Subject Matter: Technology, the Body, and Science on the Anglo-American Frontier, 1500–1676.* Cambridge, MA: Harvard University Press, 2001.

Chibka, Robert L. "'Oh! Do Not Fear a Woman's Invention': Truth, Falsehood, and Fiction in Aphra Behn's *Oroonoko*." *Texas Studies in Literature and Language* 30, no. 4 (1988), 510–37.

Chico, Tita. *The Experimental Imagination: Literary Knowledge and Science in the British Enlightenment.* Stanford, CA: Stanford University Press, 2018.

———. "From Fleece to Fleets; or, Wool and the Production of Wonder." *Eighteenth-Century Fiction* 32, no. 1 (2019): 101–21.

Clapham, Christopher. "The European Mapping of Ethiopia, 1460–1856." *Journal of Ethiopian Studies* 40, no. 1/2 (2007): 293–307.

Clark, Evert Mordecai. "Milton's Abyssinian Paradise." *University of Texas Studies in English* 29 (1950): 129–50.

Cohen, Matt. *The Networked Wilderness: Communicating in Early New England.* Minneapolis: University of Minnesota Press, 2010.

Cole, Lucinda. "Guns, Ivory and Elephant Graveyards: The Biopolitics of Elephants' Teeth." In *Animals and Humans: Sensibility and Representation, 1650–1830*, edited by Katherine M. Quinsey, 35–55. Oxford: Voltaire Foundation, 2017.

Colley, Linda. *Captives: Britain, Empire and the World, 1660–1850.* 1st American ed. New York: Pantheon Books, 2002.

Conrad, David C. "A Town Called Dakajalan: The Sunjata Tradition and the Question of Ancient Mali's Capital." *Journal of African History* 35, no. 3 (1994): 355–77.

Conrad, Joseph. *Heart of Darkness.* Edited by Paul B. Armstrong. New York: Norton, 2016.

Coppola, Al. *The Theater of Experiment: Staging Natural Philosophy in Eighteenth-Century Britain.* Oxford: Oxford University Press, 2016.

Crawford, Robert. *Scotland's Books: A History of Scottish Literature.* Oxford: Oxford University Press, 2009.

Crone, G. R. Introduction to *The Voyages of Cadamosto.* Edited and translated by Crone, xi–xlv. London: Hakluyt Society, 1967.

Crouch, Nathaniel. *The English Acquisitions in Guinea and East-India.* London: Printed for A. Bettesworth, 1700.

Crummey, Donald. *Land and Society in the Christian Kingdom of Ethiopia: From the Thirteenth to the Twentieth Century.* Urbana: University of Illinois Press, 2000.

Curley, Thomas M. *Samuel Johnson and the Age of Travel.* Athens: University of Georgia Press, 1976.

Curtin, Philip D. *Africa Remembered: Narratives by West Africans from the Era of the Slave Trade.* Prospect Heights, IL: Waveland Press, 1967.

Damrosch, Leo. *Fictions of Reality in the Age of Hume and Johnson*. Madison: University of Wisconsin Press, 1989.

Daston, Lorraine. "Description by Omission: Nature Enlightened and Observed." In *Regimes of Description: In the Archive of the Eighteenth Century*, edited by John Bender and Michael Marrinan, 11–24. Stanford, CA: Stanford University Press, 2005.

Davies, Godfrey. "Dr. Johnson on History." *Huntington Quarterly* 12, no. 1 (1948): 1–21.

Davis, Asa. "Background to the Zaga ZaAb Embassy: An Ethiopian Diplomatic Mission to Portugal (1529–39)." *Studia* 32 (1971): 211–302.

d'Avity, Pierre. *The Estates, Empires, and Principallities of the World*. Translated by Edw. Grims. London: Printed by Adam Islip, 1615.

Defoe, Daniel. *Atlas Maritimus and Commercialis; Or, a General View of the World, So Far as Relates to Trade and Navigation*. London: Printed for James and John Knapton, 1728.

———. *Captain Singleton*. Edited by Manushag Powell. Peterborough, Ontario: Broadview Press, 2019.

———. *Defoe's Review Reproduced from the Original Editions*. Introduction and notes by Arthur Wellesley Secord. 22 vols. New York: Columbia University Press, 1938.

———. *The History of the Principal Discoveries and Improvements, in the Several Arts and Sciences*. London: Printed for W. Mears, F. Clay, and D. Browne, 1721.

Dickson, Vernon Guy. "Truth, Wonder, and Exemplarity in Aphra Behn's *Oroonoko*." *SEL* 47, no. 3 (2007): 573–94.

DiPiero, Thomas. *Dangerous Truths and Criminal Passions: The Evolution of the French Novel, 1569–1791*. Stanford: Stanford University Press, 1992.

Dolfsma, Wilfred, and Antoon Spithoven. "'Silent Trade' and the Supposed Continuum between OIE and NIE." *Journal of Economic Issues* 42, no. 2 (2008): 517–26.

Donaldson, Ian. "Samuel Johnson and the Art of Observation." *ELH* 53, no. 4 (1986): 779–99.

Duncan, Ian. "The Pathos of Abstraction: Adam Smith, Ossian, and Samuel Johnson." In *Scotland and the Borders of Romanticism*, edited by Leith Davis, Ian Duncan, and Janet Sorensen, 38–56. Cambridge: Cambridge University Press, 2004.

Duverdier, Gilbert Saulnier. *The Love and Armes of the Greeke Princes*. London: Printed by Thomas Harper, 1640.

Dyer, John. *The Fleece: A Poem in Four Books*. London: Printed for R. and J. Dodsley, 1757.

Edson, Evelyn. *The World Map, 1300–1492: The Persistence of Tradition and Transformation*. Baltimore: Johns Hopkins University Press, 2007.

Edwards, Jess. "Daniel Defoe and the *Atlas Maritimus & Commercialis*." In *Topographies of the Imagination: New Approaches to Daniel Defoe*, edited by Katherine Ellison, Kit Kincade, and Holly Faith Nelson, 141–66. New York: AMS Press, 2014.

———. "Defoe the Geographer: Redefining the Wonderful in *A Tour Thro' the Whole Island of Great Britain*." In *Travel Narratives, the New Science, and Literary Discourse, 1569–1750*, edited by Judy A. Hayden, 179–98. Farnham: Ashgate, 2012.

———. "How to Read an Early Modern Map: Between the Particular and the General, the Material and the Abstract, Words and Mathematics." *Early Modern Literary Studies* 9, no. 1 (2003): 1–58.

Estow, Clara. "Mapping Central Europe: The Catalan Atlas and the European Imagination." *Mediterranean Studies* 13 (2004): 1–16.

Evelyn, John. *Numismata: A Discourse on Medals, Antient and Modern*. London: Printed for Benj. Tooke, 1697.

Fage, J. D. "Upper and Lower Guinea." In the *Cambridge History of Africa: Vol. 3, c. 1050–c. 1600*, edited by Roland Oliver, 463–518. Cambridge: Cambridge University Press, 1977.

Farias, P. F. de Moraes. "Silent Trade: Myth and Historical Evidence." *History in Africa* 15, no. 1 (1974): 9–24.

Farr, Jason S. "Colonizing Gestures: Crusoe the Signing Sovereign." *Eighteenth-Century Fiction* 29, no. 4 (2017): 537–62.

Fauvelle, François-Xavier. *The Golden Rhinoceros: Histories of the African Middle Ages*. Translated by Troy Tice. Princeton, NJ: Princeton University Press, 2018.

Ferguson, Moira. *Subject to Others: British Women Writers and Colonial Slavery, 1670–1834*. London: Routledge, 1992.

Festa, Lynn. *Sentimental Figures of Empire in Eighteenth-Century Britain and France*. Baltimore: Johns Hopkins University Press, 2006.

Festa, Lynn, and Daniel Carey. Introduction to *The Postcolonial Enlightenment*, edited by Lynn Festa and Daniel Carey, 1–36. Oxford: Oxford University Press, 2009.

Fisher, Humphrey J. "Leo Africanus and the Songhay Conquest of Hausaland." *International Journal of African Historical Studies* 11, no. 1 (1978): 86–112.

Folkenflik, Robert. "'Rasselas' and the Closed Field." *Huntington Library Quarterly* 57, no. 4 (1994): 337–52.

Foucault, Michel. *The Order of Things: An Archaeology of Human Sciences*. 1971. Translated by Alan Sheridan. New York: Vintage, 1994.

Freedman, Paul. *Out of the East: Spices and the Medieval Imagination*. New Haven, CT: Yale University Press, 2008.

Fromont, Cécile. *The Art of Conversion: Christian Visual Culture in the Kingdom of Kongo*. Chapel Hill: University of North Carolina Press, 2014.

Furbank, P. N. "The Naked White Man." In *The Novels of Daniel Defoe: The Life, Adventures, and Pyracies, of the Famous Captain Singleton (1720)*, edited by P. N. Furbank, 227–29. London: Pickering and Chatto, 2008.

Furbank, P. N., and W. R. Owens. *A Critical Bibliography of Daniel Defoe*. London: Pickering and Chatto, 1998.

Furtado, Júnia Ferreira. "Evolving Ideas: J. B. d'Anville's Maps of Southern Africa, 1725–1749." *Imago Mundi* 69, no. 2 (2017): 202–15.

Gallagher, Catherine. *Nobody's Story: The Vanishing Acts of Women Writers in the Marketplace, 1670–1820*. Berkeley: University of California Press, 1994.

Garrard, Timothy F. *Akan Weights and the Gold Trade*. New York: Longman, 1980.

———. "Myth and Metrology: The Early Trans-Saharan Gold Trade," *Journal of African History* 23, no. 4 (1982): 443–61.

Gates, Henry Louis, Jr. *The Signifying Monkey: A Theory of African American Literary Criticism*. 2nd ed. Oxford: Oxford University Press, 1998.

Geddes, Michael. *The Church History of Ethiopia*. London: Printed for Ri. Chiswell, 1696.

Gevirtz, Karen Bloom. "Behn and the Scientific Self." In *The New Science and Women's Literary Discourse: Prefiguring Frankenstein*, edited by Judy A. Hayden, 85–100. New York: Palgrave, 2011.

Gikandi, Simon. *Slavery and the Culture of Taste*. Princeton, NJ: Princeton University Press, 2011.

Glover, Jeffery. *Paper Sovereigns: Anglo-Native Treaties and the Law of Nations, 1604–1664*. Philadelphia: University of Pennsylvania Press, 2014.

Gold, Joel J. Introduction to *A Voyage to Abyssinia (Translated from the French)*, by Samuel Johnson, xxiii–lviii. Edited by Joel J. Gold. New Haven, CT: Yale University Press, 1985.

The Golden Coast, or a Description of Guinney. London: Printed for S. Speed, 1665.

Gomberville, Marin le Roy de. *The History of Polexander in Five Bookes*. 1632–37. Translated by William Browne. 5 vols. London: Printed by Tho. Harper, 1647.

Gomes, Diogo. "The Voyages of Diogo Gomes." In *The Voyages of Cadamosto*, by Alvise Cadamosto, 91–102. Edited and translated by G. R. Crone. London: Hakluyt Society, 1967.

Gomez, Michael A. *African Dominion: A New History of Empire in Early and Medieval West Africa*. Princeton, NJ: Princeton University Press, 2018.

Goodwin, Stephan. *Africa in Europe: Antiquity into the Age of Global Expansion*. Plymouth: Lexington Books, 2009.

Guasco, Michael. "Agents of Empire: Africans and the Origins of English Colonialism in the Americas." In *Entangled Empires: The Anglo-Iberian Atlantic, 1500–1830*, edited by Jorge Cañizares-Esguerra, 42–63. Philadelphia: University of Pennsylvania Press, 2018.

Guffey, George. "Aphra Behn's *Oroonoko:* Occasion and Accomplishment." In *Two English Novelists, Aphra Behn and Anthony Trollope: Papers Read at a Clark Library Seminar,* edited by George Guffey and Andrew Wright, 3–41. Los Angeles: William Andrews Clark Memorial Library, 1975.

Green, John. *The Construction of Maps and Globes.* London: Printed for T. Horne, 1717.

Greenblatt, Stephen. *Shakespearean Negotiations: The Circulation of Social Energy in Renaissance England.* Berkeley: University of California Press, 1988.

Gregory, Derek. *Geographical Imaginations.* Cambridge: Blackwell, 1984.

Griffin, Megan. "Dismembering the Sovereign in Aphra Behn's *Oroonoko.*" *ELH* 86, no. 1 (2019): 107–33.

Gruber, Elizabeth D. "Dead Girls Do It Better: Gazing Rights and the Production of Knowledge in *Othello* and *Oroonoko.*" *LIT* 14, no. 2 (2003): 99–117.

Haddad, Emily A. "Florence Nightingale, Felicia Hemans, and James Bruce's Fountains of the Nile." *Journal of African Travel Writing* 5 (1998): 53–69.

Haggard, H. Rider. *King Solomon's Mines.* 1885. New York: Longmans, 1924.

———. "The Real King Solomon's Mines." *Cassell's Magazine* 44 (1907): 144–51.

Haguet, Lucile. "J.-B. d'Anville as Armchair Mapmaker: The Impact of Production Contexts on His Work." *Imago Mundi* 63, no. 1 (2011): 88–105.

Haile, Getatchew. *The Ethiopian Orthodox Church's Tradition on the Holy Cross.* Leiden: Brill, 2018.

———. "The Works of Ras Səmʿon of Hagärä Maryam." *Journal of Ethiopian Studies* 38, no. 1/2 (2005): 5–95.

Hair, P. E. H. "Attitudes to Africans in English Primary Sources on Guinea up to 1650." *History in Africa* 26 (1999): 43–68.

Hall, Bruce S. "Arguing Sovereignty in Songhay." *Afriques* 4 (2013). doi.org/10.4000/afriques.1121.

———. *A History of Race in Muslim West Africa.* Cambridge: Cambridge University Press, 2011.

Hall, Joseph. "Sea-Floor Property and Imperial Futures in Thomas Heyrick's 'The Submarine Voyage' (1691)." *Eighteenth-Century Fiction* 31, no. 4 (2019): 639–57.

Hall, Kim F. "*Othello* and the Problem of Blackness." In *A Companion to Shakespeare's Works,* vol. 1, edited by Richard Dutton and Jean E. Howard, 357–74. London: Blackwell, 2003.

———. *Things of Darkness: Economies of Race and Gender in Early Modern England.* Ithaca, NY: Cornell University Press, 1996.

Hammond, Dorothy, and Alta Jablow. *The Africa that Never Was: Four Centuries of British Writing about Africa.* New York: Twayne, 1970.

Handler, Jerome S. "Slave Revolts and Conspiracies in Seventeenth-Century Barbados." *Nieuwe West-Indische Gids/New West Indian Guide* 56, no. 1/2 (1982): 5–42.

Hannig, Anita. "The Pure and the Pious: Corporeality, Flow, and Transgression in Ethiopian Orthodox Christianity." *Journal of Religion in Africa* 43, no. 3 (2013): 297–328.

Harley, J. B. *The New Nature of Maps: Essays in the History of Cartography*. Baltimore: Johns Hopkins University Press, 2001.

Harol, Corrinne. "The Passion of *Oroonoko*: Passive Obedience, the Royal Slave, and Aphra Behn's Baroque Realism." *ELH* 79, no. 2 (2012): 467–75.

Hartman, Saidiya. *Lose Your Mother: A Journey along the Atlantic Slave Route*. New York: Farrar, 2008.

———. "Venus in Two Acts." *Small Axe* 12, no. 2 (2008): 1–14.

Hayden, Judy A. "'As Far as a Woman's Reasoning May Go': Aphra Behn, *Oroonoko*, and the New Science." In *Travel Narratives, the New Science, and Literary Discourse, 1569–1750*, edited by Judy A. Hayden, 123–43. Farnham: Ashgate, 2012.

Hegel, Georg Wilhelm Friedrich. *The Philosophy of History*. Translated by J. Sibree. New York: Dover, 1956.

Heidegger, Martin. *The Question Concerning Technology and Other Essays*. Translated by William Lovitt. New York: Garland, 1977.

Heller, Henry. "Bodin on Slavery and Primitive Accumulation." *Sixteenth Century Journal* 25, no. 1 (1994): 53–65.

Herman, Margaux. "Towards a History of Women in Medieval Ethiopia." In *A Companion to Medieval Ethiopia and Eritrea*, edited by Samantha Kelly, 365–94. Leiden: Brill, 2020.

Heylyn, Peter. *Cosmographie in Four Books*. London: Printed for Henry Seile, 1652.

Heyrick, Thomas. *Miscellany Poems by Tho. Heyrick*. Cambridge: Printed by John Hayes, 1694.

Heywood, Linda M., and John K. Thornton. *Central Africans, Atlantic Creoles, and the Foundation of the Americas, 1585–1660*. Cambridge: Cambridge University Press, 2007.

Hiatt, Alfred. "Blank Spaces on the Earth." *Yale Journal of Criticism* 15, no. 2 (2002): 223–50.

Hickey, Alison. "'Extensive Views' in Johnson's *Journey to the Western Islands of Scotland*." *SEL* 32, no. 3 (1992): 537–53.

The History of Little Goody Two-Shoes. 3rd ed. London: Printed for John Newbury, 1766.

Hopkins, J. F. P., and Nehemia Levtzion, eds. *Corpus of Early Arabic Sources for West African History*. Princeton, NJ: Markus Wiener Press, 2000.

Hudson, Nicholas. "'Open' and 'Enclosed' Readings of 'Rasselas.'" *Eighteenth Century* 31, no. 1 (1990): 47–67.

Hulme, Peter. *Colonial Encounters: Europe and the Native Caribbean, 1492–1797*. London: Methuen, 1986.

Hulton, Paul F., Nigel Hepper, and Ib Friss. *Luigi Balugani's Drawings of African Plants: From the Collection Made by James Bruce of Kinnaird on His Travels to Discover the Source of the Nile 1767–1773.* New Haven, CT: Yale Center for British Art, 1991.
Hunwick, John, ed. *Timbuktu and the Songhay Empire: Al-Sa'dī's Ta'rīkh Al-sūdān down to 1613 and other Contemporary Documents.* Translated by Hunwick. Leiden: Brill, 1999.
Insalaco, Danielle. "Thinking of Italy, Making History: Johnson and Historiography." In *Johnson Re-Visioned: Looking Before and After,* edited by Philip Smallwood, 99–113. Lewisburg, PA: Bucknell University Press, 2001.
Iwanisziw, Susan B. "Behn's Novel Investment in 'Oroonoko': Kingship, Slavery, and Tobacco in English Colonialism." *South Atlantic Review* 63, no. 2 (1998): 75–98.
Jay, Martin. *Force Fields: Between Intellectual History and Cultural Critique.* 1993. New York: Routledge, 2013.
Jehlen, Myra. "History before the Fact: Or, Captain John Smith's Unfinished Symphony." *Critical Inquiry* 19, no. 4 (1993): 677–92.
Jobson, Richard. *The Golden Trade: or, A Discovery of the River Gambra, and the Golden Trade of the Aethiopians.* London: Printed by Nicholas Okes, 1623.
Johnson, Carina L., and Catherine Molineux. "Putting Europe in Its Place: Material Traces, Interdisciplinarity, and the Recuperation of the Early Modern Extra-European Subject." *Radical History Review* 130 (2018): 62–99.
Johnson, John William. "The Dichotomy of Power and Authority in Mande Society and in the Epic of *Sunjata.*" In *In Search of Sunjata: The Mande Oral Epic as History, Literature, and Performance,* edited by Ralph A. Austen, 9–24. Bloomington: Indiana University Press, 1999.
Johnson, Samuel. "Essay on the *Description of China* in two Volumes Folio. From the French of Pere Du Halde." *Gentleman's Magazine* 12 (1742): 320–23.
———. *The Idler and the Adventurer.* Edited by W. J. Bate, John M. Bullitt, and L. F. Powell. New Haven, CT: Yale University Press, 1963.
———. *Johnson on Demand: Reviews, Prefaces, and Ghost-Writings.* Edited by O. M. Brack and Robert DeMaria. New Haven, CT: Yale University Press, 2019.
———. *The Rambler.* Edited by W. J. Bate and Albrecht B. Strauss. 3 vols. New Haven, CT: Yale University Press, 1969.
———. *Rasselas and Other Tales.* Edited by Gwin J. Kolb. New Haven, CT: Yale University Press, 1990.
———, ed. and trans. *A Voyage to Abyssinia (Translated from the French),* by Jeronimo Lobo and Joachim Le Grand. Edited by Joel J. Gold. New Haven, CT: Yale University Press, 1985.
Jordan, Winthrop. *White over Black: American Attitudes toward the Negro 1550–1812.* 1968. 2nd ed. Chapel Hill: University of North Carolina Press, 2012.

Joseph, Betty. *Reading the East India Company, 1720–1840: Colonial Currencies of Gender.* Chicago: University of Chicago Press, 2003.

Kaul, Suvir. *Eighteenth-Century British Literature and Postcolonial Studies.* Edinburgh: University of Edinburgh Press, 2008.

Kenshur, Oscar. *Dilemmas of Enlightenment: Studies in the Rhetoric and Logic of Ideology.* Berkley: University of California Press, 1993.

Kiern, Tim. "Daniel Defoe and the Royal African Company." *Historical Research* 61 (1988): 243–47.

Klein, Bernhard. *Maps and the Writing of Space in Early Modern England and Ireland.* London: Palgrave, 2001.

———. "*Oroonoko* and the Mapping of Africa." In *English Literature and the Disciplines of Knowledge, Early Modern to Eighteenth Century: A Trade for Light,* edited by Jorge Bastos da Silva and Miguel Ramalhete Gomes, 25–55. Leiden: Brill, 2018.

Knox-Shaw, Peter. "Defoe and the Politics of Representing the African Interior." *Modern Language Review* 96, no. 4 (2001): 937–51.

———. *The Explorer in English Fiction.* New York: Palgrave, 1986.

Kolb, Gwin J. Introduction to *Rasselas and Other Tales,* by Samuel Johnson, xviii–lxx. Edited by Gwin J. Kolb. New Haven, CT: Yale University Press, 1990.

———. "The 'Paradise' in Abyssinia and the 'Happy Valley' in *Rasselas.*" *Modern Philology* 56, no. 1 (1958): 10–16.

Korounos, Michael. "*Rasselas* and the Riddle of the Caves: Setting Eternity in the Hearts of Men." *Age of Johnson* 16 (2005): 39–58.

Krebs, Verena. *Medieval Ethiopian Kingship, Craft, and Diplomacy with Latin Europe.* Cham, Switzerland: Springer, 2021.

Kroll, Richard. "'Tales of Love and Gallantry': The Politics of *Oroonoko.*" *Huntington Library Quarterly* 67, no. 4 (2004): 573–605.

Kroupa, Sebestian. "Humanists and Travellers, Gorgons and Gorillas: Hanno the Navigator's *Periplus* and Early Modern Geography (1530–1630)." *International History Review* 41, no. 4 (2019): 793–820.

Kugler, Emily M. N. *Sway of the Ottoman Empire on English Identity in the Long Eighteenth Century.* Leiden: Brill, 2012.

Lamb, Jonathan. *Preserving the Self in the South Seas, 1680–1840.* Chicago: University of Chicago Press, 2001.

Late Travels of S. Giacomo Baratti. London: Printed for Benjamin Billingsley, 1670.

Latour, Bruno. *Science in Action: How to Follow Scientists and Engineers through Society.* Cambridge, MA: Harvard University Press, 1987.

Leask, Nigel. *Curiosity and the Aesthetics of Travel Writing 1770–1840.* Oxford: Oxford University Press, 2002.

———. "*Kubla Khan* and Orientalism: The Road to Xanadu Revisited." *Romanticism* 4, no. 1 (1998): 1–21.

Lee, Sungho. "Mercantile Gentility out of Reach: Moral Cartography and Rhetorical Guidance in Defoe's *Captain Singleton*." *Modern Language Review* 112, no. 2 (2017): 299–319.

Le Grand, Joachim. "Dissertations Relating to the History of Abyssinia." In *A Voyage to Abyssinia (Translated from the French)*, by Jeronimo Lobo and Joachim Le Grand, edited and translated by Samuel Johnson, 151–318. Edited by Joel J Gold. New Haven, CT: Yale University Press, 1985.

———. "Septie'me Dissertation, de la Reine de Saba." In *Voyage Historique D'Abissinie du R. P. Jerome Lobo*, by Jeronimo Lobo, 266–72. Paris: Printed for Chez P. Gosse and J. Neaulme, 1728.

———. "Sixie'me Dissertation, de la Mer Rouge." In *Voyage Historique D'Abissinie du R. P. Jerome Lobo*, by Jeronimo Lobo, 257–65. Paris: Printed for Chez P. Gosse and J. Neaulme, 1728.

Leo Africanus. *Geographical Historie of Africa*. Translated by John Pory. London: Printed by Georg Bishop, 1600.

le Roux, Magdel. "In Search of the Origin of the Merchants of the Sea." *Religion and Theology* 10, no. 1 (2003): 24–50.

———. "Kohenim Travelling South: The Queen of Sheba in Ethiopian and Lemba Tradition." *Journal for Semitics* 13, no. 1 (2004): 59–71.

Levtzion, Nehemia. "The Western Maghrib and Sudan." In the *Cambridge History of Africa: Vol. 3, c. 1050–c. 1600*, edited by Roland Oliver, 331–462. Cambridge: Cambridge University Press, 1977.

Leyburn, Ellen Douglass. "'No Romantick Absurdities or Incredible Fictions': The Relation of Johnson's *Rasselas* to Lobo's Voyage to Abyssinia." *PMLA* 70, no. 5 (1955): 1059–67.

Lipking, Joanna. "At London and Paris: Pursuing Behn's French Connections." In *Aphra Behn (1600–1698): Identity, Alterity, Ambiguity*, edited by Mary Ann O'Donnell, Bernard Dhuicq, and Guyonne Leduc, 259–76. Paris: L'Harmattan, 2000.

———. "Confusing Matters: Searching the Backgrounds of *Oroonoko*." In *Aphra Behn Studies*, edited by Janet Todd, 259–81. Cambridge: Cambridge University Press, 1996.

Liu, Alan. "Wordsworth: The History in 'Imagination.'" *ELH* 51, no. 3 (1984): 505–48.

Livingstone, David N. *Putting Science in Its Place: Geographies of Scientific Knowledge*. Chicago: University of Chicago Press, 2003.

Loar, Christopher. *Political Magic: British Fictions of Savagery and Sovereignty, 1650–1750*. New York: Fordham University Press, 2014.

Lobo, Jeronimo. "A Voyage to Abyssinia." In *A Voyage to Abyssinia (Translated from the French)*, by Jeronimo Lobo and Joachim Le Grand, edited and translated by

Samuel Johnson, 7–117. Edited by Joel J. Gold. New Haven, CT: Yale University Press, 1985.

Lock, F. P. "Samuel Johnson's View of History." *Clio* 45, no. 2 (2016): 159–80.

Lockhart, Donald M. "The Fourth Son of the Mighty Emperor: The Ethiopian Background of Johnson's *Rasselas*." *PMLA* 78, no. 5 (1963): 516–28.

Ludolf, Hiob. *A New History of Ethiopia*. 2nd ed. Translated by J. P. Gent. London: Printed for Samuel Smith, 1684.

Lydon, Ghislaine. *On Trans-Saharan Trails: Islamic Law, Trade Networks, and Cross-Cultural Exchange in Nineteenth-Century Western Africa*. Cambridge: Cambridge University Press, 2009.

Lyttelton, George. *The Works of George Lord Lyttelton*. 2nd ed. London: George Edward Ayscough, 1775.

Mack, Ruth. "The Limits of the Senses in Johnson's Scotland." *Eighteenth Century* 54, no. 2 (2013): 279–94.

Mafe, Diana Adesola. "From Ògún to Othello: (Re)Acquainting Yoruba Myth and Shakespeare's Moor." *Research in African Literatures* 35, no. 3 (2004): 46–61.

Mallipeddi, Ramesh. *Spectacular Suffering: Witnessing Slavery in the Eighteenth-Century British Atlantic*. Richmond: University of Virginia Press, 2016.

Marana, Giovanni Paulo. *Letters Writ by a Turkish Spy* Vol. 4. 6th ed. London: Printed for H. Rhodes, 1707.

Marees, Pieter de. *Description and Historical Account of Guinea (1602)*. Translated and edited by Albert van Dantzig and Adam Jones. Oxford: Oxford University Press, 1987.

Mark, Peter. *"Portuguese" Style and Luso-African Identity: Precolonial Senegambia, Sixteenth–Nineteenth Centuries*. Bloomington: University of Indiana Press, 2002.

Markley, Robert. *The Far East and the English Imagination, 1600–1730*. Cambridge: Cambridge University Press, 2006.

———. "Global Analogies: Cosmology, Geosymmetry, and Skepticism in some Works of Aphra Behn." In *Science, Literature, and Rhetoric in Early Modern England*, edited by Juliet Cummins and David Burchell, 188–212. Farnham: Ashgate, 2007.

Masolo, D. A. *African Philosophy in Search of Identity*. Bloomington: Indiana University Press, 1994.

Mayhew, Robert J. *Enlightenment Geography: The Political Languages of British Geography*. London: MacMillan, 2000.

———. *Landscape, Literature and English Religious Culture, 1600–1800*. London: Palgrave, 2004.

M'Baye, Babacar. *The Trickster Comes West: Pan-African Influences in Early Black Diasporan Narratives*. Jackson: University Press of Mississippi, 2009.

Mbembe, Achille. *Critique of Black Reason*. Translated by Laurent Dubois. Durham, NC: Duke University Press, 2017.

———. *On the Postcolony*. Berkeley: University of California Press, 2001.

McClintock, Anne. *Imperial Leather: Race, Gender, and Sexuality in the Colonial Contest*. New York: Routledge, 1995.

McKendry, Andrew. "The Haphazard Journey of a Mind: Experience and Reflection in Samuel Johnson's *Journey to the Western Islands of Scotland*." *Age of Johnson* 20 (2010): 11–34.

McKeon, Michael. *The Secret History of Domesticity: Public, Private, and the Division of Knowledge*. Baltimore: John Hopkins University Press, 2005.

McLeod, Bruce. *The Geography of Empire in English Literature, 1580–1745*. Cambridge: Cambridge University Press, 1999.

McRae, Kenneth Douglas. Introduction to *The Six Bookes of a Commonweale*, by Jean Bodin, A3–A68. Edited by Kenneth Douglas McRae. Translated by Richard Knolles. Cambridge, MA: Harvard University Press, 1964.

Miller, Christopher. *Blank Darkness: Africanist Discourse in French*. Chicago: University of Chicago Press, 1985.

Milton, John. *Paradise Lost*. Edited by Alastair Fowler. London: Routledge, 1997.

Mitsein, Rebekah. "Trans-Saharan Worlds and Worldviews in Aphra Behn's *Oroonoko*." *Eighteenth-Century Fiction* 30, no. 3 (2018): 340–68.

———. "Upon a Voyage and No Voyage: Mapping Africa's Waterways in Defoe's *Captain Singleton*." *Digital Defoe* 10, no. 1 (2018). http://digitaldefoe.org/category/issues/issue-10-1-fall-2018/.

Mitsein, Rebekah, and Manushag Powell. "Defoe, Africa, and the Levant." In *Oxford Handbook of Defoe*. Oxford: Oxford University Press, forthcoming.

Molineux, Catherine. *Faces of Perfect Ebony: Encountering Atlantic Slavery in Imperial Britain*. Cambridge, MA: Harvard University Press, 2012.

———. "False Gifts/Exotic Fictions: Epistemologies of Sovereignty and Assent in Aphra Behn's *Oroonoko*." *ELH* 80, no. 2 (2013): 455–88.

Moll, Herman. *A System of Geography*. London: Printed for Timothy Childe, 1701.

The Monthly Review, from May to August, Inclusive. Vol. 2. London, 1790.

Moore, Francis. *Travels into the Inland Parts of Africa*. London: Printed by Edward Cave, 1738.

Moore, John Robert. "*Rasselas* and the Early Travelers to Abyssinia." *MLQ* 15, no. 1 (1954): 36–41.

Moorefield, Arthur A. "James Bruce: Ethnomusicologist or Abyssinian Lyre?" *Journal of the American Musicological Society* 28, no. 3 (1975): 493–514.

Morgan, Jennifer L. *Reckoning with Slavery: Gender, Kinship, and Capitalism in the Early Black Atlantic*. Durham, NC: Duke University Press, 2021.

Morris, Rosalind C. Introduction to *Can the Subaltern Speak? Reflections on the History of an Idea*, edited by Morris, 1–20. New York: Columbia University Press, 2010.

Mudimbe, V. Y. *The Invention of Africa: Gnosis, Philosophy, and the Order of Knowledge*. Bloomington: Indiana University Press, 1988.

New General Collection of Voyages and Travels. Vol. 2. London: Printed for Thomas Astley, 1745.

Newman, Ian. "Property, History, and Identity in Defoe's *Captain Singleton*." SEL 51, no. 3 (2011): 565–83.

Newton, John. *Thoughts upon the African Slave Trade*. London: Printed for J. Buckland, 1788.

Northrup, David. *Africa's Discovery of Europe 1450–1850*. Oxford: Oxford University Press, 2002.

Novak, Maximillian E. *Daniel Defoe: Master of Fictions*. Oxford: Oxford University Press, 2001.

Nussbaum, Felicity. "Between 'Oriental' and 'Blacks So Called.'" In *The Postcolonial Enlightenment: Eighteenth-Century Colonialism and Postcolonial Theory*, edited by Lynn Festa and Daniel Carey, 137–66. Oxford: Oxford University Press, 2009.

———, ed. *The Global Eighteenth Century*. Baltimore: Johns Hopkins University Press, 2003.

———. *The Limits of the Human: Fictions of Anomaly, Race, and Gender in the Long Eighteenth Century*. Cambridge: Cambridge University Press, 2003.

———. *Torrid Zones: Maternity, Sexuality, and Empire in Eighteenth-Century English Narratives*. Baltimore: Johns Hopkins University Press, 1995.

Oestigaard, Terje, and Gedef Abawa Firew. *The Source of the Blue Nile*. Newcastle: Cambridge Scholars, 2013.

Ogborn, Miles. *Spaces of Modernity: London's Geographies 1680–1780*. New York: Guilford, 1998.

Ogborn, Miles, and Charles W. J. Withers. "Travel, Trade, and Empire: Knowing other Places, 1660–1800." In *A Concise Companion to the Restoration and Eighteenth Century*, edited by Cynthia Wall, 13–35. London: Blackwell, 2005.

Ogilby, John. *Africa*. London: Printed by Tho. Johnson, 1670.

O'Mahony, Anthony. "Between Islam and Christendom: The Ethiopian Community in Jerusalem before 1517." *Medieval Encounters* 2, no. 2 (1996): 140–54.

O'Quinn, Daniel. *Engaging the Ottoman Empire: Vexed Mediations, 1690–1815*. Philadelphia: University of Pennsylvania Press, 2019.

Orr, Bridget. *Empire on the English Stage, 1660–1714*. Cambridge: Cambridge University Press, 2001.

Pacheco, Anita. "Royalism and Honor in Aphra Behn's *Oroonoko*." SEL 34, no. 3 (1994): 491–506.

Páez, Pedro. *Pedro Páez's History of Ethiopia, 1622*. Edited by Isabel Boavida, Hervé Pennec, and Manuel João Ramos. Translated by Christopher J. Tribe. 2 vols. Farnham: Hakluyt Society, 2011.

Pankhurst, Richard. "Early Contact between Italy and Ethiopia, and the Beginnings of Italian Scholarship on Ethiopia." *Africa* 50, no. 3 (1995): 399–403.

——. "Ethiopia's Alleged Control of the Nile." In *The Nile: Histories, Cultures, Myths*, edited by Haggai Erlich and Israel Gershoni, 25–38. Boulder, CO: Lynne Reinner, 2000.

——. "The Medical Activities in Eighteenth-Century Ethiopia of James Bruce the Explorer." *Medizinhistorisches Journal* 17, no. 3 (1982): 256–76.

Park, Katharine, and Lorraine Daston. *Wonders and the Order of Nature, 1150–1750*. New York: Zone, 1998.

Park, Mungo. *Travels in the Interior of Africa*. Vol. 1. London: Cassell, 1893.

Parker, Fred. "The Skepticism of Johnson's *Rasselas*." In *The Cambridge Companion to Samuel Johnson*, edited by Greg Clingham, 127–42. Cambridge: Cambridge University Press, 1997.

Parrish, Susan Scott. *American Curiosity: Cultures of Natural History in the Colonial British Atlantic World*. Chapel Hill: University of North Carolina Press, 2006.

Parry, Benita. "Problems in Current Theories of Colonial Discourse." *Oxford Literary Review* 9, no. 1/2 (1987): 27–58.

Paxman, David. "Oral and Literate Discourse in Aphra Behn's *Oroonoko*." *Restoration* 18, no. 2 (1994): 88–103.

Pearl, Jason H. *Utopian Geographies and the Early English Novel*. Charlottesville: University of Virginia Press, 2014.

Perkins, Pam. "Regulating Reality by Imagination: Fact, Fiction, and Travel in the Scottish Enlightenment." In *The Scottish Enlightenment and Literary Culture*, edited by Kenneth Simpson, Ralph McLean, and Ronnie Young, 37–52. Lewisburg, PA: Bucknell University Press, 2016.

Pettigrew, William A. *Freedom's Debt: The Royal African Company and the Politics of the Atlantic Slave Trade, 1672–1752*. Chapel Hill: University of North Carolina Press, 2013.

Pinto, Fernão Mendes. *The Voyages and Adventures of Fernand Mendez Pinto*. Translated by Henry Cogan. London: Printed by J. Macock, 1653.

Pliny, the Elder. *The Historie of the World: Commonly Called, the Natural Historie*. Translated by Philemon Holland. London: Printed by Adam Islip, 1634.

Poncet, Charles-Jacques. *Voyage to Aethiopia*. London: Printed for W. Lewis, 1709.

Poovey, Mary. *A History of the Modern Fact: Problems of Knowledge in the Sciences of Wealth and Society*. Chicago: University of Chicago Press, 1998.

Porter, David. *The Chinese Taste in Eighteenth-Century England*. Cambridge: Cambridge University Press, 2010.

Pory, John. Introduction to *Geographical Historie of Africa*, by Leo Africanus, 1–60. Translated by Pory. London: Printed by Georg Bishop, 1600.

Potkay, Adam. *The Passion for Happiness: Samuel Johnson and David Hume*. Ithaca, NY: Cornell University Press, 2000.

Powell, Manushag N. Introduction to *Captain Singleton*, by Daniel Defoe, 9–46. Edited by Manushag N. Powell. Peterborough, Ontario: Broadview Press, 2019.

———. *Performing Authorship in Eighteenth-Century English Periodicals*. Lewisburg, PA: Bucknell University Press, 2012.

Pratt, Mary Louis. *Imperial Eyes: Travel Writing and Transculturation*. 1992. 2nd ed. New York: Routledge, 2008.

A Proposal for Settling the Trade to Africa. London, 1713.

Purchas, Samuel. *Purchas His Pilgrimage. Or Relations of the World and the Religions Observed in All Ages and Places Discovered*. London: Printed by William Stansby, 1613.

———. *Purchas His Pilgrimage. Or Relations of the World and the Religions Observed in All Ages and Places Discovered*. 4th ed. London: Printed by William Stansby, 1626.

———. *Purchas His Pilgrimes in Five Books*. 4 vols. London: Printed by William Stansby, 1625.

Rees, Christine. *Johnson's Milton*. Cambridge: Cambridge University Press, 2010.

———. *Utopian Imagination and Eighteenth-Century Fiction*. New York: Longman, 1996.

Reid, J. M. *Traveller Extraordinary: The Life of James Bruce of Kinnaird*. London: Eyre and Spottiswoode, 1968.

Ridley, Glynis. *Clara's Grand Tour: Travels with a Rhinoceros in Eighteenth-Century Europe*. New York: Grove, 2004.

Rivero, Albert J. "Aphra Behn's *Oroonoko* and the 'Blank Spaces' of Colonial Fictions." *SEL* 39, no. 3 (1999): 443–62.

Rogers, Katharine M. "Fact and Fiction in Aphra Behn's 'Oroonoko.'" *Studies in the Novel* 20, no. 1 (1988): 1–15.

Rogers, Pat. "Speaking within Compass: The Ground Covered in Two Works by Defoe." *Studies in the Literary Imagination* 15, no. 2 (1982): 103–13.

Romm, James. "Biblical History and the Americas: The Legend of Solomon's Ophir, 1492–1591." In *The Jews and the Expansion of Europe to the West, 1450–1800*, edited by Fiering Bernardini, 27–46. New York: Berghahn, 2001.

Ruffhead, Owen. Review of *Rasselas*. In *Rasselas*, by Samuel Johnson, edited by Jessica Richard, 166–69. Peterborough, Ontario: Broadview, 2008.

Runge, Laura L. "Constructing Place in *Oroonoko*." In *Gender and Space in British Literature, 1660–1820*, edited by Mona Narain and Karen Bloom Gevirtz, 19–32. Farnham, UK: Ashgate, 2014.

Said, Edward. *Culture and Imperialism*. New York: Vintage, 1993.
———. *Orientalism*. New York: Vintage, 1979.
Salt, Henry. *A Voyage to Abyssinia*. London: F. C. and J. Rivington, 1814.
Salvadore, Matteo. *The African Prester John and the Birth of Ethiopian-European Relations, 1402–1555*. London: Routledge, 2017.
———. "The Ethiopian Age of Exploration: Prester John's Discovery of Europe, 1306–1458." *Journal of World History* 21, no. 4 (2010): 593–627.
Saur, Elizabeth. *Milton, Toleration, and Nationhood*. Cambridge: Cambridge University Press, 2014.
Schmidgen, Wolfram. *Exquisite Mixture: The Virtues of Impurity in Early Modern England*. Philadelphia: University of Pennsylvania Press, 2013.
Schmidt, Benjamin. *Inventing Exoticism: Geography, Globalism, and Europe's Early Modern World*. Philadelphia: University of Pennsylvania Press, 2015.
Scrimgeour, Gary J. "The Problem of Realism in Defoe's *Captain Singleton*." *Huntington Library Quarterly* 27, no. 1 (1963): 21–37.
Shakespeare, William. *Othello*. In *The Norton Shakespeare Based on the Oxford Edition*, edited by Stephen Greenblatt, Walter Cohen, Jean E. Howard, and Katharine Eisaman Maus, 2nd ed., 2109–91. New York: Norton, 2008.
Shalev, Zur. "Sacred Geography, Antiquarianism, and Visual Erudition: Benito Arias Montano and the Maps in the Antwerp Polyglot Bible." *Imago Mundi* 55 (2003): 56–80.
Sher, Richard B. *The Enlightenment and the Book: Scottish Authors and Their Publishers in Eighteenth-Century Britain, Ireland, and America*. Chicago: University of Chicago Press, 2006.
Sills, Adam. "Eighteenth-Century Cartographic Studies: A Brief Survey." *Literature Compass* 4, no. 4 (2007): 981–1002.
———. "Surveying the Map of Slavery in Aphra Behn's *Oroonoko*." *Journal of Narrative Theory* 36, no. 3 (2006): 314–40.
Smith, Cassander L. *Black Africans in the British Imagination: English Narratives of the Early Atlantic World*. Baton Rouge: Louisiana State University Press, 2016.
Smith, Courtney Weiss. *Empiricist Devotions: Science, Religion, and Poetry in Early Eighteenth-Century England*. Richmond: University of Virginia Press, 2016.
Smith, Malvern van Wyk. "Father Lobo, Ethiopia, and the Transkei: Or, Why *Rasselas* was not a Mpondo Prince." *Journal of African Travel Writing* 4 (1998): 5–16.
———. "Would the Real James Bruce Please Stand Up? Bruce's *Travels to Discover the Source of the Nile* (1790) in Alexander Murray's edition of 1813." *English Academy Review* 23 (2006): 59–83.
Smith, William. *New Voyage to Guinea*. London: Printed for John Nourse, 1744.
Sobel, Mechal. *The World They Made Together: Black and White Values in Eighteenth-Century Virginia*. Princeton, NJ: Princeton University Press, 1989.

Sparks, Randy J. *Where the Negroes Are Masters: An African Port in the Era of the Slave Trade.* Cambridge, MA: Harvard University Press, 2014.

Spear, Thomas, ed. *The Oxford Encyclopedia of African Historiography: Methods and Sources.* 2 vols. Oxford: Oxford University Press, 2019.

Spencer, Steffan A. "Matrifocal Retentions in Ethiopian Orthodox Traditions: The Madonna as Ark and Queen Makeda as Prefiguration of Mary; with Egyptian Queen Tiye and Pharoh Hatshepsut as Reference." *African Identities* 19 (2021): 1–22. doi.org/10.1080/14725843.2021.1995325.

Spivak, Gayatri Chakrovorty. *Critique of Postcolonial Reason: Toward a History of the Vanishing Present.* Cambridge, MA: Harvard University Press, 1999.

Sprat, Thomas. *History of the Royal Society.* London: Printed for J. Knapton, 1667.

Starr, G. Gabrielle. "Objects, Imaginings, and Facts: Going beyond Genre in Behn and Defoe." *Eighteenth-Century Fiction* 16, no. 4 (2004): 499–518.

Stiebel, Lindy. "Creating a Landscape of Africa: Baines, Haggard and Great Zimbabwe." *English in Africa* 28, no. 2 (2001): 123–33.

———. *Imagining Africa: Landscape in H. Rider Haggard's African Romances.* Westport, CT: Greenwood Press, 2001.

Sudan, Rajani. *The Alchemy of Empire: Abject Materials and the Technologies of Colonialism.* New York: Fordham University Press, 2016.

———. *Fair Exotics: Xenophobic Subjects in English Literature, 1720–1850.* Philadelphia: University of Pennsylvania Press, 2002.

Sundström, Lars. *The Trade of Guinea.* Lund, Sweden: Lund University Press, 1965.

Sutton, Elizabeth A. *Early Modern Dutch Prints of Africa.* London: Taylor and Francis, 2017.

Svalastog, Julie M. *Mastering the Worst Trades: England's Early Africa Companies and Their Traders, 1618–1672.* Leiden: Brill, 2021.

Sweet, James H. *Domingos Álvares, African Healing, and the Intellectual History of the Atlantic World.* Chapel Hill: University of North Carolina Press, 2011.

Táíwò, Olúfẹ́mi. "Exorcizing Hegel's Ghost: Africa's Challenge to Philosophy." *African Studies Quarterly* 1, no. 4 (1998): 3–16.

———. *How Colonialism Preempted Modernity in Africa.* Bloomington: Indiana University Press, 2009.

———. "Looking Back, Facing Forward: (Re)-Imagining A Global Africa." *Black Scholar* 45, no. 1 (2015): 51–69.

Tally, Robert T., Jr. *Topophrenia: Place, Narrative, and the Spatial Imagination.* Bloomington: Indiana University Press, 2019.

Tamrat, Taddesse. *Church and State in Ethiopia, 1270–1527.* Oxford: Clarendon, 1972.

Taylor, David Francis. "Johnson's Textual Landscape." *Eighteenth Century* 59, no. 1 (2018): 66–75.

Taylor, Diana. *The Archive and the Repertoire: Performing Cultural Memory in the Americas.* Durham, NC: Duke University Press, 2003.

Tellez [Telles], Balthasar. *The Travels of the Jesuits in Ethiopia.* Translated by John Stevens. London: Printed for J. Knapton, 1710.

Thell, Anne M. *Minds in Motion: Imagining Empiricism in Eighteenth-Century British Travel Literature.* Lewisburg, PA: Bucknell University Press, 2017.

Thornton, John. *Africa and Africans in the Making of the Atlantic World, 1400–1800.* Cambridge: Cambridge University Press, 1998.

Tomarken, Edward. *Johnson, Rasselas, and the Choice of Criticism.* Lexington: University Press of Kentucky, 1989.

———. "Perspectivism: The Methodological Implications of 'The History of Imlac' in *Rasselas.*" *Age of Johnson* 2 (1989): 262–90.

Turk, Edward Baron. *Baroque Fiction-Making: A Study of Gomberville's Polexandre.* Chapel Hill: University of North Carolina Press, 1978.

Turley, Hans. "Piracy, Identity, and Desire in *Captain Singleton.*" *Eighteenth-Century Studies* 31, no. 2 (1997): 199–214.

Ullendorff, Edward. *Ethiopia and the Bible.* Oxford: Oxford University Press, 1968.

———. "James Bruce of Kinnaird." *Scottish Historical Review* 32 (1953): 128–43.

Van Donzel, Emery. "The Legend of the Blue Nile in Europe." In *The Nile: Histories, Cultures, Myths,* edited by Haggai Erlich and Israel Gershoni, 121–30. Boulder, CO: Lynne Reinner, 2000.

Visconi, Elliot. "A Degenerate Race: English Barbarism in Aphra Behn's *Oroonoko* and *The Widow Ranter.*" *ELH* 69, no. 3 (2002): 677–91.

Vitkus, Daniel J. *Turning Turk: English Theater and the Multicultural Mediterranean.* London: Palgrave, 2003.

Wahrman, Dror. *The Making of the Modern Self: Identity and Culture in Eighteenth-Century England.* New Haven, CT: Yale University Press, 2004.

Walker, William. *Victorious Love, a Tragedy.* London: Printed for Ralph Smith, 1698.

Walmsley, Peter. "The African Artisan Meets the English Sailor: Technology and the Savage for Defoe." *Eighteenth Century* 59, no. 3 (2018): 347–68.

Watt, James. "What Mankind Has Lost and Gained: Johnson, *Rasselas,* and Colonialism." In *Reading 1759: Literary Culture in Mid-Eighteenth-Century Britain and France,* edited by Shaun Regan, 21–36. Lewisburg, PA: Bucknell University Press, 2013.

Wear, Jeremy. "No Dishonour to Be a Pirate: The Problem of Infinite Advantage in Defoe's *Captain Singleton.*" *Eighteenth-Century Fiction* 24, no. 4 (2012): 569–96.

Weinbrot, Howard D. "The Reader, the General, and the Particular: Johnson and Imlac in Chapter Ten of *Rasselas.*" *Eighteenth-Century Studies* 5, no. 1 (1971): 80–96.

Welch, Ellen R. *A Taste for the Foreign: Worldly Knowledge and Literary Pleasure in Early Modern French Fiction*. Newark: University of Delaware Press, 2011.

Wheeler, Roxann. *The Complexion of Race: Categories of Difference in Eighteenth-Century British Culture*. Philadelphia: University of Pennsylvania Press, 2000.

White, Robert. Preface to *The Golden Regions of South East Africa*, by Thomas Baines, v–ix. London: Edward Stanford, 1877.

Whitney, Lois. "Did Shakespeare Know Leo Africanus?" *PMLA* 37, no. 3 (1922): 470–83.

Wilks, Ivor. "The History of the *Sunjata* Epic." In *In Search of Sunjata: The Mande Oral Epic as History, Literature, and Performance*, edited by Ralph A. Austen, 25–58. Bloomington: Indiana University Press, 1999.

———. "Wangara, Akan and Portuguese in the Fifteenth and Sixteenth Centuries. 1. The Matter of Bitu." *Journal of African History* 23, no. 3 (1982): 333–49.

Wilson, Kathleen. *The Island Race: Englishness, Empire, and Gender in the Eighteenth Century*. New York: Routledge, 2003.

Wise, Christopher. "Leo Africanus and the Songhay Dynasty of the Askiyas: Plundering Northern Mali, Past and Present." *Arena* 39/40 (2012/2013): 140–57.

Withers, Charles W. J. *Placing the Enlightenment: Thinking Geographically about the Age of Reason*. Chicago: University of Chicago Press, 2005.

———. "Travel and Trust in the Eighteenth Century." In *L'invitation au voyage: Studies in Honour of Peter France*, edited by John Renwick, 47–54. Oxford: Voltaire Foundation, 2000.

Wright, Michelle. *Physics of Blackness: Beyond the Middle Passage Epistemology*. Minneapolis: University of Minnesota Press, 2015.

Yang, Chi-ming. "Asia out of Place: The Aesthetics of Incorruptibility in Behn's *Oroonoko*." *Eighteenth-Century Studies* 42, no. 2 (2009): 235–53.

———. *Performing China: Virtue, Commerce, and Orientalism in Eighteenth-Century England, 1660–1760*. Baltimore: Johns Hopkins University Press, 2011.

Yewbrey, Graham. "John Dee's 'Brytish Impire': 'A Laborious Treatise' on Ophir of 1577." *Journal of the Warburg and Courtauld Institutes* 78 (2015): 247–76.

Zhiri, Oumelbanine. "Leo Africanus and the Limits of Translation." In *Travel and Translation in the Early Modern Period*, edited by Carmine di Biase, 175–86. Amsterdam: Rodopi, 2006.

Zouche, Richard. *The Dove: Or Passages of Cosmography*. 1613. Reprinted and edited by Richard Walker. Oxford: H. Slatter, 1839.

Zuroski, Eugenia. *A Taste for China: English Subjectivity and the Prehistory of Orientalism*. Oxford: Oxford University Press, 2013.

INDEX

Page numbers in italics designate maps and figures in the text.

Abay/Blue Nile, 30, 130, 132; entire course of the, 148; as the "Father of Waters," 130, 156, 174, 229n112; source of the, 142–43. *See also* Nile River
Abba Salama, 193–94
Abu Bakr, 44
Abu Marwan Abd al-Malik I, 63
Abyssinia: biblical connections of, 40, 152, 165; control over the Nile of, 131, 156, 196–97; early modern impressions of, 129–34, 137–38, 142–46; emperor of, 67; geopolitical reach of, 20, 133, 156; gold of, 163; historical scope of, 40; impressions of, 124–49, 165, 177–99; as land of exotic exports, 133; literary or pseudo-historical representations of, 151; Milton on, 34–36, 66, 145, 151, 229n4; mines of, 19, 160; as nation ruled over by the *negusa nagast*, 226n5; obsession with prophecy and the interpretation of dreams of, 188; Royal Chronicles of, 179, 184, 188, 197, 202; scholarship on, 9, 161; Solomonic claims of, 20, 35, 135–36, 149, 152, 167; as the source of the Nile, 3, 29–30, 39, 61–64, 125, 129–34, 142–43, 148–49, 153, 165, 180, 191, 196; topography of, 145, 196; travel narratives on, 9, 124–49, 150–99. *See also* Africa; African empires; Church of Our Lady Mother of Zion; empire; Ethiopia; Ethiopian exceptionalism; Ge'ez; Gondar; Habesha; Happy Valley; Land of Prester John; *negus* (Emperor of Abyssinia); *negusa nagast*; Nubia; Paradise; Sheba, Queen of; Solomonic Dynasty; *Zemene Mesafint* (Era of the Princes, Era of the Judges)
Adal, 165–66
Adal Sultinate, 138
Africa: as absolute other, 5, 7, 30; as blank space, 8, 111; British contact with, 11, 90; circumnavigation of, 115; colonization of, 5, 112, 201; cosmopolitanism of, 13; in drama, 68, 87; as eastern margin of the Atlantic world, 13, 70; in eighteenth-century mock travel narratives, 125, 147; in eighteenth-century travel narratives, 114, 125, 146, 153–54, 167, 177–99; European circumnavigation of, 62; European discourse about, 209n33; European exploration of the interior of, 98–99, 112, 115, 119–21, 178, 195, 201; in European literature as theorized by literary scholars, 7–8, 37–38, 65; as fantasy space, 79, 111; geopolitical clout of elites of, 3, 41–47; gold trade and geography of, 41–44, 46, 51–55; inter-African politics and trade, 65; interconnectivity with the early modern world of, 41–76; invention of, 5–6, 10; Islamic states of, 84; justification for the colonization of, 111; as the "Land of the Blacks," 2, 34, 39, 65, 83; North Africa vs. sub-Saharan Africa, 65; partition at the Berlin Conference

Africa (*continued*)
from a map of Africa of, 30; physical topography of, 39, 42, 106, 110; poetic mappings of, 33–38; pre-colonial Africa vs. colonial Africa, 14; as real place, 37, 72, 79; in romance, 68–69, 71, 78–79, 179; southern tip of, 62; symbolic role of the Sahara in European impressions of, 65; trade potential of, 118; in verse, 40, 150–76. *See also* Abyssinia; African expressions; African impressions; Atlantic coast; Atlas Mountains; East Africa; Eastern Sudan; Great Zimbabwe; Horn of Africa; North Africa (Barbary); Sahara Desert; sub-Saharan Africa; West Africa; Western Sudan

African agency: in the archive, 13; in the contact zone with Europeans, 8–9, 42, 90, 129; in the literary record, 13. *See also* African expressions

African empires: African gold and the shape of, 42–47, 49, 72; interior, 72–76; Solomonic Dynasty, 125–29; spatial grammar of, 107–12; of Western Sudan, 41–42, 72–76, 83. *See also* Abyssinia; empire; Ghana Empire; Mali Empire; Songhai Empire; trade; Wolof Empire

African expressions: of African elites, 3, 9, 14, 42–47, 52, 58, 69, 75, 125–29, 133; African strategies of self-representation as, 1, 10–12; in European literary traditions, 1, 3, 9–10, 13, 33–37, 100–123, 153–65, 230n15; in European travel writing, 20–33, 110, 177–99, 202–3; as geographical evidence, 28, 69, 103, 110, 123, 202–3; of geopolitics and culture, 106; literary and cultural, 157; oral traditions as, 10, 18, 47, 172; preservation in popular geographical texts of recognizable elements of, 29, 110; written traditions as, 10, 47, 129–34, 172. *See also* Africa; African agency; African impressions; African literature

African historiography, 8–9; state of, 14. *See also* historiography

African impressions: African self-representations in, 11, 79; creation and perpetuation of, 2–3, 61–66; early Enlightenment, 11, 100, 201–3; as an epistemological form, 3, 81; European dependence on, 111–14, 122; and European imperial idioms, 33–38; extratextual, 2, 81; geographical genres and the consolidation of, 25–33, 104; geographical ideas as, 1, 52, 196; of Habesha pilgrims and dignitaries, 130, 177–99; of interior of Africa, 110–12, 121–22, 195; intertextual, 2; precolonial European and Arabic contact narratives and other kinds of geographical writing as, 14, 23, 70, 75–76; rivers for want of empires in, 98–123; romance and, 77–97; as a structural idea, 4; of Western Sudan, 50–77. *See also* Africa; African expressions; contact narratives; geographical genres; imagination; representation of geography; Sofala-Ophir impression

Africanism, 5

African literature: Epic of Askia Muhammad I, 58–60; Epic of Sundiata, 45, 214n11; Ethiopian Synaxarium, 189; in European languages, 13; Royal Chronicles of Abyssinia, 179, 184, 188, 197, 202. *See also* African expressions; *Kebra Nagast*

African titles: *askia*, 61, 69, 72, 84, 114; *itege*, 140–42, 180–82, 185–90, 192–93; *mansa*, 69, 114; *negus*, 34, 36, 69, 114; *sonni/sunni*, 69, 114

age of discovery, 16

Ahmad ibn Ibrahim al-Ghazi (Grahn), 138–39, 145–46, 157, 185

Akan (Coramantees), 54; brokers of the, 84–85

Aksum/Axum, 17, 27, 34, 132, 135–37, 144–45; as city of Queen of Sheba, 166;

INDEX   263

Empire of, 158; pre-Zagwe king of, 126; ruins of, 19, 144, 161, 163, 166; stone steles of, 136, 166. *See also* Ethiopian Highlands
al-Bakri, 58
Alborn, Timothy, 203
Albuquerque, Afonso de, 131
Alexander the Great, 195
Algiers, Kingdom of, 82
Aljoe, Nicole, 24
allegory, 181, 184
al-Umari. *See* Ibn Fadlallah al-Umari
Álvares, Francisco, 17, 22, 27, 129, 169, 185; informants of, 166; *Prester John of the Indies*, 134–37, 140–41, 143–44
Amara (hill), 143–45, 169. See also *amba* (mountain prison, fortress); Amba Geshen; Amhara (region); Debre Damo
amba (mountain prison, fortress), 130, 139, 169. *See also* Amara (hill); Amba Geshen; Debre Damo
Amba Geshen, 144–45. *See also* Amara (hill); *amba* (mountain prison, fortress)
Amda Seyon I, 127, 133, 136
Americas, 7; seventeenth-century natural history writing in the, 95. *See also* New World
Amhara (region), 132, 144. *See also* Amara (hill)
Andrea, Bernadette, 57, 61
Angola, 87
Arabian Peninsula, 18–19, 163, 165; as periphery of Makeda's domain, 184; ruins of the palace of Sheba in the, 163
Arabic, 14
Aravamudan, Srinivas, 151; *Tropicopolitans*, 77, 97, 99
archive: nontextual, 7; problem of the, 208n22; written, 13–14. *See also* history; recovering African voices
Ariosto, Ludovico: *Orlando Furioso*, 125, 129–34
Ark of the Covenant, 126, 129, 135, 143–44, 162, 166

Ashanti, 85
Asia, 7, 149, 164
Askia Muhammad I, 29, 56–60, 65, 127; imperial reach of, 62; overthrow of, 60; pilgrimage of, 58; rise to power of, 58–59. *See also* Epic of Askia Muhammad I
Association for Promoting the Discovery of the Interior Parts of Africa (African Association), 11, 123, 201
Aster Iyasu, 180, 183, 191–95, 197, 236n67
Astley, Thomas: *New General Collection of Voyages and Travels*, 29, 106
Atlantic coast, 41, 50–51; European explorations of the, 55, 100; slave ports of the, 78; states of the, 50, 83. *See also* Africa
Atlantic creoles, 78
Atlantic Ocean, 62
Atlas Mountains, 42–43, 48, 50, 62–63. *See also* Africa
Aylo, 190, 192

Baines, Thomas, 203–4; *Golden Regions of South East Africa*, 203
Bakaffa, 181–82, 186–88
Baltasar, Juan de, 143–45
Balugani, Luigi, 202
Banks, Joseph, 154, 201
Baratti, Giacomo: *The Late Travels of S. Giacomo Baratti*, 145
Barbary, 62, 74. *See also* Barbary traders; North Africa (Barbary)
Barbary traders, 58, 74. *See also* Barbary
Barbauld, Anna Letitia, 179
Barbot, Jean, 22, 85
Barker, Anthony, 8
Barros, João de: *Décadas da Ásia*, 18–20, 27, 32, 34, 146, 205
Bartels, Emily, 8, 61, 65, 217n87
Bati del Wambara, 185
Beach, Adam, 8, 78, 80, 221n51
Behn, Aphra, 4, 38, 76, 219n11; *Oroonoko*, 39, 77–97, 221n51

Belcher, Wendy Laura: *Abyssinia's Samuel Johnson: Ethiopian Thought in the Making of an English Author*, 9–10, 37, 131, 152, 157, 160, 162, 164, 170, 230n15, 231n41; "Sisters Debating the Jesuits," 192

Benin, 124; Oba of, 124

Bennett, Herman, 8, 25, 43

Berington, Thomas: *News from the Dead*, 147–48

Berlin Conference (1884–85), 30

Bermudes, João, 138–41

Bible, 16, 27; Psalm 45 in the, 181

Bilad al-Sudan (Land of the Blacks), 2, 41, 46, 49, 53, 58–60; contact narratives of the western reaches of the, 134; in early Enlightenment geographical imagination, 72–76; eyewitness accounts of the, 149; fourteenth-century impression (Catalan Atlas) of the, 47–50; geographical impressions of the, 69, 75, 78, 82–86, 90, 94, 99, 101–11, 134, 137; impressions of the hydrography of the, 101–7; literary geography of the, 61–66, 87; as place of kings and empires, 85. See also Western Sudan

Blaeu, Willem Janszoon, 60, 102, 142

Blair, Hugh, 179, 195

Blue Nile. See Abay/Blue Nile

Bochart, Samuel: *Geographia Sacra*, 163–64

Bodin, Jean, 66–72, 89–90; *Les Six livres de la République* (*Six Bookes of a Commonweale*), 66–68, 71

Borno, 58, 63, 83

Bosc-Tiessé, Claire, 182

Boswell, James, 150, 154–55, 172

Boulukos, George, 8, 57, 65, 78

Bourdieu, Pierre, 15

Bovill, E. W., 215n48

Boyle, Robert, 28, 80; *General Heads for the Natural History of a Country Great or Small Drawn out for the Use of Travellers and Navigators*, 21, 26, 79

Britain, 17; expansionist interests of, 12, 112–13, 118; geopolitical interests of, 19; global trade of, 37, 112; imperialism of, 35–37; nationalism of, 230n8; ruins of Great Zimbabwe as a foundation for empire of, 37; settlements in Africa of, 195; and the slave trade, 98; West African trade ports of, 78. See also empire

Brooks, Christopher, 229n2

Brooks, Lisa, 25

Brown, Laura, 37

Browne, Patrick: *Civil and Natural History of Jamaica*, 231n19

Bruce, James, 4, 17, 19–20, 38, 148–50, 202, 205, 234n1, 234n7; debates about the credibility of, 179; epistemological strategies of, 178–79; medical skills of, 190; sexualization of Ethiopian women by, 235n18; support of Mentewab for, 184; synopsis of the *Kebra Nagast* of, 184; *Travels to Discover the Source of the Nile*, 32–34, 40, 125, 146, 177–99, 201

Brue, André, 102

Brydges, James (Duke of Chandos), 98–99, 102, 112

Bucker, 52–53, 109

Buckor Sano, 72–75

Buffon, Comte de, 177

Bumi Jeleen, 51–52, 69

Burchett, Josiah, 18, 114

Burney, Frances, 179

Burton, Jonathan, 57, 61, 204

Buzi River, 17. See also rivers

Cadamosto, Alvise, 52–55, 74, 81, 99

Caillié, René, 201

Cairo, 43–44, 48, 68, 133; Mamluk sultan in, 46. See also Egypt

Cambyses, 195

Campbell, Mary Baine, 94

Candace (Kandake), Queen, 135; temple dedicated to, 143

Cantor, 52–53

Cape of Good Hope, 66, 132

INDEX   265

Caribbean, 87; plantations of the, 66, 77; settlers in the, 211n77; and the slave trade, 72
Carignano, Giovanni Mauro da, 130
cartography: ancient, 27; classical worldviews in African, 142, 148; depiction of uncharted territory as easily accessible in, 49; early modern, 60, 108; eighteenth-century, 148; empirical, 30–31; exotic appeal in, 32; history of, 30–32, 47–50, 148; Jewish, 214n24; literary, 61, 86–88; prose, 69; scientific, 101, 104, 148; seventeenth-century, 142; single-river theory in, 104; sixteenth-century, 142; systematic and empirical, 201, 203; verse, 61–62, 64, 83–84, 88, 132–34; written and oral evidence in, 172. *See also* Catalan Atlas; *mappae mundi*; maps; portolan; speculative maps
Castanhoso, Miguel de, 138–41, 143–45, 169, 185
Catalan Atlas, 47–50, *48*, 61, 65, 94, 102, 124, 220n30. *See also* cartography
Catholic missions in Ethiopia, 157, 180, 189. *See also* Ethiopia; Franks; Jesuits
Certeau, Michel de, 15
Ceuta, 82
Ceylon, 159–60
Chandos. *See* Brydges, James (Duke of Chandos)
Charles II, King of England, 78
Charles V, King of France, 47
Chibka, Robert, 97
Chico, Tita, 37
Christianity: in Abyssinia, 12, 133–36, 143, 160; in Britain, 12–13; conversions of Africans to, 57, 127, 141; primitive, 162. *See also* Catholic missions in Ethiopia; Ethiopian Orthodox Church; religion; Virgin Mary
chronometer, 201
Church of Our Lady Mother of Zion, 135–36, 166. *See also* Abyssinia

Clark, Evert Mordecai, 145
Coleridge, Samuel, 179; *Kubla Khan*, 195
colonialism, 5, 34; British, 107, 112. *See also* empire
Columbus, Christopher, 16
comedy, 145
Congo. *See* Kongo, Kingdom of
Congo River, 107. *See also* rivers
Conrad, Joseph: *Heart of Darkness*, 5, 8, 30, 122. *See also* Marlow
contact narratives, 14, 23; Abyssinian-European, 129, 134–37, 152, 166; of coastal states of West Africa, 85–86; early Atlantic, 50–55. *See also* African impressions; geographical genres
Cook, James, 154
copper, 107
Coramantien (Kormantin), 39, 77–82, 86–90, 94, 97
Council of Florence, 128
Crummey, Donald, 126, 197
Curley, Thomas M., 151–52, 230n9
cycle of accumulation, 26–27
cycle of discursive reiteration, 1, 12, 27, 29, 33, 62

da Gama, Cristóvão, 138, 140
Damot, 191
d'Anville, Jean Baptiste Bourguignon, 28, 30, 104, 106, 229n112; *Afrique publiée sous les auspices de Monseigneur le Duc d'Orléans Prémier Prince du Sang*, 30–32, *31*
Dapper, Olfert, 82
Daston, Lorraine, 26
Dawit I, 131
Dawit II (Lebna Dengel), 128–29, 134–36, 138–41, 144, 146, 185
Debre Damo, 130, 138, 145, 169. *See also* Amara (hill); *amba* (mountain prison, fortress)
Dee, John, 16, 37
Defoe, Daniel, 4, 38, 76, 99–100, 106, 222n5; *Atlas Maritimus and*

Defoe, Daniel (*continued*)
Commercialis, 39, 101, 106–14, 117, 120–23, 223n31; *Captain Singleton*, 39, 100–101, 106, 112–22, 223n31, 223n33; defense of the Royal African Company's monopoly by, 99; *History of the Principal Discoveries*, 124–25; *Review*, 111, 114, 117–18, 223n31; *Robinson Crusoe*, 118, 223n33; speculative geography of, 119–23; valorization of empiricism of, 106
de Gama, Vasquez, 70
Delisle, Guillaume, 148
Democratic Republic of the Congo, 142. *See also* Kongo, Kingdom of
de Ruyter, Engel, 78
diamonds, 20; mining of, 204
DiPiero, Thomas, 69
divine right of kings, 71, 88. *See also* political theory; sovereignty
Djenné (Jenné), 58, 83, 108–9
Dominicans, 144
Donaldson, Ian, 154
Doster Esther, 202
Dürer, Albrecht, 96
Dyer, John: *The Fleece*, 33, 35–38, 61, 66

earthen ablution, 46, 59, 65, 67, 86
East Africa, 4, 16–19, 34–37, 147, 151, 184; centrality of the Abyssinian emperor to the geopolitics of, 156; Muslim expansion in, 127; narrative traditions of, 17, 125; Portuguese explorers in, 204. *See also* Africa
Eastern Sudan, 83. *See also* Africa
East Indies, 165
economy, 54. *See also* trade
Edson, Evelyn, 49
Edwards, Jess, 100, 110, 119–20, 223n31
Egypt, 61–62, 153, 158, 165; famine in, 131; flood of the Nile in, 63, 131, 156–57, 198; voyage along the Nile into, 116. *See also* Cairo

Eleni, Queen Regent, 128, 135–36, 139–42, 166, 181–82, 185, 188–89
empire: European colonization of Africa in the nineteenth century, 5, 34, 107, 112; European motivation for exploring Africa, 19–20, 120; representations of non-European, 6, 19. *See also* Abyssinia; African empires; Britain; colonialism; Ghana Empire; ideology, imperial; Mali Empire; Ottoman Empire; Songhai Empire; Wolof Empire
empiricism, 21–23; of Bruce's *Travels*, 178; of Johnson's *Rasselas*, 169; methodological constraints of, 153; of Royal Society, 79, 81, 91–97; scientific, 219n11. *See also* epistemology; gaze; science; seeing man
Enlightenment: in cultural studies, 6; early, 1–8, 11–13, 19, 25–33, 66, 78, 152; epistemology of the, 4–6; global thinking and expansionist desire of the early, 29–30, 35–36, 69, 88, 101; in literary studies, 6–8; as set of epistemological values and practices, 11; as temporal designation, 11. *See also* Europe
enslaved Africans, 5, 68, 77; sold to Arab traders, 42. *See also* slavery; slave trade
Epic of Askia Muhammad I, 58–60. *See also* Askia Muhammad I
Epic of Sundiata, 45, 214n11. *See also* Sundiata Keita
epistemology: changing nineteenth-century ideas of, 204; commentary of Behn's *Oroonoko* on, 77–97; commentary of Bruce's *Travels* on, 177–99; commentary of Defoe's *Atlas* on, 101, 106–14, 120–23; commentary of Defoe's *Captain Singleton* on, 100–101, 106, 112–22; commentary of Johnson's *Rasselas* on, 168, 173–75; hybridization of a range of strategies of, 97; local, 26; of the organizational schemas of the Royal Society, 92–93; of Western geographical discourse, 14, 38, 92, 101,

152, 161, 168, 178–79. *See also* empiricism; geographical discourse; Johnson, Samuel; knowledge; Royal Society
Eritrea, 142
Ethiopia: Christian empire of, 17, 157; conversion to Christianity of, 144; Emperor of, 124; languages of, 177, 180, 202; in mapmaking, 104; modern-day, 142; religious destiny of, 135; royal prisons of, 169; traditional poetry of, 131. *See also* Abyssinia; Catholic missions in Ethiopia; Ethiopian exceptionalism; Ethiopian Highlands; Ethiopian Orthodox Church; Ge'ez; Solomonic Dynasty; Zagwe Dynasty
Ethiopian-Adal War, 127, 137–42, 146, 185
Ethiopian exceptionalism, 9, 34–35; geographical, 125; national, 132, 196–97; religious, 39, 125–29, 132, 135, 143, 149; Solomonic, 136. *See also* Abyssinia; Ethiopia; religion
Ethiopian Highlands, 9, 19; Christianity in the, 12, 226n5; rule of the Solomonic Dynasty in the, 126–27; wartime occupation of the, 138–39. *See also* Aksum/Axum; Ethiopia; Habesha
Ethiopian Orthodox Church, 127, 130, 189; communion for women in the, 197; patriarch of the, 138; typology of the, 182. *See also* Christianity; Ethiopia; religion
Ethiopian Synaxarium (Lives of the Saints), 189
Eugene IV, Pope, 128
Europe: coast of, 47; invention of Africa by, 5–6; mathematical charting of, 64; slave trade to, 63; terminology of, 12; tradition of racial or cultural superiority of, 5; travelers from, 3. *See also* Enlightenment
Evelyn, John: *Numismata*, 61, 217n78

Farias, P. F. de Moraes, 215n48
Farr, Jason, 113

Fasil, 191–93, 196
Fasilides, 157
Ferrer, Jaume, 49–50
Fouta Djallon, 53. *See also* Guinea Highlands
Fra Mauro: *Planisfero*, 132
France, 47, 62, 178; *Fronde* in the history of, 69; kings of, 67
Franks, 180, 182, 190–94. *See also* Catholic missions in Ethiopia; Jesuits
Freedman, Paul, 49
Fromont, Cécile, 8
Frumentius, 135
Furbank, P. N., 121, 223n31

Galawdewos, 138–40, 185
Gambia River, 41–42, 49, 51–52, 72–76, 102, 106, 110, 116; European attempts to travel up the, 99, 103–4, 123; interior states along the, 103; navigability of the, 114; source of the, 99, 102; valley of the, 46, 55, 75, 104. *See also* rivers
Gao, 43–48, 53, 58, 83, 102, 108, 218n105; court at, 87; gold of, 85. *See also* Western Sudan
Gaoga, 58, 83; king of, 67–68; location of, 218n105
Gastaldi, Giacomo, 60, 102, 142
gaze: curious native, 95; disinterested native, 92; imperial, 92–95; single, 30. *See also* empiricism; seeing man
Geddes, Michael: *Church History of Ethiopia*, 146–47
Ge'ez, 14, 179, 226n5. *See also* Abyssinia; Ethiopia
geographical discourse: "Africa" as an invention of Enlightenment, 4–40; African, 10, 103, 111–12, 153; eyewitness accounts as, 78–79, 142, 152; fact vs. fancy in, 2, 100, 114, 149–76, 199; imaginative representations of Africa in, 2, 5, 9–10, 211n88; importance of narrative to, 86–90; justification of enslavement of Africans in European, 13;

geographical discourse (*continued*)
in literature, 34–36, 61–66, 77–97, 132–34, 173; nonempirical, 86–97; romance in, 68–71, 78–79; wonder in, 21, 32, 57, 68, 97. *See also* epistemology; geographical traditions; representation of geography

geographical evidence: African, 104, 111–12; archaeological, 14; biblical, 16, 161; changes in attitude to, 27, 76, 201–4; classical, 161; credibility of, 20, 30, 97, 101–7, 114, 180; eyewitness/empirical, 20–25, 30, 52, 57, 76, 81–86, 90, 97, 101–4, 113, 134, 149, 169, 178–79; historical linguistics, 14; mathematical, 161; nonempirical, 165; scholastic, 30, 106. *See also* geographical method; local testimony/native testimony

geographical genres: architecture, 14; art, 5, 14; atlases, 28; canonical narratives, 84–85, 125, 130; dictionaries, 28; ecclesiastical writings, 125; edited compendiums and epitomes, 84–85; gazetteers, 25–26; grammars, 25–26; heroic romances, 87; histories, 5; literature, 5, 14, 33–38, 132–34, 150–76; local oral histories, 14; maps, 25–26, 28–32, 87, 125, 142; mock travel narratives, 125, 147; oral literature, 14; periodical serials, 125, 147; plays, 87; travel guides, 130; travel writing, 1–8, 14, 20–33, 41, 57, 77–98, 103, 115, 125, 155–58, 170, 173–75. *See also* African impressions; contact narratives; geographical traditions

geographical method: debates regarding, 86, 103, 114, 149, 171–76; early modern practices of, 142; empirical, 171, 178–79, 201; reliability of eyewitness accounts in, 52, 79, 101, 149; reliability of scholastic traditions in, 30, 100, 103, 106, 149; as specifically defined discipline, 211n88. *See also* geographical evidence

geographical traditions: Arabic, 2, 12, 27, 30, 41, 82, 109, 131; biblical, 16, 27, 132; classical, 27, 30, 99, 102, 142, 148, 160, 198; empirical, 27, 81, 85–86, 91–97, 100, 106, 152; European, 2–3, 12, 27, 47, 82–83, 115; Ptolemaic, 132, 142, 148; scholastic/humanist, 100, 103, 161, 179. *See also* geographical discourse; geographical genres

Germany, 17, 131

Ghana Empire, 46; early medieval, 102. *See also* African empires; empire

Gihon, 130, 133, 196

global majority, 6, 10; agency and resistance of the, 7; epistemologies of the, 38; worlds and worldviews of the, 11

Glorious Revolution, 88

Glover, Jeffrey, 24

Goa, 115, 131

Góis, Damião de, 17

Gojjam, 132, 142, 165

gold: African, 107, 121; Defoe's imagery of the rivers of, 110, 120; in exchange for salt, 109; houses covered with, 74–75; as motivating European exploration of Africa, 72–76, 114; rivers offer access to, 39, 42, 50, 98–99, 110–11, 114, 117; search for the location of gold mines/gold fields, 18, 73; and the shape of empire, 42–47; sources of East African, 35–36, 125, 160, 202; sources of West African, 3, 72–76, 84, 102; as symbol in Mansa Musa's pilgrimage, 42–47; ubiquity of, 111. *See also* gold mines; gold trade

Gold, Joel J., 159, 164, 231n41, 232n64

Gold Coast, 3, 22, 39, 54, 77–86, 111; books published about the, 84; brokers of the, 111; early Enlightenment accounts of the, 79–86; earwitness accounts of the coastal states of the, 85; interior states and trade of the, 84–85; travel to the interior from the, 110; Wangara or "Mandiguas" and the, 54–55, 85. *See also* West Africa

Golden Coast, or a Description of Guinney (anonymous compilation), 84–85

gold mines: debates over the location of King Solomon's, 17–19; debates over the location of Queen of Sheba's, 18–19, 125, 160; debates over the location of the King of Tombut's, 102; of the Gambia River, 102; information about inland towers and, 202; as south of the Niger River, 42, 44. *See also* gold

gold trade, 41–46, 51–55, 63, 66, 72–73, 83–84, 118; from interior states where gold is bartered for salt, 84. *See also* gold; trade

Gomberville, Marin le Roy de, 89; *Polexandre (Polexander)*, 69–72, 87–89, 124

Gomes, Diogo, 52, 74, 99

Gomez, Michael, 8, 45–46, 215n49

Gondar, 40, 146, 177, 180–82, 184, 187–94, 202. *See also* Abyssinia

Gorgoryos, 17, 20, 34, 104, 131, 156, 160, 164–65

Great Zimbabwe, 17, 27, 34; "discovery" of, 203; ruins of, 19, 36–37, 160, 204; sensationalized archaeological digs of, 204–5. *See also* Africa

Green, John, 27–29, 81, 106, 148, 172

Greenblatt, Stephen, 23

Gualata, 58, 83; incorporation into Songhai Empire of, 71; king of, 68, 87

Guber, 59

Guinea, 2, 39, 83–84, 109; Akan-occupied territories of, 84; coastal states of, 66, 77; gold of, 44; Islam in, 13; Lower, 77, 84

Guinea Highlands, 99. *See also* Fouta Djallon

Habesha, 9, 16–19, 33, 137–45; attitudes toward asceticism and self-denial of the, 153; elites of the, 196; informants of the, 32; narrative traditions of the, 21, 39, 125–35, 143–44, 149, 156, 163, 190; pilgrimages to Jerusalem of the, 127–28, 130; Solomonic ties of the, 125–29; suspicion of Western Europeans of the, 180; symbolic importance of the Nile to the, 131; unique Christianity of the, 125, 132; women of the, 40, 181. *See also* Abyssinia; Ethiopian Highlands; *Kebra Nagast*

Haggard, H. Rider: *King Solomon's Mines*, 20, 203–5

Hair, P. E. H., 8

Hajj, 29, 42–47, 49, 56, 59, 76. *See also* pilgrimages

Hall, Bruce, 14, 56

Hall, Joseph, 36

Hall, Kim, 57, 64

Happy Valley, 151, 165–70; materiality of, 168–69. *See also* Abyssinia

Harley, J. B., 29–30, 32

Harol, Corrinne, 93

Hartman, Saidiya, 14, 24

Hegel, G. W. F.: *The Philosophy of History*, 5, 8, 12–13

Helena, Mother of Constantine, 141–42, 181–82, 185, 188

Heliodorus, 161

Hemans, Felicia, 179

Henry the Navigator, Prince, 51

Herman, Margaux, 140, 182

Herodotus: *Histories*, 54, 215n48

Heylyn, Peter: *Cosmographie*, 83–85, 145, 229n4

Heyrick, Thomas: "The Submarine Voyage," 33, 35–38, 61, 66

Hispaniola, 16

historiography: African self-representation in, 8–9; centrality of Africa to the early Enlightenment in, 8; debates about, 175–76; royal, 186; theory of transcultural intertextuality in, 9. *See also* African historiography; history

history: enslaved voices and perspectives in the records of, 14; of southeastern Africa, 19; written archives of, 13–14. *See also* archive; historiography

Holy Lands: Christian pilgrimages to the, 15, 25, 127, 141, 166; economic and ecclesiastical connections of Abyssinia to the, 158; European attempt to reopen the route to the, 166; joint effort to take back the, 128–29; Muslim pilgrimages to the, 15, 25; voyage to the, 16. *See also* pilgrimages; religion
Holy Sepulchre, 197. *See also* Jerusalem
Horn of Africa, 130. *See also* Africa
human diversity, 100
hydrography. *See* rivers

Iberia, 128, 130
Ibn Battuta, 46, 48, 65
Ibn Fadlallah al-Umari, 54–55
Ibn Khaldun, 53, 214n11
identity: national, 6, 127; racial, 6; religious, 127
ideology, imperial, 26, 33. *See also* empire
imagination: African sovereignty in European, 66–72, 75–76, 90; cycle of discursive reiteration and European, 152; early Enlightenment, 7, 20, 72–76, 90–97; European geographical, 2–4, 11, 20, 28, 35–37, 50, 70–76, 86–90, 119, 122–25, 146, 169–76, 204; European speculative, 100, 120; literary, 7, 10, 35, 75, 151; manipulation of both fact and, 100; romantic, 179; in travel writing, 154. *See also* African impressions; representation of geography
India, 128, 140, 165; Portugal's holdings in, 141
Indian Ocean, 13, 19, 158
Indonesia, 18
intertextuality, 2; transcultural, 9
Islam: building of mosques by African sovereigns, 46; conversion of local Abyssinian populations to, 138; expansion in Africa of, 128, 134; holy places of, 45; mix of Islamic and traditional religious and cultural practices in Western Sudan, 42, 65, 67; spread through sub-Saharan Africa of, 12–13. *See also* Islamic world; Koran; religion
Islamic world, 43, 46, 56, 65, 75, 87–88; Christian access to the Holy Lands cut off by the, 165–66; slavery in the, 78. *See also* Islam
Islamophobia, 7
Italy, 62, 88, 132
ivory, 16, 107, 121; rivers offer access to, 39, 98–99, 117; trade in, 118; ubiquity of, 111. *See also* trade
Iyasu I, 146
Iyasu II, 181–82, 189; portrait of, 183
Iyoas I, 181–82, 189, 191

jeliw (griots), 45–46, 65, 214n11
Jerusalem, 19, 127–30, 135–38, 163, 189, 196–97; Christian pilgrimages to, 127, 141–42; as contact zone, 166; Solomonic, 158, 162. *See also* Holy Sepulchre; pilgrimages
Jesuits, 144, 179; early modern, 148; in Ethiopia, 144, 157; missionaries of the, 157. *See also* Catholic missions in Ethiopia; Franks
Jewish merchants, 109
João II, King, 51, 124
Jobson, Richard, 106; *The Golden Trade*, 72–76, 81, 85, 99, 102, 218n124
Johnson, Samuel, 4, 9–10, 38, 149–78, 229n4, 233n88; anticolonial sentiments of, 166; attitudes toward poetry of, 233n98; *Dictionary*, 154; *The History of Rasselas, Prince of Abissinia*, 40, 150–76, 229n4, 230n9, 230n15, 233n97; *Idler*, 153–55; *Journey to the Western Islands of Scotland*, 155, 160, 164; *A Voyage to Abyssinia*, 164, 231n41. *See also* epistemology
Jolof, 51
Julius Caesar, 195

Karounos, Michael, 168
Kaul, Suvir, 207n12

Kebra Nagast, 34, 135, 147–48, 158, 162, 182; circulation in Europe of the, 129; copy in the Church of Our Lady Mother of Zion of the, 166; Johnson's defense of the, 164; prophecy of the, 126; Solomonic narrative in the, 127, 129, 181; story of the Queen of Sheba in the, 16–17, 125–26, 129, 147–48, 167. *See also* African literature; Habesha; Solomonic Dynasty
Kenshur, Oscar, 169
Khartoum, 195
Kilwa, 17
Kircher, Athanasius, 179
Klein, Bernhard, 217n87
Knolles, Richard: *The Six Bookes of a Commonweale* (translation), 66
knowledge: absence of geographical, 104, 115; African expressions fill gaps in European geographical, 3, 11, 76, 115, 122–23; canonically accepted, 86; "cycle of accumulation" in European acquisition of global, 26–27; empirical, 3, 86, 178; Enlightenment, 4–5, 11; European dependence on indigenous, 7, 111–12, 115, 122, 148; geography as a knowledge-making practice, 79, 81–82, 86; local points of view in the production of global, 153; of medicine, 177; of navigation and trade, 26; nonempirical, 152; slowness of production of knowledge about Africa, 11; systematized method for the production of accurate and useful, 168; universalization of, 26; Western knowledge as imperial, 5–6, 24; Western literature as constituting the other as an object of, 10. *See also* epistemology
Knox-Shaw, Peter, 100, 121
Kolb, Gwin, 151
Kongo, Kingdom of, 2, 83, 158, 165. *See also* Democratic Republic of the Congo
Koran, 203. *See also* Islam
Krebs, Verena, 44, 127, 226n11
Kuskuam, 190, 194

Labat, Jean-Baptiste, 102, 104, 106, 121, 123
Lake Chad, 41, 57
Lake T'ana, 146, 191
Lake Victoria/Lake Nyanza, 195
Lalibela, 144–45
Lamb, Charles, 179
Lamb, Jonathan, 22
Land of Negroes, 62, 84, 108. *See also* Bilad al-Sudan (Land of the Blacks)
Land of Prester John, 3, 61–63, 99, 146–48; Abyssinia as the Christian kingdom of, 29, 39, 124–25, 128–29, 132–38, 142, 225n2; in Italian literature, 227n33. *See also* Abyssinia
Land of the Blacks. *See* Bilad al-Sudan (Land of the Blacks)
language: figurative, 93; organizing geographical knowledge through, 82
Latour, Bruno, 26–27
Leask, Nigel, 178
Le Grand, Joachim, 151–53, 158–67; Johnson's translations of, 153–65, 171
Lemba, 18–19, 33, 35–36, 205; narrative traditions of the, 20
Leo Africanus, 22, 30, 56–57, 62–64, 78, 137, 216n64; *Description of Africa*, 56–65, 67–68, 71, 81, 83, 87, 94, 102–4, 108–9. *See also* Pory, John
Levtzion, Nehemia, 56
Libya, 62
Lipking, Joanna, 78
Livingstone, David, 21, 204
Lobo, Jerónimo, 146, 148, 158, 177, 179, 230n15; *Voyage to Abyssinia*, 151–54, 156–57, 162, 164–65, 171
local testimony/native testimony: changes in attitude toward, 160, 201–4; credibility of, 23, 34, 112, 115, 118, 121, 137; criticism of, 111–12, 118, 123, 160; European dependence on, 3–4, 7, 20–25, 34, 97, 106, 111–15, 122–23, 137, 148, 160–63, 202, 230n15; eyewitness accounts required from, 4, 22, 121;

local testimony/native testimony (*continued*)
  reconciliation of local evidence and details with global ideas, 27. *See also* geographical evidence
London, 80–81; literati of, 177; menagerie in, 96; publishing in, 124
London Magazine, 150
longitude, 201
Lopez, Thomas, 17–18, 27
Louis XIV, King, 69
Ludolf, Hiob, 104, 131, 160; *Historia Aethiopica,* 17, 20, 34, 146, 151–53, 156, 165
Lydon, Ghislaine, 64
Lyttelton, George, 147

Mack, Ruth, 155, 160
Madagascar, 115–16
Makeda, 17, 20, 29, 127, 135–37, 140–48, 162, 165, 181–82, 188; empire of, 19, 125; imaginative power of, 146–48; prohibition on women becoming heads of state of, 184; Solomonic connections of, 19, 125–29, 162, 184; temple dedicated to, 143. *See also* Sheba, Queen of
Malacca, 159
malaria, 201
Mali, 45, 58; merchants of, 54, 110; regional anecdotes of, 53. *See also* Mali Empire
Mali Empire, 2, 29, 39, 41–51, 66, 70, 108; cities of the, 43; consolidation of the, 45–46, 214n11; fragmentation of the, 86; gold of the, 55; Musa's vision for the, 50; travelers visit the, 48, 50. *See also* African empires; empire; Mali
Mande-speaking peoples: Mandinka, 51–55, 72–73, 83, 99–103, 106, 109–10, 123; Soninke, 56; traders of the, 54, 102–3; Wangara, 54, 84–85, 220n38
Mandeville, John: *Travels,* 27, 64, 128
Mandinka. *See* Mande-speaking peoples
Mansa Musa I, 29, 42–50, 48, 54–56, 59, 62, 65, 76, 127; pilgrimage of, 42–47,
109, 214n11; source of the gold of, 99, 102
Mansa Suleyman, 46, 59
Manuel I, King, 141–42
mappae mundi, 47, 102. *See also* cartography
maps: aesthetics of early modern, 32, 199; complex production of, 212n101; early Enlightenment, 30, 100–101; early modern, 101–2; eighteenth-century, 101, 199; as imaginative projections, 30, 132; medieval, 101–2, 130; as mirrors of reality, 29; as politically neutral products of Euclidean geometry, 29; untrustworthy, 115–18; valorization of the geological narratives of, 119. *See also* cartography; speculative maps
Marana, Giovanni Paolo: *Letters Writ by a Turkish Spy,* 145
Marees, Pieter de, 84
Markley, Robert, 79
Marlow, 5, 30. *See also* Conrad, Joseph
Massaio, Pietro del, 130
Mauch, Karl, 203; excavation of, 205
Mayhew, Robert, 25
Mbembe, Achille, 5, 14
McCleod, Bruce, 34
Mecca, 42–43, 56, 58
media: artworks as, 9; coronations as, 9; diplomatic performances as, 9; manipulation by elite Africans of, 9; pilgrimages as, 9; processions as, 9; religious devotion as, 9; written texts as, 9
Mediterranean Sea, 13
Mendes, Afonso, 146, 157–58; *Expeditionis Aethiopicae,* 162–64, 166
Menelik I, 126–29, 135–37, 144, 147–48, 162, 181, 184
Mentewab, 180–92, 195; identity of, 189; melancholy of, 195–99; narrative of lineage and power in narrative about, 182; portrait of, *183*; retirement of, 182–84
Mercator, Gerardus, 142
Middle Ages: early, 126; late, 13

Middle Passage, 13. *See also* slave trade
Mikael Sehul, 182–83, 191–94, 236n67
Miller, Christopher, 6
Milton, John: *Paradise Lost*, 33–38, 61, 66, 124–25, 133, 145–46, 151–52, 169, 203, 205
modernity: and the European self, 7; Western assumptions about Enlightenment and, 6
Molineux, Catherine, 89, 92
Moll, Herman: *System of Geography*, 28–29, 81, 94, 104, *105*, 106, 226n5
Montano, Benito Arias, 16, 159
Moore, Francis, 103–4, 106, 121, 123; *Travels into the Inland Parts of Africa*, 103, 223n25
Morocco, 60, 63, 83
Mountains of the Moon, 63, 132–33, 147
Mozambique, 16, 31, 37, 114–15; coast of, 114
Muhammad al-Idrisi, 27, 30, 49, 58, 102–4
Mumbarre, 73
Münster, Sebastian, 142
myth of the silent traders, 109–10, 215n48; Mande origins of, 53–55, 99; origin of the, 85; repetition by coastal brokers of, 52, 73–75, 84, 110. *See also* trade
mythology: mythological Abyssinian lineage, 182; Solomonic, 38; of the Songhai Empire, 58, 83. *See also* sovereignty

Natal, 204
Near East, 43
negus (Emperor of Abyssinia), 34, 36, 69, 114. *See also* Abyssinia
negusa nagast, 35, 131–33, 138, 146, 225n2, 226n5; grandeur of the, 137; historical regalia of the, 133. *See also* Abyssinia
Newbery, John: *The History of Little Goody Two-Shoes*, 147–48
Newton, John, 22–23

New World, 89–90; slavery in the, 221n51; voyages to the, 16. *See also* Americas
Nigeria, 13
Niger River, 107–8, 116; in books published about the Gold Coast, 84; Bure on the, 84; course of the, 123; European search for city-states along the, 3, 83, 85–86, 123; Gambia and Senegal Rivers as branches of the, 42, 99, 103, 106–10; reunification of the kingdoms along the, 58; source of the, 99, 102; trade cities of the, 50, 75, 102; trade routes of the, 54, 83–84; Upper, 84; valley of the, 41, 46, 50–51, 62, 69–70, 75–76, 83, 104, 108–9; as western branch of the Nile, 165. *See also* rivers
Nile River: Abyssinia as the home of the source of the, 3, 29–30, 39, 61–64, 125, 129–34, 142–43, 148–49, 153, 165, 180, 191, 196; cause of the inundation of the, 170–71, 198; conflation with the biblical river of Gihon, 130, 196; Ethiopian emperor's ability to divert the course of the, 131, 156; images of the, 170; literary survey on the, 170–74; paternalistic greatness of the, 131, 156; religious associations of the, 130; search for the source of the, 116–17, 132, 171, 177, 179, 195–96, 199; significance to Egypt of the, 131–32; significance to Ethiopia of the, 130–31, 172, 174, 196; significance to Europe of the, 130, 132; source of the Senegal River and Niger River same as the source of the, 66; as symbol of geographical or epistemological indeterminacy in literature, 171, 173–75. *See also* Abay/Blue Nile; rivers; White Nile/Egyptian Nile
North Africa (Barbary), 43, 65, 87, 109, 151; coast of, 47–48, 64; merchants of, 109; princes of, 70; slave trade to, 63; sovereigns of, 67. *See also* Africa; Barbary

Novak, Maximillian, 100, 110, 120
Nubia, 2, 62, 124, 133; Christians of, 124. See also Abyssinia

Ogilby, John: *Africa*, 82–85
Ophir, 4, 16–20, 27, 29–32, 36, 179; biblical, 204; Fura as, 30; gold of, 181; location of, 158–61, 184, 202
Orientalism, 5, 7, 150, 229n2
oriental tales, 88, 150–76
Ortelius, Abraham: *Africa Tabula Nova*, 60, *60*, 102, 142; *Geographia Sacra*, 16, 18
Ottoman Empire, 88. See also empire; Ottoman Turks
Ottoman Turks, 70; problems of succession of the, 145. See also Ottoman Empire
Ozoro Esther. See Aster Iyasu

Páez, Pedro, 137, 144–45, 148, 157–58, 163, 171, 177–80, 205; missionary efforts of, 179
Palestine, 165
Paradise, 34, 133; images of, 142–46; of Milton, 145–46, 169; Nile as the conduit to, 125. See also Abyssinia
Park, Mungo, 123, 204
Parrish, Susan Scott, 23–24, 95
Pearl, Jason, 100, 119
periodical publications, 125, 147
Persia, 67, 165
Peru, 16, 18, 159–60
Pettigrew, William, 98
Phoenicians, 203
pilgrimages, 9; Christian pilgrimages to Jerusalem, 127, 141–42; Muslim pilgrimages to Mecca (Hajj), 42–47, 49–50, 56, 58. See also Hajj; Holy Lands; Jerusalem; religion; theater of pilgrimages and state appearances
Pina, Ruy de: *Chronica del Rey João II*, 51
Pinto, Fernão Mendes, 140–43, 185–86
piracy, 113

Pliny, 62, 161
political theory, 69–71, 88–89; abstract, 72, 88–89. See also divine right of kings; sovereignty
Poncet, Charles-Jacques, 146, 179
Poovey, Mary, 155, 164
portolan, 47. See also cartography
Portugal, 17, 51–52, 138–42, 182; alliance of Abyssinia with, 185; geopolitical interests of, 19; holdings in India of, 141; king of, 138; missionaries from, 195; supremacy in West Africa of, 72; traders from, 205
Pory, John, 57, 61, 63, 65, 68, 216n77. See also Leo Africanus
Pratt, Mary Louise, 21, 178, 210n65
Prester John. See Land of Prester John
Ptolemy, 132, 142, 148
Purchas, Samuel, 17, 37, 143, 145–46, 220n38, 229n4

Quatermain, Allan, 204

race: blackness or complexion in European geographical descriptions, 64, 82, 89, 113–14; moor (blackamoor), 64–65, 107
Ramusio, Giovanni Battista, 68
Ras Mikael Sehul. See Mikael Sehul
realism, 100; realism vs. romance, 78–79, 100
recovering African voices, 7, 22–25. See also archive
Red Sea, 19, 128, 133, 149, 158, 184; African side of the, 164; Arabian side of the, 164; European access to the, 131
religion: Catholicism in Ethiopia, 157, 180, 189; Christianity in Africa, 12; Christianity in Ethiopia, 9, 39, 125–32, 135, 138, 143, 149, 189; Islam in Africa, 12; religious exceptionalism of Africans, 3, 9; religious imagery of Christ and Mary, 182; traditional African conceptual schemes in the Western Sudan

of, 42–47, 56. *See also* Christianity; Ethiopian exceptionalism; Ethiopian Orthodox Church; Holy Lands; Islam; pilgrimages

representation of geography: African, 10–12; critical approaches to European, 10, 111–13, 153–65, 155–65, 172; critique of cartographic, 119; without embellishment, 91–97, 117; empirical geographical knowledge and other forms of, 101, 122–23, 153–65; fictional forms of, 121; imperial, 49; indirect and mediated images that can be traced back to African impressions in the, 97; instruction and delight in the, 28, 35, 81; of interior geography and geology of Africa, 111–23, 195; literary cartography of the, 39, 61, 86–88, 101, 106–14, 117–23; moral purpose of the, 91–92; nationalistic purpose of the, 35–36, 147; nonempirical, 120, 129–30; nonfiction, 223n33; and social or political questions of early Enlightenment Europeans, 90; stakes and methods of global, 100; theological purpose of the, 36; treatment of African sovereignty in the, 42–47, 49, 55, 66–72, 75, 86, 111. *See also* African impressions; geographical discourse; imagination

Rio Grande/Corubal River, 108. *See also* rivers

Ripon Falls, 195

rivers: of Africa, 101–7, 122–23, 195; criticism by Defoe of cartographical speculation about African, 112, 116; expeditions into the interior through, 98–99, 117, 119; exploration of, 50, 98–99, 123; sub-Saharan, 50. *See also* Congo River; Gambia River; Niger River; Nile River; Rio Grande/Corubal River; Senegal River; single-river theory (Senegambia, Gambia, and Niger Rivers are one river); single-source theory (Senegambia, Gambia, Niger, and Nile Rivers share a source); Zaire River; Zambezi River

Rogers, Pat, 99, 119

romance, 68, 78–79; African, 91–97; early modern, 69; heroic, 71

Rome, 128, 130

Royal African Company, 98, 102–3, 112, 114, 121

Royal Society, 21, 28, 39, 80–82; empiricism of the, 79, 81, 91–97; repository of the, 92–93; taxonomical projects of the, 22, 79–80. *See also* epistemology

Ruffhead, Owen, 150

Runge, Laura, 79–80

Sabla Wangel, 135, 138–41, 169, 185, 188

Saga za Ab, 17–18, 20, 27, 129

Sahara Desert, 41–43, 62–65, 70, 76, 110. *See also* Africa

Said, Edward, 26, 37, 208n26; *Culture and Imperialism*, 7; *Orientalism*, 5

Saint Domingo, 159

salt, 53–54, 63, 73–74, 84; in exchange for gold, 109. *See also* trade

Salt, Henry: *Voyage to Abyssinia*, 201–3

Salvadore, Matteo, 8, 128, 130, 138

Santos, João dos, 18, 27, 114, 160–61

science: early Enlightenment transition from wonder to, 32; fiction and, 100; maps at the intersection of aesthetics and, 212n101; and navigation, 177. *See also* empiricism

Scotland, 155, 160, 199

Scott, Walter, 179

Scrimgeour, Gary, 119

Sebastian I, 63

Second Anglo-Dutch War, 78

seeing man, 21–22, 178. *See also* empiricism; gaze

self: Cartesian, 23–24; narratives designed to communicate ideas about the, 15

Senegal River, 41–42, 49, 51, 72, 99, 102, 106–7, 110, 116; Bambouk on the, 84, 123; navigability of the, 114; source of

Senegal River (*continued*)
the, 66, 99; valley of the, 46, 51, 104. *See also* rivers

Senegambia, 3, 51–52, 57, 69–76, 83–85; British political and economic ties in the, 72; brokers of the, 50–55, 73–76, 102–3, 110–11; coastal peoples of the, 76; Europeans drawn to the, 99; king of, 69–70; merchants and traders of the, 39, 72–76; trade cities of the, 75; trade routes of the, 54, 72–76, 99. *See also* West Africa

Senex, John, 104, 106

Shakespeare, William, 217n93; *Othello*, 63–66, 87–88, 217n87

Sheba (Saba), 18, 149, 158, 160–65. *See also* Sheba, Queen of

Sheba, Queen of: books collected by, 143; claim of Abyssinia to, 17, 29, 33–34, 40, 125–29, 134–37, 144–46, 161–63, 184; debates about the origins (Arabia or Africa) of, 19, 163–64; domains of, 27, 125, 158, 184; ruins in Great Zimbabwe of the palace of, 203; visit to Solomon of, 143, 147, 162, 166, 184. *See also* Abyssinia; Makeda; Sheba (Saba)

Sher, Richard, 234n1

Shona, 17, 19

silk, Yemeni, 43

Sills, Adam, 77, 79, 92

Simien, 132

single-river theory (Senegambia, Gambia, and Niger Rivers are one river), 99, 101–8, 117. *See also* rivers

single-source theory (Senegambia, Gambia, Niger, and Nile Rivers share a source), 99, 104, 123. *See also* rivers

slave narratives: Caribbean, 24; as traveling narratives, 211n77. *See also* slavery

slavery: ideas of Africa as influenced by debates about race and, 13; losers in military conflicts sold into, 86. *See also* enslaved Africans; slave narratives; slave trade

slave trade: growth of the, 72; inter-African, 83, 88, 221n51; trans-Atlantic, 13, 66, 77, 88, 218n124; trans-Saharan, 41, 63, 88. *See also* enslaved Africans; Middle Passage; slavery; trade

Smith, Cassander, 23–24

Smith, William, 22

Sofala, 16–19, 27, 29–32, 36–37, 66, 163, 165, 184

Sofala-Ophir impression, 15–20, 27, 30–38, 40, 133, 146, 159–61, 203. *See also* African impressions

Solomon, King, 4, 16–20, 36–37, 125–26, 136, 142, 162; diamond mines of, 204; gold mines of, 18; great power over the djinn of, 17; reliance on trade rather than conquest of, 19, 37. *See also* Solomon's Temple

Solomonic Dynasty: Bruce's annals of the, 181, 184–89; legitimizing the right to the throne in the, 136; Makeda as the mother of the, 181–82; Mentewab as one of the most influential queens in the history of the, 182; mythopoetic national narrative of the, 16–17, 125–29; names and dates of the reigns in the, 144; origin story of the, 126, 128, 147, 184; as unbroken line, 126, 147, 162–63. *See also* Abyssinia; *Kebra Nagast*

Solomonic exceptionalism, 15–20

Solomon's Temple, 16, 37, 125, 133, 136. *See also* Solomon, King

Songhai Empire, 2, 29, 39, 41, 50, 66–67, 70, 108, 127; conquests of the, 109; consolidation of the, 55–71, 84; economic power of the, 59; fall of the, 60; founding myths and projected imperial self-image of the, 58, 83; fragmentation of the, 86; history of the, 216n70; military might and conquest narrative of the, 71, 84; rise of the, 55–61. *See also* African empires; empire

Sonni Ali, 56, 58; traditional occult power of, 56

INDEX 277

Southerne, Thomas: *Oroonoko* (adaptation), 68, 87
South Sudan, 142
sovereigns: absolute and perpetual power of true, 67; associations made with other sovereigns or significant people by, 44; European writing about sophisticated African kingdoms ruled by, 8, 41–42, 177–99; legitimacy of, 44, 136, 181; medieval Ethiopian, 226n11; North African, 63; representation in literature of African, 8, 34–36, 61–66; tyrannical, 70–72, 89. *See also* sovereignty
sovereignty: abstract concept of, 72; divinely ordained, 127; European political theories on ideas of African, 69–71, 88; idealized concept of, 90; narratives of African sovereigns about their, 42–44, 55, 65–72, 125–29; performances of, 42–47, 49, 55, 66–72, 75, 86–90, 127, 134–37; scholarly treatments of African, 43, 68; spectacle of dress and person in manifestation of, 89; symbolic registers of African, 47, 55; universal account of, 67. *See also* divine right of kings; mythology; political theory; sovereigns; theater of pilgrimages and state appearances
Spain, 51, 62, 69, 157–58
speculative maps, 31, 115–18. *See also* cartography
Speke, John Hanning, 195, 197, 204
Spivak, Gayatri Chakravorty, 14, 23
Sprat, Thomas, 80; *History of the Royal Society*, 91–93
Stanley, Henry Morton, 204
steamboat, 201
Stibbs, Bartholomew, 102–4, 121, 123
Strabo, 161
sub-Saharan Africa, 3, 22, 25, 39, 41, 50, 53, 64, 109; cosmopolitan cities of trade and learning in, 75; geographical regions of, 82–83; Islam in, 12–13; kingdoms of, 51, 70; sources on, 56–58; as universally uncivilized, 85. *See also* Africa
Sudan, 142
Sumatra, 16
Sundiata Keita, 44–45, 55, 214n11. *See also* Epic of Sundiata
Surinam, 39, 78–81, 90–97
Susenyos I, 157, 180
Susenyos II, 191, 194–95
Sutukho, 74
Swahili, 14, 17–19, 33, 35–36, 205; elites of the, 114; Muslim, 18; narrative traditions of the, 20, 160; traders who speak with Europeans, 17–18, 36
Swahili Coast, 3, 29
Syria, 128

Tagaza, 53
Táíwò, Olúfẹ́mi, 6, 14
Tally Jr., Robert, 37
Tamrat, Taddesse, 135, 138
Tamrin, 17, 125, 148, 165
Tanzania, 17
Tarshish, 161
Tartary, 67
Taylor, David Francis, 155
Taylor, Diana, 15, 25
Tekle Haymanot II, 191–94, 196
Telles, Balthazar, 140, 146, 166
Temporal, Jean, 68
theater of pilgrimages and state appearances: European impressions and expansionist desires combined with African, 69, 88; of Habesha pilgrimages, 127; of Musa's Hajj, 42–47, 49. *See also* pilgrimages; sovereignty
Thell, Anne, 22–23, 100, 119, 155
Thomas, Dalby, 121
Thompson, George, 72, 74
Tigre, 182, 191
Timbuktu (Tombut, Thombut, Tombutto), 43, 45–48, 52, 58–59, 83, 102, 108, 165; capture by Sonni Ali of, 56; court of, 87; eyewitness accounts

Timbuktu (Tombut, Thombut, Tombutto) (*continued*)
of, 201; gold of, 85; location of, 123; travel of Leo Africanus to, 57–58. *See also* Tombut, King of; Western Sudan
Tomarken, Edward, 151, 169
Tombut, King of, 59–61, 66–71, 83, 89; legacy of the, 88. *See also* Timbuktu (Tombut, Thombut, Tombutto)
trade: African kingdoms at crossroads of, 8, 41–46, 73, 165–66; of Arab traders, 42, 53, 73, 75; ceremony of, 73–74; Defoe's ideas about and attitude toward global, 112, 125; European coastal, 87–88, 108, 113, 117; inland, 108–9, 118; inter-African, 83, 88, 113; routes of, 13, 43–44, 49, 63, 77, 83, 85, 125, 166. *See also* African empires; economy; gold trade; ivory; myth of the silent traders; salt; slave trade; trans-Atlantic trade; trans-Sahara trade; wealth
trans-Atlantic trade, 77. *See also* trade
trans-Sahara trade, 15, 25, 39, 41, 49–53, 70, 83, 87, 109–10. *See also* trade
Travels of the Jesuits in Ethiopia (compilation), 140
Turk, Edward Baron, 69
Turkey, 67
tyranny, 71, 89

Ullendorff, Edward, 126
Urreta, Luis de: *Historia de la sagrada Orden de predicadores, en los remotos reynos de la Etiopia*, 143–46, 151–52, 169

van Wyk Smith, Malvern, 234n9
Verdier, Gilbert Saulnier du, 89; *Le Romant des Romans* (*The Love and Armes of the Greeke Princes*), 68
Virgin Mary, 181, 188; paintings of the, 182. *See also* Christianity

Walker, William: *Victorious Love* (play), 68, 87
Wall, Cynthia, 37
Walpole, Horace, 177
warfare, inter-African, 88
Watt, James, 229n2
wealth: of African elites, 3, 42–47, 75, 86, 134, 137; of Happy Valley, 166–67; of Timbuktu, 59. *See also* trade
Wedem Arad, 127, 136
Welch, Ellen R., 69
Welleta Georgis, 186–87
West Africa: central, 45–48, 56, 58, 72, 108; coastal slave ports of, 78; coastal states of, 2, 66, 84, 90; cosmopolitan centers of trade and learning of, 46; geopolitical control of, 56, 61; gold of, 3, 84; interior states of, 41, 72–76, 83–86, 108; major rivers of, 117; self-displays of imperial power in, 72, 87; sophisticated kingdoms and empires of, 41–47, 55–61; supremacy of Portugal in, 72; transatlantic connections of, 77. *See also* Africa; Gold Coast; Senegambia
Western Sudan, 3, 22, 39, 83; conquest by Askia Muhammad I of, 29, 58; as Country of the Blacks, 41, 46; descriptions of, 29, 86; fourteenth-century Arabic accounts of the, 214n11; hybridized culture of the, 42; hydrography of the, 103; imperial history of, 86; imperial performances of, 55, 58, 86–88, 127; impressions of, 41–76, 86–87, 99; interior trade of, 55, 72–76; interior world of, 82, 86–87; Islam in, 13, 42; as Negroland, 41; as Nigritarum Regio, 41; as outpost of the Muslim world, 46; rivers of, 108; as Terra Nigritarum, 41, 84. *See also* Africa; *Bilad al-Sudan* (Land of the Blacks); Gao; Timbuktu (Tombut, Thombut, Tombutto)
West Indies, 88
Wheeler, Roxann, 8, 113, 114, 117, 225n79
White, Robert, 203

White Nile/Egyptian Nile, 156–57, 173, 195. *See also* Nile River
Wilkins, John, 80, 92
Wilks, Ivor, 54, 85
Wise, Christopher, 216n64
Withers, Charles, 211n88
Wolof Empire, 51–52, 70, 99. *See also* African empires
women: African women as geographical authorities, 177–99; cultural power of Abyssinian court, 191–95; detailed narratives about historical Ethiopian, 181; elite Abyssinian, 135–36, 139–40, 180–95; Habesha, 137–42, 195–97; lineage of archetypal African, 40; monastic or ascetic life chosen by older Ethiopian, 197; significance of, 135, 195
Wordsworth, William, 179
World War II, 4
Woyzero Aster Iyasu. *See* Aster Iyasu

Yang, Chi-ming, 79
Yekuno Amlak, 126–27, 136
Yemen, 161–64

Za Dengel, 157
Zagwe Dynasty, 126. *See also* Ethiopia
Zaire River, 107. *See also* rivers
Zambezi River, 107, 205. *See also* rivers
Zambia, 142
Zara Yaqob, 127
Zemene Mesafint (Era of the Princes, Era of the Judges), 183–84, 191. *See also* Abyssinia
Zhiri, Oumelbanine, 57
Zimbabwe, 13
Zouche, Richard: *The Dove: Or Passages of Cosmography*, 61–62, 64, 83–84
Zulu, 203
Zuroski, Eugenia, 89

RECENT WINNERS OF THE
WALKER COWEN MEMORIAL PRIZE

Against Better Judgment: Irrational Action and Literary Invention in the Long Eighteenth Century
Thomas Salem Manganaro

Voices from Beyond: Physiology, Sentience, and the Uncanny in Eighteenth-Century French Literature
Scott M. Sanders

The Usufructuary Ethos: Power, Politics, and Environment in the Long Eighteenth Century
Erin Drew

Staging Civilization: A Transnational History of French Theater in Eighteenth-Century Europe
Rahul Markovits, translated by Jane Marie Todd

The Shortest Way with Defoe: "Robinson Crusoe," Deism, and the Novel
Michael B. Prince

Public Vows: Fictions of Marriage in the English Enlightenment
Melissa J. Ganz

Citizens of Convenience: The Imperial Origins of American Nationhood on the U.S.-Canadian Border
Lawrence B. A. Hatter

Empiricist Devotions: Science, Religion, and Poetry in Early Eighteenth-Century England
Courtney Weiss Smith

Nationalizing France's Army: Foreign, Black, and Jewish Troops in the French Military, 1715–1831
Christopher J. Tozzi

Prose Immortality, 1711–1819
Jacob Sider Jost

The Evil Necessity: British Naval Impressment in the Eighteenth-Century Atlantic World
Denver Brunsman

Be It Ever So Humble: Poverty, Fiction, and the Invention of the Middle-Class Home
Scott R. MacKenzie

Backstage in the Novel: Frances Burney and the Theater Arts
Francesca Saggini, translated by Laura Kopp

The Nation's Nature: How Continental Presumptions Gave Rise to the United States of America
James D. Drake

Our Coquettes: Capacious Desire in the Eighteenth Century
Theresa Braunschneider

Virginians Reborn: Anglican Monopoly, Evangelical Dissent, and the Rise of the Baptists in the Late Eighteenth Century
Jewel L. Spangler

Ending the French Revolution: Violence, Justice, and Repression from the Terror to Napoleon
Howard G. Brown

www.ingramcontent.com/pod-product-compliance
Lightning Source LLC
Chambersburg PA
CBHW030610230426
43661CB00053B/1922